EAT, DRINK, AND BE MERRY (LUKE 12:19) – FOOD AND WINE IN BYZANTIUM

Society for the Promotion of Byzantine Studies

Publications

13

EAT, DRINK, AND BE MERRY (LUKE 12:19) – FOOD AND WINE IN BYZANTIUM

Papers of the 37th Annual Spring Symposium of Byzantine Studies, in Honour of Professor A.A.M. Bryer

edited by
Leslie Brubaker and Kallirroe Linardou

ASHGATE
VARIORUM

Published by Variorum for the Society for the Promotion of Byzantine Studies

Published by
Ashgate Publishing Limited
Gower House
Croft Road
Aldershot
Hampshire GU11 3HR
England

Ashgate Publishing Company
Suite 420
101 Cherry Street
Burlington, VT 05401-4405
USA

Ashgate website: http://www.ashgate.com

British Library Cataloguing in Publication Data
Spring Symposium of Byzantine Studies (37th : 2003: University of Birmingham)
Eat, Drink, and Be Merry (Luke 12:19) – Food and Wine in Byzantium: Papers of the 37th Annual Spring Symposium of Byzantine Studies, in Honour of Professor A.A.M. Bryer. – Publications for the Society for the Promotion of Byzantine Studies)
1. Food habits – Byzantine Empire – Congresses. 2. Byzantine Empire – Civilization – Congresses. I. Title. II. Bryer, Anthony. III. Brubaker, Leslie. IV. Linardou, Kallirroe. V. Society for the Promotion of Byzantine Studies (Great Britain).
394.1'2'09495'0902

Library of Congress Cataloging-in-Publication Data
Spring Symposium of Byzantine Studies (37th : 2003 : University of Birmingham)
Eat, Drink, and Be Merry (Luke 12:19) – Food and Wine in Byzantium: Papers Delivered at the 37th Annual Spring Symposium of Byzantine Studies under the Auspices of the Society for the Promotion of Byzantine Studies, in Honour of Professor A.A.M. Bryer, at the University of Birmingham, 29–31 March 2003 / edited by Leslie Brubaker and Kallirroe Linardou.
p. cm. – (Publications for the Society for the Promotion of Byzantine Studies ; 13)
1. Dinners and dining – Byzantine Empire – Congresses. 2. Food habits – Byzantine Empire – Congresses. 3. Wine festivals – Byzantine Empire – Congresses. 4. Byzantine Empire – Civilization – Congresses. I. Bryer, Anthony. II. Brubaker, Leslie. III. Linardou, Kallirroe. IV. Society for the Promotion of Byzantine Studies (Great Britain) V. Title.
TX360.B97S67 2007
641.59495–dc22 2007005527

ISBN 978-0-7546-6119-1

This volume has been printed on acid-free paper.

Printed and bound in Great Britain by MPG Books Ltd, Bodmin, Cornwall.

SOCIETY FOR THE PROMOTION OF BYZANTINE STUDIES – PUBLICATION 13

Contents

Acknowledgements

It is also a pleasure to thank the sponsors of the original symposium – the Society for the Promotion of Hellenic Studies, the A. G. Leventis Foundation and *History Today* – and especially the postgraduate students who helped ensure that it ran smoothly, all under the expert supervision of Anna Williams, who also organized the logistics of the conference with extraordinary patience and goodwill. In the publication process, I would like to extend my thanks to Elizabeth Jeffreys, who, among her many other duties, chairs the publications board of the Society for the Promotion of Byzantine Studies; to John Smedley and the team at Ashgate, for patience that went beyond the professionalism for which they are justly well known; and especially to my co-editor, Kallirroe Linardou, without whom, it is no exaggeration to say, this volume would never have been completed. And, as always, I would like to thank my husband, Christopher Wickham, for services above and beyond the call.

Abbreviations

AD	*Archaiologikon Deltion* (*ἈρχαιολογικὸνΔελτίον*)
AE	*Archaiologike Ephemeris* (*Ἀρχαιολογικὴ Ἐφημερίς*)
AIPHOS	*Annuaire de l'Institut de philologie et d'histoire orientales et slaves*
ANRW	*Aufstieg und Niedergang der römischen Welt*
AntT	*Antiquité tardive*
ArchP	*Archeion Pontou* (*Ἀρχεῖον Πόντου*)
ArtB	*Art Bulletin*
AS	*Art Studies*
BAV	Biblioteca Apostolica Vaticana, Vatican City
BCH	*Bulletin de correspondance hellénique*
BEFEO	*Bulletin d'études francaises d'extreme Orient*
BF	*Byzantinische Forschungen*
BHG	*Bibliotheca hagiographica graeca*, ed. F. Halkin (Brussels, 1957)
BICS	*Bulletin of the Institute of Classical Studies*
BL	The British Library, London
BMFD	*Byzantine Monastic Foundation Documents: A Comparative Translation of the Surviving Founders' Typika and Testaments*, 5 vols, ed. J. Thomas and A.C. Hero, Dumbarton Oaks Studies 35 (Washington, DC, 2000)
BMGS	*Byzantine and Modern Greek Studies*
BN	Bibliothèque nationale de France, Paris
BNM	Biblioteca Nazionale Marciana, Venice
BollBG	*Bollettino della Badia di Grottaferrata*
BSA	*The Annual of the British School at Athens*
BSl	*Byzantinoslavika*
Budé	Bulletin de l'Association Guilaume Budé
BV	Byzantina Vindobonensia
BZ	*Byzantinische Zeitschift*
CahArch	*Cahiers archéologiques*
CahCM	*Cahiers de civilisation médiévale, Xe–XIIe siècles*
CCCM	Corpus Christianorum, continuatio mediaevalis
CCSG	Corpus Christianorum, series graeca
CCSL	Corpus Christianorum, series latina
CFHB	Corpus fontium historiae byzantinae
CSCO	Corpus scriptorum christianorum orientalium
CSHB	Corpus scriptorum historiae byzantinae
DChAE	*Deltion tes Christianikes Archaiologikes Etaireias* (*Δελτίον τῆς Χριστιανικῆς Ἀρχαιολογικῆς Ἑταιρείας*)

DOP	*Dumbarton Oaks Papers*
EchCl	*Echos du monde classique*
EEBS	*Epeteris Etaireias Byzantinon Spoudon* (*Ἐπετηρὶς Ἑταιρείας Βυζαντινῶν Σπουδῶν*)
GCS	*Die griechischen christlichen Scriftsteller der ersten [drei] Jahrhunderte*
GRBS	*Greek, Roman and Byzantine Studies*
ICS	*Illinois Classical Studies*
IRAIK	*Izvestiia Russkogo arkheologicheskogo instituta v Konstantinopole*
IstMitt	*Istanbuler Mitteilungen*, Deutsches Archäologisches Abteilung, Istanbul
JECS	*Journal of Early Christian Studies*
JHS	*Journal of Hellenic Studies*
JMA	*Journal of Mediterranean Archaeology*
JMC	*Journal of Material Culture*
JMedHist	*Journal of Medieval History*
JÖB	*Jahrbuch der Österreichischen Byzantinistik*
JRA	*Journal of Roman Archaeology*
LBG	*Lexicon zur Byzantinischen Gräzität*
Loeb	Loeb Classical Library
LSJ	H.G. Liddell, R. Scott and H.S. Jones, *A Greek–English Lexicon*
Mansi	G. D.Mansi, *Sacrorum conciliorum nova et amplissima collectio* (Paris and Leipzig, 1901–27)
MGH	Monumenta germaniae historica
MonAnt	*Monumenti antichi*
NHell	*Neos Hellenomnemon* (*Νέος Ἑλληνομνήμων*)
NL	National Library of Greece, Athens
OCA	*Orientalia christiana analecta*
OCP	*Orientalia christiana periodica*
ODB	*The Oxford Dictionary of Byzantium*, ed. A. Kazhdan (Oxford, 1991)
OED	*The Oxford English Dictionary*, ed. J.A. Simpson and E.S.C. Weiner (Oxford, 1989)
ON	Österreichische Nationalbibliothek, Vienna
PG	*Patrologiae Cursus Completus, Series graeca*, ed. J.-P. Migne
PO	*Patrologia Orientalis*, ed. R. Graffin and F. Nau
RA	*Revue archéologique*
RACr	*Rivista di archeologica cristiana*
REA	*Revue des études anciennes*
REAu	*Revue des études augustiniennes*

REB	*Revue des études byzantines*
RJ	*Rechtshistorisches Journal*
RK	*Repertorium für Kunstwissenschaft*
SBS	*Studies in Byzantine Sigillography*
SC	Sources chrétiennes
SemKond	*Seminarium kondakovianum*
SRM	Scriptores rerum Merovingicarum
StT	*Studi e testi*
StVen	*Studi veneziani*
Teubner	Bibliotheca scriptorum Graecorum et Romanorum Teubneriana
TLG	*Thesaurus Linguae Graecae. A Digital Library of Greek Literature*
TM	*Travaux et mémoires*
TT	*Tools and Tillage*
VizVrem	*Vizantiiskii vremennik*
ZDPV	*Zeitschrift des deutschen Palästina-Vereins*
ZU	*Skyllis. Zeitschrift für Unterwasserarchäologie*

Figures

Table

Preface

Leslie Brubaker

It was my great pleasure to be the symposiarch at the 37th Spring Symposium of Byzantine Studies, held in Birmingham in March 2003 under the auspices of the Society for the Promotion of Byzantine Studies.

The theme of the symposium was 'Eat, drink and be merry (Luke 12:19): the production, consumption and celebration of food and wine in Byzantium'. In the papers delivered, many of which follow in this volume, speakers covered this topic from many angles and – in a feature that made us distinct from most academic conferences – we practised what we preached: A. A. M. Bryer, Emeritus Professor of Byzantine Studies at the University of Birmingham, created a genuine Byzantine feast for the Sunday-night banquet.

The celebration part of the title was my remit. As a Byzantinist among Byzantinists, I felt it imperative to open the symposium with a bow to tradition: the ritual of the daffodils. As always in Birmingham, following the tradition of the Fathers (in this case, Bryer), we placed a bowl of daffodils in bud on the front table at the opening of the symposium; these burst into flower as the symposiasts spoke over the course of the symposium and, I fear, drooped a bit, as we did, by the end.

But, braving the wrath of the 787 Council at Nicaea and numerous Byzantine churchmen,[1] we also introduced an innovation: the daffodil ritual was followed by a dedication ceremony. It was my honour to dedicate the 37th Annual Spring Symposium of Byzantine Studies to its *ktetor* (founder), and the founder of Byzantine Studies in Britain, Anthony Bryer. Bryer's first symposium, held in Birmingham in 1966, was followed by his establishment of Britain's first Centre for Byzantine Studies, also in Birmingham, in 1975 (a foundation commemorated by the celebrated *Iconoclasm*, edited by Bryer and his first postgraduate student, Judith Herrin).[2] As in all proper dedication speeches, I could truly claim in this one that we would not be here but for Bryer. We thanked him then, and we thank him now.

---

[1] 'As for ourselves, we gain nothing but the certainty that we, who have come to a reverence of God, introduce no innovation, but rather remain obedient to the teachings of the apostles and fathers and to the traditions of the church': Mansi 13, 208C; tr. D. Sahas, *Icon and Logos: sources in eighth-century iconoclasm*, Toronto Medieval Texts and Translations 4 (Toronto, 1986), 52.

[2] A .A. M. Bryer and J. Herrin, eds, *Iconoclasm* (Birmingham, 1977).

I think, and hope, that Bryer did not know in advance that this symposium was created to honour him. This, at any rate, seemed to be demonstrated by the fact that he sent in a registration form the same as everyone else did. But you cannot register for a symposium in your own honour, and so the first ceremonial act of the symposium was to rip up his registration cheque. Next came the official dedication ceremony, at which we emulated Byzantine donor portraits (rather badly) and presented Bryer with a model of Hagia Sophia (that of his special city, Trebizond, of course).

Speeches and celebrations in Bryer's honour followed, and a series of *enkomia* to Bryer, written by his former students, are sandwiched between this introduction and the chapters dedicated to food and drink in Byzantium that follow.

These chapters present food in nearly every conceivable guise, ranging from its rhetorical uses – food as a metaphor for redemption (Cunningham); food as politics (Crostini and Korobeinikov); eating as a vice (James and Eastmond); abstinence as a virtue (Karlin-Hayter) – to more practical applications such as the preparation of food, processing it (Stathakopoulos), preserving it (Grünbart), and selling one product, wine, abroad (Harris). We learn how the Byzantines viewed their diet (Koder), and how others viewed it (Zhiqiang). Different chapters unpick the protocols of eating in a monastery (Talbot), in the palace (Malmberg), or on a picnic or military campaign (Mango); or consider what serving dishes and utensils were in use in the dining room (Lymberopoulou and Vroom). Throughout, the terminology of eating – and especially some of the more problematic terms (Dalby) – is explored. These themes are, we hope, fitting tributes to the scholar who first told the world about Byzantine agricultural implements:[3] it is, once again, an honour and a pleasure to dedicate this volume to Bryer.

---

[3] A. A. M. Bryer, 'Byzantine agricultural implements: the evidence of medieval illustrations of Hesiod's *Works and Days*', *BSA* 81 (1986), 45–80.

Bibliography of publications by A. A. M. Bryer

There is also a bibliography of Pontic opuscula by Bryer in A. K. Savvides and S. Lampakes, *Genike Bibliographia peri tou Byzantinou Pontou* (Athens, 1992), 106–28.

1956 'The Breton Bisquine', *Sailing Time* 4: 28–29.

1960 'Trebizond', *History Today* 10, 2 (February): 125–35.
'Aghthamar and Digenis Akrites', *Antiquity* 34: 295–7 (= Bryer 1988, I).

1961 'The littoral of the Empire of Trebizond in two fourteenth-century portolano maps', *ArchP* 24: 97–127.
'Ochrida', *History Today* 11: 418–28.

1962 'Skanderbeg', *History Today* 12: 426–34.
'Pisanello and the Princess of Trebizond', *Apollo*, n.s., 76: 601–3.

1963 *Colliers Encyclopaedia* (New York): 'Justin I', 'Justin II'.

1964 'Trebizond and Rome', *ArchP* 26: 290–307.
'Edward I and the Mongols', *History Today*, 14 [10]: 696–704.

1965 'A molybdobull of the imperial protospatharios Constantine, krites of the theme of Chaldia', *ArchP* 27: 244–6.
'Ludovico da Bologna and the Georgian and Anatolian Embassy of 1460–61', *Bedi Kartlisa* 19–20: 178–98 (= Bryer 1980, X).
'The Great Idea', *History Today* 15: 159–68; reprinted in *Universal Rome*, ed. A. Birley (Edinburgh, 1967), 100–17.
'Trebizond and Serbia', *ArchP* 27: 28–40.
with R. Milner-Gulland, 'Two Metropolitans of Trebizond in Russia', *ArchP* 27: 21–7.
Review of D. Talbot Rice and W. Swaan, *Constantinople*, in *History Today* 15 (December).
Review of Philip Sherrard, *Constantinople*, in *History Today* 15 (July).
Review of Steven Runciman, *The Fall of Constantinople*, in *History Today* 15 (August).

1966 'Some notes on the Laz and Tzan (I)', *Bedi Kartlisa* 21–2: 174–95 (= Bryer 1988, XIVa).

'From Damaskinos to Tzanes: Cretan painting, 1453–1669', *Apollo* 84: 10–19.

with S. Ballance and D. Winfield, 'Nineteenth-century monuments in the city and vilayet of Trebizond: architectural and historical notes', Part 1, *ArchP* 28: 233–308.

'Rural Society in the Empire of Trebizond', *ArchP* 28: 152–60.

'Shipping in the Empire of Trebizond', *Mariner's Mirror* 52: 3–12 (= Bryer 1980, VIII).

Review of Steven Runciman, *The Fall of Constantinople*, in *JHS* 86.

Review of V. Lazarev, *Old Russian Murals*, in *Apollo* 84 (November).

1967 'Byzantine Games,' *History Today*, 17: 453–9; tr. into Greek, *Kathemerine* (Athens, 1968).

'The XIIIth International Congress of Byzantine Studies (Oxford 1966)', *Bedi Kartlisa* 23–4: 169–70.

'Some notes on the Laz and Tzan (II)', *Bedi Kartlisa* 23–4: 161–8 (= Bryer 1988, XIVb).

Encyclopaedia Britannica (13th edn, 1967; 14th edn, 1970): 'Trabzon'.

Review of J. J. Norwich, *The Normans in the South*, in *History Today* 17 (June).

Review of Spiro K. Kostof, *The Orthodox Baptistery of Ravenna*, in *Architectural Design* 37: 7.

Review of U. Vogt-Goknil, *Ottoman Architecture*, in *Architectural Design* 37: 2.

1968 'An introduction to Byzantine Art', in *Byzantium* (London, BBC Publications), 24–40.

'Nineteenth-century monuments in the city and vilayet of Trebizond: architectural and historical notes', Part 2, *ArchP* 29: 89–132.

'The tomb of Solomon II, last king of Imereti', *Bedi Kartlisa* 25, 214–17; tr. K. Emiroglu, 'Trabzon'da Yok Olan Bir Anit: Gurcu Krali Solomon II'nin Turbesi', *Trabzon* 3 (1989): 79–80.

'Notes on the function and vocabulary of Byzantine art', in Anton von Kassel, *Golden Icons* (London, The Grecian Gallery), 2.

Review of *Cambridge Medieval History, IV (1)*, in *JHS* 88.

Review of P. A. Underwood, *The Kariye Djami* (Princeton, NJ), in *Architectural Design* 38: 2.

Review of Patrick Leigh Fermor, *Roumeli*, in *Apollo* 87 (April).

1969 'Aghthamar', *Ararat* 10: 10–16.
'Byzantine Studies at the University of Birmingham', *Balkan Studies* 10.
'The Armenian Dilemma', *History Today* 19: 345–52.
'The last Laz risings and the downfall of the Pontic Derebeys, 1812–1840', *Bedi Kartlisa* 26, 191–210 (= Bryer 1988, XV).
'The church of Haghia Sophia in Trebizond,' *Apollo* 89, 268–74.

1970 with D.Winfield, 'Nineteenth-century monuments in the city and vilayet of Trebizond: architectural and historical notes', Part 3, *ArchP*, 30, 228–385.
with L. K. Young and T. Trautman, *Byzantium and the Ancient East*, ed. M. Gough (London, Hamlyn).
'A Byzantine family: the Gabrades, c.979–c.1653', *University of Birmingham Historical Journal* 12: 164–87 (= Bryer 1980, IIIa).
'A seal of Epiphanios, Archbishop of Cyprus', *Kypriakai Spoudai* 34: 19–24 (= Bryer 1988, III).
'The *Tourkokratia* in the Pontos, some problems and preliminary conclusions', *Neo-Hellenika* 1: 30–54 (= Bryer 1980, XI).
Review of C. A. Frazee, *The Orthodox Church and Independent Greece, 1821–1852*, in *Oxford Magazine* 1 (Hilary).
Review of D. M. Nicol, *The Byzantine Family of Kantakouzenos (Cantacuzenus), ca.1100–1460*, in *The Classical Review* 20 (2): 219–22.

1971 'Europe and the wider world to the fifteenth century', in *The Making of the Modern World, I, Europe Discovers the World*, ed. D. Johnson (London, Ernest Benn; New York, Barnes & Noble), 50–92.
'Nicaea, a Byzantine City', *History Today* 21: 22–31 (= Bryer 1988, IX; reprinted by American Research Institute in Turkey, Ankara, c.1993).
'The Byzantine monuments and topography of the Empire of Trebizond: the bandon of Trikomia,' *XIVe Congrès Internationale des Etudes Byzantines. Communications* (Bucarest), 104–6.
'The first encounter with the West, 1050–1204', in P. D. Whitting, ed, *Byzantium: an introduction* (Oxford, Blackwell), 83–110. The book ran into several British and US editions, to which A. A. M. B. added eight maps from 1981.
Review of 'Against Oblivion. Monuments of Byzantium' [review of 12 books, by Grant, Birley, Brown, Browning, Lang, Gimbutas, Vlasto, Dvornik, Whitting, Vacalopoulos, Haussig], in *Encounter* 37 (4)(October): 73–9.

Review of V. Laurent, *Corpus des sceaux de l'empire byzantin,* V, in *Erasmus* 23 (1971): 48–51.

1972 'Anthony Gervase Mathew, O.P.: a bibliography', *Eastern Churches Review* 4: 153–5.
Mereyamana Manastir (Soumela): a brief history (Trabzon) (cyclostyled guide).
The Christian East (London, BBC Publications).

1973 'Cultural relations between East and West in the twelfth century', in D. Baker, ed, *Relations between East and West in the Middle Ages* (Edinburgh), 77–94.
with J. Isaac and D. Winfield, 'Nineteenth-century monuments in the city and vilayet of Trebizond: architectural and historical notes', Part 4, *ArchP* 32: 126–310 (= Bryer, with Winfield, Ballance and Isaac; reprinted Ashgate 2002).
'The fate of George Komnenos, ruler of Trebizond (1266–1280)', *Byzantinische Zeitschrift* 66: 332–50 (= Bryer 1980, IV).
Review of D. Talbot Rice, *Byzantine Art and Its Influences,* in *Times Literary Supplement* (anonymous).
Review of *DOP* 26 (1972), in *Times Literary Supplement,* 20 July (anonymous).

1974 'A National Trust for Greece', *Eastern Churches Review* 6: 202.
Review of *DOP* 17 (1973), in *Times Literary Supplement,* 8 November (anonymous).

1975 with D. Winfield, 'A bibliography of travellers' reports on the Pontos: addenda', *ArchP* 33: 25–7.
with S. Fassoulakis and D. M. Nicol, 'A Byzantine family: the Gabrades. An additional note,' *BSl;* 36: 38–45 (= Bryer 1980, IIIb).
'Greeks and Turkmens: the Pontic exception', *DOP* 29: 113–49 (= Bryer 1980, V).
'Who was Eudokia/Euphemia?' *ArchP* 33: 17–24.
Review of K. Kalokyris, *The Byzantine Wall Paintings of Crete,* in *Times Literary Supplement* (anonymous).
Review of Michael Angold, *A Byzantine Government in Exile,* in *Times Literary Supplement,* 5 September.

1976 'Some Trapezuntine monastic obits', *REB* 34: 178–98 (= Bryer, 1980, IX).

'The Latins in the Euxine', *XVe Congrès International d'Etudes Byzantines. Rapports et co-rapports* (Athens), I, 1–12.

'The Pontic Revival and the New Greece', in N. P. Diamandouros and others. eds, *Hellenism and the First Greek War of Independence (1821–1830)* (Thessalonike), 171–90 (= Bryer 1980, XIII).

1977 'Excursus on Mananalis, Samosata of Armenia and Paulician Geography', in *Iconoclasm*, 83–4 (= Bryer 1980, II).

ed. with Judith Herrin, *Iconoclasm. Proceedings of the Ninth Spring Symposium of Byzantine Studies, Birmingham, March 1975* (Birmingham) (= reproduced 2006 by ACLS History E–Book Project).

Review of Douglas B. Hague and Rosemary Christie, *Lighthouses* (Gomer Press, 1975) and Dudkey Witney, *The Lighthouse* (New York, 1975), in *Journal of the Society of Architectural Historians*, xxxvi (4): 174–275.

1977–78 'Historical Note on Zil Kale', *ArchP* 34: 49–56.

1978 with T. S. Brown, 'Cities of Heraclius', *BMGS* 4: 15–30 (= Bryer 1980, I).

'The estates of the Empire of Trebizond: evidence for their resources, products, agriculture, ownership and location', *ArchP* 35: 270–477 (= Bryer 1980, VIII).

'Twelfth Spring Symposium of Byzantine Studies: "The Byzantine Black Sea", 18–20 March 1978', *ArchP* 35: 7–21.

A Cadaster of the Great Estates of the Empire of Trebizond (Birmingham).

1979 'The Late Byzantine monastery in town and countryside', in D. Baker, ed., *The Church in Town and Countryside*, Studies in Church History 16 (Oxford), 219–41 (= Bryer 1980, VI).

Review of Clive Foss, *Ephesus after Antiquity*, in *Times Literary Supplement*, 12 December.

The Empire of Trebizond and the Pontos (London, Variorum Reprints; reproduced 2006 by ACLS History E-Book Project).

1981 '"The Byzantine Saint": The XIVth Spring Symposium of Byzantine Studies', in *The Byzantine Saint*, ed. S. Hackel (London, Sobornost), 4–8.

with J. F. Haldon, P. Karlin-Hayter, R. Loverance and H. W. Lowry, 'Continuity and change in Late Byzantine and early Ottoman

society: case studies from Macedonia, Lemnos and the Pontos', *JÖB* 31 *Beiheft = XVI. Internationaler Byzantinistenkongress,* Akten I/ Beiheft 2.2., n.p.
'Greek historians on the Turks: the case of the first Byzantine–Ottoman marriage', in R. H. C. Davis and J. M. Wallace Hadrill, eds, *The Writing of History in the Middle Ages: essays presented to Richard William Southern* (Oxford), 471–93 (= Bryer 1988, IV).

1982 'The question of Byzantine mines in the Pontos: Chalybian iron, Chaldian silver, Koloneian alum and the mummy of Cheriana', *Anatolian Studies* 32: 133–50 (= Bryer 1988, XI).
'Une église "à la demande du client" à Trebizonde', *Proche-Orient Chrétien* 32: 216–34 (= Bryer 1988, V).
'Alexios I of Trebizond', in *Dictionary of the Middle Ages* I (New York)

1983 'Greeks and Turks', in T. Winnifrith and P. Murray, eds, *Greece, Old and New* (London, Macmillan), 95–110.
'The crypto-Christians of the Pontos and Consul William Gifford Palgrave', *Deltio Kentrou Mikrasiatikon Spoudon* 4: 13–68 (= Bryer 1988, XVIII).

1984 'The faithless Kabazitai and Scholarioi', in Ann Moffatt, ed., *Maistor. Classical, Byzantine and Renaissance Studies for Robert Browning,* Byzantina Australiensia 5 (Canberra), 309–28 (= Bryer 1988, VII).

1984–85 'The treatment of Byzantine place-names', *BMGS* 9: 209–14 (= Bryer 1988, VIII).

1985 'Byzantine porridge', in H. Mayr-Harting and R. I. Moore, eds, *Studies in Medieval History Presented to R. H. C. Davis* (London, Hambledon Press), 1–6 (= Bryer 1988, XIII).
with D. Winfield, *The Byzantine Monuments and Topography of the Pontos,* Dumbarton Oaks Studies 20 (2 vols, Washington, DC; reproduced 2006 in ACLS History E-Book Project).

1986 'Byzantine agricultural implements: the evidence of medieval illustrations of Hesiod's *Works and Days*', *BSA* 81: 45–80.
'Eclipses and epithalamy in fourteenth-century Trebizond', in *Byzantium:. a tribute to Andreas N. Stratos,* ed. Nia Stratos, I (Athens), 347–52 (= Bryer 1988, VI).

ed. with H. Lowry, *Continuity and Change in Late Byzantine and Early Ottoman Society* (Birmingham and Washington, DC); including 'Rural Society in Matzouka', 51–96 (= Bryer 1988, XI); 'The Three Cyrils', 155–8 (= Bryer 1988, XVI) and 'The structure of the Late Byzantine town: *Dioikismos* and the *Mesoi*', 263–79 (= Bryer 1988, X).

review of Lyn Rodley, *Cave monasteries of Byzantine Cappadocia* (Cambridge University Press, 1985), in *Times Literary Supplement*, 14 November.

1987 '*Han* Turali rides again', *BMGS* 11: 193–206 (= Bryer 1988, II).

1988 'Anaphora apo ten Imera kai to Mpirmigcham', in *HIMEPA*, ed. P. G. Tanamanides (Thessalonike), 191–3; reprinted in the Proceedings of the *B! Pagkosmio Synedrio Pontiakou Hellenismou* (Thessalonike, 1988), I, 83–8.

'Byzantine and Modern Greek Studies: a partial view', *BMGS* 12: 1–26

Past Worlds: The Times Atlas of Archaeology (London), 'The Byzantine Empire'.

Peoples and Settlement in Anatolia and the Caucasus, 800–1900 (London, Variorum) (= reproduced 2006 in ACLS History E-Book Project).

Review of *The Holy and Great Monastery of Vatopaidi* , ed. The Fathers of the Holy and Great Monastery of Vatopaidi (Mount Athos, 1998), in *Friends of Mount Athos Annual Report*, 51–4.

The Blackwells Dictionary of Historians, ed. J. Cannon (Oxford): 'Norman Hepburn Baynes', 'Byzantine Historiography', 'Charles Diehl', 'Henri Gregoire', 'George Grote', 'George Ostrogorsky', 'Steven Runciman'.

1988–89 'David Komnenos and Saint Eleutherios', *ArchP* 42: 161–88 (= *Dedicatio* [*Festschrift* for Mariam Lordkipanidze], ed. I. A. Dzhavachishvili [Tbilisi, 2001], 39–77).

1989 *Dictionary of the Middle Ages* XII (New York), 'Trebizond, Empire of'.

1990 'A view from the Byzantine side of the river Akampsis', in *The Georgian Chronicle. The period of Giorgi Lasha,* ed. S. Qaukhchshvili, tr. Katharine Vivian (Amsterdam), i–xxi.

Review of Martin Harrison, *A Temple for Byzantium* (University of Texas, 1989), in *Times Literary Supplement*, 10 January.

1991 'Byzantium and the Pontos during the "Time of Troubles" (1332–63)', *XVIIIth International Congress of Byzantine Studies, Major Papers* (Moscow), 246–66; reprinted in *Acts XVIIIth International Congress of Byzantine Studies. Selected Papers: Main and Communications. Moscow, 1991*, I, History, ed. I. Ševčenko and G. G. Litavrin (Sheperdstown, WV, 1996), 93–105.

'The Pontic Greeks before the Diaspora', *Journal of Refugee Studies* 4 (4): 315–34 (= Bryer, with Winfield, Ballance and Isaac; reprinted, Ashgate 2002).

ed. with Michael Ursinus, *Manzikert to Lepanto: The Byzantine World and the Turks, 1071–1571. Papers given at the Nineteenth Spring Symposium of Byzantine Studies, Birmingham, March 1985* (= *BF*, 16 [Amsterdam], and 1–8 [= reproduced 2006 in ACLS History E-Book Project].

Review of Donald M. Nicol, *Byzantium and Venice: a study in diplomatic and cultural relations* (Cambridge University Press, 1989), in *Journal of Theological Studies* 42 [1]: 381–2.

1992 'Santa Sophia', *Cornucopia* 1, 64–5.

'The Black Sea Coast', in *The Berlitz Guide to Turkey*, ed. Toni Cross (New York, 1992), 534–62; expanded and emended (New York), 596–628 and subsequently.

Review of Donald Nicol, *A Biographical Dictionary of the Byzantine Empire* (London, 1991), in *Minerva* III (3): 39

1993 'Black Sea', *Cornucopia* 3: 35–40.

'Byzantynistyka coraz atrakcyjniejska', tr. Malgorzata Dabrowska, *Kronika* (University of Lodz), 6: 29–31.

'Family planning in Trebizond: the AIMA of the Grand Komnenoi', in *TO HELLENIKON. Studies in Honor of Speros Vryonis, Jr.*, ed. Milton V. Anastos et al., I, *Hellenic Antiquity and Byzantium* (New York), 85–90.

with J. Crow, 'Survey at Bozluca, Trabzon Vilayet, Turkey 1992', *University of Durham and University of Newcastle upon Tyne Archaeological Reports 1992* (Durham), 35–8.

'Tamara and David Talbot Rice', *Cornucopia* 4: 22–7.

'The Historian's Digenes Akrites', in *Digenes Akrites. New Approaches to Byzantine Heroic Poetry*, ed. R. Beaton and D. Ricks (London, Variorum), 93–102.

'The Pontic Greek Diaspora' [Hippocratic Oration 1992], *Bio-Medical Bulletin of Hellenic Diaspora* 3 (1): 2–3.

'Trabzon Imperatorlugu'nda Gemicilik', tr. K. Emiroglu, *Trabzon* 7: 18–27.

Review of Bettina Selby, *Beyond Ararat* (London, John Murray, 1993), in *Times Literary Supplement*, 16 April.

Review of *Hagioreitike Photographia* (Thessalonike, 1993), I, II, in *Friends of Mount Athos Annual Report*, 37–9.

Review of Michel Kaplan, *Les Hommes et la terre à Byzance du Vie au Xie siècle. Propriété et exploitation du sol* (Paris, 1992), in *English Historical Review* 108 [429]: 966–8.

ed. with G. S. Georghallides, *The Sweet Land of Cyprus. Papers given at the Twenty-fifth Jubilee Spring Symposium of Byzantine Studies, Birmingham 1991* (Birmingham and Nicosia), with introduction.

1994 'Foreword' to P. M. Kitromilides, *Enlightenment, Nationalism, Orthodoxy* (London, Variorum), ix–xi.

'St Asteios and the amphitheatre chapel at Dyrrhachion', in *THYMIAMA: ste mneme tes Laskarinas Mpoura* (Athens), I, 41–45.

'The Grand Komnenos and the Great Khan at Karakorum in 1246', in *Itinéraires d'Orient. Hommages à Claude Cahen = Res Orientales* VI, 257–61.

'Zaro Agha (1774–1934)', *Cornucopia* 7: 80–82.

1995 with S. Hill, 'Byzantine Porridge: *Tracta, Trachanas and Tarhana*', in D. Harvey and M. Dobson, eds, *Food in Antiquity* (Exeter), 44–54.

Review of D. Braund, *Georgia in Antiquity* (Oxford, 1994), in *Times Literary Supplement*, 20 January.

Review of P. M. Straessle, *Der Internationale Schwarzmeerhamdel und Konstantinopel, 1204–1464*, in *Speculum* 70: 204–5.

1996 'Bryer broods on Braund', *Pegasus* 39: 28–30.

'Byzantium and the Pontos during the 'Time of Troubles' (1332–63)', in I. Ševčenko, G. Litavrin and W. Hanak, eds, *Acts, XVIIIth International Congress of Byzantine Studies. Selected Papers: Main and Communications, Moscow 1991* (Shepherdstown, WV), I, 93–105.

'Gibbon and the Later Byzantine Empires', in Rosamond McKitterick and Roland Quinault, eds, *Gibbon and Empire* (Cambridge), 101–16.

'The Late Byzantine identity', in *Byzantium: Identity, Image, Influence. Major Papers XIX International Congress of Byzantine Studies* (Copenhagen), 49–50.

ed. with Mary Cunningham, *Mount Athos and Byzantine Monasticism. Papers from the Twenty-eighth Spring Symposium of*

Byzantine Studies, Birmingham, March 1994 (SPBS,Variorum, Aldershot).
The Macmillan Dictionary of Art (London), 'Trebizond'.

1997 'From Selly Oak to Sinai: *Sparagmata Syriaca*', *Sinaiticus* 2: 6–8.
with James Crow, 'Survey in Trabzon and Gumushane Vilayets, Turkey, 1992–1994', *DOP* 51: 283–89.
'The rise and fall of the Macedonian school of Byzantine art (1910–1962)', in Peter Mackridge and Eleni Yannakakis, eds, *Ourselves and Others: the development of Greek Macedonian identity since 1912* (Oxford), 79–87.
'Trabzon Imparatorlugu'nda Gimicilik' [in Turkish], in I. G. Kayaoglu, O. Ciravoglu and C. Akalin, eds, *Bir Tutkudur Trabzon* (Istanbul), 97–105.
'Trabzon Imperatorlugu'nda Gemicilik', tr. K.Emiroglu, in *Bir Tutkudur Trabzon,*'XXXth Spring Symposium of Byzantine Studies', *Bulletin of British Byzantine Studies* 23: 80–81.
Review of Peter Lock and G. D. R. Sanders, eds, *The Archaeology of Medieval Greece,* in *Anglo-Hellenic Review* 15: 20–21.
The Oxford Companion to Archaeology (New York), 'Constantinople'.

1998 'Byzantium and the Roman Orthodox world, 1395–1492', in Christopher Allmand, ed., *The New Cambridge Medieval History*, VII (Cambridge), 771–95; revised and reprinted in Jonathan Shepard, ed., *The Cambridge History of the Byzantine Empire* (Cambridge, 2007), chapter 24.
'He episteme pou askei einai paradeigmatike' [in Greek] (Nikolaos Panayiotakis), *Anti* II, 672 (30 October), 21.
'Ottoman Athos', *Friends of Mount Athos Annual Report*, 22–9.
'The Black Sea in Crisis', *Anglo-Hellenic Review* 17: 11.
'The Holy Mountain', *Cornucopia* III, 15: 42–63.
Review of Lyn Rodley, *Byzantine Art and Architectur: an introduction* (Cambridge University Press, 1994), in *JHS* 118: 254–55.
Review of *The Journals and Letters of George Finlay*, ed. J. M. Hussey, in *English Historical Review* 103 [454], 1344–5.

1999 'What time is it?', *Bulletin of British Byzantine Studies* 25: 85.
Review of Martin Biddle, *The Tomb of Christ*, in *History Today*, 49 (10) (October 1999): 54.
Review of N. Malcolm, *Kosovo: a short history* (Macmillan, 1998), in *Cornucopia* III (17): 21–2.

Review of *The Theotokos Evergetis*, ed. Margaret Mullett and Anthony Kirby, 2 vols (= BBT&T 6.1 and 6.2), in *Anglo-Hellenic Review* 19: 19.

2000 'Alice Lindsell's Botanical Sketchbook', in J. E. Raven, *Plants and Plant Lore in Ancient Greece* (Leopard's Head Press, Oxford), xiii.
'*Intervista*', *Ngjallja* 12 (99) (Dhjetor): 6, 8, 10 (in Albanian).
'Xeroun oti einai Christougenna?', *Archaeologia* 74 (June): 8–15.
Encyclopedia of Greece and the Hellenic Tradition (London): 'Political History, 1453–1832', 'Ani', 'Trebizond', 'Black Sea', 'Crimea', 'Pontus', 'Conversion to Islam'.
Review of Andrew Sharf, *Jews and Other Minorities in Byzantium* (Jerusalem, 1995), in *English Historical Review* 105 [460]: 175–6.
Review of Jonathan Harris, *Greek Emigres in the West, 1400–1520* (Camberley, 1995), in *English Historical Review* 105 [460]: 192–3.
Review of Nicholas Coureas, *The Latin Church in Cyprus, 1195–1323* (London, 1997); Nicholas Coureas and Christopher Schabel, *The Cartulary of the Cathedral of the Holy Wisdom of Nicosia* (Nicosia, 1997); and Gillian Webster, *Philia and Philiotes before and after 974* (London, 1999), in *BMGS* 24: 282–6.
Review of Robert Ousterhout, *Master Builders of Byzantium* (Princeton University Press, 1999), in *Times Literary Supplement* 30 June.
The Archaeology of Anatolia: an encyclopedia (Ankara), 'Pontos', 'Trapezous'.

2001 'Byzantium and its Pontic neighbours', Abstract of keynote lecture, *Second International Congress on Black Sea Antiquities* (Ankara, 5 September)
'Do they know it's Christmas?', *History Today* 51, 1 (January): 16–18.
'The Pilgrim monastery of Soumela as an economic paradigm', *XXe Congrès International des Etudes Byzantines, Pré-Actes* (Paris), II, *Tables Rondes* 90–91.
'Who won the Battle of the Acropolis? The evidence of William James Muller in 1838', *Anglo-Hellenic Review* 24 (Autumn): 4–6.

2002 'Cruise Control: Runcie at Sea with Swan', in Stephen Platten, ed., *Runcie: on reflection. An archbishop remembered* (London), 116–24.
'The Means of Agricultural Production: Muscle and Tools', in Angeliki E. Laiou. ed., *The Economic History of Byzantium from the Seventh through the Fifteenth Century* (Dumbarton Oaks and Athens),

I, 101–13; Greek translation (Athens, National Bank Cultural Foundation, 2006), I, 181–204.
with D. Winfield, Selina Balance and Jane Isaac, *The Post-Byzantine Monuments of the Pontos: a source book* (Ashgate, Variorum Collected Studies CS707), 'Introduction', vii–xix.

2003 'Kultet e tre shenjtore've martire' ne' Shqipe'ri', in *2000 Vjet Art dhe Kulture' kishtare ne' Shqipe'ri: Aktet e Simpoziumit nde'rkomb'tar, Tirane', 16–18 N'entor 2000*, ed. Archbishop Anastasios and the Autocephalous Orthodox Church of Albania (Tirana), 53–7.
with Archibald Dunn and John Nesbitt, 'Theodore Gabras, Duke of Chaldia (+1098) and the Gabrades: portraits, sites and seals', in Anna Avramea, Angeliki Laiou and E. Chrysos, eds, *Byzantio Kratos kai Koinonia / Byzantium State and Society. In memory of Nikos Oikonomides* (Athens), 51–70.

2004 Review of Antony Eastmond and Liz James, eds, *Icon and Word: the power of images in Byzantium. Studies presented to Robin Cormack* (London, 2003), in *Times Literary Supplement*, 2 April.
Review of Helen C. Evans, ed., *Byzantium: faith and power, 1261–1557* (Yale, 2004), in *The World of Interiors* 24 (September): 36.
Review of James Knox, *Robert Byron: A Biography* (London, 2004) and Graham Speake, *Mount Athos: renewal in paradise* (Yale, 2003), in *Cornucopia* 5 [31]: 25–6.

2006 'Foreword', in *Proceedings of the 21st International Congress of Byzantine Studies, London 21–26 August 2006*, ed. Elizabeth Jeffreys and others (London), I, viii; and 'Who goes there? Jacob d'Ancona and other travellers', in ibid., II, 291–2.
'People get the heroes and martyrs they deserve', in *Ritual and Art: Byzantine essays for Christopher Walter*, ed. Pamela Armstrong (London, Pindar Press), 122–8.
'Welcome', in Programme of 21st International Congress of Byzantine Studies (London), i.

2007 'Byzantium on display', in *Cornucopia*.
'Epilogue', in G. Erkut and S. Mitchell, *The Black Sea: past, present and future*, (London/Istanbul).
'R. M. Dawkins, F. W. Hasluck and the crypto-Christians', in M. Llewellyn-Smith and P. Kitromilides, eds, *Scholars, Travels, Archives* (Athens).

Oxford Handbook to Byzantium (Oxford 2007): 'Chronology and dating', 'Food and feasting'.

Professor Bryer, celebrating the Symposium (photo credit: A. Dunn)

Section I

A tribute to A. A. M. Bryer

1. A tribute to Professor Bryer

Joseph A. Munitiz, S.J.

My contribution to our celebrations will take the form of reminiscences: I propose two, both connected with walks, and both with Professor Bryer. They are both, you might say, examples of 'serendipity', and if any of you are unfamiliar with that term, let me recall a description of it that I heard recently: serendipity is the experience one has when one is looking for a needle in a haystack and comes across the farmer's daughter.

I had known Bryer since one of the early Birmingham symposia back in the 1970s, but our acquaintance remained a remote one. Although I am older than he, at that stage I was a lowly PhD student, struggling to complete a thesis, and he was already an established professor. By chance, we both decided to attend the International Byzantine Conference held in Athens in 1976. And we met when we both decided to play truant from the main activity of the day, and to get off the bus taking the group to Delphi, as we wanted to spend more time at Hosios Loukas. So there you have the pair of us, tramping along the dusty road that forked off to the left, while the bus careered on along the main road to Delphi. As you all know, Bryer is one of the most sociable beings that exist. We began to chat as we walked along, and to my astonishment I discovered that this bearded man, looking very like an Orthodox pope, was also one of the kindest persons I have ever known.

So much for the first reminiscence and the first walk: the second comes nearly twenty-five years later, when I found myself posted to Birmingham, where we Jesuits have our novitiate house, semi-retirement if you like because my duties in the house were light and I could continue working on editions of Greek texts. On the first weekend I borrowed a map of the vicinity and set off to explore; in fact the area of Harborne consisted, not many years ago, of a series of farms, and one can still follow the boundaries of what have since become various golf courses. As I returned that Sunday afternoon, whom should I meet coming along the dusty path in the opposite direction but Bryer with his wife and a group of locals also exploring the bounds. Bryer welcomed me like a long-lost friend, and it is thanks to him that I have been able to find a place as an emeritus scholar at the Centre here, with access to the library, an inestimable joy for any scholar.

It is obvious that if Bryer and I have known one another it is largely thanks to our admiration for the Byzantine world; it is that initially which drew us together. But it seems to me that there is at least one other condition that had to exist if we were to find a certain harmony of spirit. And this I think is an openness of mind.

On a recent visit to Athens I have had the joy of discovering the works of a remarkable scholar-politician, Panayotis Kanelopoulos (you may know more of him than I do). But this man who reached the highest political posts – though probably he was less successful there – was also someone who in his seventies could write a historical novel of life in fourteenth-century Patras, which also shows an extraordinary breadth of spirit. Later he was to write an even more ambitious work, his ten-volume *History of the European Spirit,* which covers with equal magnanimity Luther and Ignatius of Loyola and Lenin. It is that breadth, that openness, that attracts me also in Bryer. He can show it in unexpected ways at times, as his culinary interests show, but it is thanks to that gift of his that he has been able to do so much, and for which we are truly grateful.

2. *Polla ta ete* (repeat three times) to Bryer

Judith Herrin

Among the many things Bryer has taught me, there is one in which I was a less than willing student: the art of writing obituaries. This field, in which he excels partly because of long and brilliant experience as the Public Orator at the University of Birmingham, was forced on me when Robert Browning died. Bryer instructed me to ring up the *Guardian* and insist that it carry an obituary; he would deal with the *Independent* and arrange for others to cover *The Times*. I was thus obliged to try and master a new art form, quite distinct from the writing of history.

By 2000, when Nikos Oikonomides died, this task had become established and I was again instructed to call the *Guardian*. The paper agreed to commission 600 words and requested a photograph of the deceased. I found a lovely picture of Nikos taken when he gave the Runciman Lecture at King's College London, which showed him with Bryer and Sir Steven. After identifying the individuals, I sent off the photo with my text, asking for it to be returned as it was a favourite. The *Guardian* duly focused on the bearded guy, assumed to be the Greek, cropped the picture and published a close-up of Bryer with my obituary of Nikos on 21 June 2000. While his daughters protested and I fumed, Bryer himself was away in Belfast, and the first he knew of this crass error was on the plane returning the following day. As usual, with the *Guardian,* he turned first to the erratum column, which he knew to be the only reliable and accurate part of the news, and there was the apology. Although he saw the funny side, it was not amusing for Nikos's family and for those who only saw the original text, which continued to circulate without the apology.

When I first came to Birmingham in 1965, Bryer was a research fellow in the History Department. He and Liz were living in a flat off the Hagley Road and their first daughter, Theo, had recently been born. I recall walking over there with Bryer to admire his collection of travel books in a small glass-fronted case beside the nappies drying on a clothes horse in front of the gas fire – those were the days!

Before that momentous meeting, I didn't even know that Birmingham had a Byzantinist. I had written to the Department of Classics, asking if I could study Greek. Ron Willetts had invited me to come at once because the beginners' course had started and I would have to catch up. So I rushed into what became my seven-year attachment to Birmingham. First, I studied ancient Greek with Ron (Homer, *Odysseia,* and Aristotle, *Poetics,* stick in the mind); medieval Byzantine Greek with Meg Alexiou (Romanos and Theodore Prodromos among many authors), and Modern Greek with George Thomson, who loved the *Δωδεκάλογος τοῦ Γύφτου* of Palamas. Over two years I received a very full introduction to most aspects of Greek. Thanks to Bryer, who was rapidly promoted to lecturer, I then started my PhD using the letters of Michael Choniates, Metropolitan of Athens from 1180 to 1205, as a source for the social and economic history of Hellas.

In the 1960s the Arts Faculty at Birmingham was crammed with brilliant intellectuals, many of a left-wing persuasion, and the nearby Social Science Tower and Barber Institute both contributed their own wealth of distinction. Anthony Lewis brought Janet Baker to sing in his productions of unfamiliar Handel operas every year, Bob Davies ran the Centre for Russian Studies, and Norbert Elias filled in for a sociology professor on leave. But it was the group of communist or ex-communist scholars in Arts: Rodney Hilton, Roy Pascal and George Thomson, along with fellow socialists Douglas Johnson and Richard Hoggart, who set the agenda. When the latter retired, Stuart Hall took over the Centre for Contemporary Cultural Studies and raised it to a leading position, pioneering Media Studies as well. Birmingham was exciting. While Bryer, I think, missed Oxford, I was delighted to transfer to a university so different from Cambridge, a place where people were so engaged, so politically aware, so committed to improving university life and standards.

Our Vice-Chancellor was not quite so committed to change, however, and we had one of the best sit-ins of 1968–69, which lasted several weeks and turned the administration upside down. Although the teachers were not keen on the disruption, when the VC threatened to ask the police to come and arrest everyone who was still occupying the Great Hall, they all joined the thousands of students and stood at the back waiting. No arrests were made and the sit-in was only called off at the end of term because everyone felt the need of a holiday. Bryer put up with my involvement with very good grace. In fact, he put up with most of my graduate activities outside the field of Byzantine Studies and supported my research in every way. I was the first of a long line of graduate students, most of whom attended the Food and Drink Symposium as a tribute to their teacher.

Bryer expected me to get on with my research and so I did. Whenever I managed to write a chapter, I gave it to him and he was unfailingly clear in his corrections, which included my spelling mistakes as well as more serious conceptual problems. He insisted that I should go with him to a conference in Venice so that I could look at manuscripts in the Marciana Library. Similarly, when the Byzantine Congress met in Bucharest in 1971, he helped me to apply for funding and we both had the dubious pleasure of seeing Ceauşescu at close quarters. When the *University of Birmingham Historical Journal* proposed that he edit a special Byzantine number, he insisted that all local Byzantinists should contribute. His own article is a model of detailed prosopography devoted to the Gabrades, members of a Byzantine family from the Pontos, set in the wider context of Bryer's rich knowledge of the region's connections – Arab, Seljuk, Armenian, Georgian and Cretan. By then, John Haldon had joined the band of graduates and Margaret Mullett and Wesam Farag were not far behind. We felt that Byzantine Studies were on a roll; we were riding the crest of a thundering big wave and Bryer was the wave-maker.

This was evident from Bryer's immense triumph in creating the Centre for Byzantine and Modern Greek Studies, which later expanded to include Ottoman. The process began in a modest fashion with a committee formed to promote Byzantine Studies at Birmingham, chaired by Ellis Waterhouse, Professor of Art History. The huge Department of Theology, established by the Cadburys, contributed courses on New Testament and Orthodox theology, with help from the Syriac Institute down the road, inspired by Sebastian Brock. Bryer provided courses on Byzantine history for the History Department, and the teaching of Greek from Homer to the present day established the linguistic foundation. With the help of an enlightened librarian with expanding resources, and the donation of specialist book and coin collections put together by the numismatist Philip Whitting, Birmingham rapidly acquired magnificent holdings in the field of Byzantine Studies. Outsiders undoubtedly helped: I recall Bryer's visits to the Talbot Rices and Steven Runciman for guidance and encouragement; connections from Oxford (Gervase Matthews, Dimitri Obolensky and Father Kallistos), and George Avery and others from the Fellowship of St Alban and St Sergius. All this came together thanks to Bryer's indefatigable persistence and imagination.

At the same time, he continued his own research into the monuments and institutions of the empire of Trebizond, based on his PhD thesis at Oxford, which was eventually expanded into the two-volume publication with David Winfield. He regularly took students to Trabzon and other remoter regions of eastern Turkey looking at Byzantine monuments, and tracking down speakers of Pontic Greek dialects, and this at a time when such activity was not considered appropriate by the authorities. Reports of their fieldwork made clear his debt to local foresters – particularly the one responsible for the region near the Soumela monastery – village chieftains and transhumant farmers who helped them to find isolated churches. Bryer was an assiduous contributor to the journal *Archeion Pontou* and the less familiar *Bedi K'art'lisa*, a Georgian periodical, which published many of his articles on the region's medieval monuments.

In their grander accommodation at Crosbie Road, the Bryers were dedicated hosts who entertained students lavishly with home cooking and good wine. How Liz put up with making huge trays of lasagne and mountains of cream-filled meringues, I can't imagine. Everything was delicious and unusually grand, and she was always most welcoming. Overnight guests were required to sign the visitors' book. Their comments must be a vital source for Bryer anecdotes. This aspect of the Bryers' hospitality was later extended to the invited speakers for spring symposia, who set out from the university on a double-decker bus for Harborne with glasses of champagne. How the symposia developed is perhaps another topic, but I recall the events of one Saturday afternoon in 1971 – three lectures, I think, on the Holy Man. A. H. M. Jones laid down the context in a fashion so dry that it might have discouraged even the most enthusiastic audience, and then Peter Brown and Sebastian Brock took over. The thrill of those lectures set the pattern for what gradually became a regular symposium and rapidly began to attract larger numbers. With *Iconoclasm* (1975; published 1977), I feel it really got into its stride, not only because the papers given were so interesting, but also because Bryer and I edited them into a privately published volume, which became in effect number 1 in the series. That volume is still in demand and thanks to the American Council of Learned Societies it will soon be available as an e-book.

Food and drink have always been an important part of the symposium – not just the Byzantine feast, which usually falls in Lent and is therefore a bit restricted in its scope – but also the consumption of curries and beer in restaurants and pubs up and down the Bristol Road, which brings together so many Byzantinists. As symposiarch, Bryer is unmatched, and if he suspected the choice of subject for the spring of 2003, he did not let on. Since he had always refused to countenance any idea of a Festschrift, we thought it would be neat to set up a symposium in which he could participate and which could then be turned into a volume in his honour. To my great delight, this is what has happened.

Finally, let no one forget that Bryer is the world's expert on one aspect of Byzantine food and drink – porridge. This food was obviously one of the mainstays of the transhumant pastoralists encountered in the Pontic Alps, who dried their summer grain and formed it into compressed blocks, which they broke up and heated with water or milk to make into porridge during the winter. In typical fashion Bryer had observed a traditional foodstuff, made notes about it in his black pocket book, and then traced it back into medieval times. His colleague at Birmingham, Ralph Davis, was honoured with this important article, which gets overlooked because it was published in a Festschrift! And worse, in a Festschrift for a western medievalist where Byzantinists would not think of looking for it. So I end by drawing attention to yet another highly original article by our great teacher, patron, benefactor and friend – A. A. M. Bryer.

3. Bryer the anthropologist

Rosemary Morris

Over thirty years ago, Bryer gave me my 'big break'. The theme of the Spring Symposium in 1974 was 'Byzantine Society and Economy' and Bryer, in his customarily eclectic way, had invited the eminent French numismatist Cécile Morrisson to give a paper. Unfortunately for her, but very fortunately for me, Professor Morrisson had an accidental fall off the tailgate of a French army lorry ferrying citizens about during one of the many transport strikes which characterize *la vie parisienne.* She injured her leg and was thus unable to travel. This led to a terse last-minute communication from Bryer to me. I should say that all he hitherto knew of me was that I had written for permission to consult his embargoed D.Phil thesis on the empire of Trebizond in the Bodleian Library and that I was working for a doctorate on 'something to do with church lands'. Bryer's note a) invited me to give a main paper and b) reassured me that 'they will not notice the difference; your names are almost identical.'

Having since had the great pleasure of meeting Cécile Morrisson, I must say that there can, in fact, have been very little resemblance between the erudite and chic Professor Morrisson and the extremely tatty and somewhat confused graduate student that I then was. One thing, however, led to another. My paper on the 'Poor and the Powerful' at the symposium was taken up for publication in *Past and Present* by the late, great Rodney Hilton (whom, I suspect, had been told by Bryer that I was a distinguished economic historian from Paris), and, in the summer of 1974, when faced by a table full of suits (no women, of course, on appointment committees in the University of Manchester then, and precious few since … but I digress), I was able to maintain – fingers firmly crossed behind my back – that I was 'quite used' to speaking to large audiences. The fact that the then Professor of Medieval History (a somewhat 'unreconstructed' individual) was able to report back, with some surprise, to his colleagues – and here you must imagine the rich tones of Accrington – 'We have appointed a young woman; we have not had One of Them since the War, when the chaps went to the

Forces', I attribute in great measure to the immense boost in my confidence provided by Bryer's invitation.

Bryer, as is well known, is, above all, interested in people – in you, me and the whole human zoo, particularly the specimens in the capacious enclosure labelled 'Byzantinists. Please take care as these creatures may bite!' He is an anthropologist of rare insight and often alarming discernment. Let me illustrate my point with a few case studies, drawn from my own dossier on *Homo bryerensis*. Like all anthropologists, Bryer is interested in hierarchies, though he dislikes and distains most of them. His views on the multiplicity of administrative worthies that has proliferated in the British university system in recent years are surely influenced by long experience of explaining the implications of Byzantine *taktika* to generations of students. When he conjures up the grand entrance of an academic VIP into the staff bar at Birmingham, accompanied by 'metrognomes, protochancellors, triple-liners, diet-lager bearers and understrappers', the heady mixture of self-importance and vacuity is precisely located. When he comments, in an official report on a conference attended in the US in 1987, that 'I do not think there was much the speakers learned at the Conference, but perhaps that was not the point,' the *real* point is gently to remind his sponsors that some things, which are touted as very important by their protagonists, might not turn out to be quite so earth-shattering as they suppose. Bryer's dislike of pomposity is more than manifest in the way Birmingham (and other places that have hoped to emulate the unique atmosphere generated at the symposia there) conducts its Byzantine business. Not for us the spectacle of grand professors arriving in state with a suite of graduate students carefully walking three paces behind. It is this sense of equality which has now successfully permeated the international gatherings, too. No longer does one sit through endless hour-long addresses by 'great names'; we actively participate as speakers and interlocutors at *tables rondes* and seminars. Long (and further) may this trend continue!

Bryer is, therefore, no respecter of reputations. In 1986, when working on entries for the *Oxford Dictionary of Historians*, he took little notice of the editorial instructions about which figures to concentrate upon. As he wrote to me in characteristically irreverent mode:

> I've extravagantly changed the wording to make Grégoire the greatest. Liberal but Walloon; the reason why he epigraphised East from 1905 to Leopold II's death was his damning report on the Belgian Congo. Have you ever read *Le Flambeau* [Bryer *always* assumes you are as unnervingly well read as he is], his mag. before *Byzantion*, first circulated as *samizdat* during the first German occupation and again in the second? It is a sort of *Encounter* watered down by the end. 783 publications and not a book: I like that. Diehl merited three times as much on the editors' system and has been reversed. After degeneration

> into a *salon* Byzantinist from 1917, we only put in his first – *Ravenna* (1888) – and last *grands problèmes* books as survivable. Admirable chap: Vassiliev sang rounds with him in Wisconsin.

If we reluctantly tear ourselves away from the intriguing spectacle of this glee club of eminent Byzantinists, we can note that Bryer's stalwart defence of scholarship in all its forms (often the best is *not* in hard covers), his dislike of the superficial and the glib – however elegantly put – and his support for those who persist in preserving the integrity of their beliefs, are, as ever, presented with a light, but precise touch.

Like all good anthropologists, Bryer has preternaturally sensitive powers of observation. If anyone wanted a really impressive dose of 'deep description', he should read Bryer's highly detailed, sometimes scurrilous and always hilarious account of a trip to Finland in 1987. Here we are in the Zausilow Collection of 11,000 agricultural implements in the Helsinki Museum: 'I found one tray labelled "Troy" and another labelled "Anglo-Saxon England". It was a temptation to transfer them …' Here we are late at night in Crosbie Road, Harborne, in the same year. Bryer wonders whether the *Archives de l'Athos* team would 'do' the *Archives du Pont* (the 'lost' archive of Soumela – nineteen bulls and *sigillia*, the first dating from 1364) and the 195 charters of Vazelon and writes that 'I was about to ring Peter Mackridge in Oxford about my Soumela archive and the 1364 bull and what a great discovery it was, when he rang to say that he had just got back from Trebizond (or rather from Ophis along the coast) and had, at long last, tracked down and recorded THE PONTIC INFINITIVE. It's funny what people think is important.'

It is indeed, and this might well serve as my closing text. Bryer – luckily for me all those years ago and for all of us now – thinks we are *all* important. He watches us with great erudition and with the 'gentle and perceptive blue eyes behind all that hair', which an Extremely August Personage, still clearly highly observant as she approached her hundredth birthday, noted at a lunch party held in a Scottish tower a few years ago. Although the Byzantine tribe is, like any other, often quarrelsome, stubborn, misguided, confused and sometimes very stupid indeed, like all great anthropologists, he still persists in studying us, he still finds us interesting and, I suspect, he still quite *likes* us, too!

4. Bryer the enthusiast

John Haldon

When I was invited to give this very short appreciation at the symposium, I was asked to focus on a particular attribute of Bryer's, something by which I and others might readily recognize him and his activities. It was not hard to work out what to talk about – his phenomenal, infectious and all-encompassing enthusiasm! This symposium was dedicated to Bryer as a scholar and as the man who, in the view of very many people, above all worked and organized and raised awareness, to put Byzantine Studies on the map of British teaching and research. For myself, Bryer was also the mentor who awakened my interest in Byzantium and who encouraged me to pursue that interest beyond my undergraduate work, and so it is with particular pleasure that I recall one specific moment, which summed up Bryer the Enthusiast and confirmed the course of study I was set to follow!

In the summer of 1969 I was one of five people, including Bryer, who met up in Trebizond to look at aspects of the Byzantine and more recent Greek presence – up until 1922 – in the region behind Trebizond. Our attention was to be focused in particular on standing monuments, which had hitherto received little or no attention from archaeologists, architectural and art historians or other scholars concerned with the history of the region's Byzantine fortresses, as well as to follow up work done by Bryer and David Winfield in earlier years. The work was fairly grueling, involved a lot of walking up and down hills and mountains and across pretty rough terrain at times, occasionally being threatened or challenged by fierce guard dogs who could only be called off when the shepherd to whom they answered chose to appear – at one point we waited unable to move for fear of being attacked for nearly an hour! – or walking through dense mountain woodland with the clack-clack of the bear-scarers in the background … we never saw a bear, but they probably saw us! Some time was spent in Trebizond itself, of course, where – apart from a couple of near-arrests for doing survey work on the citadel walls without permits, or being forced to remove ourselves somewhat hastily from the former church of the Holy

Wisdom after Bryer had begun to incant part of the Greek liturgy – we marvelled at the old city and its walls and monuments, the last outpost of the Byzantine empire.

On a hot August day we had proceeded across one of the passes behind Trebizond towards Maçka (Matzouka) and had noted a steep, shale-covered outcrop towering above the minor road along which we were walking. There appeared to be a small structure on the summit, and since in many similar locations this was frequently a fortification of some sort, it was decided that we would scale the heights and see what was there. It was slow, laborious and sometimes painful work as we skidded about precariously trying to move up across the shale, and every few yards one of us would start to slide very slowly backwards: we quickly learned to keep as still as possible on such occasions in the hope that minimal movement would arrest the slithering. After a while I found myself, as one of the lightest and certainly the skinniest member of the team (a mere nineteen-year-old, remember, and long before I discovered the benefits of south German beers!) some distance ahead, so Bryer shouted that I should just get to the top and see what was there. On arriving at the ridge I discovered that there was indeed a building – a small, low stone structure, not particularly impressive, with a vaulted roof and no door, although the remains of hinges were still to be seen at the entrance. Part of the roof had fallen in, but when I went in, it was clear that this had been a chapel of some sort, for the walls and the remaining plastered areas were still covered in painted religious images, obviously late Byzantine! This was both unexpected and exciting, so of course I immediately went out and shouted down to the others what I had found.

Imagine my surprise, then, when Bryer, who had until then had the greatest difficulty of us all in ascending the shale, with frequent stops as he began to slide back downhill, looked up and suddenly appeared to take off: arms and legs working overtime, he moved up that steep slope quicker than I had ever seen him move before (or since), spraying shale and scree down as he roared up to meet me, a look of manic delight on his face as he approached ... His enthusiasm and excitement were infectious, but I never realized until then that they also provided motive power and traction! It is a small thing, but it stands out in my memories of Bryer as someone who motivated and enthused everyone he taught and many he did not, and who certainly motivated me, for good or ill, to pursue my own Byzantine adventure!

5. Not the champagne bus

Margaret Mullett

Some time between 1118 and 1133 Michael Italikos asked a young friend to dinner. It was to be some dinner, a *pandaisia,* a complete banquet at which no one and nothing fails: there was to be venison, hare, peacock and partridge, boiled and roast meats, swans and sausages, tarts and custards, sesame-cakes and honey-cakes. But it was a strictly wordy banquet: the deer is philosophical, the swan is musical, the partridge poetic, the deer scientific.

It seems to me that Bryer has been offering us wordy banquets for nearly forty years. There have been thirty-nine symposia of which twenty-four have been in Birmingham, and at twenty of these he was sole symposiarch. We sometimes forget the way he has created our national institutions: the Society, the Symposium, the Bulletin, *Byzantine and Modern Greek Studies,* the Centre at Birmingham. And the way in which he has created them: everything he touches becomes a party, a *logike pandaisia* in Michael Italikos's phrase. And what a party-giver he is. He has invented whole new genres of party. The Mongol special-subject feast, sitting cross-legged in the garden, spitting apricot stones, hurling lamb bones and occasionally vomiting in the direction of the Young Conservatives' barbecue next door. The champagne bus, setting out delightedly from the Barber steps and returning tipsily to snooze through the first paper after lunch. Reconstructions of feasts for the Buckland Society: Byzantine, Ottoman, Pontic, Georgian, Albanian, all complete with whole sets of the appropriate crockery made for the occasion. That now is *pandaisia.* Anyone else can have a dish named after her, or a drink – and Bryer's mint drink is regularly made by his academic grandchildren as far away as Toronto. But whole new genres of party? That requires genius.

Reconstruction, of course, is a great Bryer skill. When we were research students in the early 1970s we would trail back, bruised and exhilarated from the expeditions which John Haldon recalls here, to find that every first-year student knew what this year's project was to be – and what part we were to play in it. It is the *Book of Ceremonies* and you're going to be a court official. It is a Cretan play and Paul Tuffin is playing the lead. But they never quite knew how it would turn out by the end of the year … It is Greek Fire, the entire symposium, the *THES* and the Birmingham Fire Brigade are all waiting and you are going to be sent into a room with the physicist and a case of bubbly to persuade him that the show must go on ... The life skills Bryer teaches are unparalleled: no Dearing Report or White Paper could map them. After we had created Athonite feasts, *agiozoumi* and *trachana,* we began to make books: where would it stop? Donald Nicol, lecturing once on chrism, stopped and played to the gallery: if Bryer were here he would want to make it! We did not laugh: we knew that Bryer could.

Bryer inspired that kind of confidence. His brilliant first-year lectures and radio broadcasts recruited a cadre of special-subject students who were seduced into further work by being asked to catalogue the slide collection, or read a seal, or give a party or look after a visitor. He led by example: we learned to dream collaborative research projects by seeing how he set up the demography project; we learned to build bricks without straw by looking around us. He looked after his people too. If you showed signs of writer's block just before finals you were given a treat, like a visit to the Serbian church in Bournville, or taken home to Liz's good cooking; if you could not face looking at the degree results, you were told the result en route to see the new coin collection. If you showed signs of not accepting a job you had been offered somewhere in Ultima Thule, Bryer turned up at 8 a.m. on the doorstep in Oxford to make sure that you did. Bryer focused always on what was important. His academic supervision was acute and detailed, but he inspired rather than directed; he gave infinite amounts of rope for students to shin up to the heights. How would the QAA have regarded this supervision style? I like to think that they would have benchmarked student support and guidance, for all time, on this paragon of good practice.

And when his students went away to build Byzantine Studies elsewhere, he maintained his support and mentoring. I can only speak of my own experience, as Bryer the Brummie, Bryer the Byzantine traveller, became Bryer in Belfast. The first thing to note is that he had circumnavigated Ireland in a small boat before ever he visited anything Byzantine on the island. He succumbed, however, to George Huxley's persuasive invitations to lecture in the early 1970s and despite his failure to parse Greek inscriptions at a height of twenty feet above street level was invited back, to be the first external examiner, to attend and then give the Wiles Lectures, to preside over the AHRC Centre and the validation of the new Centre MAs and to nourish the subject as it grew there, in every way imaginable.

As Crow says, 'as we get older, we turn into Bryer.' So during the semester of the food symposium I found myself on a scaffold working with artist-in-residence Colin McGookin, Leverhulme Professor Jeffrey C. Anderson and five undergraduates to paint a monastic refectory programme in the backyard of our institute. The composition is called *The Feast of Wisdom* and it features a banquet worthy of Michael Italikos: the Marriage at Cana, the Hospitality of Abraham, Elijah and the Ravens, the Last Supper and the Tree of the Knowledge of Good and Evil. All our research projects are there, a donor portrait with Sophia herself, various serpents and their nemesis, St Patrick, and (yes, Jenny) our very own King Billy, heavily disguised as St George. Bryer has made many friends in Ireland, and, by specific demand of the undergraduates who acted as patrons, he is immortalized in the yard painting in Belfast. All I can tell you is that he has red socks, but to find where he is you will have to track him on the internet or visit in person. Is he the consummate public orator Chrysostom? Or, the greatest teacher we know, Constantine-Cyril, the patron saint of university teachers? Or, a wonderful host, Aberkios, the patron saint of wine?

All of us who passed through his hands have inherited a standard of how to do things properly, with integrity and style. How to write, how to build, how to travel, how to look after students, how to bring our subject before a wider public, how to tease out a research problem, as we advance upon it crabwise. But we shall never manage to do any of these things with quite the panache, the style, the passion, the omnifarious learning, the subtlety, the absolutely serious purpose which characterizes everything that Bryer turns his hand to. His wordy banquets are *panhyperpandaisiai*, feasts of wisdom to which no dinner guest is ever equal. In this volume we all raise a glass (of Bryer's mint drink) to him in admiration and gratitude.

6. Bryer and I – and the class of 1980–1985

Catia Galatariotou

In 1978 I applied from Cyprus to the Centre for Byzantine Studies for a post-graduate degree. In due course, I received a letter: one 'A. A. M. Bryer, Professor of Byzantine Studies' was inviting me to come up to the Centre for an interview! My initial joy at receiving this invitation was soon overcome by anxiety, as in my mind the future interview took the imaginary shape of an ordeal, culminating in the humiliation of a polite rejection. Unable to contain my anxiety, I decided to seek professional help. And so it was that a few days before embarking on this dangerous assignation I found myself seated opposite a highly reputable professional in downtown Lemessos. In exchange for a not inconsiderable fee she sat in silence for quite a while, reflecting upon the dregs in my coffee cup. She finally exclaimed excitedly that she saw me – 'There! See?' – standing before a *Megale Porta*. Ah, I thought, the Centre! 'Do I go through it?' I asked with trepidation. The *kafetzou* sighed and shrugged her shoulders: Ah, she couldn't tell me that, she said, *that* wasn't in my coffee cup ...

It was thus in a rather fragile state of mind that I arrived at the University of Birmingham for the dreaded interview. I remember standing at the far end of the long first-floor corridor in the Arts building, having no idea what this 'A. A. M. Bryer, Professor of Byzantine Studies' looked like, and half-expecting a stern and stuffy old man to appear to claim the name. I had begun to walk slowly down the corridor, looking to locate Professor Bryer's room, when suddenly, from the far end of the corridor I saw, speeding towards me, a – well, I am *sure* that what I first saw speeding towards me was – *a beard*! I saw this long beard, which obviously belonged to a Greek Orthodox priest, closely followed by a man incongruously dressed in layman's clothes, plus red socks, the whole uncanny assemblage topped by an endearing boyish haircut. 'I'm Bryer,' said the apparition, 'Who are you?' My distracted mind managed to grab hold of my name and blurt it out. Still in the corridor, I called him 'Professor Bryer' and he cut me short. 'Call me Bryer,' he said – as indeed, I soon discovered, everybody did, including his wife, dear Liz. I do not know if it is the same with you, good reader, but

Bryer is one of only two persons known to me who do not seem to have a first name. The other one, in case you are wondering, is Inspector Morse – and he, as you know, is a fictional character. Anyway, that day, which ended for the first of innumerable times in the bar, I was surprised and delighted to see that 'A. A. M. Bryer, Professor of Byzantine Studies' was – *Bryer*. I thought, well, this might be interesting.

And interesting it certainly was. Not only Bryer, but 'the whole package'. I did find a *Megale Porta* to Byzantium, and I did go through it. But I never thought that at a Centre for Byzantine Studies I would also find so many other gateways, to so many other places. Passing through them surprised, fascinated and changed me. There was a big gate to Marxism, oiled and polished by John Haldon's Marxist seminar, religiously attended by Aglaia Kasdagli, Alan Harvey, Stephanie White and myself, and supported by an unholy alliance between Byzantine and Western Medieval knights encamped further down the corridor, led by Rodney Hilton and Chris Wickham. There was another door, to Feminism, guarded with passion by Stephanie and the other women I was soon meeting at parties, readings, seminars; indeed we had soon organized and were running our own seminar at the Centre, on Pre-Industrial Women. Another gate led me to Social Anthropology – a revelation, at the time, and years later, together with History, one of my bridges to Psychoanalysis. And yes, I also read, in big quantities, Byzantine sources, alone and with others, in seminars. My goodness, if 'Empire' means 'Big and Complicated', we certainly got the message while trying to work out what else was contained in that interminable imperial train we all boarded every week at the Constantine Porphyrogennetos seminar. We even read the Bible. I guess that if there was a guardian angel for that this must have been Jill Storer, but she was not the only committed Christian amongst us. There was a whole group of them – Jill, Zaga Gavrilović, Mary Cunningham, Susan Ashbrook. In fact there were so many groups at the Centre, we even had a group for those who did not belong to a group – the non-allied, like Archie Dunn, Anna-Maria Kasdagli and, indeed, Bryer: clearly, they were the bravest of us all. And we were soon joined by a group of new-arrivals: Vassilis Karabatsos, George Kalophonos, Anna Frangedaki, Eugenia Petrides, Halil Berktay; while at the outskirts of our little *oikoumene* there was Katerina Krikos-Davies, Meg Alexiou, Michael Hendy, Demetris Tziovas, Marianna Spanaki, Fane Balamotte ... But it is, of course, silly and artificial to speak of separate 'groups' at the Centre, for more often than not we all met in the big, inclusive melting pot that was our love and fascination for Byzantium and its culture.

Apart from 'Us' there were also 'The Foreigners' – the (mostly British) guest speakers at the Byzantine seminars. We soon realized that these *xenoi* were 'foreigners' to us but not to Bryer. A number of them were former students of his; all of them were full of fondness, respect and admiration not only for his scholarship but also for his unbounded energy and enthusiasm. This was not surprising; for it seems to me that if Bryer has single-handedly done more for Byzantine Studies than anyone else of his generation in this country, this is above all because he has always invested far more in promoting the Empire than in promoting his own career. Hence the creation of the Centre for Byzantine Studies, of the seminars, of the spring symposia ...

The 'whole package' here was so alive, creative and fun because Bryer had assembled it. It was he who pulled these people together, who allowed them to be and to just get on with whatever each wanted to do, never imposing his view or 'a line', yet unfailingly supporting our efforts. He did not just tolerate the pluralities that existed at the Centre, he actually invited them in, contained them and gave them room to be. To us, the students, he was the very embodiment of English liberalism, as we sensed that he not only tolerated but positively cultivated pluralism.

I look back at us, students and staff of those days, 1980–85, and I see *such* an incongruous bunch of people! – English, Greek, Turk, Serb, North American; feminists, Marxists, atheists, Christians and Muslims. And each one of us intensely individualistic, different and, let's face it, *difficult* – weren't we, Bryer? – and yet we all got on really well with each other. We all worked together at the seminar room and, after work, we played. Because another great gate we found here was a gate to friendships: at this Centre – and I can say this safely by now – were forged true and lifelong friendships. And the atmosphere at the Centre has a lot to do with this, imbued as it was with Bryer's openness and generosity. Bryer looked after us; and he did this so effortlessly that we all came to expect it and even demand it, like spoiled children.

As for me and Bryer, well, from that first meeting we got on like a house on fire. So much so that once or twice the heat and the flames got a bit out of control, and bucketfuls of water – or was it wine? – had to be brought in to cool things down. But hey ... If I am telling you all this today it is only because I can honestly say that the Centre, with Bryer at its heart, was and has remained a very important part of my life; and I know this to be the same for others. With hindsight, I now know that when I arrived here I was ready to go through many doors; but I would not have gone through them had they not been here. So: for what you created, and for what you allowed to be created; for making so much possible for so many of us, Bryer, after all these years I have come here and walked down that same corridor to meet you again – this time, to thank you.

Section II

Practicalities

7. Between the field and the plate: how agricultural products were processed into food

Dionysios Stathakopoulos

Around 570, the villagers of Aphrodito in Upper Egypt hired the scribe Dioskoros (also known as the 'Worst Poet of Antiquity') to write for them a petition to the dux of the Thebais. Therein they complained about the misdeeds of the pagarch (governor). He had taken away their livestock and used up the fodder destined for them. Because of these actions they had been driven to starvation (line 21). Furthermore their region had been subject to a year-long drought, which caused their animals to die (lines 54–6). At present, they were not able even to sow sufficient fodder for those animals that had survived. Due to this shortage of victuals during the winter they had been forced to consume raw vegetables (*droxima*) instead of bread (lines 93–4). In short, they had been left with nothing.[1] In comparison with today's exaltation of raw vegetables as healthy foodstuffs (consult the debate in such Internet forums as: 'Is cooked food poison?' or the site of the Living and Raw Food Community[2]) this seems a strange statement: why would the people of Aphrodito consider themselves as if in a state of starvation when they had vegetables to eat? The key to understanding this passage is that these vegetables had been raw.

As Lévi-Strauss has shown, food destined for human populations must be cooked in order to separate cultured people from animals or savages: it is through the process of cooking that food is transformed into a signifier of culture.[3] Naturally there were numerous instances where raw vegetables,

---

[1] P. Lond. V 1674 in *Greek Papyri in the British Museum* V, ed. H. I. Bell (London, 1917), 55–64. On this incident, see D. Ch. Stathakopoulos, *Famine and Pestilence in the Late Roman and Early Byzantine Empire: a systematic survey of subsistence crises and epidemics*, Birmingham Byzantine and Ottoman Monographs 9 (Aldershot, 2004), no. 142, 312–13; on Dioskoros, see L. S. B. MacCoull, *Dioscorus of Aphrodito: his works and his world*, Transformation of the Classical Heritage 16 (Berkeley, CA, 1988), esp. 47–51.

[2] Http://www.living-foods.com/articles/rawfreshproduce.html.

[3] C. Lévi-Strauss, *The Raw and the Cooked: introduction to the science of mythology I* (New York, 1969).

for example, were consumed, but this occurred as a rule either for medicinal purposes, as an accompaniment to other, cooked dishes, or where the vegetables were dipped in sauces and therefore not eaten utterly raw.[4]

Since other contributions to this volume deal with cooked food, I would like to step back and to examine plant foodstuffs after they were harvested but before they were consumed. I will concentrate on specific groups of agricultural products. Among the vast number of cultivated plants utilized in the Mediterranean basin in the Middle Ages it seems natural to focus on the so-called 'Mediterranean triad': cereals, olives and grapes and their chief by-products bread, oil and wine. Because, however, space is limited, I will focus on just cereals and olives, or, rather, olive oil and flour. The aim of this paper is to provide a short description of some agricultural procedures, focusing on recent literature. The work of A. A. M. Bryer on agricultural implements and techniques has been of cardinal importance to this area of scholarship, as the author combines an excellent knowledge of Byzantine sources with the recording of the function of such agricultural devices still in use and observed during his long travels in the Pontos.[5] Emphasis will be placed on recent Greek publications illustrating a renewed interest in the survival of pre-modern agricultural tools and techniques as fostered by – among others – the workshops organized since 1986 by the cultural and technological foundation of the Hellenic Industrial Development Bank, ETBA, devoted to topics such as bread, wine, oil, honey and salt.[6]

We can follow the necessary procedures that these products had to undergo across the agricultural year, and our focus will be mostly on those implements instrumental in this process. But first we must note the problems and shortcomings of the material.

Although (or perhaps because) agricultural processing was among the most common procedures in the pre-industrial Mediterranean,

---

4 See Cassianus Bassus, *Geoponika* XII.22.5, ed. H. Beckh (Leipzig, 1895), 370, on eating radishes raw to prevent one from being harmed by poisons; furthermore, the *Geoponika* (XII.17.21, p. 364) notes, one should eat raw cabbage in order to drink a lot of wine without getting drunk. On the consumption of radishes, see further the chapters by Joanita Vroom and Angeliki Lymberopoulou in this volume.

5 See especially Bryer's 'The estates of the Empire of Trebizond: evidence for their resources, products, agriculture, ownership and location', *ArchP* 35 (1979), 392–413; furthermore his 'Byzantine agricultural implements: the evidence of medieval illustrations of Hesiod's *Works and Days*', *BSA* 81 (1986), 45–80. His latest study on this subject, 'The means of agricultural production: muscle and tools', in A. E. Laiou, ed., *The Economic History of Byzantium*, vol. 1 (Washington, DC, 2002), 101–13 is, in principal, a reprise of his earlier work.

6 The foundation no longer exists, as the ETBA bank has been bought by the Piraeus Bank. Its own cultural foundation (see www.piop.gr) has taken over and expanded the scope of the ETBA one. The relevant publications of the ETBA foundation of conferences held so far are still available through the new foundation; see, on bread, *Ο άρτος ημών. Από το σιτάρι στο ψωμί* (Athens, 1994); on olive oil, *Ελιά και λάδι* (Athens, 1996).

contemporaries took little trouble to record any details. The sources at our disposal dealing with the technical aspects of such matters are scarce. Remarkably, though, the extant texts show a striking resemblance and an even more striking continuity. In 1634 a Cretan monk from Athos, Agapios Landos, published a book called *Geoponikon* in Venice; it was the first of numerous subsequent re-impressions. Its first part, which deals with agriculture, is in fact a paraphrased version of Cassianus Bassus's *Geoponika*, a work composed in the sixth century that has come down to us in a slightly updated version from the time of Constantine Porphyrogennetos.[7] Even later, in 1930, Cassianus's work was translated into modern Greek and published in the *Agricultural Report*, an organ of the Ministry of Agriculture, and intended to be used in practice.[8] Because of the conservative character of agricultural techniques and implements, it was, perhaps, not deemed necessary to elaborate on matters already well known – a fact which should not be confounded with neglect. On the other hand, the material evidence of such implements at hand today is strikingly poor compared to their significance in Byzantine daily life. Tools made of wood perished, naturally. The fact that many agricultural implements continued to be used throughout the Middle Ages and until at least the Second World War (in some parts of the Mediterranean even more recently[9]) provides further difficulties. First, it means a lack of typological criteria that would enable us to date with accuracy a number of them: a tool was used until it was worn out and then replaced – probably – by a fairly similar one, perhaps even modelled on its predecessor. Secondly, there is still relatively little published archaeological material on Byzantine villages and rural communities; extensive fieldwork on such habitats, encompassing the remains of all kinds of implements and their role within those communities – as well as a body of amassed evidence – is only now emerging.[10] In order to

---

7 Agapios Landos, *Γεωπονικὸν περιέχον ἑρμηνείας τινὰς ὠφελιμοτάτας τῆς τε γεωργίας καὶ ἰατρικῆς* (Venice, 1636; new edn 1850). On the *Geoponika*, see J. Koder, *Gemüse in Byzanz. Die Versorgung Konstantinopels mit Frischgemüse im Lichte der Geoponika*, Byzantinische Geschichtschreiber, Ergänzungsband 3 (Vienna, 1993), 27ff.

8 *Georgikon Deltion*, 2 (1930), 6–156 and 3 (1930), 5–148.

9 For example the implements and techniques described in Bryer, 'Estates', as witnessed in the 1960s and 1970s and the case of the Ropas valley in Corfu, in which a primitive type of ard plough was in use; see A. Sordinas, 'The Ropas plow from the island of Corfu', *TT* 3 (1979), 139–49, as discussed in P. Horden and N. Purcell, *The Corrupting Sea: a study of Mediterranean history* (Oxford, 2000), 233–4.

10 This is mainly the result of a number of archaeological surveys conducted in Greece, particularly at Melos, Methana, Southern Argolid, Boeotia, Nemea, Sphakia and Lakonia. For bibliographical data on these surveys, see J. Bintliff, 'Reconstructing the Byzantine countryside: new approaches from landscape archaeology', in K. Belke, F. Hild, J. Koder and P. Soustal, eds, *Byzanz als Raum*, Veröffentlichungen der Kommission für die Tabula Imperii Byzantini 7 (Vienna, 2000), 49–63, and P. Armstrong 'The survey area in the Byzantine and

reconstruct the use of agricultural implements and the techniques used for food processing, scholars have been turning to ethnoarchaeological studies of modern practices to build or test models of parallel ancient practices.[11] However, in all such cases significant caution is required, to save one from constructing the past rather than reconstructing it, as most ethnographers did in the early twentieth century.[12]

The Byzantine year began with the indiction cycle on 1 September. A great number of tasks were set for each month of the agricultural year. Regarding the products we will be discussing, the initial task was the making of the first olive oil of the year – that made from unripe olives, called *omphakinon*, the modern-day *agourelaion*.[13] This was done around mid-October, while in the course of the following month the rest of the olives were left to mature and then harvested. The olives were harvested little by little: only the quantity that could be processed within the same day was picked.[14] They were laid on a mat made of withy-branches until dry and then made into oil. There were two stages to this process: first, the separation of the oil from the flesh and, second, the removal of the bitter watery fluid (*amurca*); during both procedures it was vital to avoid crushing the kernel.[15] The first task, the crushing of the olives, was achieved by two devices both familiar since late Hellenistic times.[16] The *trapetum* (*trapetes*), the oil mill par excellence, consisted of a large cup made of lava with a solid column in its middle, a little higher than the lip of the cup. On top of the column there was a square hole, through which passed a wooden beam on each side of which rested two millstones. When properly adjusted they would keep a distance of exactly one Roman inch from the column, from the bottom of the hollow and from its outer side. Olives were placed

---

Ottoman periods', in W. Cavanagh et al., eds, *The Laconia Survey* I, *BSA*, supplementary vol. 26 (London, 2002), 398–402.

11 W. E. Lee, 'Pylos Regional Archaeological Project, Part IV', *Hesperia* 70 (2001), 51.

12 See P. Koukoules's grand narrative of continuity manifest through, inter alia, tools and techniques in his *Βυζαντινῶν βίος καὶ πολιτισμός*, 9 vols, (Athens, 1948–55).

13 *Geoponika* III.13, p. 100.

14 *Geoponika* IX.19, p. 250.

15 R. J. Forbes, *Studies in Ancient Technology*, vol. 3 (Leiden, 1993), 105–7.

16 I here follow S. Hadjisavvas, *Olive Oil Processing in Cyprus from the Bronze Age to the Byzantine Period*, Studies in Mediterranean Archaeology 99 (Nicosia, 1992) and M.-C. Amouretti, *Le Pain et l'huile dans la Grèce antique: de l'araire au moulin*, Centre de Recherches d'Histoire Ancienne 67 = Annales littéraires de l'Université de Besançon 328 (Paris, 1986), 153–75. The continuity of the techniques employed is attested; see Hadjisavvas, *Olive Oil Processing in Cyprus*, 121: 'The crushing methods based on the classical *mola olearia* and probably the *trapetum*, which were introduced during the Hellenistic period continued to be used with no significant variation as far as the last quarter of the twentieth century. As such devices were used over long periods of time and in some cases reused in entirely different periods their dating when found without context is extremely difficult.'

in the cup and the millstones made a double rotation round the column, at the same time turning on their axes. The gaps ensured that the olives were compressed without crushing their pits. A device similar in principal was the *mola olearia*. It consisted, as a rule, of two cylindrical stones rotating on a horizontal axle carried by a vertical beam that also turned, placed in the middle of a flat surface where the grinding took place. Sometimes the *mola olearia* had only one millstone and could be operated by an animal. Another device that could be used for pressing was a screw-press, like the one utilized for wine production.

During the next step the kernels were separated from the pulp and the first oil recovered. The pulp was subsequently often soaked in hot water (as oil is lighter than water and so could then easily be skimmed off) and subjected to a second pressing. Finally, the pulp was put in baskets and with the help of weights (stones moved by a lever) the oil was extracted. In the *Geoponika*, the same procedure is described but the author seems to imply that the weights used could be lifted by humans.[17] Between pressings, the crushed pulp was spread on raised mats to get rid of the bitter *amurca* contained in the olives. Each of the pressings produced more olive oil, but of a progressively lower quality. The leftovers from the procedure of oil pressing (stones, olive pulp) were used for heating and as animal fodder, both important at the micro-level of local farmers.[18]

The liquid obtained from the crushed and pressed olives represents on average 60 per cent of the weight of the used olives; of this about two-thirds is water and other substances and only a third is oil. When the fluid from the press is allowed to stand in the tank, oil being lighter floats to the top. It can then be collected either by hand or with the help of a ladle. Another method consisted in drawing off the water through a hole at the base of the tank. Finally, the floating oil could be conveyed into a lateral tank through an outlet at the rim. The last stage of purification took place in settling vats; after some time the impurities settled at the bottom of the vat and could be thus easily separated from the oil.

Of course, these were not the only ways to produce oil, though they certainly were the most widespread ones. An example from modern-day Greece may give us an idea of what a much smaller, family-centred unit for the production of olive oil may have looked like.[19] The fruit is crushed with the help of a small cylindrical stone operated by one person; with the help

[17] *Geoponika* IX.19, pp. 250–51.

[18] Armstrong, 'Survey area', 385; Lee, 'Pylos', 64; see also M.-C. Amouretti, 'Les sous-produits de la fabrication de l'huile et du vin', in M.-C. Amouretti and J.-P. Brun, eds, *La Production du vin et l'huile en Méditerranée*, *BCH*, Supplément 26 (Athens, 1993), 464–7.

[19] A. Oikonomou, 'Το χειροκίνητο λιοτρίβι στην Έλαφο Αγιάς', *Technologia*, 8 (1998), 12–14.

of a little shovel the olives are pushed towards it. The pressing again occurs with only human power; the pulp is put into a large bag made of hair and pressed either with both feet or with a device following the principle of a see-saw, while hot water is poured to facilitate the process. Finally, the liquid is put into a large wooden barrel, which has a small hole in its bottom side to help separate it from impurities and water. A work day of eight hours of pressing some 100 kg of olives produced roughly 20 kg of oil.

Oil presses and similar devices were naturally important in regions that produced oil.[20] Examination of the peninsula of Methana helps us visualize their expansion and importance. Only 50 km^2, the area holds the remains of some twenty oil presses dating from the late Roman to the early modern period.[21] The Southern Argolid survey also produced a significant number of Roman *trapeta* dating from between the early Roman to the medieval period.[22] It is remarkable that a region surveyed in Lakonia, a territory in which the olive crop played a very important role, produced only two oil presses, both dating from the Ottoman period.[23] This warns us against facilely projecting modern landscape appearance and use (in this case the preponderance of olive trees and oil production) into the past. The example of Crete, a region today dominated by the olive tree, is salutary: though oil was produced on the island in Byzantine times, its production was much more limited than at present.[24] Similarly, when addressing the antiquity of the (now dominating) olives in a region in Southern Argolid one discovers that their cultivation does not go back much before the nineteenth century.[25]

Even if oil presses existed in sufficient numbers, not every family or farming-unit would have owned and operated one. Modern practice (though reflecting a pre-industrial attitude) in Maryeli (Pylos) has it that 10 per cent of the produced oil went as a fee to the press and was then split in half between the owner and the press workers.[26] Perhaps there were similar arrangements in Byzantium as well.

---

[20] For an overview, see A. Liberi, 'Βυζαντινά γεωργικά εργαλεία και μηχανές', *DChAE*, Periodos 4, 21 (2000), 283–4.

[21] C. Mee and H. Forbes, eds, *A Rough and Rocky Place: the landscape and settlement history of the Methana Peninsula, Greece* (Liverpool, 1997), 262–7.

[22] M. H. Jameson, C. N. Runnels and T. H. van Andel, *A Greek Countryside: the Southern Argolid from prehistory to the present day* (Stanford, CA, 1994), table 6.9, 400.

[23] P. Armstrong, 'The survey area', 385.

[24] C. Gaspares, 'Η ελιά και το λάδι. Παραγωγή και εμπόριο στη μεσαιωνική Κρήτη (13ος–14ος αιώνας)', in *Ελιά και λάδι*, 151.

[25] H. Forbes, 'The place of the olive in the Southern Argolid', in Amouretti and Brun, eds, *La Production du vin*, 213–26.

[26] Lee, 'Pylos', 64; for a similar arrangement in Lakonia, see A. Oikonomou, 'Προβιομηχανικές τεχνικές παραγωγής ελαιολάδου στην περιοχή Πετρίνας Λακωνίας', in *Ελιά και Λάδι*, 371.

In late June the wheat harvest took place. The *Geoponika* is quite stern on the matter: 'On June 23 [that is, July 6, after the calendar reform] threshing begins; in these days there is neither rainfall nor dew.'[27] The grain was transported tied in sheaves to the threshing floors. These were sometimes adjacent to the fields, but in any case near to them. The *Geoponika* gives advice on their construction: they must be built on high places, where the winds can pass through; caution is necessary to prevent the straw flying off the floor from reaching houses or gardens, for it can pierce the eyes of people, damage vines and harm vegetables.[28] Threshing floors were stone-paved circles with a diameter of 10 to 13 m, sometimes with stones set upright at the edge to contain the chaff during winnowing.[29] Simpler forms of these *alonia* were made of stamped dung and earth.[30] Cereals were to be placed with their cut sides facing south (according to the *Geoponika*) to facilitate the threshing.[31] *Alonia* were probably communally owned; privately owned ones could be leased out to neighbours in return for chores, favours or small amounts of money.[32]

Threshing was usually a two-step process.[33] First, the cut stalks of grain were spread on the threshing floor and a threshing sledge was pulled over the stalks by a pair of oxen (or occasionally two pairs) or a horse. The sledge (*tribulum, dokani*) was a simple wooden sled or heavy board with stone or metal spikes or flints on the bottom that would break the heads of grain from the stalks. A person must stand on it to ensure it is weighed down. Oxen were sometimes fitted with a kind of muzzle to prevent them from eating the hay.[34] A team of archaeologists measured a threshing session of a full floor with a reconstructed Mesopotamian sledge; it amounted to around two hours.[35]

The second step (winnowing, *likmesis*) was to toss the broken stalks into the air with a large forked tool, usually made of wood.[36] As with the sledge,

---

27 *Geoponika* III.6.8, p. 95.

28 *Geoponika* II.26, pp. 66–7.

29 Bryer, 'Means', 109; J. C. Whittaker, 'Alonia: ethnoarchaeology of Cypriot threshing floors', *JMA* 12 (1999), 7–25.

30 Lee, 'Pylos', 62; Bryer, 'Means', 109.

31 *Geoponika* II.26, pp. 66–7.

32 See M. Givens, 'Agriculture, settlement and landscape in Ottoman Cyprus', *Levant*, 32 (2000), 215–36; Whittaker, 'Alonia'.

33 On threshing and winnowing, see L. Cheetham, 'Threshing and winnowing – an ethnographic study', *Antiquity*, 56 (1982), 127–30. Older ways of threshing involved oxen walking over the stalks or beating the stalks with heavy sticks (flails, *dirabdia*).

34 Koukoules, *Βυζαντινῶν βίος καὶ πολιτισμός*, 5.264.

35 P. C. Anderson, J. Chabot, A. van Gijn, 'The functional riddle of "glossy" Canaanean blades and the Near Eastern threshing sledge', *JMA* 17.1 (2004), 87–130, esp. p. 105.

36 For the illustration of a *likmeterion* in Venice, BNM MS Z 464, fol. 34r see Bryer, 'Means', fig. 2.

such wooden utensils have not been preserved, and we are dependant on ethnoarchaeology for our understanding of these procedures. The wind blew the lighter chaff to one side, while the heavier grain fell into a pile, which could then be gathered. The grain could then be ground to produce flour.

There were four basic types of mills: hand mills, animal mills, watermills and windmills. Extant written records have been interpreted as recording the use of windmills from the twelfth century onwards; however archaeological evidence is missing (and the scarce documentary evidence presented is not entirely convincing).[37]

In contrast, hand mills or rotary hand querns were certainly very popular. They were made of two flat, round stones (often of volcanic stone) of about 30 to 40 cm in diameter with a hopper on the upper stone to provide a lateral horizontal handle. Such artefacts were found throughout Mediterranean rural communities until quite recently. They covered domestic needs and offered the advantage of making it possible to grind as much grain as one needed whenever it was required.[38] Hence, they were also quite important for the supply of armies during campaigns.[39] The flour produced by them is very coarse. Furthermore, if it is not passed through a fine sieve it may contain not only hard leftover seed fragments but also splinters of the millstones, which would then pass into the bread made from it.

The donkey mill (*mola asinaria*) was a great improvement.[40] It was driven by blindfolded horses, mules or donkeys (more rarely, in the earlier periods, by slaves). A conical lower stone is topped by an hourglass-shaped upper stone, which turns on the spindle of the lower one, separated by an iron bridge. It always had grooved surfaces and it was moved by pushing the handle projecting horizontally from the waist of the mill and attached to the upper stone.[41] It was widespread in Rome and remained common throughout the Byzantine period. It is important to note its presence in Constantinople as attested in the *Book of the Eparch*,[42] and it is also attested

[37] G. Demetrokalles, 'Οἱ ἀνεμόμυλοι τῶν Βυζαντινῶν', *Parnassos*, 20 (1978), 141–4; T. G. Koukoulis, 'A Late Byzantine windmill at Kythera', in J. M. Sanders, ed., *Φιλολάκων: Lakonian Studies in Honour of Hector Catling* (London, 1992), 155–63.

[38] Bryer, 'Estates', 411–12; idem, 'Means', 110; Forbes, 'The place of the olive in the Southern Argolid', III 148–51.

[39] K. Karaple, 'Το σιτάρι, το ψωμί και ο βυζαντινός στρατός', in *Ο άρτος ημών*, 109.

[40] A. Liveri, 'Παρασκευή και πώληση ψωμιού σε ρωμαϊκά ανάγλυφα', in *Ο άρτος ημών*, 82–3.

[41] Forbes, 'The place of the olive in the Southern Argolid', III 151–2.

[42] *Book of the Eparch* 18.1, ed. J. Koder, *Das Eparchenbuch Leons des Weisen*, CFHB 33 (Vienna, 1991), 128.

in the monastic *typika* of Kosmosoteira, Pantokrator and Petritzonitissa in Bačkovo (in the latter two co-existing with watermills).[43]

This last type of mill was introduced in the Mediterranean at some time between the last pre-Christian century and the first century AD and is still used today. Watermills are hard to reconstruct because all wooden parts have perished. Regardless of their early presence, watermills took almost four centuries to establish themselves.[44] In Diocletian's price edict they are valued at 2,000 denarii, as opposed to 1,250 for donkey mills, 1,500 for horse mills and 250 for hand mills.[45] Their spread and success in the later centuries has been linked to the decline of cheap slave labour, which made an initial investment in the construction of a mill more attractive than before.[46] The first mention of watermills within a genuinely rural environment occurs in the *Farmer's Law* (chaps 82–3), dated to the late seventh to ninth century: according to this text, mills were erected by individuals and sometimes shared within a community.[47]

There is an extensive record of watermills in Late Byzantine documents of chiefly monastic nature.[48] They were seemingly abundant in the areas of Macedonia belonging to Athonite monasteries.[49] Watermills often co-existed with donkey mills. The latter were deemed safer because they remained unaffected by climatic phenomena and in cases of siege could operate within the city or *castrum* walls.[50]

There are two basic types of watermills, the 'Greek' or horizontal type, and the 'Roman' or vertical one. Both types were known to the Byzantines, but scholarly consensus has it that the Greek one prevailed. The wheel

---

43 P. Gautier, 'Le typikon du sébaste Grégoire Pakourianos', *REB* 42 (1984), 43, 112 and *BMFD* 2.507–63; L. Petit, 'Typikon du monastère de la Kosmosotira près d'Aenos (1152)', *IRAIK* 13 (1908), 60 and *BMFD* 2.782–858; P. Gautier, 'Le typikon du Christ Sauveur Pantocrator', *REB* 32 (1974), 90, 92, 104 (horse- rather than donkey-drawn) and *BMFD* 2.725–81.

44 J. H. Munro, *Industrial Energy from Water-Mills in the European Economy, Fifth to Eighteenth Centuries: the limitations of power*, University of Toronto, Department of Economics, Working Papers 16 (Toronto, 2002).

45 S. Laufer, ed., *Diokletians Preisedikt*, Texte und Kommentare 5 (Berlin, 1971), 15.52–5, 146–7.

46 Munro, *Energy*, 5–6.

47 W. Ashburner, 'The Farmer's Law', *JHS* 32 (1912), 94–5.

48 *BMFD*, Index s.v. 'mills', 1943.

49 See J. Lefort, *Villages de Macédoine: 1.-La Chalcidique occidentale*, *TM*, Monographies 1 (Paris, 1982), Index s.v. 'moulins', 203; idem, ed., *Paysages de Macédoine: leur caractères, leur évolution à travers les documents et les récits des voyageurs*, *TM*, Monographies 3 (Paris, 1986), Index s.v. 'moulins', 228; and also A. Harvey, *Economic Expansion in the Byzantine Empire, 900–1200* (Cambridge, 1989), 131.

50 Harvey, *Expansion*, 131. For the siege, see Prokopios, *De Bello Gothico* I.19.19–27, 99–101, which describes how Belisarios had a floating mill installed in the Tiber as the water supplies in Rome had been cut off (hence no watermills could be operated), while donkey mills could not be used as there was not enough fodder in the city.

is attached to a vertical axle, passing through the lower millstone and fixed to the upper one by a crossbar. This type of mill is as a rule found in mountainous regions, but a mill race and chute is often necessary since the wheel will turn only if water is directed against one of its sides. Water is then channelled off upstream by sluices to create a head of water. Then the water falls on the mill wheel with twenty to fifty wooden scoop vanes. It is not very efficient, utilizing only 15 to 20 per cent of the available water pressure, but seems to have served the limited needs of small landholders.

The vertical or Roman mill was a more sophisticated machine.[51] Vitruvius described it as follows:

> Wheels on the principles that have been described above are also constructed in rivers. Round their faces float-boards are fixed, which, on being struck by the current of the river, make the wheel turn as they move, and thus, by raising the water in the boxes and bringing it to the top, they accomplish the necessary work through being turned by the mere impulse of the river, without any treading on the part of workmen. Watermills are turned on the same principle. Everything is the same in them, except that a drum with teeth is fixed into one end of the axle. It is set vertically on its edge, and turns in the same plane with the wheel. Next to this larger drum there is a smaller one, also with teeth, but set horizontally, and this is attached (to the millstone). Thus the teeth of the drum, which is fixed to the axle make the teeth of the horizontal drum move, and cause the mill to turn. A hopper, hanging over this contrivance, supplies the mill with corn, and meal is produced by the same revolution.[52]

This is the so-called undershot watermill, turned by the mere force of the current without a dam or mill-race; as such it requires fairly swift flowing rivers. The more complicated, and much more efficient overshot type, requires water to be diverted from the river by a mill race, stored in a millpond and passed through a chute. It is then poured on the mill wheel into inclined buckets or other receptacles fixed into the rim–circumference of the wheel. The overshot mill was able to harness between 50 to 70 per cent of the water force.[53]

The Greek type is admittedly less efficient than the Roman one; but it is much easier to build, requiring less mechanical gear; it is therefore decidedly less expensive and requires less water for its operation. The Roman type, especially the overshot mill, prevailed in the late medieval west, where it was constructed and controlled by feudal lords, who had

[51] T. S. Reynolds, *Stronger Than a Hundred Men: a history of the vertical water wheel* (Baltimore, MD, 1983).

[52] Vitruvius, *The Ten Books on Architecture*, tr. M. H. Morgan (Cambridge, MA, 1914), X 5, 1–2.

[53] Munro, *Energy*, 10.

the power to forbid the use of hand mills, and thus direct all milling work to their property.[54] This type, though more efficient, was rarely used by the Byzantines.[55]

Some watermills could operate only seasonally, relying on the power of winter streams, others – notwithstanding the power of water currents in the winter and the amount of mud they transported – only in the summer. In places where water was scarce in the summer, the mill's use was suspended during the day and the mill race channelled towards the fields; the mill would be put back to use in the evening.[56]

Millstones, called 'eyes', could be single, but were double, or even triple, whenever possible. Grain was 'fed' to them through a hopper, an inverted pyramid, standing on a cradle; the supply was regulated by a string to a show below the hopper, while a spatula agitated the shoe to shake grain into the eyes of the upper millstone. After a specific time (in modern practice, a fortnight) the miller had to sharpen the millstones again with a hammer (a procedure termed *charaé* in modern Greek). The first flour that was ground after this procedure was full of splinters and thus inedible. To deal with this, millers would first grind lower-quality grain and feed the flour produced to hens, who needed the mineral substance to produce hard eggshells.[57]

In recent years, renewed interest in the material culture of Byzantine daily life,[58] the rise of ecological consciousness – which has raised respect for pre-industrial agricultural techniques – and the proliferation of long-lasting, intensive archaeological surveys of various regions of the Byzantine countryside, have enriched our knowledge of this until recently neglected topic, and are beginning to bring about a change in the way Byzantine social and economic history is perceived. There are voices urging us to stop seeing the history of technology as a one-way linear path to modernity in which every new invention or technical improvement is adopted in a conscious effort to maximize production. As Peregrine Horden and Nicholas Purcell have illustrated with the example of the plough, sometimes communities simply do not adopt modern practices; on the contrary, they may stick to techniques and implements which, from an economical point of view, seem

54 Harvey, *Expansion*, 132.

55 Harvey, *Expansion*, 129.

56 A similar problem is alluded to in the *Farmer's Law* (chap. 83; see above, n. 47): 'If the water which comes to the mill leaves dry cultivated plots or vineyards, let him make the damage good; if not, let the mill be idle'; A. Karzes and M. Maglaras, *Μύλοι και μυλωνάδες. Προβιομηχανική Ήπειρος* (Patra, 2002), 26.

57 Karzes and Maglaras, *Μύλοι*, 48–9.

58 See, for example, D. Stathakopoulos and M. Grünbart, 'Sticks and stones. Byzantine material culture', *BMGS* 26 (2002), 298–327.

to us insufficient.[59] The same may be said about watermills: the Byzantines did not use the more efficient Roman type but clung to the Greek type instead. With such observations we enter the realm of anthropology and the history of mentalities. Though reliance on surviving 'archaic' practices, allegedly reflecting pre-modern or even medieval usage, as a method to fill in blanks not covered by Byzantine texts or archaeological remains, is at times controversial (a result of its misuse being the construction of nationalistic narratives of continuity), used with caution it nevertheless provides modern scholars with a set of tools to test hypotheses about the medieval world. Experimental archaeology, as in the case of the reconstructed sledge mentioned above, provides plausible ways to confirm or correct historical texts. The renewed interest in such topics leads to better recording of agricultural accoutrements in excavations; their accumulation produces a body of artefacts and buildings that will ultimately lead to more refined typologies and more secure dating – in short, to a better understanding of these essential procedures that occurred between the field and the plate.

[59] Horden and Purcell, *The Corrupting Sea*, 233–4.

8. Store in a cool and dry place: perishable goods and their preservation in Byzantium

Michael Grünbart

Preliminary remarks

Today we in the western world do not think as much as ancient and medieval societies did about the preservation of food because we are accustomed to refrigeration and have easy access to supermarkets to provide and store our daily products. The long-term preservation of food products in private households is a notion that has disappeared from our consciousness; we just make sure we have enough to eat for a weekend or bank holiday.

Unlike the modern industrialized world, societies in the past were aware of the importance of storage in each household because food was not available in great quantities all the time and everywhere. The need to store food arose from natural causes (crop failures due to bad weather conditions such as long and cold winters)[1] and human action (military campaigns, sieges or systematic destruction of arable land). Storage can be a household or community matter and both aspects can be found in Byzantine society. I will focus on the Byzantine 'private' household,[2] and I will not discuss public, imperial, monastic or military storage.[3] I will also exclude treasure hoards, an expression, or a manifestation of elite behaviour in Antique and

[1] See D. Ch. Stathakopoulos, *Famine and Pestilence in the Late Roman and Early Byzantine Empire: a systematic survey of subsistence crises and epidemics*, Birmingham Byzantine and Ottoman Monographs 9 (Aldershot, 2003).

[2] H. Forbes and L. Foxhall, 'Ethnoarchaeology and storage in the ancient Mediterranean: beyond risk and suvival', in J. Wilkins, D. Harvey and M. Dobson, eds, *Food in Antiquity* (Exeter, 1995), 69–86.

[3] On a granary on the island of Tenedos for ships transporting grain from Egypt to Constantinople, see A. E. Müller, 'Getreide für Konstantinopel: Überlegungen zu Justinians Edikt XIII als Grundlage für Aussagen zur Einwohnerzahl Konstantinopels im 6. Jahrhundert', *JÖB* 43 (1993), 1–20; on granaries and wine cellars for soldiers in Kallipolis: Prokopios, *De Aedificiis* 4, 10, 23, ed. J. Haury and G. Wirth, vol. 4 (Leipzig, 1964), 142.21–3.

medieval times that is defined as the act of collecting and storing valuable and rare products such as silk textiles until danger is past.[4]

Storage facilities

Before we touch on the subject of food-preservation strategies, we must consider where the Byzantines stored their daily products. Let us, first, turn to the archaeological evidence.

Excavation data from recent archaeological fieldwork in Pergamon and Corinth has contributed greatly to our ability to reconstruct an average Byzantine house.[5] The excavations of the Late Byzantine settlement on Pergamon's acropolis have shown that nearly every house or household had a section or a room in which products were stored,[6] as remains of jars or barrels indicate. About sixty large jars, called *pithoi* (πίθοι), have been excavated there, some of them up to 1.50 m high, and able to hold about 100 to 1,100 litres.

Because of their large volume, some had to be brought into a projected room before erecting its surrounding walls. Many jars were embedded in the floor; the bigger the jar the deeper it was in the ground. This was not only to save space, but also to stabilize the weight and to provide a regular temperature. Storing products in jars was effective against infestation and damage from insects and mice, because they could be sealed hermetically.

What kind of products were stored in such *pithoi*? Traces of pine and cypress resin have been found in them, but chemical analysis showed no other organic substances, because the acidity of the soil neutralized the remainder of the contents. Klaus Rheidt concluded that those traces that remained belonged to the sealing of the jars and the preserving ingredients of wine.[7] Fruits or wheat were also stored in such containers. *Pithoi* are often mentioned in agronomical literature such as the *Geoponika* or by post-Byzantine authors such as Agapios Landos, whose works reflect older habits. Agapios mentions, for example, the storage of sun-dried grapes, poured together with mustard or salted water into *pithoi*.[8] The excavator

[4] P. Horden and N. Purcell, *The Corrupting Sea: a study of Mediterranean history* (Oxford, 2002), 357.

[5] C. Bouras, 'Houses in Byzantium', *DChAE* 4/11 (1982–83), 1–26. Archaeological research adds considerable material to our knowledge of Byzantine housing; though there are too many recent publications to quote them all; see, for example, K. Dark, *Secular Buildings and the Archaeology of Everyday Life in the Byzantine Empire* (Oxford, 2003).

[6] K. Rheidt, 'Byzantinische Wohnhäuser des 11. bis 14. Jahrhunderts in Pergamon', *DOP* 44 (1990), 195–202; on *pithoi*, see 198f.; and idem, 'The urban economy of Pergamon', in A. E. Laiou, ed., *The Economic History of Byzantium: from the seventh through the fifteenth century*, Dumbarton Oaks Studies 39 (Washington, DC, 2002), 623–9.

[7] Rheidt, 'The urban economy', 628.

[8] P. Koukoules, *Βυζαντινῶν βίος καὶ πολιτισμός*, vol. 5 (Athens, 1952), 137.

also suggested that they could have been used to collect water, since there is no evidence of a larger cistern or a developed water supply system in Late Byzantine Pergamon.

Who used these huge jars? Nicholas Oikonomides analysed legal documents and testaments dating from the tenth to the fifteenth century,[9] and observed that large jars or barrels for storing oil, wine or wheat were found only in the households of laymen or monks living in the countryside, who had to keep a year's harvest in their houses.[10] In contrast, it appears that city households did not need large storage facilities as, for example, Constantinopolitans had permanent access to local shops and markets, from which they could purchase their daily products in smaller quantities.[11] In the thirteenth century, Pergamon was not a city but a larger settlement in a region that was permanently raided by the Seljuks and other Turkish peoples. As the inhabitants were living in continuous fear of devastation, it was necessary for them to have emergency supplies. Pergamon was captured peacefully without heavy destructions around 1315 and after twenty years under the reign of the Seljuk Karasi it was passed over to the Ottomans. The Byzantine settlement survives because the Ottomans moved the remaining Christian inhabitants to the fertile plain of the Kaikos beneath the acropolis.

My second example of a (probable) storeroom comes from Corinth. The Antique city of Corinth continued to be an important centre for international trade during the Middle Ages and its material culture remained essentially unchanged.[12] A large Frankish building that can be identified as a hospice or hostel, serving sick people and pilgrims travelling through Corinth to the Near East, was excavated from 1989 to 1997. The complex was erected in the last third of the thirteenth century. A vaulted chamber connected to room no. 12 has been interpreted as a root cellar for the storage of supplies demanding a cool place or for the hanging of various provisions from a

---

9 N. Oikonomides, 'The contents of the Byzantine house', *DOP* 44 (1990), 205–14, esp. 211.

10 Sharon Gerstel and her team excavated some *pithoi* in the small Late Byzantine village at Panakton (between Athens and Thebes); see S. E. J. Gerstel et al., 'A late medieval village at Panakton', *Hesperia*, 72 (2003), 147–234.

11 On storehouses in Late Byzantium, see V. Kidonopoulos, *Bauten in Konstantinopel 1204–1328*, Mainzer Veröffentlichungen zur Byzantinistik 1 (Wiesbaden, 1994), 204–5; for markets and trading of fresh food, see G. C. Maniatis, 'The perishable produce market in Byzantium: organization, marketing and pricing policies', *BSl* 61 (2003), 143–50.

12 G. D. R. Sanders, 'Corinth', in Laiou, ed., *The Economic History of Byzantium*, 647–54, esp. 651.

wooden beam which can be reconstructed. The chamber is too small to allow occupation.[13]

To continue our series of storerooms we will move from archaeological data to written sources. Eustathios of Thessalonike recounts for us in a letter the problems caused in his storeroom by mice that greedily ate his stored victuals:[14]

> The mice are no parasites for us, they are *katasitoi* [commensals], if we could name them so, since we nourish from what they leave us with ... No machine exists as a weapon against them. Traps are useless and amount to nothing. The archer Smintheus [meaning Apollo the mouse-slayer], bends his bow in vain ...[15]

Then, Eustathios describes his irritation during the small hours of several successive nights.[16] He had woken up because he heard a mouse gnawing and walked to his storeroom holding a light in the one hand and a whip in the other. He saw a mouse sitting on a wine vessel hung from a line. Noticing its persecutor, the mouse fled instantly. The following night, the mouse gnawed through the line and the vessel fell down, broke and produced a tremendous noise. Eustathios was startled and tried to catch the intruder, but he only heard it squeaking a triumphant song. The battle of man against mouse, we may call it *anthropomyomachia,* continued. Some dried grapes were hanging from a wooden construction. They were of the variety *krystallinoi* and derived their name from their harvesting time. They looked like crystals when they were collected during the first frost.[17] They were not of the finest quality, as Eustathios admits, but they did not get mouldy and they were resistant to putrefaction. The voracious mice consumed almost everything. Eustathios also mentions other stored

---

13 C. K. Williams II and O. H. Zervos, 'Frankish Corinth: 1994', *Hesperia*, 64 (1995), 1–60, esp. 6–10, fig. 6. (I thank Dionysios Stathakopoulos for this reference). Another example of a storeroom from late antiquity is discussed by C. Kosso, 'A Late Roman complex at Palaiochora near Karystos in Southern Euboia, Greece', *Classical Views / Echos du Monde Classique*, 40, n.s., 15 (1996), 201–30.

14 *Eustathii Metropolitae Thessalonicensis opuscula*, ed. T. L. F. Tafel (Frankfurt am Main, 1832; repr. Amsterdam, 1964), Epistle 6. New edition by F. Kolovou (Munich, 2006).

15 *Eustathii Metropolitae Thessalonicensis opuscula*, Epistle 6 (313.37f.): οὐδὲ γὰρ οἱ καθ' ἡμῶν μύες οὗτοι παράσιτοι· κατάσιτοι μὲν οὖν, εἴπερ ἦν ἡμῖν ὀνοματοθετεῖν ... οὐκ ἔστι κατ' αὐτῶν μηχανή. Τὰ τῶν παγίδων εἰς κενὸν διαχάσκει καὶ τέλεον ἀπρακτεῖ. Ὁ ἐκ ξύλου τοξότης Σμινθεὺς εἰς μάτην ἐντείνεται ...

16 *Eustathii Metropolitae Thessalonicensis opuscula*, Epistle 6; P. Koukoules, *Θεσσαλονίκης Εὐσταθίου τὰ λαογραφικά*, vol. 1 (Athens, 1950), 206.

17 Koukoules, *Βυζαντινῶν βίος καὶ πολιτισμός*, 5.106, 288; idem, *λαογραφικά*, 1.206; A. Karpozilos, 'Realia in Byzantine epistolography X–XIIc.', *BZ* 77 (1984), 20–37, 22; idem, 'Realia in Byzantine epistolography XIII–XVc.', *BZ* 88 (1995), 68–84.

fruits, medlar and quinces, which the mice hollowed into cave-like hiding places.

What do we learn from this nocturne? First, the problem of pests is presented. It goes without saying that mice and other vermin devoured large quantities of stored products. In 384/385 mice, snakes and locusts diminished Antioch's victuals during a severe famine;[18] in 604/605 mice ate up stored crops in Italy.[19] Andreas Müller has estimated the loss of wheat by pests and transport damages at approximately 10 to 30 per cent, but the activity of mice and other household pests is seldom reported.[20] And second, we also learn something about the contents of Eustathios's storeroom, which included dried fruits (maybe from his garden). It is well known that Eustathios was a proud gardener.[21]

Fruits and plants

Fruits, plants and fresh vegetables played an important part in the Byzantine diet.[22] To make them available the whole year, they had to be preserved, and drying is the oldest and simplest way to achieve this. Dehydration – the process of removing water from fruits and so on – destroys the breeding-ground of bacteria.[23] Plants and various spices are easier to preserve because they can be dried almost anywhere. The drying process needs air and warmth, but no admixtures.

Epistolography is a valuable source of information for Byzantine economic history, including aspects of transport and exchange of goods. Many letters were accompanied by edible gifts – fresh, living or processed. Dried fruits such as figs or raisins lost most of their weight during their dehydration,

18 Stathakopoulos, *Famine and Pestilence*, 209–10 (no. 30).

19 Stathakopoulos, *Famine and Pestilence*, 335–7 (no. 166).

20 Müller, 'Getreide für Konstantinopel', 17.

21 Gardens were important for providing fresh vegetables and fruits; Demetrios Kydones (*Démétrius Cydonès, Correspondance*, ed. R. J. Loenertz, Studi e Testi 188, 206 (Vatican City, 1956–60), Epistle 143, 208) mentions medlar fruits from his garden, which he sent to the emperor; see C. N. Constantinides, 'Byzantine gardens and horticulture in the Late Byzantine period, 1204–1453: the secular sources', in A. Littlewood, H. Maguire and J. Wolschke-Bulmahn, eds, *Byzantine Garden Culture* (Washington, DC, 2002), 87–103, 100; this volume contains several articles relevant to our topic: A.-M. Talbot, 'Byzantine monastic horticulture: the textual evidence', 37–67; R. Rodgers, 'Κηποποιΐα: garden making and garden culture in the *Geoponika*', 159–75.

22 J. Koder, *Gemüse in Byzanz: Die Versorgung Konstantinopels mit Frischgemüse im Lichte der Geoponika*, Byzantinische Geschichtsschreiber, Ergänzungsband 3 (Vienna, 1993); for an English summary, see idem, 'Fresh vegetables for the capital', in C. Mango and G. Dagron, eds, *Constantinople and Its Hinterland: papers from the Twenty-Seventh Spring Symposium of Byzantine Studies, Oxford, April 1993* (Aldershot, 1995), 49–56.

23 R. W. Lacey, *Hard to Swallow: a brief history of food* (Cambridge, 1994), 85–6.

which eased transportation. Moreover, because of their durability, the time or distance that elapsed during letter exchange did not matter.[24]

But what if somebody needed a living plant? It was no problem to send fresh flowers within the walls of Constantinople, as Michael Psellos did to the empress Eudokia or Demetrios Kydones to John V Palaiologos.[25] But what if a plant required transportation over a long distance?

An example extracted from Tzetzes's letters, an underestimated source for the reconstruction of daily life in mid-twelfth-century Byzantium, provides some evidence.[26] John Tzetzes suffered from a lung disease (*orthopnoia*), and he often deplores it (not as a literary topos of the poor and ill poet but as a genuine illness that may have caused his death). He needed a remedy found near Amastris, today Samastrus, a coastal city on the Black Sea, and east of Constantinople.[27] In a letter to the *grammatikos* Nikephoros, who was travelling by ship from Constantinople to Amastris, he described the desired tree in detail.[28] The plant can be identified as myrtle (ὁ μύρτος): Tzetzes's description follows Theophrastos's *Enquiry into Plants*.[29] Myrtle is very common in the Black Sea regions. Because of its healing properties, it was used to treat lung diseases, especially bronchitis.[30] Tzetzes asked Nikephoros to send him seeds or, if he could not find them, seedlings, which would guarantee provision of the product he needed. He told Nikephoros how to send the plants: he should place some little seedlings together with their surrounding earth into a basket or a pot and have them delivered

---

24 See Karpozilos, 'Realia in Byzantine epistolography X–XIIc.' and 'Realia in Byzantine epistolography XIII–XVc.'.

25 Michael Psellos, Epistle 132, ed. K. N. Sathas, *Mesaionike Bibliotheke*, vols 4–5 (Athens, 1872–94; repr. Hildesheim, 1972); Demetrios Cydones, *Correspondance*, ed. Loenertz, Epistle 233, p. 208.

26 Paul Magdalino demonstrated how reliable Byzantine letters are as a source for daily life; see his 'The literary perception of everyday life in Byzantium: some general considerations and the case of John Apokaukos', *BSl* 47 (1987), 28; for a brief overview, see A. A. Demosthenous, 'The scholar and the partridge: attitudes relating to nutritional goods in the twelfth century from the letters of the scholar John Tzetzes', in W. Mayer and S. Trzcionka, *Feast, Fast or Famine: food and drink in Byzantium*, Byzantina Australiensia 15 (Brisbane, 2005), 25–31.

27 K. Belke, *Paphlagonien und Honorias*, Tabula Imperii Byzantini 9 (Vienna, 1996), 161–70.

28 P. A. M. Leone, ed., *Ioannes Tzetzes Epistulae* (Leipzig, 1972), Epistle 100, pp. 146–7; see M. Grünbart, 'Prosopographische Beiträge zum Briefcorpus des Johannes Tzetzes', *JÖB* 46 (1996), 175–226.

29 A. Hort, ed., *Theophrastus. Enquiry into Plants and Minor Works on Odours and Weather Signs, with an English translation*, Loeb 70 (Cambridge, MA, 1968), 1.3.3.

30 See G. E. Thüry and J. Walter, *Condimenta. Gewürzpflanzen in Koch- und Backrezepten aus der römischen Antike* (Vienna, 1997), 61; P. Timplalexi, *Medizinisches in der byzantinischen Epistolographie* (1100–1453), Europäische Hochschulschriften, Reihe VII, Abt. B. Geschichte der Medizin 8 (Frankfurt am Main, 2002), 159–60; A. Gutsfeld, in *Der Neue Pauly* 4 (Stuttgart, 1998), 1062.

to Constantinople. The earth should be moistened in order to make the extraction easier.

What would have Tzetzes done with this plant if it reached him safely in Constantinople? At the time he wrote this letter (in 1157) he lived in the Pantokrator monastery, where a garden almost certainly existed. The *typikon* of the monastery mentions gardeners (κηπουροί).[31] From this reference, and a twelfth-century dedicatory poem that mentions grass, flowers, fountains, cypress trees and gentle breezes, we may conclude that there was something like a garden within the precincts of the monastery, where the seedling could be planted.[32] The letter of Tzetzes provides a rare allusion to the transportation of living plants; only a few additional references can be found in ancient sources.[33]

Meat

But Byzantines did not live only on fruit; they also ate meat.[34] Freezing and freeze-drying of food was nearly unknown to Byzantines.[35] The use of snow or ice for preserving meat is mentioned in the *Geoponika*, but this seems to be an exception and not for daily use.[36] Other strategies had to be found in order to keep meat edible.

Since meat turns bad quickly, the simplest way to have it at hand is by keeping live animals as a reserve. Military campaigns habitually travelled with live animals.[37] Armies were followed by herds of sheep and cattle, resulting in a constant need for fresh fodder and water to keep them alive. The importance of collecting fodder, and the danger of being ambushed during this activity, is mentioned in every military treatise and recorded in historiographical sources. Every time the Byzantine emperor intended

---

31 P. Gautier, 'Le typikon du Christ sauveur Pantocrator', *REB* 32 (1974), 1–145, lines 542–4: ἀπὸ δὲ τῶν δουλευτῶν οὐκ ἀρτοποιοὶ καὶ κηπωροὶ καὶ μάγειροι μόνον γενήσονται ... See also *BMFD* 2.725–81.

32 A. M. Talbot, 'Byzantine monastic horticulture', 37–67, esp. 59 and 64.

33 K. Hornig, 'Pflanzentransporte zu Wasser im antiken Mittelmeerraum', *ZU* 2 (1999), 126–37.

34 See O. Schmitt, 'Zur Fleischversorgung Konstantinopels', *JÖB* 54 (2004), 135–57, mainly based on the *Book of the Eparch* and almost neglecting all epistolographic evidence.

35 U. Hellmann, *Künstliche Kälte: Die Geschichte der Kühlung im Haushalt*, Werkbund-Archiv 21 (Giessen, 1990).

36 *Geoponika* XIX.9.2, ed. H. Beckh (Leipzig, 1895). For the preservation of meat with snow, see T. Weber, 'Essen und Trinken im Konstantinopel des 10. Jahrhunderts nach den Berichten Liutprands von Cremona', in J. Koder and T. Weber, eds, *Liutprand von Cremona in Konstantinopel: Untersuchungen zum griechischen Sprachschatz und zu realienkundlichen Aussagen in seinen Werken*, BV 8 (Vienna, 1980), 71–99, esp. 83.

37 T. Kolias, 'Eßgewohnheiten und Verpflegung im byzantinischen Heer', in W. Hörandner, J. Koder, O. Kresten and E. Trapp, eds, *Βυζάντιος. Festschrift für Herbert Hunger zum 70. Geburtstag* (Vienna, 1984), 193–202.

to start a military expedition 'each *protonotarios* supplied the requirements of the imperial cortège from the *aerikon* and the *synone* in his thema, that is: animals for slaughter, lambs, and such like, and the provisions for the largesses and the remaining feasts'.[38] Furthermore:

> For the departure of the baggage-train, the head of the table should load the eighty pack-animals with all the imperial requirements, and should obtain from the *protonotarios* one-hundred suckling lambs, 500 rams, fifty cattle, 200 chickens and one-hundred geese, for consumption at the imperial table and for feasts.[39]

Food supply for the army was essential for military success. But the most important provision for both men and animals was water. If there was no access to fresh water, it had to be stored and kept sweet.[40] Some methods are mentioned in the so-called *Sylloge Tacticorum*. A wooden vessel should be dipped in a cistern and the water should flow into the vessel. After it has been filled up, the water should be poured again into the cistern. Another recipe was to throw flint stones into the water to keep it in a steady movement.[41]

Keeping animals for slaughter was not, of course, restricted to the military. Skimming through Byzantine letter collections, we find some references to the exchange of living or recently killed animals between correspondents. In general, however, correspondents were not very happy about receiving fresh fish or meat because it had to be consumed instantly or processed, a procedure that demanded a certain stock of salt and a place to hang.

In his epistle to Alexios Pantechnes, John Tzetzes communicates his greetings to him and thanks him for his gifts: spices (ἀρώματα) and a living partridge, and, earlier, some birds. Unfortunately Tzetzes did not know – or, more precisely, did not want to know – what to do with them. He responded that he disliked seeing blood from slaughtered animals;[42] if Alexios wants to send him meat, he should dispatch meat prepared by cooks, namely processed (τάριχα) or fresh meat.[43] Tzetzes distinguishes between cooked, processed and freshly slaughtered meat. According to

[38] J. F. Haldon, ed. and tr., *Constantine Porphyrogenitus. Three Treatises on Imperial Military Expeditions. Introduction, edition, translation, and commentary*, CFHB 28 (Vienna, 1990), 88–9 (B.101–6).

[39] Haldon, ed. and tr., *Constantine Porphyrogenitus*, 128–9 (C.532–5).

[40] It was recommended to erect camps at rivers or lakes in order to have enough water; the waterfront of a camp is easier to defend, too.

[41] *Sylloge Tacticorum*, ed. A. Dain (Paris, 1938), 55.2; Kolias, 'Eßgewohnheiten', 200.

[42] John Tzetzes, Epistle 4, ed. Leone, 7.20–22.

[43] John Tzetzes, Epistle 93, ed. Leone, 135.27–136.1: ᾧ δὲ βουλητὸν ἀποστολῶν κρεωδῶν ἡμᾶς ἅπτεσθαι, ἢ ἐσκευασμένα ταῦτα τέχνῃ μαγείρων στελλέτω ἢ τάριχα. εἴτ᾽ οὖν πρὸ ἡμερῶν ἐσφαγμένα μηδὲ νεοχύτῳ περριρεόμενα αἵματι.

the *Book of the Eparch*, it was forbidden for butchers, fishmongers and pig-sellers to process and store meat or fish for times of shortage; they were only allowed to sell freshly butchered meat and freshly caught fish.[44] Meat and fish appear to have been processed at home for private consumption.

In another letter, John Tzetzes referred to his living conditions in a Constantinopolitan flat. He lived on the second floor while on the third a priest resided with his children. In an often-quoted passage, he describes his situation:

> I live in between the horrors of fire and watery deluge. For, beneath me the hay is strewn about, while above my head and around the lintel of my doorway rain flows in as a great stream. For, the house is a three-storey [building] and a holy priest, although of a lower rank, resides on the second floor above me … Together with his children he raises little pigs. These children and the piglets do just the opposite of what the cavalry of Xerxes did. For, [Xerxes's] horses leaned over to drink [water] and completely dried up the rivers ... On the contrary, these little ones produce so much water [literally, urine] that it flows together to form navigable rivers.[45]

We may conclude that, in the absence of storerooms or stables, animals lived together with human beings.

It has been noted that pigs are constantly mentioned in Greek and Roman sources concerning dietary habits.[46] Why? The pig produces meat and leather but, unlike sheep or goats, no milk or wool. Pigs are easy to feed because they eat almost everything (even the remains of pigs that have been slaughtered). What the pig produces is more pigs, as many as twelve per litter. Moreover, a sow's gestation period is only 110 days (40 days less than sheep or goats).[47] Pigs produce and provide a lot of usable meat and anyone who keeps them has to face the question of preservation, if the piglets are not simply sold.

How was meat processed in Byzantine times? Smoking appears to have been unknown in Byzantium. The most effective way to preserve meat was drying combined with salting.[48] The process of making salted meat

---

44 *The Book of the Eparch*, ed. J. Koder, *Das Eparchenbuch Leons des Weisen*, CFHB 33 (Vienna, 1991), 15.6, 16.5, 17.2.

45 John Tzetzes, Epistle 18, ed. Leone; see G. T. Dennis, 'The Byzantines as revealed in their letters', in J. Duffy and J. Peradotto, eds, *Gonimos. Neoplatonic and Byzantine Studies Presented to Leendert G. Westerink at 75* (Buffalo, NY, 1988), 155–65; Schmitt, 'Fleischversorgung', 142.

46 F. Frost, 'Sausage and meat preservation in antiquity', *GRBS* 40 (1999), 241–52.

47 Frost, 'Sausage', 243; Schmitt, 'Fleischversorgung', 142.

48 In general, see R. J. Forbes, *Studies in Ancient Technology* (Leiden, 1965), 191–6; 'Konservierung', in *Lexikon des Mittelalters*, vol. 5 (Zürich, 1991), 1370.

is described by ancient authors like Varro Cato,[49] and is also discussed in the *Geoponika*.[50] To begin the process properly, animals were not watered the day before they were slaughtered. The first step in conservation is to dry the meat in order to stop the growth of bacteria. Bones were removed and the meat was lightly salted to extract moisture and blood. Some texts recommend pouring sweet wine over the pieces, for greater flavour. We do not know how meat processed like this tasted, but if Frank Frost's attempts to make sausages and to process meat based on ancient recipes are trusted – and if we accept his judgement of their flavour – it was tasty food.[51] If meat was too salty, it was simply washed, as soldiers did in a river in the region of Amida in the summer of 503.[52]

A similar process was applied to produce dried fish. Skimming through Byzantine letter-collections, we smell the odour of salted sea and river fishes because they were highly appreciated gifts, and the transport of such tasty pieces was easy.[53] Both dried meat and dried fish demanded a considerable amount of salt, and salt production needed to keep pace.[54]

Other perishable products

A third category of perishable animal products consists of milk and eggs. Milk was made into butter and cheese. This process facilitated both its transport and storage. Again epistolographical sources provide information.

Depending on the duration of transportation, letter-gifts had to be durable. Nicholas Mystikos received cheese from Leo, *protospatharios* and

[49] Frost, 'Sausage' 244f: 'salt is laid down in the bottom of a large jar. The hams are placed skin down on the salt and are covered with another layer of salt. Then more hams and layers of salt are added until the jar is full and covered with a final layer of salt. After five days the hams are taken out and put back in reverse order. After twelve days the hams are taken out, brushed off, and dried for two days. Then they are cleaned, coated with oil, and cold smoked for another two days before being hung to store in the meat house (Rust. 162.1–3).'

[50] *Geoponika* XIX 9.1–6, ed. H. Beckh (Leipzig, 1895).

[51] Frost, 'Sausage', 252.

[52] Prokopios, *De Bello Persico* I.8.14–17, ed. J. Haury and G. Wirth, *Wars*, vols 1–2 (Leipzig, 1962–63), 39.5–19; mentioned by Kolias, 'Eßgewohnheiten', 199.

[53] See both articles by Karpozilos on 'Realia' in Byzantine epistolography.

[54] K. P. Matschke, 'Bemerkungen zum spätbyzantinischen Salzmonopol', in *Studia Byzantina II. Beiträge aus der byzantinistischen Forschung der Deutschen Demokratischen Republik zum XIV. Internationalen Byzantinistenkongreß Bukarest 1971*, Berliner Byzantinistische Arbeiten 44 (Berlin, 1973), 37–60; in general *Το Ελληνικό Αλάτι. Η' Τριήμερο Εργασίας, Μυτιλήνη, 6/8 Νοεμβρίου 1998* (Athens, 2001).

judge of Paphlagonia,[55] and Michael Psellos appreciated cheese from the same region, which lies beyond Constantinople's hinterland.[56]

If products are not carefully produced or stored, the health of consumers can be damaged seriously. A classic case is recorded by Prokopios. Byzantine troops waited in Methone to sail to Italy and Africa. It was a hot summer and many soldiers died after the consumption of bread that was half-baked in order to save money, so Prokopios says. The bread fell apart, turned to flour, rotted, and became mouldy and smelled badly. The commander Belisarios forbade the consumption of this lethal bread.[57] Another example appears in the *Life* of Theodore of Sykeon. The inhabitants of Apokumis slaughtered an ox and everybody who consumed its meat died instantly. The rest of the meat was black and smelled badly. But Theodore of Sykeon brought them back to life.[58]

Written sources almost entirely neglect information on storing because it was a household matter. Nevertheless, some glimpses of this daily habit and necessity are preserved especially in Byzantine letters. Hagiographic and monastic sources (for example *typika*) will add more information. The most important source for the reconstruction and interpretation of storing facilities is archaeological research as it provides an increasing number of data. By combining both types of sources a more comprehensive and detailed picture of preservation can be given.

---

55 R. J. H. Jenkins and L. G. Westerink, eds, *Nicholas I Patriarch of Constantinople, Letters*, CFHB 6 (Washington, DC, 1973), Epistle 127.

56 See Karpozilos, 'Realia in Byzantine epistolography X–XIIc.', 26; J. Koder, in 'Maritime trade and the food supply for Constantinople in the Middle Ages', in R. Macrides, ed., *Travel in the Byzantine World*, Society for the Promotion of Byzantine Studies Publications 10 (Aldershot, 2002), 109–24, 112–13, supposes this.

57 It has been pointed out by Dionysios Stathakopoulos that its consumption may have produced a case of mass poisoning by ergotism; see Stathakopoulos, *Famine and Pestilence*, 263–4 (no. 90).

58 A.-J. Festugière, *Vie de Théodore de Sykéon*, Subsidia Hagiographica 48 (Brussels, 1970), 1.113 (143).

9. Some Byzantine aromatics

Andrew Dalby

As part of a sketch of Byzantine food and cookery,[1] I compiled a 'phrase-book of Byzantine foods and aromas'. I expressed the hope that it would be useful not only to time-travellers but to those conducting research on or interested in Byzantine history. It grew out of the personal glossary that I myself found it essential to compile as I worked on the sources for post-classical Greek food: this work seemed to be needed because existing dictionaries and translations tend to slip out of focus when approaching a technical field such as food and contain some serious misunderstandings. This short paper explores a few identifications that have caused difficulty. It ends with a Byzantine spice that does not appear in the phrase book because I can give it no Byzantine name.

Byzantine Greek ἄμβαρ, ἄμπαρ: *ambergris*

The erroneous gloss 'amber' is often given in modern dictionaries and translations. It is adopted by Freshfield, for example, in his translation of the brief list of aromatics and dyes in the *Book of the Eparch*.[2] Why?

Amber is a fossil resin found on beaches in several parts of the world, especially the Baltic shores. It is used as a semi-precious stone and is very slightly aromatic when warmed in the hand. It was formerly ground and used as an ingredient in medicines. Amber was already well known to ancient Greeks and Romans: it is *elektron* in classical Greek and *succinum* in classical Latin. *Elektron* remained the usual term in Byzantine Greek.[3] The Latin loanword *soukinon* is also found occasionally, in Artemidoros[4] and in

[1] A. Dalby, *Flavours of Byzantium* (Totnes, 2003).

[2] E. H. Freshfield, 'Ordinances of Leo VI (c.895) from the Book of the Eparch', in idem, *Roman Law in the Later Roman Empire* (Cambridge, 1938).

[3] See, for example, Michael Psellos, *Opuscula logica, physica, allegorica, alia*, ed. J. M. Duffy, Teubner (Leipzig, 1992), nos 34, 35.

[4] *Artemidoros, Oneirokritika, ed. R.A. Pack, Artemidori Daldiani Onirocriticon libri V, Teubner (Leipzig, 1963), 2.5.*

the *Souda*.[5] Amber was correctly understood to be the 'tears', or resin, of trees, though its prehistoric origin was not realized.

Ambergris is an intestinal secretion of the sperm whale, *Physeter macrocephalus*, and is found on the shores of the Indian Ocean. It is a powerful and very costly aromatic, resembling musk in the range of its uses in perfumery; it was also highly prized in traditional medicine, both European and Chinese. Because of its medicinal reputation, it was used in foods, notably in sweets. Small pieces of ambergris can be used as jewellery. The early geographer Ktesias heard of ambergris and was told it was the sperm of elephants;[6] his view is reported disbelievingly by Aristotle,[7] whose opinion is repeated by Aristophanes of Byzantium,[8] and later by Psellos.[9] Meanwhile the substance itself was forgotten. For some reason it was never imported into the Graeco-Roman world. Psellos was therefore probably not even aware that the *elephanton sperma* he found in Aristophanes of Byzantium was the same as the *ambar* on sale in his time in the spice market of Constantinople. To judge by surviving texts, its spread into medieval Europe had begun, in Constantinople, in the sixth century. In the view of many medieval and early modern Europeans ambergris was the sperm of whales.[10] Meanwhile it was also marketed eastwards: it reached medieval China about the ninth century and was believed there to be the spittle of dragons.[11]

Amber and ambergris have certain things in common: they are both gathered on beaches, they are both translucent aromatic solids, which can be ground. Ktesias had already noted the similarity between them. Their differences, however, are substantial. They are never confused in ancient or medieval texts.

The Arabic word *anbar*, 'ambergris', is the direct origin of most of the names for ambergris in medieval Europe, naturally enough, because in medieval times the substance was usually bought from Arab traders. Hence Byzantine Greek *ambar*, *ampar*, medieval Latin *ambar*, Italian *ambra*, Spanish *ambre*, Portuguese *âmbar*, French *ambre*, English *amber*, German *Ambra*. The

---

5 *Souda*, ed. A. Adler, *Suidae Lexicon*, 5 vols (Leipzig, 1928–38), s.v. 'soukinon'.

6 F. Jacoby, *F Gr Hist: die Fragmente der griechischen Historiker* (Berlin, 1923–58), no. 688 F 48b.

7 Aristotle, *Generation of Animals*, ed. H. J. Drossaart Lulofs, *Aristotelis de generatione animalium* (Oxford, 1965), 736a2; cf. *History of Animals*, ed. P. Louis, *Aristote: Histoire des animaux* (Paris, 1964–69), 523a26.

8 Aristophanes of Byzantium, *Epitome*, ed. S. P. Lambros, *Excerptorum Constantini de natura animalium libri duo; Aristophanis historiae animalium epitome* (Berlin, 1885), 1.57.

9 Psellos, *Opuscula logica*, ed. Duffy, no. 16.

10 See the quotation from the *Grete Herball* below.

11 E. H. Schafer, *The Golden Peaches of Samarkand* (Berkeley, CA, 1963), 174–5; A. Dalby, *Dangerous Tastes: the story of spices* (London, 2000), 67–8.

Greek word is found first (so far as I know) in Aetios of Amida's *Medicine* and occurs seven more times in Byzantine sources, in recipes containing many costly aromatics, spanning the period from the sixth century to the eleventh.[12] In many of them ambergris is listed alongside musk, as it might well be by perfumiers today.

In all European languages, until about the seventeenth century, *amber* or its equivalent usually meant 'ambergris' and not what we now call amber. In English, for example, from the *Grete Herball* of 1526: '*Ambre is hote and drye ... Some say that it is the sparme of a whale.*'[13]

In the languages of western Europe, however – and in English as early as the late fourteenth century – the same word came also to be used for the yellow resin that we now know as amber. The first indubitable evidence comes in mentions of *lamber beads* and of a *lamber colour* (meaning the colour of saffron) in manuscripts of about 1400 and 1430.[14] French lexicographers have not found the French word used in the sense of 'amber' until the early seventeenth century, and, even then, nearly always in the collocation *ambre jaune*, 'yellow amber'; yet they have traced the parallel collocations *ambre blanc* and *ambre gris* as far back as 1562. Clearly the lexicographers should go on looking. English *ambergris* is borrowed from the last of these French collocations, and it is first recorded as early as 1490 in the form *imbergres*.[15]

German *Ambra* and French *ambre* (or *ambre proprement dit*) still mean 'ambergris'. But the switch of meaning that began in English has spread into some other languages. Just as English *amber* now means 'amber', so do the Portuguese, Spanish and Italian words listed above. It is because of this later change of meaning – which had scarcely begun when Constantinople fell, and affected only certain languages of western Europe – that Byzantine *ambar, ampar* is often wrongly translated 'amber'.

---

12 Aetios of Amida, *Medicine*, ed. S. Zervos, *Gynaekologie des Aëtios* (Leipzig, 1901), 16.130. Elsewhere it is found in pseudo-Galen, *On Similar Remedies*, ed. C. G. Kühn, *Galeni opera omnia*, vol. 14 (Leipzig, 1821–33), 547, in a recipe attributed to 'the monk Ioachos'; *Corpus hippiatricorum graecorum*, ed. E. Oder and C. Hoppe, Teubner (Leipzig, 1924–27), *Appendices ad Hippiatrica Berolinensia*, section 7 (three occurrences); *Book of the Eparch*, ed. Freshfield, section 10; Constantine Porphyrogennetos, *Book of Ceremonies*, ed. J. J. Reiske, *Constantini Porphyrogeniti imperatoris de cerimoniis aulae Byzantinae* (Bonn, 1829), 468; Simeon Seth, *On the Properties of Foods*, ed. B. Langkavel, *Simeonis Sethi syntagma de alimentorum facultatibus*, Teubner (Leipzig, 1868), 26.

13 *The Grete Herball* (London, 1526). The quotation, taken from *OED*, is from signature B v b in the 1529 printing.

14 See *OED*, s.v. 'lamber': this form of the word is borrowed from French *lambre* or *l'ambre*.

15 See *OED*, s.v. 'ambergris'.

Byzantine Greek ζυγαία: storax

Another problematic word encountered by Freshfield in translating the list of aromatics and dyes in the *Book of the Eparch* was *zygaia*. In the form *zygia* this word also occurs in pharmaceutical recipes in the *Medicine* of Paul of Aigina and in *Hippiatrica Berolinensia*;[16] in both sources it is listed among aromatic resins – bdellium, ladanum, mastic, lentisk, frankincense, pine and terebinth.

For a reason unknown to me, Freshfield translates *zygaia* as 'capers', although capers are not an aromatic in the usual sense, nor a dye, and their name in Greek – ancient, medieval and modern – has always been *kappari(s)*. In the botanical works of Theophrastos, *zygia* is the name of a tree sufficiently familiar to be used several times as an example;[17] Hort,[18] followed by the ninth edition of Liddell and Scott's *Lexicon*,[19] identifies it as 'field maple, *Acer campestre*', while Andrews, in his index to plant names in Pliny,[20] proposes 'hornbeam, *Carpinus betulus*'. These identifications would work well enough for Theophrastos and Pliny but they do not work for the *zyg(a)ia* of the medical authors and the *Book of the Eparch*, because neither field maple nor hornbeam produces an aromatic. So what does the Byzantine word really mean?

A clue is provided by the Russian narrative of the pilgrim Daniel, who gives an interesting, though confused, description of the production of storax in Caria.[21] Daniel claims that this important incense-like resin is the mixture of products from two trees, one of which is called *raka* or *styuryaka* and the other *zygia* or *izygia*. Storax was familiar in the classical world, under the name *styrax*, and that name continues to be used in Byzantine sources, though it does not occur in Paul of Aigina or in the *Hippiatrica*.

Storax has several sources. Ancient supplies are usually said to have come from the Syrian tree *Styrax officinalis*, a point that requires further investigation. The modern source of storax in the Mediterranean region is the tree *Liquidambar orientalis*, which grows where Daniel saw it growing in south-western Asia Minor, and which possibly began to be exploited after

16 Paul of Aigina, *Medicine*, ed. I. L. Heiberg, *Paulus Aegineta* (Leipzig, 1921–24), 4.4.3, 7.18.8; *Appendices ad Hippiatrica Berolinensia*, ed. Oder and Hoppe, section 7.

17 *History of Plants* 3.11.1-2 and elsewhere; cf. Pliny, *Natural History*, ed. C. Mayhoff, *C. Plinii Secundi Naturalis Historia*, Teubner (Leipzig, 1875–1905), 16.67.

18 Theophrastos: A. Hort, ed. and tr., *Theophrastus, Enquiry into Plants*, Loeb 70–79 (Cambridge, MA, 1916–26), 2.451.

19 H. G. Liddell and R. Scott, *A Greek–English Lexicon* (Oxford, 1925–1940), 9th edn by H. S. Jones and R. McKenzie, s.v. 'zygia'.

20 A. C. Andrews, 'Index of plants', in *Pliny, Natural History Books XXIV–XXVII*, ed. and tr. W. H. S. Jones (Cambridge, MA; 2nd edn, 1980), 485–550.

21 *Pilgrimage*, ed. M. A.Venevitinov, *Zhitye i khozhenye Danila Russkaya zemli igumena* (St Petersburg, 1885), section 4.

Syria was lost to the Byzantine Empire. This liquidambar species, though not closely related to maple, has maple-like leaves. I suggest that Byzantine Greek *zyg(a)ia* is an alternative term for storax, and specifically the storax from *L. orientalis*, and that it acquired this name because of the superficial resemblance between the field maple and the liquidambar tree. In the Latin translation by Leonhard Fuchs of the Byzantine prescriptions of Nicholas Myrepsus, at least one recipe calls for a quantity of *styracis liquidi*.[22] This, again, is likely to be a precise designation for the storax from *L. orientalis*.

Byzantine Greek ἰάσμη: *jasmine;* ζάμβαχ: *sambac*

Two species of jasmine are familiar as sources of modern perfumes. A resemblance between the plants and the perfumes is evident, but they have different uses. Both jasmines are to be found – though rarely – in Byzantine sources, and there is every reason to suppose that the two were kept apart by name.

Jasminum officinale is jasmine or Persian jasmine and is native to south-western Asia. Its medieval Persian name, in the form *yâsam* or *yasmîn*, was borrowed both into Chinese, as early as the fourth century AD, and into Greek (*iasme*) by the sixth century, though the word is not recorded in Persian until the tenth century.[23]

Jasminum sambac is sambac or mogra or Arabian jasmine, native to Yemen. Like Persian jasmine, it had been introduced to southern China by the fourth century AD by Persian merchants: this is the jasmine that lends its aroma nowadays to Earl Grey tea. It reached the Mediterranean world later than Persian jasmine, though it seems likely that it is the unnamed aromatic flower reported from Yemen by the Hellenistic geographer Agatharchides.[24]

The earliest Greek source for *iasme*, Persian jasmine, is the sixth-century author Aetios.[25] Oil of jasmine, *τὸ ἐξ ἰάσμιον σκευαζόμενον ἔλαιον*, is called for in an anonymous later Byzantine medical handbook.[26] Du Cange found this word, and instructions for making the oil, in an interpolated manuscript of Dioskourides, but it is not in any version available to me.[27]

---

22 *Nicolai Myrepsi Alexandrini medicamentorum opus*, tr. L. Fuchsius (Lyons, 1549), 135. I have not been able to consult the Greek text.

23 A. Dalby, *Dangerous Tastes*, 77 and note 9.

24 Fragment 99b, ed. S. M. Burstein, *Agatharchides of Cnidus on the Erythraean Sea* (London, 1989). The fragment is known from Diodoros of Sicily, *Histories* 3.46.

25 *Medicine*, ed. A. Olivieri, *Aëtii Amideni libri medicinales*, Teubner (Leipzig, 1935–50), 1.120.

26 *Peri trophon dynameos*, ed. I. L. Ideler, *Physici et medici graeci minores* (Berlin, 1841–42), 475.

27 C. du Fresne, sieur du Cange, *Glossarium ad scriptores mediae et infimae Graecitatis* (Lyons, 1688), s.v. 'iasme'.

The earliest datable Greek source known to me for sambac is Symeon Seth, who wrote in the tenth century and has a reference to *zampakelaion*, sambac oil.[28] There is a mention of *zambax* in *Hippiatrica Berolinensia*, and a careful specification of *τὰ λευκοία ἃ σαρακηνιστὶ λέγονται ζαμπάκιασμιν*, the white violets that are called 'sambac jasmine' in Arabic.[29] The interesting point about these names – and those of some other exotica – is how rarely they occur in surviving texts. Known citations are separated by hundreds of years, and yet, through all that time, the words clearly remained familiar to traders, spice merchants, pharmacists and physicians.

The three sandalwoods

Sandalwood (*Santalum album*) is the ground aromatic wood of a parasitic tree native to Indonesia and long familiar in southern India. For this species the first mention in surviving texts from the Mediterranean world comes in the *Christian Topography* of Kosmas Indikopleustes.[30] He calls it *tzandana*, which is an accurate Greek transcription of the name that would have been used in the Indian ports from which it was shipped (cf. Pali *candana*). In the few later Byzantine sources in which the word occurs, it takes a form closer to those current in medieval Europe generally: *santalon or sandalon.*[31]

But why, in the *Hippiatrica Cantabrigiensia*,[32] does the anonymous author insist that *sandalon alethinon* 'true sandalwood' must be included in the prescription? In the antidote *Dia trion sandalon* for which Nicholas Myrepsus gave a recipe,[33] what are the 'three sandalwoods'?

It is perfectly true that there are three sandalwoods available in the spice trade, and that one of them is an impostor. The two true sandalwoods are the yellow and brown, or white and black, grades of the wood of *S. album*. Both are aromatic. The third is called 'red sandalwood' or, less deceptively, 'red sanders'. It is the ground wood of the tree *Pterocarpus santolina*, and, like the others, is exported from southern India. Red sanders is not aromatic and was not usually of interest to medieval pharmacists, but it was (and occasionally still is) used by cooks as a natural red food colouring. Among late medieval recipes that call for red sanders, one printed by Hieatt

---

28 *On the Properties of Foods, ed.* Langkavel, 30.

29 *Appendices ad Hippiatrica Berolinensia*, ed. Oder and Hoppe, 7; *Peri trophon dynameos*, ed. Ideler, 475.

30 *Christian Topography*, ed. and tr. W. Wolska-Conus, *Cosmas Indicopleustès, Topographie chrétienne*, SC 159 (Paris, 1970), 11.15.

31 *Santalon* in *Peri Trophon Dynameos*, ed. Ideler, 476; *sandalon* in pseudo-Galen, *Introduction*, ed. Kühn, 14.759.

32 *Corpus hippiatricorum graecorum*, ed. E. Oder and C. Hoppe, Teubner (Leipzig, 1924–27), *Hippiatrica Cantabrigiensia*, section 58.

33 *Nicolai Myrepsi Alexandrini medicamentorum opus*, tr. Fuchsius, 91.

employs the Middle English name *sawndrys*;[34] another, in the *Mesnagier de Paris*, provides the Middle French name *alixander*.[35]

I believe that we have no Byzantine name for red sanders. Yet its presence in the Byzantine spice market is clearly signalled by the caveat in the *Hippiatrica Cantabrigiensia*; it is confirmed by Nicholas Myrepsus, whose *Dia trion sandalon* would have impressed credulous patients not only by its high cost and powerful aroma but also by its blood-red colour.

---

34 *An Ordinance of Pottage ... the fifteenth century culinary recipes in Yale University's MS Beinecke 163*, ed. C. B. Hieatt (London, 1988), no. 14: tr. in Dalby, *Dangerous Tastes*, 97.

35 Text and translation in *Le Ménagier de Paris*, ed. G. E. Brereton and J. M. Ferrier (Oxford, 1981), 2.5.84.

10. *Stew and salted meat* – opulent normality in the diet of every day?

Johannes Koder

The title of my paper needs some explanation. Stew, *μονόκυθρον* (*Τὸ ἐκ τῆς χύτρας συντεθὲν μονόκυθρον*, as it is briefly defined by Eustathios[1]), seems to have been the favourite luxury food of Ptochoprodromos, who dreams of the aromatic smell of the stew: 'The little stew gives off fumes and smells wonderful.'[2] In his poems he conveys the impression that the term *monokythron* stands for a type of popular festive hot meal,[3] which is not prepared every day, but is not reserved exclusively for the imperial court or the rich.

The same seems to be true for *τὰ παστὰ*, which principally means every foodstuff that is conserved by adding salt (*τὸ ἐπιτιθέναι ἅλας πρὸς ταριχείαν*),[4] such as salted fish or salted meat, but also pickled vegetables. In Byzantium, only conservation by drying (in the sun) and/or salting was well known, the salting of vegetables often being in combination with vinegar, under the name *toursi*. In particular, I have not found any explicit reference to *smoked* meat or fish in the Byzantine period.[5] The only Byzantine author who mentions *κρέα καπνιστά* is Eustathios of Thessalonike. But he only quotes Athenaios (second century AD), who on his part quotes Poseidonios (second century BC), who in fact says that the Romans (the ancient, real Romans) on festive occasions used to eat bread,

[1] Eustathios of Thessalonike, *Commentarii ad Homeri Iliadem* 1.471, ed. M. van der Valk, *Eustathii: Commentarii ad Homeri Iliadem pertinentes*, 3 vols (Leiden, 1971–87).

[2] *Ptochoprodromos* IV.202–3, ed. H. Eideneier, *Ptochoprodromos. Einführung, kritische Ausgabe, deutsche Übersetzung, Glossar*, Neograeca Medii Aevi 5 (Cologne, 1991); See ibid. I.235.

[3] *Ptochoprodromos* I.239, II.104, III.185 and IV.204–15: recipes. See also III.185–6.

[4] Eustathios of Thessalonike, *Commentarii ad Homeri Odysseam*, 1.32, ed. G. Stallbaum, *Eustathii archiepiscopi Thessalonicensis Commentarii ad Homeri Odysseam*, 2 vols (Leipzig, 1825–26); similar descriptions come from Pseudo-John Zonaras, *Lexicon*, ed. J. A. H. Tittman, *Ioannis Zonarae lexicon ex tribus codicibus manuscriptis*, 2 vols (Leipzig, 1808; repr. Amsterdam, 1967), T 1713.20, and Nikephoros Gregoras, *Byzantina historia* 9.5, ed. L. Schopen and I. Bekker, *Nicephorus Gregoras: Byzantina historia*, 3 vols (Bonn, 1829–55), 1.417. See also P. Koukoules, 'Βυζαντινῶν τροφαὶ καὶ ποτά', *EEBS* 17 (1941), 36–40, and idem, *Βυζαντινῶν βίος καὶ πολιτισμός*, vol. 5 (Athens, 1952), 62–6.

[5] See also *TLG* online version, January 2003.

'boiled smoked meat' and 'amply roasted fresh meat from sacrificial animals' (*τῶν προσφάτως καθιερευθέντων ὀπτὰ δαψιλῆ*).[6] Obviously, Eustathios no longer understood the original sense of 'smoked meat' because he explained the verb *kapnizein* as 'to light a fire on the occasion of a feast' (*τὸ ἐπὶ τὴν εὐωχίαν πῦρ ἀνάπτειν, ὅθεν καὶ κρέα καπνιστὰ παρὰ Ἀθηναίῳ*).[7]

Therefore, I conclude that the smoking of meat and fish was known, though it was not very common, in the ancient period – evidence is to be found in the article of Frank Frost[8] – but that it had fallen into oblivion, or, in any case, was not usual, in the Byzantine Middle Ages. This could be explained at least partially by the general shortage and the high price of firewood, an issue that will be discussed later. The problem of providing fuel, however, did not arise if victuals were only dried or salted. Indeed, it may be partly for this reason that these two methods of conservation were known in all the Levant. Ptochoprodromos gives us the impression that *pasta* formed part of festive meals for most social groups. For example, in one of his poems the poor husband, who suffers from hunger and from the cruel behaviour of his wife, dreams of a table with plenty of soup and some salted meat or salted fish: '... I saw a table with plenty of *zomos* and a little *paston*'.[9]

The dietetic treatises confirm how widespread the consumption of *pasta* was. Hierophilos, for example, in one version recommends the consumption of 'only salted and dried fish' during May, whereas in another he forbids the consumption of salted and dried fish and salted vegetables during the same month;[10] in August he recommends 'to refrain from all salted and dried fish and dried fruits', in September 'to refrain from all salted food' and in October to refrain from salted fish.[11] In the context of my paper, it is not important if the consumption of salted and dried food is recommended or forbidden; what matters most is the fact that these texts speak about this category of food so often.

Finally, Ptochoprodromos also likes the combination of 'thick *monokythron* and cooked *paston*', a thick stew and a dish of boiled salted meat (or salted fish).[12] As he furthermore describes various recipes of *monokythron* based

---

[6] Poseidonios, fragment 82, quoted at Athenaios, *Deipnosofistai* 4.38.32; see also ibid. 6.108.9.

[7] Eustathios, *Commentarii ad Homeri Iliadem*, 711.

[8] F. Frost, 'Sausage and meat preservation in antiquity', *GRBS* 40/3 (1999), 241–52.

[9] *Ptochoprodromos* I.264–5; see also III.128–9: 'first the well-boiled meat, as second course the salted meat and then the omelette ...'

[10] Hierophilos, ed. R. Romano, 'Il calendario dietetico di Ierofilo', in *Atti dell Accademia Pontaniana*, n.s. 47 (Naples, 1999), 197–222, at 208.

[11] Hierophilos, 'Il callendario dietetico', 212–15.

[12] *Ptochoprodromos* II.104.

on fish,[13] and as salted fish is mentioned comparatively often in Byzantine texts,[14] we can assume that such fish dishes were also Lenten fare, at least at the stage of *apokreas* (a period of abstinence from the consumption of meat) (not the stages of *tyrine* and *xerophagia* – periods of consumption of dairy products and dry food respectively). In this connection one should bear in mind that on the whole the Lenten periods lasted nearly half of the year,[15] though we should not overestimate the practical acceptance of Lent by the people as a whole. The patriarch of Constantinople Athanasios, for example, demands that during Lent not only should public baths and taverns be closed, but also Christians 'should stop eating fish [which is sold] by the old women at the seashore … Instead of these, *kollyba* [boiled wheat mixed with raisins, pomegranate seeds and flour, prepared today for the commemoration of the dead] and pulses and fruits and vegetables are sufficient for the Orthodox.'[16] Meat is not mentioned in these demands. So much for the title of my paper.

The question is whether the *monokythra, pasta* and similar meals described in the dreams of Ptochoprodromos were really *μεγάλα καὶ πολλὰ θρύμματα*[17] – that is, plentiful and big pieces consumed on a daily basis – and if they really belonged to everyday food for all Byzantines. Were they part of everyday diet? Taking Evelyn Patlagean's book as a starting point,[18] we have to return to the sources and to reread them, even though, sometimes, this is not very helpful. A fundamental problem is that people never – or nearly never – write down the details of everyday life, because such information is seen as commonplace or self-evident. Consequently, direct written evidence concerning everyday meals and drinks in Byzantium barely exists. Recipes for how to make gruel, how to bake bread, how to boil an egg, or how to stew cabbage, and so on, were only rarely written down. Normally, they were learned by practice and

---

13 *Ptochoprodromos* IV.204–15.

14 Examples: *Ptochoprodromos* IV.214: 'twenty salt mackerels'; see also the Appendix of book I of Constantine Porphyrogennetos's *De ceremoniis*, ed. J. J. Reiske, 2 vols (Bonn, 1829–30), 1.464, and the *Book of the Eparch* 13.1, ed. J. Koder, *Das Eparchenbuch Leons des Weisen*, CFHB 33 (Vienna, 1991).

15 14 September, the six weeks before Christmas, 5 January, the seven weeks before Easter, at least two weeks before the feast day of SS Peter and Paul, two weeks before the *Koimesis* feast day, 29 August, and every Wednesday and Friday of the non-Lenten weeks of the year except Easter time (until Pentecost): in total at least 144 days.

16 A.-M. Talbot, ed., *The Correspondence of Athanasius I Patriarch of Constantinople*, CFHB 7 (Washington, DC, 1975), 90–91 (Epistle 43.36–44, dated spring 1307).

17 *Ptochoprodromos* I.265 and II.105; see also IV.180, 382, 391.

18 E. Patlagean, *Pauvreté économique et pauvreté sociale à Byzance, 4e–7e siècles*, Civilisations et Sociétés 48 (Paris, 1977), 36–44: 'L'échelle des régimes alimentaires'; 44–53: 'Régimes et nutrition'. For further discussion (and bibliography of reviews), see D. S[imon], 'Ein gescheitertes Seminar', *RJ* 1 (1982), 18–22.

were passed on from generation to generation. Before entering into details, I would like to underline that in this paper, mainly for practical reasons, I am concentrating on observations and comments about the period between the sixth and twelfth centuries, and I shall mostly disregard two major social groups – the soldiers, and the monks and nuns.[19]

The 'normal' number of daily meals was two. The first meal was the *ariston*,[20] sometimes also called the *geuma*.[21] The 'hour of the *geuma*' was late in the morning or early at noon, *περὶ ὥραν ἕκτην*.[22] The second, richer meal, the *deipnon*, was consumed early in the evening, usually before sunset.[23] Sometimes it was served earlier in the afternoon and therefore was called *aristodeipnon*.[24] I think it is likely that in the majority of cases the *deipnon* was the hot meal, although Ptochoprodromos's famous cobbler ordered already in the morning *ekzeston* (stew), *akropaston* (salted meat) and *sphoungaton* (omelette),[25] and only then was he able to continue his work; but in this case the poet clearly exaggerated.

For the majority of people, a hot cooked meal (*mageiria*) was normally offered as *deipnon* only once a day, if served at all, and this for several reasons.[26] One obvious explanation is that warming a meal was generally time-consuming, because the cook had to start reheating the fireplace anew

---

19 This does not mean that information on monastic or military conditions is not considered, at least in order to compare them with the possibilities of daily supply for the laity. On the monastic diet, see Alice-Mary Talbot's chapter in this volume.

20 Hesychios, *Lexicon*, ed. K. Latte, *Hesychii Alexandrini Lexicon*, 2 vols (Copenhagen, 1953, 1966), A 7252; Orion, *Etymologikon*, ed. F. G. Sturz (Leipzig, 1826), D 45, and *Additamenta in Etymologicum Gudianum*, ed. E. L. de Stefani, vol. 1 (Leipzig, 1909), D 375. See also A. Karpozilos and A. Kazhdan, 'Ariston and Deipnon', *ODB*, 1.170; Koukoules, *Βυζαντινῶν βίος*, 136–40; V. Grumel, *La Chronologie*, Traité d'études byzantines 1 (Paris, 1958), 163–5, and J. Koder, 'Η καθημερινή διατροφή στο Βυζάντιο με βάση τις πηγές', in D. Papanilola-Bakirtzi, ed., *Food and Cooking in Byzantium. Proceedings of the Symposium on 'Food in Byzantium', Thessaloniki, Museum of Byzantine Culture, 4 November 2001* (Athens, 2005), 17–30.

21 George Sphrantzes, *Chronicon (minus)*, ed. V. Grecu (Bucharest, 1966), 34.1.

22 Aetios, *Iatrosophion* 9.30, ed. S. Zerbos, '*Ἀετίου Ἀμιδηνοῦ λόγος ἔνατος*', *Athina*, 23 (1911), 273–390; see also *Ptochoprodromos* III.124–5 and (in the monastery) IV.165–6.

23 *Ptochoprodromos* I.224; Michael Psellos, *Chronographia* 5.9 (13), ed. E. Renauld, *Michel Psellos: Chronographie*, 2 vols (Paris, 1926–28); Anna Komnene, *Alexias* 8.6.1, ed. B. Leib, *Anne Comnène, Alexiade*, 3 vols (Paris, 1937–45; repr. 1967); John Kantakouzenos, *Historia* 2.558, ed. L. Schopen, *Ioannis Cantacuzeni eximperatoris historiarum libri quattuor*, 3 vols (Bonn, 1828–32); Pseudo-George Sphrantzes, *Chronicon (majus)*, ed. V. Grecu (Bucharest, 1966), 7.10.

24 Hesychios, *Lexicon*, A 7262; Theophanes, *Chronographia*, ed. C. de Boor, 2 vols (Leipzig, 1883–85; repr. Hildesheim, 1963), 375; George Monachos, *Chronicon* 642, ed. C. de Boor, *Georgius Monachus, Chronicon*, 2 vols (Leipzig, 1904; repr. Stuttgart, 1978); Constantine Porphyrogennetos, *De ceremoniis* 751–2, 764–5. See also George Pachymeres, ed. I. Bekker, *Georgii Pachymeris de Michaele et Andronico Palaeologis libri trecedem*, 2 vols (Bonn, 1835), 619.

25 *Ptochoprodromos* III.127–9.

26 For example *Ptochoprodromos* II.104, III.93; Pseudo-George Sphrantzes, *Chronicon* 542.17 and 20.

every time or else to remain near the fireplace in order to stoke the fire. Even more of a problem was the fact that fuel was expensive and, in addition to this, often rare, not only in Constantinople but also in minor towns and in the countryside. When, for example, in 542 the plague reached Myra, the farmers of the surrounding villages brought to the town 'neither grain nor flour, no wine and no wood' because they wanted to avoid infection.[27] The standard firewood (*xylon kausimon*) was often brushwood of low quality and a low burning temperature. This meant that one had to burn greater quantities, but not that fuel was cheap. It is worth remembering that John the Cappadocian produced bread for the soldiers, which was not baked long enough in the oven, in order to save firewood. Thus, the bread became mouldy in the sacks (*thylakia*) and 500 of Belisarios's soldiers died.[28] Even more expensive than firewood was charcoal (*karbounin*). In regions without any significant quantity of woodland, for example in Anatolikon, 'instead of wood we use *zarzakon*, which is dung that has been processed, an extremely disgusting and smelling thing', as Leo of Synada explains in a letter to the emperor Basil II.[29] Dried dung, Turkish *tezek*, is used even today in many regions facing a shortage of other fuel.

During the pre-Turkish Middle Ages, of course, a significant primeval woodland coverage (or at least scrubland coverage) still existed in many places of northern Syria, Asia Minor and the southern Balkans that are eroded today. I also agree with Archie Dunn that scrubland is 'extremely resilient and economically productive'.[30] But two major problems remain: first, well-organized transportation, from the producer to the user, of wood and of other fuel (*chartos*, *phrygana* and *papyrus*),[31] which are bulk goods, and second, storage of this fuel near the fireplace in sufficient, but not too large, quantities, and in a safe manner, so as to avoid conflagration. The *Book of the Eparch* mentions this danger specifically regarding the *artopoioi*, the bakers, but also with respect to all *politai*, to all inhabitants of Constantinople.

The inhabitants of cities and other large settlements could easily run short of firewood, as happened, for example, during the blockade of

---

27 *Vita Nicolai Sionitae* 82, chap. 52, ed. G. Anrich, *Hagios Nikolaos. Der Heilige Nikolaos in der griechischen Kirche. Texte und Untersuchungen*, vol. 1, Teubner (Berlin, 1913).

28 Prokopios, *Wars* III.13.15–16, ed. J. Haury and G. Wirth, *Procopii Caesariensis opera omnia*, vols 1–2 (Leipzig, 1962–63). On this episode, see also Michael Grünbart's chapter in this volume.

29 Leo of Synada, ed. M. P. Vinson, *The Correspondence of Leo, Metropolitan of Synada and Syncellus*, CFHB 23 (Washington, DC, 1985), 68–9 (Epistle 43). Cf. L. Robert, *Opera minora selecta*, vol. 7 (Amsterdam, 1990), 33–8.

30 A. Dunn, 'The exploitation and control of woodland and scrubland in the Byzantine world', *BMGS* 16 (1992), 235–98, esp. 240–49.

31 *Book of the Eparch* 18.3, ed. J. Koder.

Constantinople by Michael VIII Palaiologos at the end of the year 1260.[32] But under normal conditions, too, the poor often could not afford to buy firewood or charcoal.[33] A letter of the patriarch Athanasios refers to the problem as well. When on the occasion of the famine during the winter 1306/1307 he decided to prepare gruel (*atheran hepsein*) for the poor, he soon 'ran out of wood to keep the fire going'.[34]

What was everyday food for the masses? For a period of more than a millennium and a territory of some 500,000 square miles – at least at the beginning of the eleventh century – there can be no consistent and specific answer. The authors of the relevant chapters of the *Economic History of Byzantium* seem justified when they state, very generically, that people ate bread, olives and olive oil, meat, vegetables, fruits and dairy products – at least in principle, because there were certainly regional differences due to climatic and soil conditions. Leo of Synada, for example, reports about 'his' Anatolikon: 'We do not produce olive oil' and 'Our land does not yield wine because of the high altitude and the short growing season.'[35] Nevertheless, basically, nobody doubts that the answer to the question 'whether the quantities were such as to keep the population in good health [and perhaps even better than that of western Europeans]' must be a qualified 'yes'.[36]

From the *Book of the Eparch* we learn about a number of provisions and providers.[37] First of all one had to go to the *artopoios*, who sold fresh bread every morning. The next address was the *saldamarios*, the grocer, who offered non-perishable merchandise of all kinds, including *tyron* (cheese from sheep and goats) and *boutyron* (butter, mostly from sheep and goats, but also from cows).[38] He also sold oil and olives, legumes (and dry vegetables), honey, salted meat and fish, but not the more expensive fresh fish and fresh meat, which was distributed by the *ichthyopratai*, the fishmongers, the *makelarioi*, the butchers for lamb and mutton, and the *choiremporoi*, the pork butchers; beef is not mentioned in the *Book of the*

32 Nikephoros Gregoras, *Byzantina historia* 4.1 (I.81).

33 *Ptochoprodromos* II.30.

34 ... *ἐπιλελοίπεί μοι καὶ τὰ τρέφοντα ξύλα τὸ πῦρ*: Athanasios I of Constantinople, *The Correspondence of Athanasius*, 194–7 (Epistle 78, l.39-45); see also the commentary, ibid., 400.

35 Leo of Synada, *The Correspondence of Leo*, 68–9 (Epistle 43).

36 A. E. Laiou, ed., *The Economic History of Byzantium: from the seventh through the fifteenth century*, Dumbarton Oaks Studies 39, vol. 1 (Washington, DC, 2002), 53–4.

37 *Book of the Eparch*, chaps 13, 15, 18 and 19, ed. J. Koder.

38 In my talk I proposed that *boutyron* might not be butter, but cheese from cows. Michael Featherstone, Collège de France, has kindly corrected this view. For *boutyron* as 'cream', see E. A. Wallis Budge, ed., *The Syriac Book of Medicines: Syrian anatomy, pathology and therapeutics in the early Middle Ages with sections on astrological and native medicine and recipes, by an anonymous physician* (London, 1913; repr. Amsterdam, 1976), II.644–5. The Syriac equivalent of butter (and cream) is 'hewta'.

Eparch. Wine was offered in the *kapeleion*, the tavern, together with soups and other simple prepared dishes.

These pieces of information are confirmed by the catalogue of goods which survives as an appendix of the *Book of Ceremonies*.[39] This list of provisions served primarily as a catalogue of food supplies for the soldiers, but in my view these goods can be understood as part of the common diet as well. The text mentions beans, rice, pistachios, almonds, lentils and oil; lard, salted meat, cheese, salted fish and wine; and also livestock for slaughter, namely sheep with lambs and cows with calves.[40] The animals and most of the other goods are well known; more striking is the mention of rice (*oryzin*), which would have been extremely expensive in this period.[41] Perhaps *oryzin* could here mean the so-called 'Arabic millet' (*soročinskoje přeno*) which is mentioned in the Palaeoslavic translation (c. 1060) of the *Typikon* (1034) of Alexios Stoudites.[42] Another explanation might derive from Italian *orzo* (barley).[43]

Some information also comes from the *Farmer's Law*, the *Nomos georgikos*, which belongs to the period of the *Ekloga* or some decades earlier.[44] It reflects conditions in the countryside: the breeding of sheep, pigs and cattle, and the production and marketing of cereals, legumes, grapes and figs, products of the orchard, wine and ewe's milk.[45]

There is no doubt that bread in Byzantium was really prominent above all other foodstuffs, both as a means of mass provision and as a synonym for

---

39 *De ceremoniis* 463–4; J. F. Haldon, ed. and tr., *Constantine Porphyrogenitus. Three Treatises on Imperial Military Expeditions. Introduction, edition, translation and commentary*, CFHB 28 (Vienna, 1990), 144–51.

40 From another part of the same text that mentions lambs, rams, cattle, chickens and geese (*De ceremoniis* 487; Haldon, ed. and tr., *Constantine Porphyrogenitus*, 532–5), we understand that fresh meat was served only to the imperial and other rich households and at feasts.

41 See G. Dagron, 'The urban economy, seventh–twelfth centuries', in Laiou, ed., *The Economic History of Byzantium*, 2.445–6.

42 See A. M. Pentkovskii, *Tipikon patriarcha Aleksiia Studita v Vizantii i na Rusi* (Moscow, 2001), 376 (bibliographical information from Nataliya Izmaylova).

43 See Francesco Calducci Pegolotti, *La pratica della mercatura*, ed. A. Evans (Cambridge, MA, 1936), 58, and the report from Coriolano Cippico, in K. N. Sathas, *Documents inédits relatifs à l'histoire de Grèce au moyen âge*, vol. 7 (Paris, 1888), 286: '… *buona quantità di orzo e di formento*'.

44 See S. Troianos, *Πηγές του βυζαντινού δικαίου* (Athens, 1999), 121f., and the most recent edition of the *Farmer's Law* by I. P. Medvedev, E. K. Piotrovskaja and E. E. Lipšic, *Vizantijskij zemledel'českij zakon* (Leningrad, 1984). Remarkably enough, neither olive trees nor olive oil are mentioned.

45 *Farmer's Law*, ed. Medvedev, Piotrovskaja and Lipšic: cereals and wine passim, *ospria* § 60, *ampeloi* and *sykai* § 61, *kepos* and *oporophylax* § 31–3. From a special regulation (§ 34), we deduce that milk (of sheep or goats!) was produced in quantities to be sold (... *ἀμέλγων τὰ βοσκήματα … καὶ πιπράσκων*) and that the orchards were guarded by a keeper, an indication that fruits were precious and could be sold at a high price.

nourishment as a whole. Such a meaning was underlined by the symbolic use of 'daily bread' in the Bible. Thus the word *artos* and especially the formula ἄρτος ἐπιούσιος (daily bread) was normally used in a religious or theological context, based on the Gospels,[46] as, for example, by Michael Psellos in his poem on the mysteries of the divine liturgy, when he explains the Lord's Prayer.[47] We know that since late Hellenistic times *psomion* (*psomin*), originally meaning 'morsel of bread', had become the usual word for 'bread'.[48] Ptochoprodromos normally uses the term *psomin*, and its specific connotations for him are characteristic of other writers as well. *Psomin* is normally seen positively: '... and I smell the bread (*psomin*) and have nothing to eat!' or '... Darkness without moon – so I see my gloom, from which I suffer, when I have no bread (*psomin*).'[49]

By contrast, *artos* is connected to the hardness of human life (that is, since the expulsion from the Paradise). Ptochoprodromos, who uses the word only once, refers there to the meals that were offered to him in his hated monastery: '... and with the dry bread (*artos*) the malicious holy soup (*hagiozoumin*)'.[50]

The *mesos* or *mesokatharos artos* (also called *tripton*, diminutive *triptoutsikon*), normally the bread of 'middling purity', was for Ptochoprodromos already of bad quality. He calls it explicitly 'the bread of poverty' (*psomin tes ptocheias*),[51] although normally one would identify the so-called 'dirty bread' (*ryparos artos*), made of bran or barley, with the worst grade.[52]

Finally, the importance of bread is confirmed by a catalogue enumerating the basic equipment of every household, which was composed by Ptochoprodromos. He first mentions grain as the raw material for bread and continues with various spices, salt, olive oil, linseed oil and honey; then he concentrates on vegetables: celery (*selinon*), leek (*praso*), green salad (*marouli*), cress (*kardamo*), endive (*intybin*), spinach (*spinakin*), turnip (*gongylin*), aubergine (*matzitzanin*), cabbage (*krambe*), kohlrabi (*lachanogoulo*) and cauliflower (*kounoupidin*).[53] Meat and fish are not mentioned.

---

46 Matthew 6.11 and Luke 11.3.

47 *Michaelis Pselli Poemata*, ed. L. G. Westerink (Stuttgart, 1992), Poem 56, lines 216–17.

48 See *LSJ*, Supplement, 318b, s.v.

49 *Ptochoprodromos* III.206 and 234.

50 *Ptochoprodromos* IV.245.

51 *Ptochoprodromos* III.145–6, 169–170, 173. Further evidence in I.179; III.82, 93, 97, 197, 213; IV.48, 259, 472, 480, 652. At III.82 he asks for 'τὸ ψωμὶν καὶ τοῦ ψωμιοῦ τὴν μάνναν', an allusion to Septuagint (Deuteronomy 8.3 and 16: 'He fed you in the wilderness with manna'), but see also Eideneier, ed., *Ptochoprodromos*, 192.

52 See Dagron, 'Urban economy', in Laiou, ed., *The Economic History of Byzantium*, 2.446.

53 *Ptochoprodromos* II.24–45. He also speaks about firewood and charcoal, torches and candles, soap, shoes and various pieces of clothing, and about kitchen utensils such as cooking pots, pitchers, a spit for *kokoretsi*, a water kettle and a sieve (50–52), and ends with a statement

So, how important were vegetables? Demetrios Kydones, in a letter to Isidoros Glabas dated to the year 1382/83 writes: 'You can see it yourself, that the Romaioi are more interested in the vegetables at the market than in high theoretical reflections'.[54] In fact, however, Kydones simply wants to express here that the inhabitants of Constantinople, in view of their daily problems of survival, understandably neglected philosophy (*ὑψηλῶν θεωρημάτων φροντὶς*); he does not really mean that they were enthusiastic about vegetables in particular.

In general one has to be careful not to attribute modern parameters to Byzantine thought, as for example a high esteem for vegetarian food, which corresponds to *our* (or some of our) health standards. The Byzantines were less complex; they just followed their instinctive taste and liked lavish and expensive food. In this they were in principle confirmed by the written traditions of ancient medicine. For example, Michael Psellos's general advice is simply 'Of all vegetables (*lachanika*) and pulses (*ospria*) take only a little!',[55] and he shares this opinion with Aetios's *Iatrikon* (seventh century), who recommends that 'the consumption of vegetables (*lachanika*) must occur rarely, because they cause flatulence' (*πνευματοτικὰ γὰρ*).[56] Medical handbooks like that of Aetios, or of the dietetic treatises, which formed a well-known mixture of elements of ancient medicine and popular pharmacological traditions, offered more information. This is the case, for instance, in *The Syriac Book of Medicines*. This text forbids – in a rather schematic manner – the consumption of a wide set of vegetables in (roughly) every third month, namely during November, February, April and August.[57]

Another example is provided by Hierophilos. He is more specific, as he explicitly outlines what to eat and what not to eat during every month of the year. A summary of his list of vegetables, legumes and fruits reads as follows, with the foods not to be eaten underscored:[58]

---

which gives to his list a touch of general validity (73–5): 'All these they need at home year for year, rich and poor, slaves and masters, monks and secular, old and young ...'

54 Demetrios Kydones, ed. R. J. Loenertz, *Démétrius Cydonès, Correspondance*, 2 vols, Studi e Testi 208 (Vatican City, 1956–60), 2.132, Epistle 235 (I am indebted to Martin Hinterberger for this information).

55 *Michaelis Pselli Poemata*, Poem 15.3.

56 Aetios of Amida, ed. A. Olivieri, *Libri medicinales*, 2 vols (Leipzig, 1950), IX.35.173.

57 *Second Toshrî* (November): '... no vegetables except rock parsley, gourds, leeks and carrots'; *Shebât* (February): '... no vegetables of any kind because of phlegm and cold'; *Nisân* (April): '... no radishes or beetroot or any stale vegetable'; and *Âbh* (August): '... no vegetable which has been cooked by fire, no vegetable soup'. See also *The Syriac Book of Medicines*, II.643–4; similar advice ibid., 644–5.

58 Summary of the three versions of Hierophilos, 'Il calendario dietetico di Ierofilo', 197–222 (not underlined = recommended; underlined = not recommended):

JANUARY: cabbage, turnip, carrot, leek, wild asparagus, olive shoots, bay, rape, ground peas,[59] [other] peas / raisins, almonds, pistachios, pomegranate seeds, pomegranates, pears, dates

FEBRUARY: wild herbs, cabbage, beet / fruits as in January

MARCH: beet, mallow, orache, asparagus, mushrooms, rape, bay, olives, boiled wheat, split peas, grinded peas, [other] peas, beans / fruits as in February, dates

APRIL: orache, lettuce, fresh dill, coriander, fresh garlic, leek, dry pulse, fresh pulse / dried fruits

MAY: in general as in April / olive shoots, wild asparagus, tile, dry, salt and bitter food

---

JANUARY: *krambai, gonkylia, daukin, prasa, asparagoi agrioi, elaiosparaga chamaidaphnia, bryonia, lathyrion kai auchos alesta / mela opta, staphides, amygdala, pistakia, kokonaria, roidin, apidion, phoinikes*

FEBRUARY: *agria lachana, krambe, seutlon* / fruits as in January

MARCH: *seutlon, molochin, chrysolachanon, asparagoi, amanitai, bryoniai, chamaidaphne, elaiai alika diephthon, kyamos toutesti phaba, lathyrin kai auchos alesta, phasioulos* / fruits as in February, *phoinikes*

APRIL: *chrysolachanon, maioulion, anethon chloron, koliandron, skoroda chlora, prason, ospria xera, ospria chlora / opora xera*

MAY: in general as in April / *elaiosparagos, agriosparagos, tile, xera, halmyra, pikra*

JUNE: *skoroda, krommya, raphanon, chrysolachanon, kolokynthe, thalassokrambe, seutlon, andrachne, maioulion, intybion, selinon, angourion / kerasia leuka, tetrangoura*

JULY: in general as in June / *lachana drimea kai pikra kai therma / peponai, syka leuka, staphylai, apidia, mela, damaskena, rodakina, opora xera*

AUGUST: *moloche, pan agrion lachanon, elaiai maurai, xera ospria, elaiai, seutlon, bliton, kolokynthe / chlorai oporai = syka, staphylai, apidia, damaskena leuka, rodakina pepeira, xerai oporai*

SEPTEMBER: *prasa, asparankoi, amanitai leukai, krambe, gongyle, elaiai maurai kyamos, phake, lathyron / staphylai, apidia, damaskena leuka, mela, rodakina, peponion, syka leuka, roinai, phoinikes, melokydon / pistakia, karya basilica, amygdale, kokonaria*

OCTOBER: *krambe, gongyle, asparagoi, amanitai leukoi (kyamoi, phake, lathyra) / staphylai asprai, apioi, mela, syka aspra, mespila, rodakina persika, phoinikes, roiai, melokydon / pistakia, karya basilika, amygdala, kokonaria, karya pontika, kokkodaphna.*

NOVEMBER: *prasomolocha, kyamos, phake, lupinaria = thermia / phoinikai, kokkodaphna / hola ta xera*

DECEMBER: in general as November / *krambe, skimbros, elaiai maurai, kolymbadai elaiai, phake.*

[59] *Auchos*: Souda A 4545, ed. A. Adler, *Suidae Lexicon*, 5 vols (Leipzig, 1928–38); 'osprion', *LBG* 1.245a: 'eine Erbsenart'.

June: garlic, onions, radish, orache, gourd, sea kale, beet, purslane, lettuce, endive, celery, cucumber / white cherries, bottle-gourds[60]

July: in general as in June / pungent and bitter and hot herbs / melons, white figs, grapes, pears, apples, plums, nectarines, dried fruits

August: mallow, all wild herbs, black olives, dry pulse, olives, beet, blite, gourds / fresh fruits, namely figs, grapes, pears, 'white plums'[61], ripe nectarines, dried fruits

September: leek, asparagus, white mushrooms, cabbage, turnip, black olives, (beans, lentils, peas) / grapes, pears, 'white plums', apples, nectarines, melons, white figs, pomegranates, dates, quinces / pistachios, 'imperial' nuts, almonds, pomegranate seeds

October: cabbage, turnip, asparagus, white mushrooms, [beans, lentils, peas] / white grapes, beans, apples, white figs, medlars, Persian peaches, dates, pomegranates, quinces / pistachios, 'imperial' nuts, almonds, pomegranate seeds, hazelnuts, laurel berries

November: *prasomolocha*, beans, lentils, lupines / dates, laurel berries / all dry fruits and vegetables

December: in general as in November / cabbage, watercress, black olives, olives pickled in brine, lentils

I will not repeat here what I have already said in *Gemüse in Byzanz*.[62] I just wish to sketch out some basic principles and main lines of the vegetarian aspects of Hierophilos's menu. First of all there is a clear distinction between three groups: *lachana* (vegetables, herbs), *ospria* (pulses) and *oporai* (fruits for some months, with a sub-group of 'dried fruits', *xerai oporai*).

60 *Tetrangourin*: Souda S 401; 'sikyia', *LSJ* 1598a and Supplement 275a: 'bottle-gourd'.

61 *Damaskena leuka:* greengage or yellow plums (?); see J. Diethart and E. Kislinger, 'Aprikosen und Pflaumen', *JÖB* 42 (1992), 75–8, who also take 'apricot' in consideration. For the problem of the varieties of plums, see also T. Weber, 'ΔΑΜΑΣΚΗΝΑ. Landwirtschaftliche Produkte aus der Oase von Damaskus im Spiegel griechischer und lateinischer Schriftquellen', *ZDPV* 105 (1989), 151–65; V. Hehn, *Kulturpflanzen und Haustiere in ihrem Übergang aus Asien nach Griechenland und Italien sowie in das übrige Europa* (Berlin, 1911), and J. André, *Les Noms de plantes dans la Rome antique* (Paris, 1985), s.v.

62 J. Koder, *Gemüse in Byzanz: Die Frischgemüseversorgung Konstantinopels im Licht der Geoponika*, Byzantinische Geschichtsschreiber, Ergänzungsband 3 (Vienna, 1993); see also idem, 'Fresh vegetables for the capital', in C. Mango and G. Dagron, eds, *Constantinople and Its Hinterland. Papers from the Twenty-seventh Spring Symposium of Byzantine Studies, Oxford, April 1993* (Aldershot, 1995), 49–56.

Some of the *lachana* are also mentioned separately in the group of *kodimenta* (condiments), for example *krom(m)yon* (onion) and *prason* (leek).

At first sight, looking just at Hierophilos's handling of fruits, we might reach the conclusion that some practical aspects are considered in his text. For example, baked apples and dried fruits and nuts, such as raisins, almonds and pistachios, not surprisingly, are recommended in late autumn and in winter, when fresh fruits were not available.

As regards vegetables, however, the documentation is not at all clear. There are reasonable recommendations, for example to avoid dry pulses and fruits (*xera ospria* and *xerai oporai*) in August (when enough fresh products were on the market) – but why should kale (*krambe*) be forbidden in December and February, since it is allowed in January? Why is onion (*krommydion* or *krommyon*), one of the cheapest vegetables, mentioned only once, in June, and this time only to be forbidden? I mention here again the 'malicious holy soup' (*τὸ δόλιον τὸ ἁγιοζούμιν*), which was served in the monastery and Ptochoprodromos detested so much. *Hagiozoumin* is probably a nickname, because it can only be found in the 'monastic' poem of Ptochoprodromos.[63] Whatever its normal name, it consisted only of water, onions, salt, marjoram and a tiny quantity of oil. Therefore, for the poorest of the population, a hot meal might often have consisted only of this 'holy soup' and bread, not too dissimilar from the French *soupe à l'oignon*. Another basic and cheap meal already mentioned was the *atheras*, a soup or gruel, consisting basically of semolina or bulgur (in Greek *pligouri*) boiled in water or milk, perhaps with some drops of oil or another kind of cooking fat.[64]

Here we should also mention the great variety of decoctions (*zemata*) described by Hierophilos, some of which seem to have had an importance in everyday life, thus going beyond a purely medicinal use, such as for example the brew of leek (*prasozema*) or of garlic (*skordozema*).[65]

Hierophilos also comments upon fish and meat. I will set aside fish and concentrate on meat. Here again some strange suggestions occur, although others seem to fit with recommendations from other sources. For example, meat is not mentioned at all in the diet for March. This could be explained as a result of the influence of the Christian faith (March being a Lenten month), or of the reproduction phases of livestock, or of an incomplete

---

63 *Ptochoprodromos* IV.245, 358, 375–84, 390, 394, 410; see *TLG* online version, March 2003.

64 See Athanasios of Constantinople, *The Correspondence of Athanasios*, 194–7 (Epistle 78, l.39–45); Photios, *Lexicon*, ed. C. Theodoridis, vol. 1 (Berlin, 1982), A 471.1: ἐκ πυρῶν ἑψημένων καὶ διακεχυμένων, and Hesychios, *Lexikon*, A 1581: βρῶμα διὰ πυρῶν καὶ γάλακτος ἡψημένον παρ᾽ Αἰγυπτίοις.

65 Hierophilos, 'Il calendario dietetico di Ierofilo', *apozematizein*: 204; *apozema*: 217; *zema(ta)*: 201 et passim; *zematoposia*: 209; *xerozema*: 201, 208; *prasozema*: 203, 215, 217; *skordozema*: 203.

manuscript transmission. In all other months of the year, fowl is strongly recommended, whereas mutton is recommended only until September, and goat only between April and August. Pork should be consumed only during the winter months of January and February (explicitly not in April and May). Hierophilos recommends game in summer until 15 August, and again in November and December, but he advises explicitly against hares and wild boars in September and October. Corresponding to the general Byzantine trend, beef is mentioned only once, in September, and in this case it is forbidden. On the whole, the text of Hierophilos can be seen to be a mixture of iatrosophical traditions and practical advice.

Combining the information from the *Iatrika* with that from other sources, I would conclude that in fact vegetables did not have the fame of being higher in quality, healthier or more valuable, compared to meat, as would be the case today. Meat simply tasted much better; it was more prestigious and expensive. Therefore, it was esteemed more highly. To refrain from meat during Lent was really a sacrifice: St Loukas Steiriotes 'refrained since the days of his childhood not only from meat, but also from cheese and eggs and from all sorts of food which might *give pleasure*; his only foodstuffs were bread made from barley, water, herbs and legumes if available' (my italics).[66] Vegetables 'gave no pleasure'. They were, at least partially, a non-recommended and low-esteemed category of food. This underlines the function of cheap and storable vegetables, especially legumes, as everyday provisions and staple food for all social classes.[67]

Hierophilos, as other iatrosophical authors, also discusses the advantages and shortcomings of the raw materials for sauces, soups and dressings, so he at least gives some hints of how to prepare, to dress and to spice the meals. He thus, indirectly, confirms other sources. His most important varieties of seasoning are oil with salt (*halati* and *elaion*);[68] honey mixed with wine (*oinomeli*) or with vinegar (*oxomeli, oxymeli*);[69] vinegar (*oxos*), especially vinegar conditioned with squills (*oxos skillitikos*), and also combined with

[66] D. Z. Sophianos, *Βίος του Οσίου Λουκά του Στειριώτη* (Athens, 1989), 162 (chap. 7.10–13).

[67] See Patlagean, *Pauvreté*, 38, with the disputed 'four stages of alimentation' (*ramassés – cultivés – préparés sans cuisson – préparés avec cuisson*), which in every stage contain also vegetables. The situation was fairly similar during the Ottoman period: see J. Vroom, *After Antiquity. Ceramics and Society in the Aegean from the 7th to the 20th Century A. C.* (Leiden, 2003), esp. 335–47 (chap. 12), on dining habits.

[68] Hierophilos, 'Il calendario dietetico di Ierofilo', *halati kai elaio*: 204, 207; but *aneu elaiou, anelaion*: 201.

[69] Hierophilos, 'Il calendario dietetico di Ierofilo', *meli*: 201 et passim; *oinomeli*: 200; *oxomeli* (*oxomelitos*): 204, 205, 211–13, 217; *oxymeli* (*oxymelitos*): 205, 210, 211–13 (*oxymelitátos*: 213, 217).

oil;[70] and finally *garum* mixed with oil (*elaiogaron*), or with vinegar (*oxogaron*), or with wine (*oinogaron*), or with water (*hydrogaron*).[71]

It is not necessary to refer in detail to the opinion of Liudprand of Cremona about *garum*, the *deterrimus piscium liquor* (the worst liquid made out of fish),[72] but it seems noteworthy that between the Early Byzantine period and the eleventh century the word *garon* is – with rare exceptions[73] – found only in lexica and in medical and similar scientific texts. Consequently, I do not believe that *garum* was either common or popular during these centuries.[74]

To sum up the preceding observations: normally, the Byzantines had two daily meals, the *ariston* or *geuma* in the morning and a richer meal, often cooked, the *deipnon*, before or at sunset. The basis of their everyday food was bread and soup – often both of low quality. They had a taste for unhealthy food, especially fat meat. They appreciated it highly, not only because its consumption was considered prestigious, but also because they loved the taste of meat, bacon and lard. Nevertheless, the high prices of good quality meat and fish as well as the extended Lenten periods prohibited the regular consumption of such food in big quantities. Consequently, the everyday meals consisted primarily of cheap vegetables and fruits – fresh as well as preserved – olives and low-cost dairy products.

---

70 Hierophilos, 'Il calendario dietetico di Ierofilo', 214; *oxos skillitikos*: 207, 210.

71 Hierophilos, 'Il calendario dietetico di Ierofilo', *oxogarizein*: 207, 210; *oxogaritos*: 211; *oxygarizein*: 207, 211; *oxygaritos*: 211; *oxygaron*: 210; *elaiogaron*: 201; *holelaios*: 201; *oinogaron*: 202; *hydrogaron*: 208.

72 Liudprand of Cremona, 'Relatio de Legatione Constantinopolitana', in P. Chiesa, ed., *Liudprandi Cremonensis Opera Omnia*, CCCM 156 (Turnhout, 1998), 11. See generally E. Kislinger, 'Gastgewerbe und Beherbergung in frühbyzantinischer Zeit. Eine realienkundliche Studie aufgrund hagiographischer und historiographischer Quellen' (unpublished PhD dissertation, Vienna, 1982), 90–91, and *LBG* 2, 309b.

73 Exceptions (see *TLG* online, May 2004): Athanasios, *Syntagma ad monachos* 5.7; *Basilica* XIX.1.85 (86) = C IV, 41.1, ed. H. J. Scheltema, N. van der Wal and D. Holwerda, *Basilicorum libri LX* (Groningen, 1953–88); Cassianus Bassus, *Geoponika* VII.26.1, XII.15.2, XVI.12.4, XX.12.1, XX.46.2 and 6, ed. H. Beckh (Leipzig, 1895); Michael Psellos, *Opuscula logica, physica, allegorica, alia*, ed. J. M. Duffy (Berlin, 1992), 55 line 692; Photios, *Bibliotheca*, ed. R. Henry (Paris, 1971), cod. 221.177a, and *Epistulae et Amphilochia*, ed. B. Laourdas and L. G. Westerink (Leipzig, 1987), Epistle 318.14; Gregory of Nazianzos, *Contra Julianum imperatorem* 1, *PG* 35.620, and Theodoret, *Historia ecclesiastica* 184, ed. L. Parmentier, *Kirchengeschichte*, 2nd edn (Berlin, 1954); Sozomenos, *Historia ecclesiastica* V.10.12, ed. J. Bidez and G. C. Hansen, *Kirchengeschichte* (Berlin, 1960).

74 But also in the period after the eleventh century, I found only three texts in *TLG*: *Ptochoprodromos* IV.186 and Eustathios, *Commentarii ad Homeri Iliadem* 4.95, from the twelfth century, and Nicholas Rabdas, *Epistula*, chap. 37, from the fourteenth.

Section II

Dining and its accoutrements

11. Dazzling dining: banquets as an expression of imperial legitimacy[1]

Simon Malmberg

Emperor Maximus had made himself the master of Gaul through a civil war in the 380s, but his position was tenuous because he still had two imperial rivals. At this time, Maximus turned to other means of strengthening his position than by force of arms. He entreated all the bishops of his realm to visit him at Trier and to dine with him in order to show their support for the new regime. However, Bishop Martin of Tours was not cowed that easily and refused the emperor's bidding, denouncing Maximus as a usurper. Maximus, however, maintained 'that he had simply defended by arms the necessary requirements of the empire', and that his office had been imposed upon him by the soldiers and divine appointment. Perhaps convinced by these arguments, Martin yielded and journeyed to Trier, but, as we shall see, he still held trumps. The emperor was very pleased with Martin's appearance at Trier and showed him great honour by inviting him to his own dining couch, which was otherwise reserved for only the highest of dignitaries and relations of the emperor. But Martin declined the honour, and by demonstratively sitting down on a stool he showed both his asceticism and his independence. However, Maximus would not yet admit defeat. As custom dictated, a servant presented a goblet of wine to him, in order that he might be the first to drink. But instead of raising it to his lips, in an act of outstanding honour, he ordered it to be given to Martin. The emperor expected that after Martin had drunk from it, he would then return the cup to Maximus as a sign of allegiance. But Martin, when he had drunk, handed the goblet to his own accompanying priest, invoking

[1] I am very grateful to Professor Leslie Brubaker and the Centre of Byzantine, Ottoman and Modern Greek Studies at Birmingham University for inviting me to the symposium 'Eat, Drink and Be Merry', and for giving me the opportunity to deliver one of the main papers there. I am also indebted to my tutor Dr Mats Cullhed and Dame Professor Averil Cameron who examined my doctoral thesis, 'Dazzling Dining' (unpublished PhD dissertation, Uppsala, 2003), from which this article is derived.

the divine hierarchy as taking precedence over the secular one. Thus the emperor had to admit defeat. At the emperor's own banquet Martin had done what no bishop had dared to do at even the lowest governor's feast![2]

The story about Martin and Maximus tells us how important dazzling dining was to the process of political legitimization in late antiquity. This paper examines how banquets hosted by the Roman emperor were vehicles of imperial propaganda and expressions of the ruler's political legitimacy. Five aspects are here used in the analysis of imperial banqueting:[3] traditional values, religion, precedence, acclamation and tradition.

Traditional values

World on a plate In late antiquity, banquets projected the identity of the emperor as the ruler of the Roman world by bringing together food produce from all over the empire. The quantity and the richness of food, often represented in the standard triad of earth, sea and sky, demonstrated imperial domination over the riches of the Earth. The ostentatious exhibition of wealth reinforced the ruler's sense of his own power and set him apart from the rest of Roman society, or, as Cassiodorus put it: 'A private person may eat the produce of his own district; but it is the glory of a king to collect at his table the delicacies of all lands … It becomes a king to regale himself that he may seem to foreign ambassadors to possess almost everything.'[4] Indeed, we know that banquets constituted a part of the official entertainment of foreign ambassadors at the Great Palace in Constantinople.[5] Venantius Fortunatus portrayed the emperor as the

---

2 Sulpicius Severus, *Vita Martini* XX.2–7, ed. J. Fontaine, *Sulpice Sévère. Vie de Saint Martin*, SC 133–5 (Paris, 1967–69).

3 By imperial banquets I mean public, ritual activity centred on the communal consumption of food and drink, held in the main banqueting halls of the palace, hosted by the emperor and attended by guests from outside the imperial family and immediate friends (*amici*) of the emperor. No difference will be made between the terms 'dinner', 'feast', and 'banquet'. If a dinner, feast or banquet is mentioned, it is assumed that it is imperial, if not otherwise stated.

4 Cassiodorus, *Variae* XII.4, ed. Å. Fridh, *Aurelii Cassidori variarum libri XII*, CCSL 96 (Turnhout, 1973); M. Roberts, 'Martin meets Maximus: the meaning of a Late Roman banquet', *REAu* 41 (1995), 101. S. Ellis, 'Late-antique dining: architecture, furnishings and behaviour', in R. Laurence and A. Wallace-Hadrill, eds, *Domestic Space in the Roman World* (Portsmouth, RI, 1997), 51. J. D'Arms, 'Performing culture: Roman spectacle and the banquets of the powerful', in B. Bergman and C. Kondoleon, eds, *The Art of Ancient Spectacle* (New Haven, 1999), 309, 311. On the geographical sources of food as symbols of power, see I. Cook and P. Crang, 'The world on a plate: culinary culture, displacement, and geographical knowledge', *JMC* 1 (1996), 131–56. The produce of earth, sea and sky is also especially common in descriptions of Paradise and in hymns about the universal power of God.

5 Banquet in 547 for a Persian embassy: *De ceremoniis* I.90, ed. J. J. Reiske, *Constantini Porphyrogeniti imperatoris De ceremoniis aulae byzantinae*, CSHB (Bonn, 1829).

recipient of the entire world's bounty: 'The whole world on every side hastens to do the emperor's bidding, supplying the riches and the delights that … sea, earth, and sky furnish in fish, fowl, and grain.'[6] Four centuries earlier, Aristides had claimed that Roman ships brought food produce from the whole world to the imperial capital, with Arabia, India and Central Asia in this way offering 'tribute' just as the provinces of the empire did.[7] At Justin II's coronation banquet, Corippus tells us of the different wines brought together to symbolize the different provinces of the empire. And if anyone had missed the point, the poet ended with the words: 'Who will tell of all that the world brings forth for its rulers, all the provinces that are subject to the Roman Empire?'[8]

A grotesque example of imperial world rule expressed through conspicuous food consumption is the story about Emperor Vitellius consuming his favourite dish called the 'Shield of Minerva'. This monstrosity was a mixture of pike livers, pheasant and peacock brains, flamingo tongues and lamprey milt brought by his captains and triremes from the whole empire, from Parthia to the Spanish Strait. The title alludes to military exploits, its contents to all-embracing imperial power, all symbolically consumed by the emperor.[9]

Another way to express imperial dominion through banqueting was through the use of a triumphal vocabulary. The guests at the coronation banquet of Justin II were served on golden plates with images of the Vandal triumph of Justinian.[10] Also, at the beginning of imperial banquets, the heralds acclaimed the victories of the emperor.[11] It seems to have been common to invite members of vanquished peoples as guests at imperial banquets, a tradition still practised in the tenth century.[12] This was a way both to awe the foreign 'barbarians' and to concretize imperial victory for

---

[6] Venantius Fortunatus, *Vita Martini* II.72–9, ed. S. Quesnel, *Venance Fortunat: Oeuvres 4, Vie de Saint Martin*, Budé (Paris, 1996).

[7] Aristides, *Oratio romana* 10–12, ed. C. A. Behr, *Aristides*, Loeb (Cambridge, MA, 1973).

[8] Corippus, *In laudem Iustini* III.85–91 and 103–4, ed. A. Cameron, *In laudem Iustini Augusti minoris libri IV* (London, 1976).

[9] Suetonius, *Vitellius* 13.2, ed. J. Rolfe, *Suetonius*, Loeb (Cambridge, MA, 1951). See also Pliny, *Historia Naturalis* XXXV.163, ed. H. Rackham, *Pliny: Natural History*, Loeb (Cambridge, MA, 1967–71).

[10] Corippus, *In laudem Iustini* III.121–5; Cameron, *In laudem*, 184.

[11] *De ceremoniis* I.75, ed. A. Vogt, *Le Livre des cérémonies*, Budé (Paris, 1935–39): 'Always be victor!', and 'May God guard our Empire!' It is important to note that these acclamations were still made in Latin in the sixth century (and even in the tenth), probably as part of an *imperial* and military tradition (compare the use of Latin in the army), as opposed to a *Christian* tradition (with its strong Greek influence).

[12] Eunapios, fragment 59, ed. R. Blockley, *The Fragmentary Classicising Historians of the Later Roman Empire*, vol. 2 (Trowbridge, 1983); Philotheos, ed. N. Oikonomides, *Les Listes de préséance byzantines des IXe et Xe siècles* (Paris, 1972), 169, lines 9–18; 169, line 21; 171, line 10; Harun-ibn-

the fellow guests. Most probably, it was Justinian who initiated the so-called Gothic Play, a song-and-dance act performed during banquets in the Great Palace at Constantinople in commemoration of the conquest of Italy.[13]

Provider for the people In imperial ideology, two important virtues were *providentia* and *liberalitas*: the emperor as provider for his people and the generous giver of gifts to his friends. As imperial legislation and the admonishing advice of Late Antique political philosophers show, it was essential for the emperor to emphasize his role as 'father of his subjects' and 'living wholly and finally not for himself or for his own sake but for his subjects and for their sake'.[14]

Imperial banquets were held in the palace to show the hospitality of the emperor, with a multitude of dishes to show his generosity. The architectural decoration of the dining halls should put the guests in awe, with care and expense spent on the furniture and the tableware as well.[15] The message of generosity could also be underlined by inscriptions in mosaic, oriented so as to be seen by the diners.[16]

The lavishness of imperial banquets stood in contrast to traditional Roman virtues such as simplicity and abstinence, which were especially important in connection with eating and drinking. However, the emperor's authority paradoxically rested on the use of extravagant banquets for displaying his registry of virtues. The magnificence was essential in putting forth the generosity of the emperor and showing his target group

---

Yahya 121–3, tr. A. Vasiliev, 'Harun-ibn-Yahya and his description of Constantinople', *SemKond* 5 (1932), 149–63.

[13] *De ceremoniis* I.83, ed. Vogt; K. Dietrich, *Hofleben in Byzanz* (Leipzig, 1912), 63–5; O. Treitinger, *Die oströmische Kaiser- und Reichsidee nach ihrer Gestaltung im höfischen Zeremoniell* (Jena, 1938), 179–80; A. Vogt, *Le Livre des cérémonies. Commentaire*, vol. 2 (Paris, 1940), 188–91. Compare with the 'Persian Play', mentioned in the *Historia Augustae, Alexander Severus* 57.1, ed. E. Hohl, *Scriptores historiae augustae*, Teubner (Leipzig, 1927). For further discussion, E. Bolognesi, 'Winter in the Great Palace: the persistence of pagan festivals in Christian Byzantium', *BF* 21 (1995), 120–2 and A. Dain, 'Touldos et touldon dans les traités militaires', *AIPHOS* 10 (1950), 161, 168–9.

[14] Quotations from Majorian, *Novella* 2, ed. T. Mommsen and P. Meyer, *Theodosiani libri XVI* (Berlin, 1905), and *De scientia politica* V.9, ed. C. M. Mazzucchi, *Menae patricii cum Thomae referendario de scientia politica dialogus* (Milan, 1982). See also Majorian, *Novella* 1, ed. Mommsen and Meyer; Agapetos 46, *PG* 86.1.1163–86; Corippus, *In laudem Iustini* II.195–227, and Themistios, *Orationes* I.9c–10c, ed. G. Downey and A. F. Norman, *Orationes quae supersunt*, Teubner (Leipzig, 1965–74); J. Straub, *Vom Herrscherideal in der Spätantike* (Stuttgart, 1939), 160–74; J. Vanderspoel, *Themistius and the Imperial Court* (Ann Arbor, MI, 1995).

[15] Statius, *Silvae* I.6.9–34, ed. K. Coleman, *Statius Silvae* (Oxford, 1988); Martial VIII.50.7–10, ed. D. Shackleton Bailey, *Martial: Epigrams*, Loeb (Cambridge, MA, 1993); Sidonius, *Epistulae* II.9, ed. W. B. Anderson, *Sidonius: Poems and Letters*, Loeb (Cambridge, MA, 1936–65).

[16] As in the Palace of Theodoric at Ravenna: G. Ghirardini, 'Gli scavi del palazzo di Teodorico a Ravenna', *MonAnt* 24 (1916), col. 789. See also Ellis, 'Late-antique dining', 44.

of courtiers how the riches of the empire came to be shared amongst them all. According to Agapetos, the emperor was to be lavish in giving to those who seek his help.[17] This view was embraced at imperial banquets in the *Triclinium* of the Nineteen Couches, which always seem to have included twelve paupers. Not only were they given food, but in exchange for the lead or copper token used to invite them to the banquet, they were also given a gold coin.[18] Likewise, after a devastating earthquake on 14 December 557, the Christmas banquet at the Great Palace was cancelled and the money saved as a help to the victims of the earthquake.[19] In these concrete ways the emperor was shown as a benefactor to the common people, in the latter case interestingly by *not* hosting a banquet.

As emperor, the way to combine these conflicting traditions of extravagance and abstemiousness was to give lavish banquets for your supporters, while at the same time displaying a personal frugality. However, there was a fine line between 'bad' and 'good' emperors, shown for instance by Evagrios's description of Justin II as dominated by greed and luxury, while his successor Tiberios is portrayed as epitomizing the generous ideal.[20]

First among equals The emperor's commensality, in sharing with his guests in the feast, enabled him to display his affability, his readiness to associate with his subjects and to be seen as foremost among citizens and not as a tyrant.[21] Imperial inaccessibility had to be complemented by approachability in certain circumstances, such as social contact over the dinner table, but the emperor had to take care not to slip from dignified affability into undignified camaraderie.

When Julian heard that his old teacher, the philosopher Maximos, had arrived at Constantinople, 'he started up in an undignified manner, so far forgetting himself that he ran at full speed to a distance from the vestibule, and after having kissed the philosopher and received him with

17 Agapetos 16, 19 and 46.

18 *De ceremoniis* I.72, ed. Vogt, vol. 2, p. 161, lines.2–4; Philotheos, p. 181, lines 4–9; J. Nesbitt, 'Byzantine copper tokens', *SBS* (1987), 69.

19 Theophanes *AM* 6050, ed. C. de Boor, *Theophanis chronographia,* Teubner (Leipzig, 1883–85).

20 A. Cameron, 'Early Byzantine *Kaiserkritik*: two case histories', *BMGS* 3 (1977), 9; Evagrios V.13, ed. J. Bidez and L. Parmentier, *The Ecclesiastical History of Evagrius* (Amsterdam, 1964).

21 Statius, *Silvae* I.6.46–50; Pliny, *Panegyric* 49.4–6, ed. B. Radice, *Pliny: Letters and Panegyric,* Loeb (Cambridge, MA, 1969); Suetonius, *Vespasian* 21.2. For the imperial virtues, see R. Fears, 'The cult of virtue and Roman imperial ideology', *ANRW* 2.17.1 (1981), 827–948; J. Goddard, 'The tyrant at table', in J. Elsner and J. Masters, eds, *Reflections of Nero* (Chapel Hill, NC, 1994), 67–82, and S. Braund, 'The solitary feast: a contradiction in terms?', *BICS* 41 (1996), 37–52.

reverence, brought him back with him.' This behaviour was frowned upon by Ammianus, who thought that this unseemly ostentation only made the emperor appear an excessive seeker for empty fame.[22] On the other hand, when Justinian received the holy man Sabas, 'he greeted him with reverence, kissing his godly head with tears of joy'. According to the biographer of Sabas, this was the correct way to behave towards the holy man, recognizing his divine favour.[23] But when an author wanted to condemn an emperor, even seemingly correct behaviour could be criticized, as when the commendable affability and serenity of Justinian was portrayed by Prokopios as only a façade for brutality.[24] These conflicting evaluations of correct behaviour seem irreconcilable, but they prove not only the need of the emperors to display a virtuous image, but also to promulgate *their interpretation* of it.

Pliny tells us that Trajan's meals were always taken in public, and his table was open to all. It was neither the lavishness of the golden tableware, nor the ingenuity of the dishes served that commanded the guests' respect, but the affability of the emperor.[25] Pliny's thoughts are mirrored by Sidonius's description of Theodoric II's banquet in the 450s: the food attracts by its skilful cookery, not by its costliness; the platters by their brightness, not by their weight. But the most weighty thing on these occasions is the conversation – 'you can find here Greek elegance, Gallic plenty, Italian briskness; the dignity of state, the attentiveness of a private home, the ordered discipline of royalty'.[26]

Valentinian I is said to have liked elegant but not extravagant dinner parties, while Constantius's, Julian's, Gratian's and Theodosios's moderation in eating and drinking were also praised.[27] The approachability and modesty

---

22 Ammianus Marcellinus XVII.7.3, ed. J. Rolfe, *Ammianus Marcellinus res gestae*, Loeb (Cambridge, MA, 1962–63).

23 Cyril of Skythopolis, *Vita Sabae* 173.19–25, ed. E. Schwartz, *Kyrillos von Skythopolis* (Leipzig, 1939). See also Anastasios's reception of Sabas in 511: Cyril of Skythopolis, *Vita Sabae* 142.3–21.

24 Prokopios *Anekdota* XIII.1–2, ed. H. B. Dewing, *Procopius*, Loeb (Cambridge, MA, 1953–68). On the inversion rhetoric of this text, of which this is a prime example, see L. Brubaker, 'Sex, lies and textuality: the *Secret History* of Prokopios and the rhetoric of gender in sixth-century Byzantium', in L. Brubaker and J. Smith, *Gender in Society, 300–900* (Cambridge, 2004), 83–101.

25 Pliny, *Panegyric* 49.5-8. See also E. Stein-Hölkeskamp, 'Culinarische Codes: das ideale Bankett bei Plinius d. Jüngeren und seinen Zeitgenossen', *Klio*, 84 (2002), 481–5.

26 Sidonius, *Epistulae* I.2.6.

27 Constantius II: Ammianus Marcellinus XXI.16.5; Julian, *Panegyricus in Constantium* 1.11a, ed. W. C. Wright, *Julian: Panegyric on Constantius II*, Loeb (Cambridge, MA, 1962). Julian: Libanios, *Orationes* XVIII.175, ed. R. Foerster, *Opera*, Teubner (Leipzig, 1903–08); Ammianus Marcellinus XVI.5.3; XXV.4.1; XXV.4.5; Mamertinus 11.3–4, ed. T. Nixon and B. Rodgers, *In Praise of Later Roman Emperors: the Panegyrici Latini* (Oxford, 1994). Valentinian I: Ammianus

of the emperors during banquets were always stressed, and Mamertinus and Pacatus as well as Sidonius and Corippus detailed the luxuries that each emperor disdained.[28] A standard theme was the expulsion of idle mouths and gourmet cooks from the palace, and the replacement of their culinary delights with the ordinary rations of common soldiers.[29]

However, we get a rather different picture when we are told of Emperor Jovian's great hunger, and it is said that both Valentinian I and Theodosios I died from overeating. Theodosios, the frugal emperor of Pacatus's verses, is also described as indulging in gluttony.[30] Obviously, the point is not whether an emperor was frugal or not, but that he or his encomiast wanted him to be *perceived* as such. If, on the other hand, one wanted to slander an emperor, his gluttony was a standard invective.

According to Suetonius, Domitian used to eat before his guests arrived, so he did not have to partake of the food together with them, but this also led to some scathing remarks by contemporary writers.[31] Neither was stuffing yourself with food appreciated, as is clear from the biographers of the infamous gourmand-emperor Vitellius. Instead the ideal emperor should behave like, for instance, the emperor Justin II, who ate and drank little during banquets.[32] The emperor should not overindulge in food consumption, but neither should he abstain from it totally. In this way, the commensality of the emperor was shown, without displaying the vices of gluttony or haughtiness.

Marcellinus XXX.9.4. Gratian: Ausonius, *Panegyric* 14, ed. R. P. H. Green, *The Works of Ausonius* (Oxford, 1991). Theodosios I: Pacatus 13.3–14.2, ed. Nixon and Rodgers; Claudian, *De sexto consulatu* 55–64, ed. M. Dewar, *Panegyricus de sexto consulatu Honorii Augusti* (Oxford, 1996).

[28] Stilicho: Claudian, *De consulatu Stilichonis* 2.139–45, ed. J. Hall, *Claudii Claudiani carmina* (Leipzig, 1985). Theodosius II: *Codex Theodosianus* XIV.20.1, ed. Mommsen and Meyer; Sozomen, preface 12, ed. J. Bidez, B. Grillet and G. Sabbah, *Sozomène: histoire ecclésiastique*, SC 306 and 418 (Paris, 1983–96). Theodoric: Sidonius, *Epistulae* I.2.6. In a verse letter of invitation, Sidonius uses the same strategy, detailing the splendours the guest cannot expect to enjoy: Sidonius, *Carmina* 17, ed. Anderson. Justin II: Corippus, *In laudem Iustini* III.105–10.

[29] Julian enjoying the food of the camps: Mamertinus 11.3–4; Ammianus Marcellinus XVI.5.3. Julian expelling the eunuchs, barbers, and cooks from the palace: Ammianus Marcellinus XXII.4.1. Severus of Antioch expels the cooks from the patriarchal palace and orders common bread to be served: John of Beith-Aphthonia, *Vita Severi* 243, ed. *PO* 2, 207–64.

[30] Jovian: Ammianus Marcellinus XXV.10.15; Libanios, *Orationes* XVIII.279. Valentinian I: Aurelius Victor, *Epitome* 45.9, ed. M. Festy, *Abrégé des césars*, Belles Lettres (Paris, 1999). Theodosios I: Philostorgios XI.2, ed. J. Bidez and F. Winkelmann, *Philostorgius Kirchengeschichte*, GCS 21 (Berlin, 1972); Zosimos IV.28.1, ed. F. Paschoud, *Histoire nouvelle*, Budé (Paris, 1979–2000). Both, of course, are very negative towards Theodosios, Philostorgios being an Arian and Zosimos a pagan. See also Antony Eastmond and Liz James's chapter in this volume.

[31] Suetonius, *Domitian* 21. See also Pliny, *Panegyric* 49.6.

[32] Cameron, *In laudem*, 184.

Religion

In late antiquity, the traditional values of the perfect prince became augmented by a new set of values derived from the Christian faith. As the Late Antique emperor strived to strengthen his political power by religious means, the parallel images of earthly and heavenly authority merged in him.

To Venantius Fortunatus, Paradise regularly conjured up the image of a banquet, while to Philotheos, the author of a banquet treatise at the end of the ninth century, the banquet at the Feast of Light (Epiphany) symbolized the union of the forces of heaven and earth. At this feast the banquet hall was filled by clergy dressed in white, representing angels who had come down to earth.[33] The most spectacular setting for heavenly connotations, however, was the symbolism attached to the imperial couch at banquets.

Augustus hosted a 'Banquet of the Twelve Gods', with himself as Apollo and the other guests dressed up as Olympian gods and goddesses.[34] In the reign of Constantine, this pagan symbolism was replaced by a Christian one. In connection with the *vicennalia* banquet of Constantine in 325, Eusebios tells us that when the bishops dined with the emperor it was like an imaginary representation of the kingdom of Christ.[35] Also in the mosaics of sixth-century San Apollinare Nuovo in Ravenna and in the pages of the contemporary Rossano Gospels, the Olympian gods have been replaced by Christ and his twelve Apostles. Finally, Philotheos explicitly tells us that the emperor imitated the second coming of Christ at banquets together with 'twelve friends which recline with the emperor as the twelve Apostles'.[36]

---

[33] Venantius Fortunatus, *Carmina* IV.7.21; VIII.3.29 (*paradisiacas epulas*), ed. M. Reydellet, *Venance Fortunat: poèmes*, Budé (Paris, 1994–98); Philotheos, p. 185, lines 8–11. Also, a table being laden with food could be compared by John Chrysostom to serving the faithful at an altar: A. Cutler and A. Karpozilos, 'Banquet', *ODB* (Oxford, 1991), 1.251.

[34] Suetonius, *Augustus* 70.1. For Emperor Domitian's Jovian banquets, see Martial VIII.39, IX.91, and Statius, *Silvae* IV.3.128–9. See also Corippus, *In laudem Iustini* III.179–90, who compares the imperial palace with Mount Olympos.

[35] Eusebios, *Vita Constantini* III.15, ed. F. Winkelmann, *Eusebius Werke 1.1* (Berlin, 1991).

[36] Rossano, Museo dell'Archivescovado, Codex Purpureus Rossanensis, fol. 3r, Gospels: G. Cavallo and W. Loerke, eds, *Codex Purpureus Rossanensis. Facsimile edition of MS Museo dell'Archivescovado*, Codices Selecti 81, 2 vols (Graz, 1985–87); Philotheos, p. 165, lines 21–2; p. 167, line 10 and lines 13–14. This view may, of course, be only Philotheos's personal interpretation of the banquet, but since his *Kletorologion* (*Banquet Treatise*) was an official document, approved by the emperor, this does not seem likely.

Precedence

Since rank in late antiquity was not hereditary, it continually had to be proven and displayed.[37] Thus society was highly stratified, but it also experienced considerable social mobility. That is why precedence occupied the Late Antique court to such a degree. For the system to work there had to be a means whereby people communicated their pledge as clients and by which the patron accepted that role. This was achieved through rituals of precedence, and through banquets, among other things, the political rankings were given concrete form. The presence of the emperor at banquets validated the hierarchy of all other diners, visually reinforcing these ties.[38]

Precedence at banquets can be expressed in five different ways: spatial distinctions (physical location of the guests), temporal distinctions (order of admission and order of dining), qualitative distinctions (the kind of food, drink and setting), quantitative distinctions (the relative amount of food) and behavioural distinctions (difference in table manners). Among these, spatial and temporal distinctions were the most conspicuous ways to differentiate the guests at imperial banquets, while qualitative, quantitative and behavioural distinctions were mostly used to distinguish between imperial banquets and other kinds of banquets.

The first of the spatial distinctions was the way in which you dined. The normal way was to recline on a dining couch (Figure 11.1), but some diners seem to have had the right, or the will, to sit. When Martin of Tours attended the banquet of Maximus he refused to recline and instead used a stool placed beside the emperor's place on the couch.[39] The patriarch of Constantinople also used a stool placed next to the emperor's place when he was invited to banquets in the Great Palace in the ninth century.[40] Although we have several examples of bishops and even monks reclining at dinner, the erect position of Martin and the patriarch may have been due to humility. The habit of sitting at a banquet was usually considered a demeaning position, reserved for women and social inferiors.[41] We can also recall the words of Luke 14.7–11:

---

37 For a more in-depth study, I refer to my article 'Visualising hierarchy at imperial banquets', in W. Mayer and S. Trzcionka, *Feast, Fast or Famine: food and drink in Byzantium*, Byzantina Australiensia 15 (Brisbane, 2005).

38 J. D'Arms, 'Control, companionship, and *clientela*: some social functions of the Roman communal meal', *EchCl* 28 (1984), 344. See the conspicuous position of Domitian at banquets: Statius, *Silvae* IV.2.15–18.

39 Sulpicius Severus, *Vita Martini* XX.2–7.

40 Philotheos, p. 175, lines 19–22; p. 185, lines 6–30.

41 Gregory of Tours, *De gloria martyrum* 79, ed. B. Krusch and W. Arndt, *Gregorii Turonensis opera*, MGH, SRM 1 (Hanover, 1885).

> do not take the place of honour, for a person more distinguished than you may have been invited … then humiliated, you will have to take the least important place … take the lowest place, so that when your host comes, he will say to you, 'Friend, move up to a better place.' Then you will be honoured.[42]

As we have seen, sometimes the refusal to recline is a demonstration of independence vis-à-vis the emperor, in Martin's case also coupled with a will not to acknowledge the ranks claimed by Maximus and his dignitaries. In the case of the emperor and patriarch, their relative rank is not that clear-cut: in secular matters the emperor holds sway, but the patriarch is at least as important as the emperor in religious matters. A convenient way to solve this problem of precedence seems to have been for the patriarch to sit next to the emperor, thereby occupying a place neither inferior nor superior to that of the emperor.

The second spatial distinction was provided by the precedence observed within the couch (Figure 11.2). The emperor, as host, reclined on the right extremity of the couch, while his guest of honour reclined opposite him, on the left extremity. The hierarchy of the other guests then decreased from the guest of honour towards the host, the person with the lowest rank being placed closest to the host. This hierarchy within the couch was then repeated in every couch of the banquet hall. Even the initial conversation within the couch had to be conducted according to this ranking system, with the emperor first addressing the guest of honour and then saying a word to each of the others in order of precedence.[43]

The third spatial distinction was the ranking system existing between the couches, here based on the circumstances in the *Triclinium* of the Nineteen Couches in the Great Palace in Constantinople. Since all precedence was measured by proximity to the emperor, the imperial couch was naturally considered the most elevated. Indeed, this was also arranged physically, by placing the couch on a podium, thereby underlining its special character and

---

[42] See also the paraphrase, adapted for Late Antique circumstances, by Juvencus III.614–21, ed. K. Marold, *C. Vettii Aquilini Iuvenci libri evangeliorum IIII*, Teubner (Leipzig, 1886).

[43] The hierarchy is most clearly shown in a passage from Sidonius, describing a banquet of Emperor Majorian at Arles in 461: Sidonius, *Epistulae* I.11.10–12. See also Sidonius, *Epistulae* VII.12.4. Juvencus is the first to mention the ranking on the *sigma*-couch in c. 330, although the older hierarchy with the guest of honour in the middle of the couch occasionally prevailed until the end of that century: J. Engemann, 'Der Ehrenplatz beim antiken Sigmamahl', in T. Klauser, ed., *Jenseitsvorstellungen in Antike und Christentum* (Münster, 1982), 239–50. The host's position *in cornu dextro* is also clearly shown in the mosaic of the Last Supper in San Apollinare Nuovo in Ravenna (for a good reproduction, see, A. Carile, ed., *Storia di Ravenna, II.1. Dall'età bizantina all'età ottoniana. Territorio, economia e società* [Venice, 1991], pl. 12); the Vienna Genesis, fol. 17v (Vienna, ÖN MS 31: O. Mazal, ed., *Wiener Genesis. Facsimile edition of Codex theol. gr. 31*, Österreichische Nationalbibliothek, Vienna, 2 vols [Frankfurt am Main, 1980]); Paris, BN MS 1286, fol. 19r, and the Rossano Gospels, fol. 3r (for the facsimile edition see note 36 above).

making it prominent. The ranks of the other couches, then, were estimated by their proximity to the imperial one. Since the couches were placed in two rows in the *Triclinium* of the Nineteen Couches, the first couch in each row was placed at an equal distance from the imperial couch, and so on. This problem was avoided by according the row closest, not to the imperial couch, but to the person of the emperor, a higher rank than the other row. In this way, the first couch of the so-called better row was ranked the second couch in the hall, the first couch of the other row ranked third, the second couch of the better row ranked fourth, and so on. Moreover, the first two couches in each row were often used for guests of higher rank than on the other couches. These two couches were often called collectively 'the closest couches', while the rest of the rows were lumped together as 'the other couches' or 'the inferior couches'.[44] As for the hierarchy between the couches, we may also recall the words of Sidonius, that 'the last guest at the first table is superior to the person who is first at the second table'.[45] Thus, the relationship between the couches was finely graded, and, together with the precedence observed within the couches, made it possible for every guest to visualize his exact rank in relation to the other 228 diners in the hall.

The first temporal distinction was the order of entering and leaving the banquet hall. The emperor was always the first to enter and the last to leave. If the patriarch also attended the banquet, he entered and left at the same time as the emperor. In this way, their equal rank was preserved. Next, the guests invited to the imperial table arrived. They entered the hall one by one, according to their rank, and also left after the other guests. Finally, the guests of the other couches entered in two files, also according to rank. They were the first to leave after the conclusion of the banquet, except that

[44] Two rows: Philotheos, p. 169, line 22. Nine couches in each row: Philotheos, p. 169, lines 9–18. Right row known as 'better couches': Philotheos, p. 181 line 132 – p. 183 line 1. The closest couches: Philotheos, p. 171, lines 20–22; *De ceremoniis* I.26, ed. Vogt, vol. 1, p. 136, lines 9–19. The other couches: *De ceremoniis* I.91, ed. Reiske, 416, lines 7–15; 417, lines 3–5; Philotheos, 173, line 25; p. 175, line 6. The inferior couches: Philotheos, p. 175, line 8. The *trapeza* of the Great Lavra on Mount Athos has a striking resemblance to the layout of the Nineteen Couches. We know that Athanasios built the *trapeza* with nineteen large *sigma*-tables at each of which twelve monks could be seated: *Vita Athanasii Athonitae, vita* B, XXV.20–25, ed. J. Noret, *Vitae duae antiquae sancti Athanasii Athonitae*, CCSG 9 (Turnhout, 1982). Since at least the abbot's table is of Late Antique origin (S. Popović, 'The Trapeza in cenobitic monasteries: architectural and spiritual contexts', *DOP* 52 [1998], 299), it does not seem too far-fetched to suggest that Athanasios's nineteen tables were taken by Nikephoros II Phokas from the recently demolished *Triclinium* of the Nineteen Couches to his new foundation on Mount Athos: G. Stričević, 'The Trapeza of Chilanderi', in *Fourth Annual Byzantine Studies Conference. Abstracts of Papers* (Ann Arbor, MI, 1978), 16; P. Mylonas, 'La trapéza de la Grande Lavra au Mont Athos', *CahArch* 35 (1987), 143, 145.

[45] Sidonius, *Epistulae* VII.12.4.

sometimes the guests at the two closest couches were allowed to stay as long as the guests of the imperial table.[46]

The second temporal distinction was the order of consumption. The only banqueters allowed to drink before the common consumption started were the emperor and patriarch, again stating their exceptional status.[47]

At some occasions, however, precedence was also consciously *avoided*, such as when an Arab embassy was entertained at a banquet in the *Triclinium* of the Nineteen Couches in 946. A round table was set up, in order that the legates should not think that any of them sat in a place of preference to the others.[48]

Acclamation

The price for being invited to a banquet was praise. Acclamations of the emperor constituted a prominent feature of the rituals performed at banquets. It was also one of the most recurring elements, being carried out when entertainment was performed, when a new dish was served to the guests, or generally when the music stopped. Actually, the instruments playing at banquets could in themselves be seen as an acclamation, where, according to a tenth-century Arab guest, 'each pipe according to its tune ... proclaims praise to the emperor'.[49] It seems that acclamation was intimately connected to the generosity of the emperor, in gratitude for his gift of food and other pleasantries during dinner.[50] However, the more implicit message of the acclamations was the expression of consent to the emperor's rule, and a pledge of loyalty towards him. This implicit message is shown not so much by the occasion as by the verbal content of the acclamations. The verbatim acclamations, as dictated to the guests by the imperial heralds in the sixth century, have come down to us through the *Book of Ceremonies*. At the beginning of the banquet, hopes were expressed that the emperor should rule for many years to come, a wish that was later repeated. This was obviously a pledge of general loyalty by the courtiers towards their ruler. Early on at the banquet, the emperor, together with God, was also acclaimed

[46] Emperor and patriarch: Philotheos, p. 175, lines 19–22; p. 185, lines 19–20; *De ceremoniis* I.26, ed. Vogt, vol. 1, p. 136, lines 9–12. Guests of the imperial couch: Philotheos, p. 167, line 14 – p. 169, line 1. Guests at the two closest couches: Philotheos, p. 175, lines 19–22; *De ceremoniis* I.26, ed. Vogt, vol. 1, p. 136, lines 9–12. Other guests: Philotheos, p. 169, lines 9–18; p. 169, line 21 – p. 171, line 10. The system of two admissions, as described by Philotheos in 899, corresponds with the first and second admissions (*primae* and *secundae admissiones*) known during the Principate: A. Winterling, *Aula Caesaris* (Munich, 1999), 119–20.

[47] Philotheos, p. 175, lines 19–22; p. 185, lines 19–20; *De ceremoniis* I.26, ed. Vogt, vol. 1, p. 136, lines. 9–12.

[48] *De ceremoniis* II.15, ed. Niebuhr, p. 594, lines 3–14.

[49] Harun-ibn-Yahya 121–3.

[50] Philotheos, p. 169, lines 9–18; p. 169, line 21 – p. 171, line 10.

as the defender of the empire. This was a reference to the legitimacy gained as victor in battle, but was also a way of associating the emperor with his heavenly counterpart. Later on, the emperor was admonished to live a good life; that is, to uphold the virtues of a good ruler and not degenerate into a tyrant, a reference to his rule for the common good.[51]

Communal chanting was sometimes performed in the *Triclinium* of the Nineteen Couches. At the sixth of the Christmas banquets, attended by the patriarch, abbots and monks, the beef was accompanied by chanting directed by two domestics. Also, in the same hall, at the banquet at the Feast of Light, attended by the patriarch, metropolitans, bishops and priests, four choirmasters led the communal chant. Obviously, chanting was only performed if priests or monks attended the banquet, presumably because of their religious zeal, and because they were accustomed to and trained in the singing of hymns.[52] The hymns were a way both to create and express church consent to imperial rule, but also to transform the banquet into a Christian meal, a kind of hierarchical *agape*. Non-communal chanting was sometimes performed at banquets by choral singers placed behind curtains, praising the emperor in every key.[53]

Acclamation was an audio-visual display of consensus. The emperor had a desire not only to possess power, but also to see it constantly recognized publicly in the words and gestures of others. Acclamations expressed senatorial loyalty at banquets and popular consensus at hippodrome games. In ancient terms, consensus as expressed through acclamation distinguished the *princeps* from the *tyrannus*.

Tradition

In the Roman empire, antiquity provided models of correct behaviour and conveyed legitimacy. Therefore, change was usually expressed in terms of continuity and tradition. This resulted in a constant tension between ideal and reality, which ceremony, to some degree, tried to bridge.

At the Great Palace, huge effort was placed upon maintaining the physical and psychological links with the past. We know that in the tenth century, emperors still sat on the thrones formerly used by Constantine, Arkadios and Maurice. At banquets, a large silver platter called 'Licinius' was also still used.[54] Although the custom of reclining at dinner faded during the seventh

---

51 *De ceremoniis* I.75, ed. Vogt, vol. 2, pp. 171–2.

52 Philotheos, p. 177, ll. 8–11; p. 187, l. 21 – p. 189, l. 1. It is important to note that there is no evidence for this custom in late antiquity, although considering the ubiquity of communal chanting in this period, it seems plausible.

53 *De ceremoniis* II.15, ed. Niebuhr, p. 585, ll. 9–15.

54 Thrones of Constantine and Arkadios: *De ceremoniis* II.15, ed. Reiske, p. 587, lines 4–7. Throne of Maurice and platter named 'Licinius': *Taktikon of Oikonomides*, p. 275, lines 10 and

century, it lingered on at imperial banquets with Late Antique curved couches being used until the tenth century – here Constantine VII reclined at table in the same manner as Constantine I.[55] In fact, the Late Antique apartments of the Great Palace had in the tenth century been transformed into a kind of museum, only used for the traditional rituals.[56] Constantine I was transformed, in the course of late antiquity, into a semi-legendary Christian hero.[57] It is hard to say if the *Triclinium* of the Nineteen Couches was built by Constantine or not. What is important, however, is that later sources, such as the *Patria*, wanted to associate it with Constantine, in order for the hall to receive part of his special aura and legitimacy.[58]

To sum up

Ever since the time of Augustus, the banquet had been one of the most important ways in which emperor and elite met and interacted. Through the ideology and rituals that surrounded it, the banquet became a setting for the social and moral values of Roman society, and thus a way for the emperor to disseminate political propaganda. As seen in the introductory story about Martin and Maximus, the host's and guest's actions take on exemplary force when staged at an imperial banquet. Sulpicius Severus takes pains to describe the brilliance of the palace dining arrangements, as an index of Maximus's imperial status and an appropriate location for symbolic action. Maximus demonstrated his political triumph and geographical extent of his power by summoning the most important regional power brokers, the bishops, to his banqueting hall. By feeding them in lavish fashion and honouring them (at least in the case of Martin),

---

17, ed. Oikonomides.

[55] Arethas 326, ed. O. Stählin and U. Treu, *Clemens Alexandrinus* I, GCS (Berlin, 1972); Liudprand, *Antapodosis* VI.8, ed. P. Chiesa, *Liudprandi Cremonensis opera omnia*, CCCM 156 (Turnhout, 1998).

[56] E. Bolognesi and J. M. Featherstone, 'The boundaries of the Palace: *De ceremoniis* II.13', *TM* 14 (2002), 38. Imperial banquet as fossilized avatar: C. Mango, 'Daily life in Byzantium', in *16. Internationaler Byzantinistenkongress, Wien 4.–9. Oktober 1981. Akten, 1* (Vienna, 1981), 353.

[57] A. Cameron, 'Models of the past in the late sixth century: the Life of the Patriarch Eutychius', in G. Clark, ed., *Reading the Past in Late Antiquity* (Rushcutters Bay, 1990), 217; A. Cameron, 'Eusebius's *Vita Constantini* and the construction of Constantine', in S. Swain and M. Edwards, eds, *Portraits: biographical representation in the Greek and Latin literature of the Roman empire* (Oxford, 1997), 245–74; A. Cameron and S. Hall, *Eusebius. Life of Constantine* (Oxford, 1999). As is well known, new emperors were often hailed as 'new Constantines': see, for example, P. Magdalino, ed., *New Constantines* (Aldershot, 1994). Constantine III is even said to have been acclaimed as emperor in 408 only because of his name: Olympiodoros, *Historia*, fragment 13.2, ed. R. Blockley, *The Fragmentary Classicising Historians of the Later Roman Empire*.

[58] *Patria*, ed. T. Preger, *Scriptores originum Constantinopolitanarum*, vol. 2 (Leipzig, 1907), 144.

he showed his generosity and affability. The banquet was also an excellent way of visualizing hierarchy, something that was used by Martin when he refused the seat of honour (and convivial etiquette), and instead sat down on a stool, usually a demeaning position, but turned in the hands of the skilful bishop into a political tool. Another important reason for the emperor to invite the bishops, and for them to attend, was the display of consensus and solidarity. By accepting the emperor's invitation, they became politically bound to him. In this lay the peril Martin tried to avoid, and so he refused to return the goblet of wine, a deeply political act. Martin's actions upset old traditions and the solemn order, the hallmarks of imperial banqueting, which revealed the imperial power as more majestic and awe-inspiring. Religion also played an important role at the banquet at Trier. One of the reasons that convinced Martin to accept the imperial invitation was Maximus's claim to have been appointed by God, a claim validated by success in battle. Martin's counterstroke was to claim that the hierarchy of the clerical order surpassed all secular authority, symbolized by him passing the goblet not to the emperor, but to his priest.

Imperial banquets appealed to common values shared by emperor and elite. Through banquets, the emperor showed that he adhered to these values, had the appropriate qualities of a ruler and served the common good of the elite. The emperor had to gain consent from the commonly acknowledged sources of authority, in order to secure his position. These were God, society in the past (tradition) and society in the present (court and senate). This consent was expressed at banquets by a symbolic merging of emperor and Christ, the emphasis placed on traditional imperial virtues (such as generosity, frugality and affability), the acclamation of the emperor by the guests, and a conservative banquet ritual. The presence of the emperor at banquets validated the hierarchy of all other diners, reinforcing visually the ties of the client–patron relationship, expressed through both spatial and temporal distinctions. Thus, the political power of the East Roman emperor was legitimized by projecting the ideology of imperial rule upon the medium of ritualized communal feasting.

Figure 11.1: Banquet of Pharaoh in the sixth-century Vienna Genesis, fol. 17v (Vienna, Österreichische Nationalbibliothek MS theol. gr. 31), showing the place of the ruler on the *sigma*-couch (After W. Ritter et al., *Die Wiener Genesis* [Vienna, 1895]).

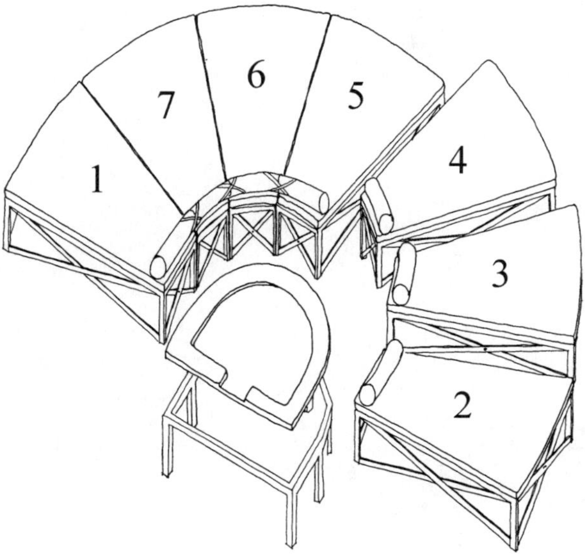

Figure 11.2: Reconstruction of a *sigma*-couch. The numbers mark the hierarchy on the couch (After G. Åkerström-Hougen, *The Calendar and Hunting Mosaics of the Villa of the Falconer in Argos: a study in Early Byzantine iconography* [Stockholm, 1974], 117, fig. 74).

12. A sultan in Constantinople: the feasts of Ghiyāth al-Dīn Kay-Khusraw I[1]

Dimitri Korobeinikov

No high-ranking Muslim ruler visited Constantinople before the twelfth century. The situation changed when the Komnenoi came to power in 1081 and brought innovations to Byzantine foreign policy. The emperor Alexios I (1081–1118), and especially his successors John II (1118–43) and Manuel I (1143–80), arranged various dynastic marriages with western rulers. The increased diplomatic contacts with Muslim sovereigns were another innovation on the part of the Byzantines; and for the first time in its history Constantinople became the meeting place where emperors received sultans.

These sultans, however, did not come from the chief Muslim centres of the time such as Damascus or Cairo; and though they belonged to the illustrious family of the Seljuks, they nevertheless represented only the minor branch of the family, whose possessions were almost surrounded by Byzantine lands. And yet, while under Byzantine influence, the sultans of Rūm were doubtlessly Muslim and asserted the title, which was considered as the highest of all secular titles in the Muslim world. The first Seljuk sultan of Rūm to visit Constantinople was Sultan Mas'ūd (1116–55) who met Emperor John II Komnenos in 1124.[2]

We do not know exactly how the meeting was conducted, for our source, Michael the Syrian only briefly mentioned, in his characteristically austere style, that: '[Sultan] Mas'ūd fled to Constantinople and took refuge with John, the emperor of the Romans (*malkā d-Rōmāyē*). For Mas'ūd's brother, the prince Malīk 'Arab, was near Konya (Iqōnīyōn), the capital of the kingdom of Sultan Mas'ūd. Emperor John joyfully received Mas'ūd and gave him

[1] I wish to express my thanks to Dr M. E. Martin who kindly read the paper and offered various suggestions concerning my style. All the possible mistakes are, however, mine.

[2] Michael the Syrian, *Chronique*, ed. and tr. J. B. Chabot, 4 vols (Paris, 1899–1910), 3.223–4 (French translation); 4.608–9 (Syriac text).

much gold.'[3] Even this scant information suggests that the reception was hardly the meeting of two equally ranking sovereigns: it was the sultan, not the emperor, who appealed for help against his brother.

However, the most detailed description of a reception given in Constantinople to a sultan is that of 1161 when Manuel I Komnenos received Sultan Kılıç Arslān II (1156–92). Before his visit to the Byzantine capital, the sultan was at war with the Byzantines (from the beginning of 1160). However, after his defeat by the armies of John Kontostephanos and then by the army of Yağıbasān ibn Dānishmand (1142–64),[4] Kılıç Arslān II was forced to sign the peace treaty in which he swore to be a military ally (*symmachos*) of the empire. In addition, the sultan became Manuel's 'friend' (*philos*), 'retainer' (*oikeios*) and 'son';[5] and he promised to be 'in obedience to the emperor' (*i hazandut'iwn t'agaworin*) until his death.[6] The treaty was ratified during Kılıç Arslān II's visit in person in Constantinople at the end of 1161.[7]

The reception of the sultan was a vivid demonstration of Manuel's power; and the 'ceremonial language' was highly symbolic, representing the sultan's submission to the empire. On his first audience outside the city walls Manuel was seated on a chair on the dais built for the occasion (whilst the sultan was on a chair below); Manuel I then arranged a solemn procession with holy icons to Hagia Sophia in which the sultan should have taken part, despite the opposition of the clergy. However, an earthquake, which was regarded as God's warning against the Muslim ruler entering the church, forced Manuel to abandon the idea. He nevertheless gave many magnificent banquets, horse races and performances in the hippodrome to honour his guest.[8] According to Paul Magdalino,

> the narrative sources, including Kinnamos, present the treaty of 1161 in terms of alliance, which suggests that the sultan became the Turkish equivalent … of the King of Jerusalem. This suggestion is confirmed, first, by the way

---

3 Ibid., 4.608.

4 John Kinnamos, *Epitome rerum ab Ioanne et Alexio Comnenis gestarum*, ed. A. Meineke (Bonn, 1836), 200.12 – 201.7; Niketas Choniates, *Historia*, ed. J.-L. van Dieten, CFHB 11 (Berlin, 1975), 118.26–9; 'Izz al-Dīn Abū al-Ḥasan 'Alī Ibn al-Athīr, *al-Kāmil fī al-tārīkh*, 11 vols (Beirut, 1998), 9.477.

5 Kinnamos, 201–8; Choniates, *Historia*, 123.74–80, 420.31.

6 Matt'ēos Uṙhayets'i, *Zhamanakgrut'iwn* (Vałarshapat, 1898), 428.

7 Kinnamos, 201.7–18, 204.22 – 208.16; Choniates, *Historia*, 118.29–32; Matt'ēos Uṙhayets'i, 425–6, 428; Gregory the Priest, 'Continuation', in Matthew of Edessa, *The Chronicle*, tr. A. E. Dostourian (Lanham, 1993), 277, 279; F. Chalandon, *Les Comnène. Études sur l'empire byzantin au XIe et au XIIe siècles*, 2 vols (Paris, 1900–1912), 2.462.

8 Kinnamos, 204–7; Choniates, *Historia*, 118–21.

> he was enthroned beside the emperor, and secondly, by the way he acted as intermediary between the emperor and other Turkish emirs ...[9]

The Byzantine sources plainly reveal the type of personal relations that existed between the emperor and the sultan after their meeting in 1161/1162. Choniates writes:

> At times, [Kılıç Arslān II] ... improved [his relations with the emperor] and did service to him; then the emperor, instead of declaring [the sultan] a wild beast in need of surveillance, honoured him by adopting him as a son. In the letters they exchanged, the emperor was addressed as father and the sultan as son. But their friendship was not honest, nor did they honour their treaties.[10]

The text of Choniates shows that the 'family' relationship between Manuel I and Kılıç Arslān II was an initiative of the Seljuk sultan. Other details confirm this statement. From the Byzantine point of view, the sultan could not have been a spiritual son of the emperor as he was Muslim, nor could he have been named the emperor's son [-in-law], as he did not marry a Byzantine princess. The Byzantines preferred to use other designations: they called the sultan 'friend' and 'retainer' of the emperor.[11] It seems strange that the emperor should consider the independent Muslim ruler as a subordinate. However, the Byzantines regarded the territory of the Sultanate of Rūm as a Byzantine land,[12] and believed that the sultan of Rūm, unlike the Grand Seljuks, was of a lower rank than that of the emperor.[13]

---

9 P. Magdalino, *The Empire of Manuel I Komnenos* (Cambidge, 1997), 77. Magdalino compares the Byzantine–Seljuk treaty of 1161 with the agreement between Manuel I and Baldwin III of Jerusalem (1143–63) in 1158: ibid., 69–72.

10 Choniates, *Historia*, 123.74–8.

11 On the sultan as an *oikeios* of the emperor, see Magdalino, *The Empire of Manuel I Komnenos*, 77; as a *philos*, see Choniates, *Historia*, 123.79, 420.31. Sometimes the terms *philos* and *oikeios* (as well as the term *doulos*, 'slave') were interchangeable: A. P. Kazhdan, *Sotsial'niy sostav gospodstvuyuschego klassa Vizantii XI–XII vv.* (Moscow, 1974), 237–8. However, in *Pouvoir et contestations à Byzance (963–1210)* (Paris, 1996), 289, J. C. Cheynet states: 'Alors que les *douloi* de l'empereur étaient des princes vaincus qui lui devaient obéissance sans en rien recevoir en contrepartie, les *philoi* disposaient d'une marge de liberté plus grande, même s'ils reconnaissaient la supériorité de l'empereur qui les récompensait de cette amitié.'

12 Choniates, *Historia*, 117.5–11. See also A. P. Kazhdan and A. Wharton-Epstein, *Change in Byzantine Culture in the Eleventh and Twelfth Centuries* (London, 1985), 167–9.

13 The Byzantines usually translated the title sultan as '*basileus*' ('emperor', 'king'), 'the king of kings' or even 'the almighty' (παντοκράτωρ): John Scylitzes, *Synopsis historiarum*, ed. I. Thurn (Berlin, 1973), 445.68–9; Nikephoros Bryennios, *Histoire*, ed. P. Gautier (Brussels, 1975), 95.26–8; Michael Psellos, *Chronographie ou histoire d'un siècle de Byzance (976–1077)*, ed. É. Renauld, 2 vols (Paris, 1926–28), 2.161.17. However, while all these 'translations' were sometimes applied to the Grand Seljuks, whose empire reminded the Byzantines of the greatest Iranian realms, the Seljuk sultans of Rūm were *never* named as '*basileus*': see G. Moravcsik, *Byzantinoturcica*, 2 vols (Berlin, 1958), 2.286–7. I presume that this was not accidental.

Little is known about the 'father–son' relations in the twelfth century as this period has few documentary sources. The Byzantine influence over the Sultanate of Rūm never ceased to exist, as long as the Greek aristocracy remained a part of the Seljuk nobility and the Greek population was numerous in Rūm.[14]

The visit of Kılıç Arslān II set an example for further receptions of the sultans in Constantinople. The fate of one of the most colourful Seljuk sultans, Ghiyāth al-Dīn Kay-Khusraw I (1195–99, 1205–11), who lingered in Constantinople in 1200–1204, is illustrative. His reception was in accord with the ceremonial of receiving Christian sovereigns, just as in the twelfth century. The historical narrative that underpins these ceremonies, banquets and receptions is the focus of the rest of this chapter.

Kay-Khusraw I was the youngest son of Kılıç Arslān II. Probably in the year 1187, Kılıç Arslān II decided to divide the sultanate between his nine sons, a brother and a nephew.[15] Soon after the division, his sons ceased to recognize Kılıç Arslān II's authority; finally, his elder son, Quṭb al-Dīn Malikshāḥ (d. 1195), who wanted undisputed power, arrested his father. The old sultan escaped to Sozopolis (Uluborlu) in the 'realm' of Kay-Khusraw I whom he recognized as his heir, apparently before his death in 1192. In the same year Kay-Khusraw entered Konya.[16]

It was Kay-Khusraw I who supported Theodore Mankaphas of Philadelphia, who had sought refuge in Konya in 1193–94. Later, while handing Mankaphas over to Byzantium at the emperor's request, Kay-

[14] On the Byzantine influence on the Sultanate of Rūm, see two important works: M. Balivet, *Romanie byzantine et Pays de Rûm Turc. Histoire d'un espace d'imbrication gréco-turque*, Cahiers du Bosphore 10 (Istanbul, 1994); O. Turan, 'Les souverains Seldjoukides et leurs sujets non-musulmans', *Studia Islamica*, 1 (1953), 65–100.

[15] Ibn al-Athīr, 10.219–20; İbn-i Bîbî, *El-Evâmirü'l-`Alâ'iyye fi'l-umûri'l-`Alâ'iyye*, ed. N. Lugal and A. S. Erzi (Ankara, 1957), 30 (hereafter cited as İbn-i Bībī [Lugal–Erzi]); *Histoire des Seldjoucides d'Asie Mineure, d'après l'abrégé du Seldjouknāmeh d'Ibn-Bībī: texte persan*, ed. M. T. Houtsma (Leiden, 1902), 5 (hereafter cited as Ibn Bibi); H. Duda, *Die Seltschukengeschichte des Ibn Bibi* (Copenhagen, 1959), 19 (hereafter cited as Ibn Bibi [Duda]); C. Cahen, *The Formation of Turkey. The Seljukid Sultanate of Rūm: eleventh to fourteenth century* (Harlow, 2001), 39. The date of 1187 is uncertain; according to Ibn Bībī and Ibn al-Athīr, the division took place before the death of Kılıç Arslān II in 1192. However, Ibn al-Athīr also writes that shortly after the division, Kılıç Arslān II arranged a match between his elder son and the daughter of Ṣalāḥ al-Dīn ibn Ayyūb (Saladin) (1169–93), sultan of Egypt and Syria. This might have happened in 1187: 'Imād al-Dīn al-Iṣfahānī, *Conquête de la Syrie et de la Palestine par Salâh ed-dîn*, ed. C. de Landberg, 2 vols (Leiden, 1888), 1.119–20; *Histoire des Seldjoucides d'Asie Mineure par un anonyme*, ed. F. N. Uzluk (Ankara, 1952), 39 (Persian text), 26 (Turkish translation); C. Cahen, 'Selgukides, Turcomans et Allemends au temps de la troisième croisade', in idem, *Turcobyzantina et Oriens Christianus* (Paris, 1974), no. 9, 28.

[16] Choniates, *Historia*, 401.2–5; Ibn Bibi, 2–6; Ibn Bibi (Duda), 17–21; Ibn al-Athīr,10.219–20; 'Imād al-Dīn al-Iṣfahānī, 1.452; Sibṭ ibn al-Jawzī, *Mir'āt al-zamān fi tārīkh al-a'yān* (Hyderabad, 1951–52), 8, 1.420.

Khusraw I insisted that his former ally should suffer no physical harm.[17] In other words, the sultan, while hostile to the central government in Constantinople, acted as a protector of local Byzantine lords.

When his brother Rukn al-Dīn Süleymānshāh became master of almost the whole territory of the sultanate which Kılıç Arslān II had ruled, Kay-Khusraw I was forced to change his policy towards Byzantium. In 1195 he signed a peace treaty with Alexios III (1195–1203), who proclaimed him the 'friend' of the emperor. Despite the short conflict with Byzantium in the same year, Kay-Khusraw I required Byzantine support,[18] for Süleymānshāh claimed Konya. In an attempt to resist his brother, in the spring of 1196, Kay-Khusraw I signed a truce with the empire and visited Constantinople where he met Alexios III. He offered to the emperor the same relationship as had existed between Manuel I and Kılıç Arslān II. Alexios III refused: he did not want to come into conflict with the real master of the sultanate. The sultan returned to Konya, only to be deprived of all of his possessions by Süleymānshāh.[19] Kay-Khusraw I was forced to leave his capital in September 1196; his two sons, 'Izz al-Dīn Kay-Kāwūs and 'Alā' al-Dīn Kay-Qubād, both future sultans, followed him.[20]

On the Byzantine border, the people of Laodikeia refused to allow the ex-sultan to enter the territory of the empire, and he was forced to go eastward – to Laranda, then to Cilician Armenia, then to his uncle, Mughīth al-Dīn Toghrulshāh, in Ablistān. The sultan was unable to stay anywhere for long;

[17] Choniates, *Historia*, 400.74 – 401.18. Mankaphas rebelled during the reign of Isaac II Angelos, c. 1188. He secured the allegiance of the inhabitants of Philadelphia and its environs and took the imperial title. Isaac II besieged Mankaphas in Philadelphia in June 1189, but the advance of Frederick I Barbarossa forced a compromise; Mankaphas gave up his imperial title, but retained control over Philadelphia. Having been defeated by Basil Vatatzes in 1193, Mankaphas fled to Kay-Khusraw I. He restored his power over Lydia and Philadelphia by 1204: Choniates, *Historia*, 603; George Akropolites, *Opera*, ed. A. Heisenberg and P. Wirth, 2 vols (Stuttgart, 1978), 1.12.5–15 (vol. 1 is cited hereafter); J.-C. Cheynet, 'Philadelphie, un quart de siècle de dissidence', in H. Ahrweiler, ed., *Philadelphie et autres études* (Paris, 1984), 47–8; P. I. Zhavoronkov, 'U istokov obrazovania Nikeiskoi imperii (otsenka deyatel'nosti Konstantina XI Laskaria)', *VizVrem* 38 (1977), 34 note 41; C. M. Brand, 'Mankaphas, Theodore', *ODB*, 2.1286–7.

[18] Choniates, *Historia*, 493–6.

[19] Ibn Bibi, 7–8; Ibn Bibi (Duda), 21–2; Choniates, *Historia*, 521–2.

[20] The dates of Kay-Khusraw I's departure in Choniates, Ibn Bībī and Bar Hebraeus (either 1198 or 1200) are wrong: Choniates, *Historia*, 493.63–6; Ibn Bibi, 7–8; Ibn Bibi (Duda), 21–2; Bar 'Ebrāyā, *Ktābā d-maktbānut zabnē*, ed. P. Bedjan (Paris, 1890), 406. The coinage of the sultan Süleymānshāh in Konya starts in AH 593 (24 November 1196 – 12 November 1197). The *Tārīkh-i āl-i Saljūq* states that Rukn al-Dīn entered Konya on Tuesday, 7 Dhū al-Qa'da (the year is omitted). It is 7 Dhū al-Qa'da AH 592 (2 October 1196), which was a Tuesday. The next month, in November 1196, the new sultan struck his first coin in the capital: İ. Artuk and C. Artuk, *Istanbul Arkeoloji Müzeleri Teşhirdeki İslâmî sikkeler kataloğu*, 2 vols (Istanbul, 1970–74), 1.355, no. 1076; *Histoire des Seldjoucides*, 1952, 41 (Persian text), 27 (Turkish translation).

he was constrained to continue his travels to Malatya, then to Aleppo. The final stage of his route lay by way of Āmid to Akhlāt. None of the rulers wanted to support him. Finally, the sultan travelled to the Pontos; thence he sailed to Constantinople in 1200.[21]

Ibn Bībī describes the reception that Kay-Khusraw I received in Byzantium. The emperor (*fāsilīyūs*), he says, 'considered the previously [concluded] treaty with the sultan[22] as [his] great achievement. He preferred to share [the power] in his realm [with the sultan] rather than [to continue to reign] independently. And during the ceremonies [literally, assembly: *ijtimā`*] they were sitting together on the throne.'[23] The whole story that Ibn Bībī goes on to tell is a fantasy about the sultan's adventures in Byzantium that circulated at the Seljuk court. For example, Ibn Bībī reports a story of how at the highly sophisticated and ceremonial Byzantine court the sultan beat a certain Frankish warrior, with whom he had quarrelled. The text has all the features of an epic story:

> There was, however, a Frank, famous for his courage and skill in warfare, notorious for his bravery and valour who [once] alone set off against a thousand warriors and fought [them]. His yearly salary was 10,000 *dīnār*s. One day he quarrelled with the ministers of the *dīwān* about his payment. He then went to the emperor (*fāsilīyūs*) and made a lengthy complaint. The emperor said to the Frank: 'The sultan is here today. Cease for a while [explaining your] circumstances. Tomorrow the remedy [for your case] will be offered according to your wish'. The Frank took no notice and did not diminish his rigour and boldness. The sultan got into rage and asked the emperor (*taqfūr*): 'What is this lord (*amīr*) saying?' The emperor answered that the people of the *dīwān* had been indolent [in paying] the wages that were due to him. The sultan said: 'Then why should this servant be so arrogant?' The Frank said foolish words to the sultan. And the sultan became furious. Having wrapped his hand with a piece of fabric from his turban, he with one strike to the ear knocked the Frank, who lost consciousness, from his chair. This caused an uproar between the Franks and the Byzantines (*rūmīyān*); they attacked the sultan and [even] intended to kill him. The emperor struck them [like] a hawk with his beak;[24] he himself came down from his throne and suppressed the riot. He sent away all the people from the palace.[25]

---

21 Ibn Bibi, 7–13; Ibn Bibi (Duda), 21–7; Choniates, *Historia*, 522; Ibn al-Athīr, 10.220, 295.

22 Ibn Bībī means the truce and the consequent treaty which was signed between the sultan and the emperor in the spring of 1196.

23 Ibn Bibi, 14; Ibn Bibi (Duda), 27.

24 The full version of Ibn Bibi contains a clearer statement: 'The emperor ordered his guardians and retainers to strike them [as strongly as] a hawk [strikes] with his beak'.

25 Ibn Bibi, 14; Ibn Bibi (Duda), 27.

At the sultan's request, the emperor appointed a special ordeal by battle. When the sultan defeated the Frank in the jousting on a square in Constantinople,

> the cry of pleasure of the Muslims, the emperor (*fāsilīyūs*), the lords (*amīrs*), the nobles (*sarwarān*) and the merchants [from all over] the world who were present there would have penetrated the spheres [of the sky]. And the Franks were disappointed losers. They wanted to stir up a rebellion. The emperor ordered the army to repulse them; and in order to calm the stormy sea of the riot he punished some of them who were the most arrogant. And for pleasure he took the sultan into his own house (*khāne*) and gave him abundant gifts and countless riches: beautiful horses, golden brocade (*saqlātūnī*) garments,[26] Byzantine brocade [cloths] (*dībā*), purses full of golden coins, well built Cuman (*qifjāq*) slaves, virginal maidservants with blossoming cheeks, cloths and other things which befit any royal household ... That night until daybreak they occupied themselves with pleasures and delights and enjoyed lute and wine until the dawn. They mixed the wine arranged for the night (*ghabūq*) with [the drink] for the morning. When the sultan left for his dwelling and rested, the emperor ordered the treasurer to bring to the banquet chamber of the sultan's palace (*sharābkhāne-i sulṭān*) the collection of various banquet items which his ancestors had preserved and decorated with gold and jewelry: the gold and silver drinking vessels and goblets, filled with excellent wines, and fruits, and sweetmeats, as numerous as [the stars in] the Pleiades. And that day they remained there, neither living nor dead because of the [immense] pleasantries of the table [that they had eaten and drunk], so that they were spilling wine from their cups (literally, 'shedding the life-giving blood of their cups').[27]

At the end of the feast the emperor exclaimed in a drunken stupor (*pāyān-i mastī*):

> The love for Khusraw of Islam is so deeply rooted in my heart and soul that they can by no means be separated ... For a while, until the throat of malice and envy of the Franks is stamped on, the sultan prefers [to stay] with *malik* Mafruzūm (Maurozomes) who is one of the greatest *caesars* of Rūm [Byzantium]. Whatever happens in the circle of power, I will [always] be with his majesty [the sultan and] will cause no harm [to him]. And that person [i.e. Maurozomes] will keep with respect these conditions, whatever these be. 'Allah may bring about something new after it' (Koran 65.1).[28]

The first scene in the palace, so unconsciously reminiscent of other descriptions of meetings between the emperor and the 'arrogant' Franks,

---

26 Dihkhudā, *Lughat-nāme*, 14 vols (Tehran, 1993–94), 8.12063–4: *saqlātūnī* meant a type of silk cloth interwoven with gold threads, usually from Baghdād or Iṣfahān.

27 I translate the original, fuller version of Ibn Bībī's work: İbn-i Bībī (Lugal–Erzi), 82.

28 Ibn Bibi, 17; Ibn Bibi (Duda), 30–31.

in particular of the famous conversation between Alexios I and a Frankish nobleman in Anna Komnene,[29] was composed by a Muslim: the Frank was called *amīr*, the imperial chancery *dīwān*, and the Byzantine emperor *taqfūr*, the latter being the Persian adaptation of the Armenian title *t'agawor* ('king') of the king of Cilician Armenia, which the Muslim chroniclers often applied to Byzantine emperors.[30] The author probably knew Greek: the fifteenth-century Ottoman translation of the text of Ibn Bībī, which may have been based on the lost manuscripts, reproduced (in vernacular Greek) the emperor's oath given to the sultan during the conversation in the palace before the ordeal as *īstim bistim metā Khristū metā banāyā*, which meant εἰς τὴν πίστιν μετὰ Χριστοῦ μετὰ Παναγίας ('by [my] faith in Christ and the Virgin').[31] The simple, unadorned language of the main body of the story, which included the quarrel between the sultan and the Frank and their consequent battle, with the possible remnants of the Greek speech, suggests that Ibn Bībī might have not composed the core of the original text. For Ibn Bībī was an émigré – he was not a native of Rūm. He was born in the city of Rughad in Central Asia; his family left Balkh in 1220 and, after a slow journey away from the Mongol threat, came to Damascus in 1231 and then to Rūm in 1234.[32] He thus knew hardly any Greek.

But Ibn Bībī's insertions in the text are clearly visible. It was he who composed the introduction, in which he described the exiled sultan as a co-ruler of the emperor, when they sat together on the throne. For the full text makes plain that it was the emperor who sat alone on his high throne whilst the sultan was placed somewhere below. Likewise, Ibn Bībī seems to have embellished the description of the celebrations after the sultan's victory.

The whole story, though almost incredible, may have some points of contact with the real circumstances of the sultan while in Constantinople. What may these have been? According to Choniates, the reception of the sultan in Constantinople was cold: 'Among the Romans, he once again failed to obtain [any support] for his aim [to return to the throne] and was not accorded the least treatment befitting his noble birth'.[33] However, this was only at the beginning. Ibn al-Athīr states that the emperor supported Kay-Khusraw I with money or land, showed him great honour and married

[29] Anna Komnene, *Alexias*, ed. D. R. Reinsch and A. Kambylis (Berlin, 2001), 316–17; eadem, *The Alexiad*, tr. E. R. A. Sewter, Penguin Classics (London, 2003), 325–6.

[30] R. Shukurov, *Velikie Komniny i Vostok (1204–1461)* (St Petersburg, 2001), 49–50.

[31] İbn-i Bībī (Lugal–Erzi), 77.

[32] Ibn Bibi (Duda), 3–4; H. Duda, 'Ibn Bībī', in *The Encyclopaedia of Islam, New Edition*, 11 vols (Leiden, 1960–2002), 3.737–8.

[33] Choniates, *Historia*, 522.21–4.

him to the daughter 'of one of the great *patrikioi*'.[34] Choniates specifies that this *patrikios* was Manuel Maurozomes.[35]

Choniates also confirms that the marriage took place shortly before Kay-Khusraw I's return to Rūm (1205). Therefore the wedding must have taken place in 1203 or 1204. From this point of view, it is important to establish who was that nameless *fāsilīyūs* in Ibn Bībī. He could have been either Alexios III (who took flight from Constantinople on the night of 17/18 July 1203)[36] or Alexios IV (who reigned from 1 August 1203 until 27/28 January 1204).[37] However, the context of the story excludes the latter. The Muslim community attended the ordeal by battle between Kay-Khusraw I and the Frank,[38] which could hardly have taken place *after* the Crusaders' attack against the 'synagogue of Agarenes called Mitaton' and the consequent destruction of the Muslim quarter by fire on 19–22 August 1203.[39] Only after the fire did Alexios IV's policy turn anti-Latin;[40] and Kay-Khusraw I had left Constantinople by this time.[41] Therefore, the *fāsilīyūs*'s words about 'the throat of malice and envy of the Franks' that 'is stamped', were Alexios III's and reflected the time when he had just received news of the approach of the Crusaders to Constantinople (May–June 1203).

The dating sheds new light on the context of the whole story. It reveals the atmosphere of hate and despair, bravado and arrogance, 'a feast in time of plague' that dominated the imperial court at the beginning of summer 1203. The story in Ibn Bībī, in which the luxury of Byzantium was described for the last time before the sack of Constantinople by the Crusaders, may serve as a sardonic illustration to Choniates's portrait of Alexios III as a short-sighted ruler, not to say worse, who had nothing but twenty rotting and worm-eaten ships against the Crusaders' armada.[42]

The impact of the relations between Alexios III and the 'Franks' (including the Crusaders) on Byzantine history is well known; the impact of the personal relations between Alexios III and Kay-Khusraw I is less so. The sultan's mother was Christian, probably of Byzantine origin.[43] The *Tārīkh-i āl-i Saljūq* writes that Kay-Khusraw I was the son of 'the sister of the wife of

---

34 Ibn al-Athīr, 10.295.

35 Choniates, *Historia*, 626.47–52.

36 Choniates, *Historia*, 546–7.

37 Choniates, *Historia*, 563–4.

38 Ibn Bibi, 16; Ibn Bibi (Duda), 29–30.

39 Choniates, *Historia*, 553–5; D. Queller and T. Madden, *The Fourth Crusade. The Conquest of Constantinople*, 2nd edn (Philadelphia, 1997), 145–7.

40 Queller and Madden, *The Fourth Crusade*, 148–63.

41 Robert de Clari, *La Conquête de Constantinople*, ed. P. Noble (Edinburgh, 2005), LII.66–7.

42 Choniates, *Historia*, 541.43–50.

43 Choniates, *Historia*, 521.87–95.

the *takfūr* Kālūyān'.[44] The statement can be deciphered. Despite the name, we must exclude from the possible candidates Kaloyan, the tsar of Bulgaria in 1197–1207, who was sent to Constantinople by his brother Theodore-Peter (1186–96) as a hostage in 1188. Kaloyan managed to flee from the Byzantine capital to Bulgaria in 1196, to become tsar the following year. He never met Kay-Khusraw I in person. Kaloyan's wife was of Cuman origin; she was probably responsible for her husband's murder in 1207; and she later married Kaloyan's nephew Tsar Boril (1207–18). Her daughter Maria became wife of Henry of Flanders (1206–16), emperor of Constantinople, in 1213. But nothing is known about the sisters of Kaloyan's wife.[45] Moreover, Kaloyan, his wife and Kay-Khusraw I must have belonged to one and the same generation, born c. 1170–80. As the chronicle often reproduced Christian names incorrectly, the most likely candidate for the '*takfūr* Kālūyān of Isṭtūnbūl' (sic; from the Greek 'the emperor Kaloyan of Constantinople') was Alexios III Angelos, whilst his wife was Euphrosyne Kamaterissa Doukaina who belonged to the family of the Kamateroi.[46] The peculiar news about the sultan's 'mother' being from one of the noble Byzantine families can be understood with the help of Akropolites. He states that while in Constantinople, Ghiyāth al-Dīn Kay-Khusraw I was baptized and adopted as son by Alexios III. The sultan even used to name the empress Anna, daughter of Alexios III and wife of Theodore I Laskaris, as his sister.[47] According to Orthodox canon law, the ties between godparents and their godchild are the same as between natural ones. That is why the author of the *Tārīkh-i āl-i Saljūq*, who was Muslim, did not manage to understand the sophisticated relations between the sultan-in-exile and the Byzantine imperial family, with the empress's sister being the godmother or adoptive mother of Kay-Khusraw I. The sultan's godfather was the emperor himself.[48]

---

[44] *Histoire des Seldjoucides*, 1952, 41 (Persian text), 27 (Turkish translation).

[45] Choniates, *Historia*, 399.51–3, 472.13–33; Akropolites, 24.1–11; K. Barzos, *Ἡ Γενεαλογία τῶν Κομνηνῶν*, 2 vols (Thessalonike, 1984), 2.602; I. Bozhilov, *Familiata na Asenevtsi (1186–1460). Genealogia i prosopografia* (Sofia, 1985), 58, 74, 93–4; Georgii Akropolit, *Istoriia*, tr. P. I. Zhavoronkov (St Petersburg, 2005) 183 notes 213 & 220 and 186 notes 248–50.

[46] On this family, see Kazhdan, *Sotsial'niy sostav*, 171; M. Angold, 'The road to 1204: the Byzantine background to the Fourth Crusade', *JMedHist* 25 (1999), 269. Gregory Kamateros, the *logothetes* of the *sekreta*, married a certain Irene Doukaina, a kinswoman of the emperor Alexios I: Choniates, *Historia*, 9.16–22. Michael Choniates mentions a certain Basil Kamateros, the empress Euphrosyne's brother, at the Nicaean court in c. 1208: Michael Choniates, *Epistulae*, ed. F. Kolovou (Berlin, 2001), Epistle 129: 125*, 208.

[47] Akropolites, 14.10–23; see the chronological stemma in C. M. Brand, *Byzantium Confronts the West, 1180–1204* (Cambridge, MA, 1968), 278.

[48] On adoptive parents and baptismal sponsors, often closely associated with each other, see the series of articles by R. Macrides, 'The Byzantine godfather', *BMGS* 11 (1987), 139–62, esp. 149–51, reprinted in eadem, *Kinship and Justice in Byzantium, 11th–15th centuries* (London,

The only author who contradicts the statement in Akropolites is Robert de Clari. According to Robert, when the participants of the Fourth Crusade had established Isaac II and his son Alexios IV on the Byzantine throne (1 August 1203), the sultan of Konya came to the Crusaders' camp. He said:

> Lords, I would like to ask you for one favour … I have a younger brother[49] who has treacherously usurped from me my land and my lordship over Konya, where I was lord and of which I am the true heir. If you are willing to help me conquer my land and lordship, I will give you great wealth from my treasure and I will become a Christian as will all those who hold themselves bound to me …[50]

The Crusaders refused to support him: they were preoccupied with their affairs in Constantinople. But did Robert de Clari really contradict Akropolites? For the sultan who lived in the Muslim environment, or at least had Muslim retainers, in Constantinople, would have had every reason to conceal his recent baptism.[51]

If we accept Akropolites, Alexios III's baptism of the Muslim ruler brought about an innovation in the traditional Byzantine policy towards the Seljuks. The sultan became not only the 'son' of the emperor, as was his father Kılıç Arslān II during the reign of Manuel I (hence Kay-Khusraw I's enthronement beside Alexios III, as Kılıç Arslān II sat beside Manuel I in 1161/1162), but he also became the godson of the imperial family. Moreover, the sultan married a daughter of Manuel Komnenos Maurozomes who, like the Angeloi, belonged to the Komnenian elite.[52]

1999), no. 1; 'Kinship by arrangement: the case of adoption', *DOP* 44 (1990), 109–18, esp. 109–11, reprinted in eadem, *Kinship and Justice*, no. 2, and 'Substitute parents and their children in Byzantium', in M. Corbier, ed., *Adoption et fosterage* (Paris, 2000), 1–11, reprinted in eadem, *Kinship and Justice*, no. 3.

[49] This is a mistake; it was Kay-Khusraw I who was the youngest: Ibn Bibi, 3; Ibn Bibi (Duda), 17.

[50] Robert de Clari, LII.66–7.

[51] Alternatively, the sultan's promise to become Christian may have been an invention of Robert de Clari. I can point to a potentially similar case; according to Otto of St Blasien, after the battle of Myriokephalon in 1176 the victorious Kılıç Arslān II sent a letter to Frederick I Barbarossa (1155–90). In order to obtain a marriage alliance with the German emperor, he promised to convert to Christianity: Ottonis de Sancto Blasio, *Chronica*, ed. A. Hofmeister (Hanover, 1912), 37; Magdalino, *The Empire of Manuel I Komnenos*, 99–100. If not a diplomatic trick, Kılıç Arslān II's promise might have been an invention on the part of Otto of St Blasien who might have shared an apocalyptic Latin visualization of Islam subject to Christianity. The mass conversion of Muslims to the Christian faith was part of this vision. See P. Krey, 'Nicholas of Lyra and Paul of Burgos on Islam', in J. V. Tolan, ed., *Medieval Christian Perceptions of Islam* (New York, 1996), 158; see also idem, *Saracens: Islam in the medieval Christian imagination* (New York, 2002).

[52] The family of the Maurozomai came into prominence in the second half of the twelfth century. In 1168 Manuel I appointed Theodore Maurozomes as commander of the armada

Kay-Khusraw I remained loyal to Alexios III and his family until the end of his life. The consequence of Alexios III's act was crucial for the survival of the future Nicaean empire.

When the Crusaders arrived at Constantinople (23 June 1203), Kay-Khusraw I was still there, as we know that he helped Alexios III to flee the capital on the night of 17/18 July 1203.[53] He then moved to the castle of his father-in-law, Maurozomes, in the environs of Constantinople.[54] Meanwhile the sultan Süleymānshāh besieged and then killed his brother Mas'ūdshāh in Ankara on 25 June 1204, thus uniting all the lands of the sultanate. When Theodore Laskaris, who acted as a deputy-in-chief of his father-in-law, Alexios III,[55] established his power in Prousa, as well as in south Bithynia, Mysia and probably Smyrna (after April 1204),[56] Süleymānshāh concluded a peace treaty with him. Theodore agreed to pay a *kharāj* (tribute) for five years.[57] However, the sultan died on 6 July 1204,[58] leaving a weak heir, the young 'Izz al-Dīn Kılıç Arslān III. Theodore I, whom Ibn Bībī with respect called *qayṣara-i Rūm* ('the *caesar* [emperor] of the Romans'), recognized him.

Meanwhile, Kay-Khusraw I and Manuel Maurozomes made haste to Rūm. In Nicaea they were detained by Theodore I. He refused to allow Kay-Khusraw I to proceed because he had previously concluded a treaty with Kılıç Arslān III. Finally, Kay-Khusraw I agreed to cede Laodikeia and Chonai to Theodore I.[59] The treaties of Theodore with Süleymānshāh and Kılıç Arslān III gave him no advantage, save the safety of his eastern borders. What Theodore needed to win over his rivals was Seljuk military help.

Kay-Khusraw I promised to give him such help. The plan worked well. According to the *Tārīkh-i āl-i Saljūq*, the *dhīsbinī* (from the Greek *despoina*),

that had to sail against Damietta in Egypt. In 1176 Theodore commanded the left wing of the Byzantine army at the battle in Myriokephalon: Choniates, *Historia*, 160.37–44; 180.84–6.

53 Akropolites, 14.14–15.

54 Ibn al-Athīr, 10.295; according to Ibn Bībī, Kay-Khusraw I stayed in the *jazīra* (the island or the peninsula). Most likely, Maurozomes's castle was one of the aristocratic *villae* in the Kocaeli peninsula, on the road between Constantinople and Nikomedeia. Ibn Bibi, 17; Ibn Bibi (Duda), 31b; Robert de Clari, LII.64–7.

55 Villehardouin, *La Conquête de Constantinople*, ed. and tr. E. Faral (Paris, 1961), 2.122, N 313.

56 Akropolites, 10.26–11.1; Zhavoronkov, 'U istokov', 31–2.

57 Ibn Bibi, 19; Ibn Bibi (Duda), 32.

58 *Histoire des Seldjoucides*, 1952, 41 (Persian text), 27 (Turkish translation); Ibn al-Athīr, 10.292.

59 Ibn Bibi, 23–6; Ibn Bibi (Duda), 36–8. According to Zhavoronkov, it was Constantine Laskaris, brother of Theodore I, who was emperor in Nicaea in 1205: Zhavoronkov, 'U istokov', 30–33. I am not convinced, as the context of Ibn Bibi's story suggests Theodore I.

Kay-Khusraw I's maternal aunt, gave the sultan lots of money and troops.[60] This is a reflection, albeit a rather fantastic one, of the 'family' relationships that existed between Kay-Khusraw I and Theodore I Laskaris. The 'aunt' of the sultan should have been the empress Euphrosyne, wife of Alexios III, as her sister was Kay-Khusraw I's adoptive mother. However, at that moment Euphrosyne was not in Nicaea.[61] Thus, the *despoina* must have been the wife of Theodore Laskaris (and Kay-Khusraw I's adoptive sister), Anna, who might have participated in the negotiations, and whom the chronicler confused with her mother. According to Ibn Bībī, the sultan also left his two sons as hostages.[62] Such was the agreement on the remnants of the once-mighty Byzantine empire between these two outstanding statesmen. Both were friends from the time they met in Constantinople in the happier days before 1204;[63] and both now needed to create a polity of their own.

With the help of his supporters in Rūm, and with the sums that were given to him in Nicaea, Kay-Khusraw I returned to the throne in Rajab AH 601 (22 February – 23 March 1205).[64] Theodore Laskaris may have attended his coronation, as we know that he visited Rūm in February–March 1205.[65] The sultan gave him a military force, which helped Theodore to become popular among the Greeks,[66] to subdue his Greek rivals in Anatolia (Theodore Mankaphas, Sabas Asidenos and probably Nikephoros Kontostephanos),[67] and finally to reconquer some of the lands which had been earlier occupied by the Latins, and to compensate himself for the heavy losses after the battle at Adramyttion (19 March 1205).[68] The defeat of the Latin army in the battle at Adrianople in April 1205 also strengthened Theodore's position.

Thus, the sultan helped Laskaris at the most crucial moment of the foundation of the Nicaean empire. Theodore I was proclaimed (but not

---

60 *Histoire des Seldjoucides*, 1952, 41 (Persian text), 27 (Turkish translation).

61 Choniates, *Historia*, 612.41–5: she was with her husband in Halmyros.

62 Ibn Bibi, 26–7; Ibn Bibi (Duda), 38–9.

63 Akropolites, 11.3.

64 Ibn al-Athīr, 10.295–6; Ibn Bibi, 27; Ibn Bibi (Duda), 39; *Histoire des Seldjoucides*, 1952, 41 (Persian text), 27 (Turkish translation).

65 Niketas Choniates, *Orationes et Epistulae*, ed. J.-L. van Dieten (Berlin, 1972), 132.21–7; Akropolites, 11.2–4; Zhavoronkov, 'U istokov', 33.

66 Choniates, *Orationes*, 132.28–33.

67 Akropolites, 12.18–21; Choniates, *Orationes*, 134.28–9; see also Zhavoronkov's translation in *Vizantiiskiye Ocherki* (Moscow, 1991), 222 and note 36. On Sabas Asidenos, see A. Savvides, *Βυζαντινά στασιαστικά καί αὐτονομιστικά κινήματα στά Δωδεκάνησα καί στή Μικρά Ἀσία 1189–c.1240* (Athens, 1987), 246–51. On Manuel Maurozomes, see: Choniates, *Historia*, 626, 638; A. Kazhdan, 'Maurozomes', in *ODB*, 2.1319–21; Cheynet, *Pouvoir*, 469; Savvides, *Βυζαντινά κινήματα*, 231–45. On Nikephoros Kontostephanos, see Cheynet, *Pouvoir*, 155 note 221. Sabas Asidenos was ruler of Sampson whilst Nikephoros Kontostephanos had possessions near the River Maeander.

68 Akropolites, 11.19–12.3.

crowned) emperor in May–June 1205.[69] Apart from the Latins, he now faced only two rivals in Asia Minor: Manuel Maurozomes in the Upper Maeander, who with Kay-Khusraw I's help ruled over Laodikeia and Chonai, and David Grand Komnenos in Paphlagonia.

Manuel Maurozomes had disappeared from the political scene by 1207: he was defeated and imprisoned by Theodore I.[70] Maurozomes's possessions, Laodikeia and Chonai, which had been given to him according to the treaty between Theodore I and the sultan by March 1206,[71] finally became Seljuk in AH 603 (8 August 1206 – 27 July 1207).[72]

One should consider Nicaean–Seljuk relations in terms of 'family policy'. The daughter of Maurozomes was wife of Kay-Khusraw I and her brother was in the service of the sultan;[73] but the Nicaean empress Anna was daughter of Alexios III, to whom Kay-Khusraw I was indebted. Indeed, the story of Kay-Khusraw I suggests how successfully Byzantine diplomacy integrated the policies of adoption of the Muslim ruler. The sultan acted as a trustworthy vassal of the emperor. Alexios III succeeded where Manuel I failed.

But the 'family policy' showed a different aspect in 1210–11 when the emperor Alexios III Angelos left Epiros and arrived at Antalya (c. 1210).[74]

---

[69] Choniates, *Historia*, 626.47–52; Akropolites, 11.5–9, 12.17–21; Cheynet, *Pouvoir*, 143–4 note 204; N. Oikonomides, 'La décomposition de l'empire byzantin à la veille de 1204 et les origines de l'empire de Nicée: à propos de la *Partitio Romaniae*', in *XVe Congrès International d'Etudes Byzantines, Rapports et co-rapports. I/1* (Athens, 1976), reprinted in idem, *Byzantium from the Ninth Century to the Fourth Crusade: studies, texts, monuments* (Hampshire, 1992), no. 20: 3–28, esp. 22–8.However, Theodore I was crowned later, most likely on 18 April 1207, by the newly elected patriarch, Michael Autoreianos (1207–14): P. Gounaridis, ''Η χρονολογία τῆς ἀναγόρευσης καί τῆς στέψης τοῦ Θεοδώρου Α΄ τοῦ Λασκάρεως', *Symmeikta*, 6 (1985), 65–71; Akropolites, tr. Zhavoronkov, 166 note 95. Another date suggested for Theodore I's coronation is 1208: M. Angold, *The Fourth Crusade* (London, 2003), 215 note 20.

[70] Choniates, *Orationes*, 127.15–17. On Maurozomes's attacks against Theodore I's territory in 1205 and 1206, see: Choniates, *Historia*, 626.47–56, 72–5; *Orationes*, 136.33 – 137.13 (tr. Zhavoronkov, 224).

[71] Choniates, *Historia*, 638.62–9; Akropolites, 14.20–23; F. Dölger, *Regesten der Kaiserurkunden des oströmischen Reiches, 565–1453*, 5 vols (Munich, 1924–77), vol. 3, Teil (with assistance of P. Wirth): *Regesten von 1204-1282* (Munich, 1977), 1668b; Cheynet, *Pouvoir*, 469; Savvides, *Βυζαντινά κινήματα*, 231–45.

[72] *İstanbul'un fethinden önce yazılmış Tarihî Takvimler*, ed. O. Turan (Ankara, 1954), 76–7; *Histoire des Seldjoucides*, 1952, 42 (Persian text), 27 (Turkish translation).

[73] Ibn Bibi, 26; Ibn Bibi (Duda), 38.

[74] Alexios III was captured by Boniface of Monferrat when the latter was on his way from Corinth to Thessalonike in November 1204. Boniface sent the ex-emperor to Monferrat. Later Michael I of Epiros ransomed Alexios III: Choniates, *Historia*, 612, 620; Akropolites, 12–14; Nikephoros Gregoras, *Historia Byzantina*, ed. L. Schopen and I. Bekker, 3 vols (Bonn, 1829–55), 1.16; Villehardouin, 2.117–18, N 309; Anonymous of Gaeta, 'Qualiter caput beati Theodori martyris de Constantinopolitana urbe ad Caietam translatum est', in *Exuviae sacrae Constantinopolitanae*, ed. P. Riant, 3 vols (Paris, 1877–1904), 1.153–4; *Annales Ianuenses. Annali*

The sultan decided to restore his godfather to the throne and wrote a letter to Theodore I saying that 'he had illegally seized the power of another [person]'.[75] He even concluded an alliance with the Latin emperor Henry I (1206–16). The Seljuk army led by the sultan himself besieged the city of Antioch-on-Maeander. Alexios III was with Kay-Khusraw I.

Theodore I had no choice but to fight. In the battle at Antioch-on-Maeander that took place after 15 June 1211, probably on 17 June,[76] the Nicaean army was almost defeated, but Laskaris met the sultan in person on the battlefield. Akropolites wrote:

> [The sultan] hastened towards the emperor with all his speed, for he had confidence in his bodily superiority over him. They recognized each other. The sultan smote the emperor's head with his mace, and the emperor fell from his horse; for he was stunned by the blow … Now without his horse, but strengthened, so to speak, by the divine power, the emperor stood on his own feet and drew his sword from the sheath. When the sultan turned from him and contemptuously exclaimed: 'Take this man!', the emperor struck the back legs of the sultan's horse (he rode a giant mare). The sultan fell down as if from the tower, and suddenly his head was cut off …[77]

The death of Kay-Khusraw I sealed the fate of the battle: Theodore I was victorious.[78]

Such was the end of this remarkable sultan. What did he recall in his last moment? His father, whom he consoled when other sons rejected him? Two sons of his own? His Greek mother? His adoptive mother, the illustrious Byzantine princess? His friend Theodore Mankaphas and his father-in-law, Manuel Maurozomes, whom he had unwisely sacrificed for Theodore I, the husband of his adoptive sister? Or the high halls of stone in Constantinople in the merrier times in which, having forgotten the rules

---

genovesi di Caffaro e de' suoi continuatori, ed. L. T. Belgrano and C. Imperiale, 5 vols (Genoa, 1890, 1901; Rome, 1923, 1926, 1929), 2.95.

75 Akropolites, 15.6 – 7. Cf. Gregoras, 1.17.8–21.

76 Ibn Bibi, 39; Ibn Bibi (Duda), 50; Abū al-Fidā', *al-Mukhtaṣar fī akhbār al-bashar*, ed. M. Dayyub, 2 vols (Beirut, 1997), 2.206; G. Prinzing, 'Der Brief Kaisers Heinrichs von Konstantinopel vom 13. Januar 1212. Überlieferungsgeschichte, Neuedition und Kommentar', *Byzantion*, 43 (1973), 414.83–90; J. Longnon, 'La campagne de Henri Hainaut en Asie Mineure en 1211', *Bulletin de l'Académie royale de Belgique* 34, facs. 8–9, Bulletin de la classe des lettres et des sciences morales et politiques, 5e série (1948), 447–50; P. I. Zhavoronkov, 'Nikeisko-latinskiye i nikeisko-seljukskiye otnoshenia v 1211–1216', *VizVrem* 37 (1976), 48–50.

77 Akropolites, 16.26 – 17.12.

78 Akropolites, 15–17; Gregoras, 1.17–21; Choniates, *Orationes*, 170–71; Michael Choniates, *Epistulae*, Epistle 179: 284–6; Ibn Bibi, 36–9; Ibn Bibi (Duda), 47–50; Abū al-Fidā', 2.206. Though the sources vary in describing the circumstances, nevertheless all of them agree that Theodore I and Kay-Khusraw I had a personal encounter during the battle.

of Islam, he participated in feasts, drank wine and rubbed shoulders with Alexios III and his courtiers? No one knows.

Postscriptum

The elder son of Kay-Khusraw I, Sultan 'Izz al-Dīn Kay-Kāwūs I (1211–19), himself the former hostage at the Nicaean court in 1205, immediately signed 'the inviolable alliances' with the Nicaean emperor.[79] Theodore I gave him his father's body and sent rich gifts and 20,000 *dīnār*s to be distributed as alms at the funeral of Kay-Khusraw I.[80] Alexios III Angelos, who was taken captive, was stripped of his imperial robes of honour and blinded on the orders of both the senate and the army. He finished his days in the monastery of St Hyakinthos (*Koimesis*) in Nicaea.[81]

79 Akropolites, 17.16–18.

80 Ibn Bibi, 46–7; Ibn Bibi (Duda), 57–8.

81 Akropolites, 17.19–23; 278.4–12; R. Janin, *Les Eglises et les monastères des grands centres Byzantins (Bythinie, Hellespont, Latros, Galèsios, Trébizonde, Athènes, Thessalonique)* (Paris, 1975), 121–4.

13. Mealtime in monasteries: the culture of the Byzantine refectory

Alice-Mary Talbot

This study will outline some of the ritual practices associated with mealtime in monasteries, the dietary regulations that reflected the weekly and annual liturgical cycle, expectations of behaviour, and punishments for infractions of the rules. In short, I hope to describe what might be termed the 'culture of the refectory' in the Middle and Late Byzantine periods. I shall draw extensively on such sources as the monastic regulations now conveniently assembled and meticulously indexed in the five-volume *Byzantine Monastic Foundation Documents* recently published by Dumbarton Oaks, with the reminder that these are normative documents, and I shall also make use of saints' lives, penitentials, satirical essays and poetry.[1]

Together with attendance at the daily church offices, sharing a common meal in the refectory or *trapeza* was one of the defining characteristics of cenobitic monasticism, the essence of communal life in a monastery. As the fourteenth-century *typikon* for the monastery of St Demetrios-Kellibara in Constantinople exhorted:

> Let there be only one table, one sort of food, one sort of drink. Let there be one time to partake of them, not some at one time, others at another. No one should eat in a special place or be served special fare. This equality brings

[1] I should like to thank my colleagues Angela Hero, Svetlana Popović, Nikolaos Bakirtzis and Alexei Pentkovskii, who commented on an earlier draft of this article and made useful suggestions for its improvement. I should also note my debt to a recent article on a similar subject in Early Christian Egypt by B. Layton, 'Social structure and food consumption in an Early Christian monastery: the evidence of Shenute's *Canons* and the White Monastery Federation A.D. 385–465', *Le Muséon*, 115 (2002), 25–55. The most complete treatment of the subject of monastic dining of which I am aware is P. Koukoules, *Βυζαντινῶν βίος καὶ πολιτισμός*, vol. 6 (Athens, 1955), 82–7.

peace and calm of soul. This is the bond of love and unity in Christ. This is what indicates progress in community life.[2]

Typically the construction of the refectory went hand in hand with that of the *katholikon* at the time of a monastery's foundation;[3] moreover, it rivalled the church in terms of the size[4] and the importance of its architecture and decorative programme.

The architecture and decoration of refectories

Visitors to Constantinople marvelled at the dining halls of the large urban monasteries of the capital, with that of Stoudios being deemed the most wonderful by the mid-fourteenth-century Russian pilgrim Stephen of Novgorod.[5] The Castilian traveller Ruy Gonzalez de Clavijo, who visited in 1403, described as follows the *trapeza* of the Peribleptos monastery: ' ... a very large and lofty refectory, in the midst of which there was a table of white marble, very well made, being thirty-five *palmos* long, and the floor was of marble flags[tones]. At the end of this refectory were two small tables of white marble, and the ceiling was covered with mosaic work.'[6]

The typical Middle and Late Byzantine refectory resembled a basilical church (Figure 13.1); it tended to be an elongated, single-aisled rectangular hall with an apse (sometimes termed the abbot's apse) at one end, often to the east.[7] The difference was, of course, the substitution in the refectory of one or more dining tables for the altar table of the church sanctuary. Sometimes, as at Nea Mone on Chios and at the Zographou monastery on Mount Athos,[8] there was a single long stone or wooden table covered with marble slabs and flanked by benches, or, as at the Great Lavra, Chilandari

---

[2] Kellibara II, chap. 4, *BMFD* 4.1508. All citations of *typika* are taken for convenience from this collection of English translations.

[3] See, for example, *BMFD* 1.206 (Great Lavra), 3.1107 and 1130 (Machairas), 3.1178 (Skoteine [properly Boreine]), and 4.1579 (Menoikeion).

[4] Large refectories might measure as much as 25–29 m in length; see A. Orlandos, *Μοναστηριακὴ Ἀρχιτεκτονική* (Athens, 1958), 45.

[5] G. Majeska, *Russian Travelers to Constantinople in the Fourteenth and Fifteenth Centuries* (Washington, DC, 1984), 40.

[6] J. P. A. van der Vin, *Travellers to Greece and Constantinople: ancient monuments and old traditions in medieval travellers' tales*, vol. 2 (Leiden, 1980), 628; Clavijo gives a similar description of the refectory at the monastery of the Prodromos in Petra, including a white marble table 30 feet in length surrounded by wooden chairs and twenty-one benches: see L. Kehren, tr., *La Route de Samarkand au temps de Tamerlan: relation du voyage de l'ambassade de Castille à la cour de Timour Beg par Ruy González de Clavijo, 1403–1406* (Paris, 1990), 110.

[7] See Orlandos, *Μοναστηριακὴ Ἀρχιτεκτονική*, 43–60; S. Popović, 'The Trapeza in cenobitic monasteries: architectural and spiritual contexts', *DOP* 52 (1998), 292–6.

[8] See C. Bouras, *Nea Moni on Chios: history and architecture* (Athens, 1982), 170 and figs 151–2. At Chios the table was 15 m in length.

and Vatopedi, there were a number of smaller *sigma*-shaped marble tables.[9] At the Great Lavra, for example, Athanasios the Athonite built a refectory (*aristerion*) with twenty-one tables made out of white marble, each one accommodating twelve monks (Figure 13.2).[10]

This is not the place to discuss in any detail the decoration of monastic refectories, a topic studied many years ago by John Yiannias. In fact, very little remains of refectory decoration from the Byzantine period, and Yiannias's dissertation focused on the sixteenth-century fresco programme of the Great Lavra.[11] His analysis of surviving refectory iconography found substantial variations in theme, although there seems to have been a tendency to include figures of saints, episodes from the Life of Christ[12] and, of course, scenes connected with eating and drinking, such as the Hospitality of Abraham, the Wedding at Cana, the Multiplication of the Loaves and Fishes, and the Last Supper. This last scene often had pride of place in the abbot's apse, as at the Pantokrator, Xeropotamou, Philotheou and Esphigmenou monasteries on Mount Athos.[13] Clavijo reports that there was also a mosaic panel of the Last Supper at the refectory of the Stoudios monastery in Constantinople.[14] One intriguing bit of information from textual evidence is that when the fourteenth-century Constantinopolitan nunnery of Maroules was converted into a male monastery, the frescoes of female saints that adorned the refectory were replaced with images of male saints.[15]

---

9 See Orlandos, *Μοναστηριακὴ Ἀρχιτεκτονική*, 51–4; Popović, 'Trapeza', 293 and figs 18 and 19b.

10 *Vita* B of St Athanasios of Athos, ed. J. Noret, *Vitae duae antiquae sancti Athanasii Athonitae* (Turnhout, 1982), chap. 25.24–5; P. Mylonas, 'La trapéza de la Grand Laura au Mont Athos', *CahArch* 35 (1987), 143–57. At Stoudios the tables provided seating for nine monks each: Stoudios, chap. 28, *BMFD* 1.109.

11 See J. J. Yiannias, 'The wall paintings in the Trapeza of the Great Lavra on Mount Athos: a study in Eastern Orthodox refectory art', (unpublished PhD dissertation, University of Pittsburgh, PA, 1971; University Microfilms, Ann Arbor, MI, 1971), chap. 4. Regrettably this dissertation was never published as a book.

12 Clavijo states that at the Peribleptos refectory the walls were covered with mosaics, 'from the salutation of the blessed Virgin Mary by St Gabriel, to the birth of Jesus Christ our God, together with his journeys with his disciples, and all his blessed life, until he was crucified': van der Vin, *Travellers*, 2.628.

13 P. M. Mylonas, *Pictorial Dictionary of the Holy Mountain Athos. I. 1. Atlas of the Twenty Sovereign Monasteries*, fasc. 1 (Wasmuth, 2000), 130 (fig. 30), 132 (fig. 31), 148 (fig. 40), 175 (fig. 57).

14 Van der Vin, *Travellers*, 2.628–9.

15 F. Miklosich and J. Müller, *Acta et diplomata graeca medii aevi sacra et profana*, vol. 1 (Vienna, 1860), 222. Paul Stephenson has called my attention to an epigram in Venice, BNM MS 524, probably dating to the late twelfth century, that describes a portrait in the refectory of St Mokios of four imperial benefactors of the monastery, Basil II, Alexios I, John II and Manuel I; see R. Janin, *La Géographie ecclésiastique de l'empire byzantin, I: Le Siège de Constantinople et le*

As a number of scholars have noted, church and refectory were both part of the 'zone of worship' within a monastic enclosure and tended to be spatially related.[16] At the Great Lavra on Mount Athos, for example, the *trapeza* entrance faced the west door of the *katholikon*. This became the pattern for many Middle and Late Byzantine *koinobia* as at Hosios Meletios, Studenica and Mount Latros.[17] Elsewhere, as at Patmos, Brontochion (Mistra), Nea Mone (Chios) and Prodromos on Mount Menoikeion, the two entrances did not face each other, but were relatively close.[18] The reason for this spatial connection was the link between the completion of the monastic office in the *katholikon* and the procession to the refectory. The influential ninth-century Rule of Stoudios prescribed that after the conclusion of the liturgy the *semandron* would be struck three times, a signal for the monks to go directly from church to *trapeza*.[19] The eleventh-century *typikon* of Alexios Stoudites (1034–43) and the twelfth-century *typika* of the Pantokrator and Evergetis monasteries follow in this same tradition, giving more details: that the monks should wait in the narthex for the signal, and that the priest who has just celebrated the Eucharist leads the way to the refectory, followed by the superior and the rest of the monks, all chanting Psalm 144 (145), a psalm of praise that begins 'I will exalt thee, my God' and includes the verse 'Thou givest them their food in due season' (verse 15).[20]

Regulations about mealtimes and seating arrangements

The actual timing of the main meal of the day varied, however, according to the rule of the monastery, the day of the week, and whether it was a feast day or a fast day. The extreme complexity of the regulations precludes their detailed review here. Suffice it to say that the liturgy was generally celebrated at the third or sixth monastic hour,[21] so that the main meal was taken in late morning or at midday. During Lenten seasons, however, the main meal (ἄριστον) followed the ninth-hour office (*nones*), in late

---

patriarcat oecuménique, 3: Les Eglises et les monastères (Paris, 1969), 355–6; and S. Lambros, 'Ὁ Μαρκιανὸς κῶδιξ 524', *NHell* 8 (1911), 127–8, no. 111, with partial English translation by C. Mango, *The Art of the Byzantine Empire, 312–1453: sources and documents* (Englewood Cliffs, NJ, 1972), 226–7. The *vita* of Lazaros of Mount Galesion mentions a Deesis panel in the refectory of the Monastery of the Resurrection; see R. Greenfield, *The Life of Lazaros of Mt. Galesion: an eleventh-century pillar saint* (Washington, DC, 2000), chap. 173.

16 Orlandos, *Μοναστηριακὴ Ἀρχιτεκτονική*, 44–5; Yiannias, 'Trapeza', 8; Popović, 'Trapeza', 282.

17 Popović, 'Trapeza', 292–6 and figs 11, 17, 20b and 23a.

18 Popović, 'Trapeza', 293 and figs 20b and 22a.

19 Stoudios, chaps 27–8, *BMFD* 1.108–9.

20 A. Pentkovskii, *Tipikon patriarkha Aleksiia Studita v Vizantii i na Rusi* (Moscow, 2001), 89–90; Evergetis, chap. 9, *BMFD* 2.478; and Pantokrator, chap. 9, *BMFD* 2.743–4.

21 Stoudios, chap. 27, *BMFD* 1.108–9.

afternoon.[22] It should also be remembered that in many monasteries the liturgy was celebrated only four times a week, and not on a daily basis, so that the mealtime had to be adjusted accordingly.

The twelfth-century Pantokrator *typikon* contains the fullest description of the protocol to be followed once the monks entered the refectory, the *synaxis* of the *trapeza*. The superior sat down first at the head table, followed by the rest of the monks. When all the monks were seated, the priest pronounced a blessing, the refectorian called for silence, and the reading began.[23] A strict seating order, prescribed by the superior, obviously induced rivalry among the monks; many *typika* repeat the statement of the Evergetis *typikon* that it is inconceivable that monks should quarrel about seating arrangements.[24] The Evergetis rule also prescribed that any monk who complained about his seat should be moved to the lowest place,[25] while the Machairas *typikon* added that a monk who persisted in such behaviour should not be allowed to sit at all, but must remain standing and wait on tables.[26] At most monasteries the seating was based on hierarchical principles, with primacy given to the superior, steward and ecclesiarch, followed by the priests, according to their seniority, and then the deacons and ordinary monks. At the monastery of Areia, by contrast, young and old monks were mixed together, so that the older monks might monitor the behavior of their junior colleagues.[27] A sketch made by Vasilii Barskii (Figure 13.2), who visited the Great Lavra in 1744, shows the seating order in his day: 1) the abbot, 2) the former superiors, 3) the priests responsible for services on that particular day, 4) the chief monks and officials, and 5) the deacons.

The seating capacity of a large monastery like the Great Lavra could be as many as 250 monks, judging from the 21 tables accommodating 12 monks each, adding up to 252. Such a figure should not, however, necessarily be taken as an accurate indication of the number of monks in a monastery, since typically, if there were too many monks to fit in the refectory at one time, some would eat at a second sitting, joined by the servitors and those whose monastic duties prevented them from arriving in time for the first sitting. If monks assigned to the first sitting were late, they could eat at the second sitting if they had a good reason for their tardiness.[28] The tables

22 Evergetis, chap. 10, *BMFD* 2.482.

23 Pantokrator, chap. 9, *BMFD* 2.744.

24 Evergetis, chap. 9, *BMFD* 2.479.

25 Evergetis, chap. 9, *BMFD* 2.479.

26 Machairas, chap. 64, *BMFD* 3.1143; this was a modification of the Evergetis rule that ordered an incorrigible monk to be expelled from the monastery.

27 Areia, chap. [T]3, *BMFD* 3.965.

28 For example, Evergetis, chap. 9, *BMFD* 2.480; Pantokrator, chap. 9, *BMFD* 2.745. The *vita* of Lazaros of Mount Galesion states that at the monastery of the Resurrection three sittings were sometimes necessary; see Greenfield, *The Life of Lazaros*, chap. 109, p. 202.

were evidently set with plates and/or bowls, spoons and wine cups;[29] there is one slim piece of evidence that monks were expected to bring their own knives and napkins to the table.[30]

The monastic diet

Let us now turn to the actual food and drink of the monks and nuns. The types of food and beverages consumed in monasteries and the complex dietary regulations prescribed by various *typika* have recently been masterfully analyzed by John Thomas in an appendix to the *Byzantine Monastic Foundation Documents*.[31] Let me summarize his overall findings, with the reminder that *typika* differed widely in their rules about foods permitted on fast days, non–fast days and feast days. On non–fast days monks and nuns normally ate twice, a substantial meal of two or three cooked dishes at midday and a lighter snack in the evening. The staple foods were bread, consumed at every meal; wine, legumes, such as beans, lentils and chickpeas, served boiled or in a soup; and green vegetables, boiled with olive oil, vinegar or water. Sometimes on non–fast days (and almost always on feast days) extra dishes of eggs, cheese, fish and shellfish (including oysters, mussels and scallops) might be added. Meat was generally prohibited at all times.[32] The evening meal (δεῖπνον), following vespers, consisted of a cold supper, with bread, seasonal fruits and vegetables, occasional leftovers from lunch, and so-called 'dry foods'. The latter were not limited to dried fruits and nuts, as one might suppose, but included uncooked foods, such as olives and *almaia*, a pickled cabbage. More abundant and more varied food was provided on feast days, as well as on days of commemoration of the deaths of members of the founder's family. Frequently a donor to a monastery would offer money or precious liturgical objects in exchange for a service of commemoration on the anniversary of his or her death, with extra lighting of lamps and candles in the church, and special fare (for example, 'fish in liberal quantities') in the refectory to gladden the hearts of the monks or nuns who had just prayed

---

29 At Pantokrator at the end of the meal, spoons were collected in one basket, plates in another, for washing: Pantokrator, chap. 9, *BMFD* 2.745, as well as Stoudios, chap. 4, *BMFD* 1.109. The penitential of Theodore of Stoudios punishes a monk who takes away a wine cup from the refectory: *Poenae monasteriales*, no. A45, *PG* 99.1737.

30 See A. Failler, ed., *Georges Pachymérès. Relations historiques*, vol. 3 (Paris, 1999), 167.10–11, where Pachymeres says that some monks were criticized for having a well-worked knife or a bleached napkin, implying that they carried their own knife and napkin to meals with them.

31 *BMFD* 5.1696–1716.

32 Svetlana Popović has informed me (private communication of 28 December 2002) that archaeological excavations at Serbian monasteries have uncovered large deposits of animal bones, suggesting that this prohibition was not always observed.

for the soul of their benefactor.[33] We learn from the *typikon* of the Bebaia Elpis nunnery that three gold coins were to be spent on the feast of the *Koimesis* for 'more costly and plentiful [food] than usual', and two gold *nomismata* on the anniversaries of the foundress's parents.[34] A story from *vita* B of Athanasios of Athos describes the disruptions such alterations in the customary regimen might cause. On the feast day of St Athanasios of Alexandria, the monk in charge of the pantry had planned a special menu including honey-cakes (μελίπηκτα) and flat-cakes (πλακοῦντας), which he set out on the refectory table. Athanasios of Athos, the *hegoumenos*, was horrified at such delicacies and swept them off the table onto the floor. This led to an unseemly scene when some disappointed monks, no doubt novices, ended up scrambling on the floor trying to pick up the discarded treats.[35]

Lenten dietary regulations varied widely, but often involved eating only one meal a day, at a later hour than usual, and the prohibition of wine, olive oil, cheese, fish and eggs, especially on Wednesdays and Fridays; the regimen tended to be more liberal on weekends. The *typika* sometimes make dietary concessions if a major feast day falls during Lent, but not always.

The primary drink was wine, consumed in quite liberal quantities; at Stoudios, for example, the ration was three cups at the main meal and two or three in the evening, depending upon the liturgical season.[36] We must remember, however, that the wine was diluted with water that was usually heated.[37] The tenth-century *vita* of Patriarch Euthymios of Constantinople provides a detailed description of the monastic ritual of wine pouring, when it relates the unexpected visit of the emperor Leo VI to Euthymios's monastery at Psamathia. Upon a signal (in the Pantokrator *typikon* it is explicitly described as striking the table three times with a gavel),[38] the wine steward said, 'Bless, father', and each monk held out his cup. A measure of wine was poured into each cup. Then hot water was blessed and passed around, and each monk could mix it into the wine according to his taste. Upon tasting the wine, which came from the monastery's own vineyard, the emperor found it execrable, and promptly donated a piece of land to Psamathia, presumably to be used for higher-quality grapes.[39]

33 See, for example, chap. 71 of the Kecharitomene *typikon*, *BMFD* 2.700–702.

34 Bebaia Elpis, chaps 112 and 114, *BMFD* 4.1555.

35 *Vita* B of Athanasios of Athos, ed. Noret, *Vitae duae*, chap. 50, pp. 186–7.

36 Stoudios, chap. 29, *BMFD* 1.109–10.

37 The dilution might be considerable; the *typikon* for the Black Mountain, where wine drinking was discouraged except on Sundays, prescribed one part of wine diluted with twenty parts of water: chap. 38, *BMFD* 1.396. On the mixing with hot water, see, for example, Evergetis, chap. 9, *BMFD* 2.479.

38 Pantokrator, chap. 9, *BMFD* 2.744.

39 P. Karlin-Hayter, *Vita Euthymii Patriarchae CP* (Brussels, 1970), 53–5.

This description of the wine-pouring ceremony is corroborated by the twelfth-century Pantokrator *typikon*, which adds the detail that each monk makes the sign of the cross over his own wine cup before the hot water is added.[40]

A tradition of a series of five toasts at the beginning of a meal is recorded only in the twelfth-century *typikon* from the monastery of Kasoulon in southern Italy:

> We take our first drink to the glory of the … Trinity …; the second for the intercession and assistance of the all-pure Mother of God; the third for the intercession of the holy and God-inspired fathers and for the salvation and benediction of our most holy and spiritual father … and of our entire august community … The refectorian serves a fourth toast and we drink for the happy falling asleep and repose of our fathers and brothers who have departed before us … We drink the fifth toast after offering the *panagia* for the intercession and assistance of the all-pure Mother of God.[41]

Wine was often prohibited on fast days, but since it was viewed as a strengthening beverage exceptions were made for the sick, and for monks who were expected to chant during lengthy nocturnal vigils or to perform heavy labour. During Lenten periods wine might be replaced by hot water mixed variously with cumin,[42] fennel, honey or grape syrup. According to the *typikon* of Blemmydes, both the cumin and fennel drinks helped prevent bloating and flatulence, which must have been common problems for monastics whose diet was predominantly based on legumes. Blemmydes added that fennel helped to maintain alertness, substituting for the caffeinated drinks of today.[43]

It is thus clear that the refectorian (the *trapezarios* or *trapezites*, the official in charge of the refectory), the cook and the wine steward had to plan ahead carefully, making sure that seasons of fasting and special feast days were observed in the dining room as well as in church; they needed to prepare menus appropriate to the day, avoid foods forbidden on fast days, and coordinate meal service with the schedule of monastic offices.

---

[40] Pantokrator, chap. 9, *BMFD* 2.744.

[41] Kasoulon, chap. 14, *BMFD* 4.1327.

[42] The cumin drink (εὔκρατον) might also be flavoured with pepper and anise: Stoudios, chap. 30, *BMFD* 1.111.

[43] Blemmydes, chap. 11, *BMFD* 3.1204.

Inequalities in monastic food and drink

A common principle of *typika* is equality of food for all, in terms of number of dishes, quality and portion size.[44] As stated in the fourteenth-century *typikon* of Andronikos II for St Demetrios-Kellibara cited at the beginning of my paper, 'the same bread should be given to all the brothers to eat, whether you are talking of the superior, the steward, the ecclesiarch, or whether it be the shoemaker, the gatekeeper, the baker or whoever it may be.'[45] The same held true of wine: 'Neither shall good wine, full-bodied and with a nice bouquet, be given to this one to drink while that one is given the opposite, like vinegar, foul smelling and hostile to one's palate and one's stomach.'[46]

Other *typika* suggest that some monks and nuns claimed the right to a more luxurious diet 'because of pride in ancestry perhaps or advanced education or supposed superior virtue, or the privilege of age, or because of a contribution of money of [read: or] property.'[47] The *typikon* of Bebaia Elpis enjoins the nuns to maintain 'custody of the eyes', and not to look around the table to see if others were receiving larger portions or different food:

> No one at table will be allowed to raise her eyes and look at her neighbor to see how she eats the food set before her, and what has been served to her. Each nun should not only have eyes for herself alone, and focus her attention on the food set before her, but should concentrate ... on the sacred readings.[48]

In similar vein Theoleptos of Philadelphia instructed the nuns at the Philanthropos monastery to keep their gaze fixed on their own food:

> When you are at table, do not look around at the portions your sisters got, nor allow your mind to be divided by nasty suspicions. As you look upon and touch what is set before you, give food to your mouth, attentiveness to the readings to your ears and prayer to your soul ...[49]

---

44 For such rules, see Bebaia Elpis, chap. 83, *BMFD* 4.1517; Athanasios I, chap. 4, *BMFD* 4.1501; Pakourianos, chap. 4, *BMFD* 2.527.

45 Kellibara II, chap. 2, *BMFD* 4.1508.

46 Kellibara II, chap. 2, *BMFD* 4.1508. A similar injunction is made by Isaac Sevastokrator Komnenos in the Kosmosoteira *typikon*, where he forbids the serving of wine that has turned sour (ὀξώδης) because it can be harmful to the monks' health: Kosmosoteira, chap. 70, *BMFD* 2.832.

47 Lips, chap. 29, *BMFD* 3.1274.

48 Bebaia Elpis, chap. 86, *BMFD* 4.1548.

49 R. E. Sinkewicz, *Theoleptos of Philadelpheia. The Monastic Discourses* (Toronto, 1992), discourse 1, chap. 31, p. 107.

The constant reminders that the same food and drink were to be served to all monastics, no matter their rank, lead to the supposition that in fact there were disparities in the quality and amount of food and beverages provided at the refectory table. This suspicion is borne out by the testimony of the twelfth-century Ptochoprodromos's satire on monastic superiors.[50] This lengthy poem, ostensibly written by Hilarion Ptochoprodromos, a former monk of the Philotheou monastery in Constantinople, was addressed to the emperor Manuel I Komnenos as a complaint about the excessive privileges of the superior and high monastic officials in contrast to the discriminatory and abusive treatment of ordinary monks. A large part of the satire deals with inequalities in food and drink, so that the abbot and his cronies gorge on gourmet delicacies, while junior monks are subjected to an almost starvation diet of virtually inedible food and wine. Ptochoprodromos reports that monks of lower station are served tiny pieces of rotten tuna, unsalted soaked beans, dry bread, hot cumin drink or vinegary wine, and the dreaded ἁγιοζούμι, literally 'holy broth'. He describes this horrid concoction as being made from water, onions and olive oil, flavoured with savory (θρυμβόξυλον) and served in bowls containing small bits of bread.[51] Additional piquancy was provided by the verdigris from the copper cauldron that floated atop the broth with a greenish sheen.[52] Meanwhile the monks of higher station were feasting, even on fast days when fish was not permitted, on untold varieties of shellfish, including oysters, clams and scallops, crab, squid and lobster, as well as caviar, accompanied by honey-flavoured rice, apples, dates, figs, nuts and grapes from Chios, quinces and pomegranates.[53] On non–fast days the senior monks enjoyed multiple courses of various fish, including mullet, red snapper, striped bass and flounder cooked with exotic spices such as cloves, cinnamon, caraway and

50 *Ptochoprodromos. Einführung, kritische Ausgabe, deutsche Übersetzung, Glossar*, ed. H. Eideneier, Neograeca Medii Aevi 5 (Cologne, 1991), IV.139–75. The vocabulary of this poem is notoriously difficult, and the English translation promised by Margaret Alexiou is eagerly awaited.

51 For the recipe, see *Ptochoprodromos* IV.361–87, pp. 159–60. This soup was a prescribed staple food at Kosmosoteira on Monday, Wednesday and Friday: Kosmosoteira, chap. 63, *BMFD* 2.826 and note 33. *Lexikon zur byzantinischen Gräzität*, ed. E. Trapp (Vienna, 1994), s.v. identifies ϑρυμβόξυλον only as a 'Pflanze', but defines ϑρύμβος as spiced cabbage; E. Kriaras, however, defines it as equivalent to ϑύμβρον or ϑύμβρα (see LSJ, s.v.); see also his Λεξικό τῆς μεσαιωνικῆς ἑλληνικῆς δημώδους γραμματείας, vol. 7 (Thessalonike, 1980), s.v. I thank Angela Hero for this reference. Another recipe for this soup is found in the *vita* of St Cyril Phileotes, singling out onions and herbs as the principal ingredients: E. Sargologos, *La Vie de saint Cyrille le Philéote, moine byzantin (†1110)* (Brussels, 1964), chap. 40.6, pp. 190–91. Cyril does not find the concoction sufficiently ascetic and calls it γαστριμαργοζώμιον!

52 *Ptochoprodromos* IV.387.

53 *Ptochoprodromos* IV.319–30.

saffron.[54] A particular treat was the casserole that included the following ingredients: cabbage, moray eel, swordfish, carp, small dried mackerel, fourteen eggs, Cretan and Vlach cheese, twelve heads of garlic and fifteen onions.[55] These succulent dishes were washed down with the finest wines from Mount Ganos, Crete, Samos and Chios,[56] while the junior monks had to be satisfied with sour and vinegary wine from Varna or large quantities of cumin drink that caused Ptochoprodromos to be afflicted with dropsy![57] The bread differed as well, the top-quality variety made from fine wheat flour, served hot and sprinkled with sesame seeds, while the other was coarse brown bread with an outer coating of ashes from the oven.[58]

Though no doubt exaggerated, this account of the abundant and tasty food to be found in at least some monasteries is borne out by Eustathios of Thessalonike's famous tale about the wedding banquet hosted by Manuel I Komnenos. The story goes that late one night the emperor decided on the spur of the moment to organize a wedding feast, but since it was Cheese-Eating Week his servants could not find appropriate foodstuffs in the Blachernai Palace on short notice. Manuel suggested that they go to the nearby monastery of St John Prodromos in Petra, where indeed they were able to obtain delicacies suitable for serving at the palace: breads of various kinds, a pure white loaf, spongy and light as foam; another well kneaded and solid; barley-cakes; sweet and dry wines; abundant cheese; dried and salted fish; red and black caviar imported from Tanais on the Sea of Azov. The imperial emissaries took so much from the monastic storerooms that it took several donkeys to carry the foodstuffs back to the palace.[59]

Readings in the refectory

The rule of silence was universal in monastic refectories; virtually every *typikon* enjoins the monks and nuns to remain silent during meals so that they could concentrate on the sacred readings that were an essential element of refectory ritual.[60] As stated in a fourteenth-century rule, 'reading aloud from sacred books ... provides nourishment for the soul as the food before

54 *Ptochoprodromos* IV.172–88.

55 *Ptochoprodromos* IV.201–16.

56 *Ptochoprodromos* IV.298, 332, 395.

57 Wine from Varna: *Ptochoprodromos* IV.396; sour wine: IV.299, 349; cumin drink: IV.337; dropsy: IV.617.

58 *Ptochoprodromos* IV.399–401. See also the Pantokrator *typikon* which prescribed a special bread for the superior made from the fine wheat used for liturgical offerings: Pantokrator, chap. 8, *BMFD* 2.742.

59 Eustathios of Thessalonike, *De emendanda vita monachica*, ed. T. L. G. Tafel, *Eustathii metropolitae Thessalonicensis opuscula* (Amsterdam, 1964), 230–31.

60 See, for example, Lips, chap. 29, *BMFD* 3.1274; Athanasios I, chap. 4, *BMFD* 4.1501; Bebaia Elpis, chap. 86, *BMFD* 4.1548; and Menoikeion, chap. 8, *BMFD* 4.1597.

you does for the body'.[61] Or, in the memorable words of the Charsianeites rule, 'A refectory without the word of God is like a stable for animals.'[62] The *typikon* for Mount Auxentios likened the sacred readings to a 'full-course spiritual banquet'.[63] The readings typically began after the monks were seated, and were selected from scripture and monastic classics such as the *Ascetical Treatises* of Basil the Great, *Gerontika*, the works of John Klimax or Theodore of Stoudios, and the lives of saints.[64] In cases where the founder of the monastery had become a saint, his *vita* would be read on the holy man's feast day.[65] Another common text was the *typikon* of the monastery, read aloud to the monastic community anywhere from once a month to three times a year.[66] When the *typikon* or other text was lengthy, it would be divided up and read out over a period of days. It was also common for a lengthy reading to be started in church and completed in the refectory.[67] Practice varied as to which monk or nun was responsible for the reading; at Prodromos on Mount Menoikeion the precentor (*kanonarches*) was charged with this task, while elsewhere texts refer to the monk or nun who is 'appointed to read' or the 'reader' (*anagnostes*).[68]

---

[61] Kellibara II, chap. 4, *BMFD* 4.1508; the same sentence is repeated in Bebaia Elpis, chap. 85, *BMFD* 4.1548. A similar expression is found in *Syméon le nouveau théologien. Catéchèses*, ed. B. Krivochéine, vol. 3 (Paris, 1965), 80–82.

[62] Charsianeites, chap. [C]10, *BMFD* 4.1658. The source of this quotation has not been identified. For a parallel sentiment, see the *typikon* of Alexios Stoudites, ed. Pentkovskii, *Tipikon patriarkha Aleksii Studita*, 372.

[63] Auxentios, chap. 10, *BMFD* 3.1227.

[64] The rule for the Great Lavra (Athonite Rule, chap. 21, *BMFD* 1.225) states that the *ekklesiarches* was responsible for choosing the reading material, while at Lips it was the *ekklesiarchissa*: Lips, chap. 29, *BMFD* 3.1274.

[65] See, for example, appendix C to Yiannias, 'Trapeza', 301–2, where a liturgical *typikon* for the Great Lavra specifies that selections from the *vita* of Athanasios of Athos are to be read on 5 July. Readings from the *vitae* and *martyria* of other saints are also prescribed for their feast days. The monastic discourses of Theoleptos of Philadelphia, originally delivered as homilies in a liturgical context, were no doubt read aloud to the monks and nuns of the Philanthropos monastery as they ate in their separate refectories. The Evergetis *Synaxarion* prescribes that the *vita* of Theodore of Stoudios would sometimes be read in the refectory instead of the *Paterikon* (a book containing tales and sayings of various fathers): see R. Jordan, *The Synaxarion of the Monastery of the Theotokos Evergetis* (Belfast, 2000), 189.

[66] For monthly readings, see, for example, Evergetis, chap. 43, *BMFD* 2.498; Kosmosoteira, chap. 59, *BMFD* 2.825; Phoberos, chap. 8, *BMFD* 3.946; Bebaia Elpis, chap. 120, *BMFD* 4.1556 ('more than any other book'); for every two months, see Heliou Bomon, chap. 16, *BMFD* 3.1062; and for three times a year, see Menoikeion, chap. 9, *BMFD* 4.1599.

[67] See, for example, the rule of Athanasios of Athos, Athonite Rule, chap. 21, *BMFD* 1.225, which specifies that the *ekklesiarches* was responsible for this division of the reading.

[68] See, for example, Pantokrator, chap. 9, *BMFD* 2.744; Lips, chap. 29, *BMFD* 3.1274; *vita* B of Athanasios of Athos, ed. Noret, *Vitae duae*, chap. 29.19, p. 118.

The refectory as a place of punishment

A medieval visitor to a Byzantine *trapeza* might observe some monks or nuns being singled out for punishment. One monk might be doing the equivalent of one hundred pushups, another standing next to the abbot holding fragments of a broken ceramic vessel, and another might be eating only olives and nuts, while his tablemates were feasting on lentil soup and boiled greens seasoned with olive oil. The refectory, as a communal gathering place for monks and nuns, was deemed an appropriate location for public penance, particularly for misbehavior and infractions of the rule related to preparation of food and refectory discipline. A particularly useful source of information in this regard is the penitential of Theodore of Stoudios. He prescribes, for example, a series of 20 to 300 penitential prostrations (*metanoiai*) for various lapses of the cooks, such as failure to add oil and salt to food at the proper time while cooking, allowing broth to boil over, spilling wine or oil or vinegar, permitting food to spoil, or leaving a pot uncovered for a long time.[69] Breaking a clay pot was viewed as a serious act of carelessness and might be punished by making the monk perform up to 300 *metanoiai* (the number probably depending upon the size of the pot) or stand at the front of the refectory holding the pieces of the pot in his hands, until he received the forgiveness of his brethren.[70] A slight variant of this punishment is found in the eleventh-century *vita* of St Neilos of Rossano. After a young monk broke a pot by overfilling it with legumes and boiling them too vigorously, he had to tie the potsherds together with a string and wear them around his neck like a necklace while standing in the refectory.[71] Misbehaviour while eating might also be punished by a prescribed number of *metanoiai*, or by deprivation of certain foods or an entire meal. Examples of infractions of refectory discipline were conversing or laughing during a meal (one hundred *metanoiai*), missing a meal altogether (standing penance in the refectory, or eating of dry foods or fasting until the following day), idle or loose talk (deprivation of wine for one day and forty *metanoiai*), and

[69] See Theodore of Stoudios, *Poenae monasteriales*, nos A36–9, 41–5; *PG* 99.1737–40. These particular penitential regulations do not specify that the prostrations are to be performed in the refectory, but others (nos A2, 8, B29, 55) do, and this practice is confirmed by the evidence of the rule of Stoudios and *vita* B of Athanasios (see next footnote).

[70] *Poenae monasteriales*, nos A40 and 46; *PG* 99.1737 and 1740; Stoudios, chap. 35, *BMFD* 1.113AB, adds the detail that the careless monk had to stand next to the abbot with his cowl covering his head, while *vita* B of Athanasios of Athos says he had to stand next to the reader (Noret, *Vitae duae*, chap. 29, p. 118).

[71] Cf. G. Giovanelli, *Βίος καὶ πολιτεία τοῦ ὁσίου πατρὸς ἡμῶν Νείλου τοῦ Νέου* (Grottaferrata, 1972), chap. 28, p. 75.

getting up from the table before dismissal (no wine for three days and one hundred *metanoiai*).[72]

Outside visitors to the refectory

Regulations for visitors to the refectory had to draw a fine line between the monastic tradition of hospitality and protection of the monks from visitors who might prove to be a distraction from the expected *taxis* of the refectory. Arrangements were made for most visitors to eat in a designated location separate from the monks or nuns; meals were typically served in the guesthouse to pilgrims, imperial officials and relatives. At the convent of Lips the male steward (*oikonomos*) ate in the hospice,[73] and at St Lazaros's various monasteries on Mount Galesion pilgrims and lay brothers were routinely directed to a guesthouse for their meals, while visiting monks ate in the refectory.[74] Nonetheless some lay visitors were accommodated in the refectory, especially if they were noble benefactors; sometimes these guests brought special treats with them, such as enough fish to feed all the monks.[75]

Concluding ceremonial

When the monks finished eating, the spiritual reading was concluded and the monks helped to clear the table by placing their dirty plates and spoons in the baskets provided; baskets were also used to collect any leftover bread that would be distributed to beggars at the monastery gate. The conclusion of the meal was marked with singing of hymns and prayers and the blessing of the superior. Then the priest recited two psalms, pronounced a thanksgiving and a prayer, and dismissed the monks.[76] The Pantokrator *typikon* also describes the ritual of the 'elevation of the Panagia', as follows:

> The revered name of the Mother of God should be set as a seal to mark the end of all meals of the monks, both the midday meal and supper, and with this invocation the refectorian at the bidding of the superior should take a piece of bread of reasonable size, bless it with the sign of the cross, and then all the monks taking a portion of it should also drink a final drink [of wine] in the name of the Mother of God, so that they may be sanctified both in their souls

[72] See Theodore of Stoudios, *Poenae monasteriales*, nos B29, A12, B37, B36; *PG* 99.1735 and 1753.

[73] Lips, chap. 26, *BMFD* 3.1273.

[74] Greenfield, *The Life of Lazaros*, chap. 150, p. 238 and note 577; chap. 211, p. 306.

[75] See, for example, Pakourianos, chap. 8, *BMFD* 2.534, and Evergetis, chap. 10, *BMFD* 2.481.

[76] See Pantokrator, chap. 9, *BMFD* 2.745, for the most complete description of this closing ritual.

> and bodies through the invocation of her divine name and by what is eaten and drunk in its honor.[77]

Depending on the monastery and the season of the liturgical year, the monks were then dismissed either to their cells, or to return to the narthex of the church for a service of thanksgiving.[78]

This closing ritual of the Panagia emphasizes once more the close connection between church and refectory, with the *trapeza* serving as a 'functional extension of the church', in the words of John Yiannias.[79] The partaking of bread and wine in the name of the Theotokos is the counterpart of the Eucharist previously celebrated in the *katholikon*[80] and provides a fitting conclusion to the meal, which has satisfied the bodily needs of monastics, while the readings and prayers have sated their spiritual hunger.

---

[77] Pantokrator, chap. 12, *BMFD* 2.747.

[78] According to the *typikon* of Alexios Stoudites, ed. Pentkovskii, *Tipikon patriarkha Aleksii Studita*, 93, the priest stood before the Royal Doors in the narthex to make a prayer of thanksgiving, and then dismissed the monks.

[79] Yiannias, 'Trapeza', 261.

[80] For more extended discussion of the elevation of the Panagia, see J. J. Yiannias, 'The elevation of the Panaghia', *DOP* 26 (1972), 227–36.

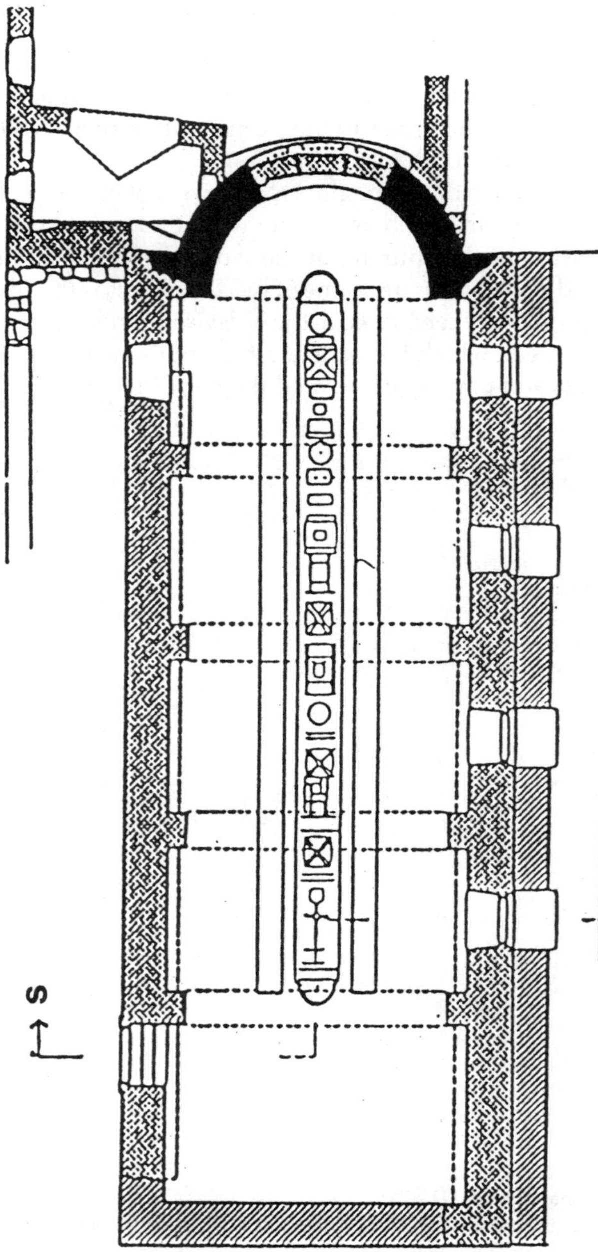

Figure 13.1: Plan of refectory of Nea Mone, Chios (After S. Popović, 'The trapeza in cenobitic monasteries: architectural and spiritual contexts', *DOP* 52 [1998], fig. 19b).

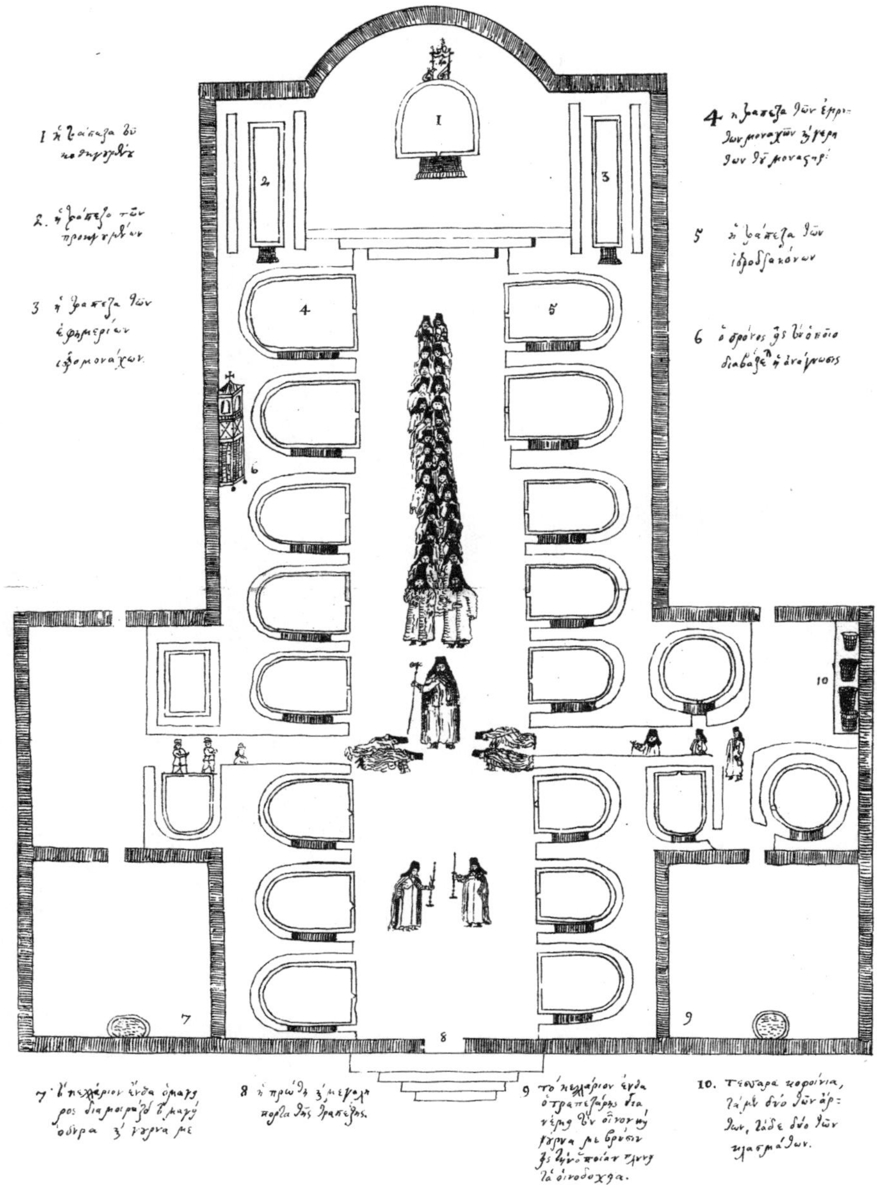

Figure 13.2: Sketch by V. Barskii of refectory of Great Lavra, Mount Athos (After V. Grigorovich-Barskii, *Vtoroe poseshchenie sviatoi Afonskoi gory Vasiliia Grigorivicha-Barskago* [St Petersburg, 1887], inserted between pp. 76 and 77).

14. From 'glittering sideboard' to table: silver in the well-appointed *triclinium*

Marlia Mundell Mango

In the mid-sixth century, John Lydos criticized the frivolous conduct of his detested civil-service boss, John the Cappadocian, saying: '... he dined on everything that flew in the air and swam in the sea accompanied by various wines ... the needs of his table exhausted the Bosporos and the Hellespont. His purveyors had to ransack the Black Sea for fish and fowl.'[1] Legal texts, inventories, anecdotal accounts, contemporary representations and extant plate provide a good idea of the pretentious silver available to enhance such occasions. Even Attila the Hun's symposium given for Priskos, envoy of Theodosios II, featured wine waiters and silver platters.[2] Sidonius Apollinaris refers repeatedly to 'glittering sideboards' loaded with silver for display. But such silver was put to use: he also refers to 'silver set by panting attendants on sagging tables' and 'heads bent by chased metal on laden shoulders'.[3] In the sixth century, Severos of Antioch refers to 'meals [taken] from silver plates carried by numerous servants'.[4] Justinian's *Digest* contains forty legal opinions from Roman law of the first to the third centuries, still relevant in the sixth, which concerned legacies of gold and silver. The opinions attempt to distinguish between types of *vasa argentea*,[5] notably *argentum escarium* and *argentum potorium* – that is, silver for eating and drinking. Numbers, weights and/or names of silver vessels are provided by three inventories or lists from

---

1 John Lydos, *De magistratibus* 3.62, ed. R. Wünsch (Leipzig, 1903).

2 R. C. Blockley, *The Fragmentary Classicising Historians of the Later Roman Empire: Eunapius, Olympiodorus, Priscus, and Malchus* (Liverpool, 1983), 2.267, 285.

3 W. B. Anderson, ed. and tr., *The Poems and Letters of Gaius Sollius Apollinaris Sidonarius* (London, 1980–84), *Carmina* 1.2.6; *Epistulae* 1.2, 2.2, 8.7, 9.13.

4 I. Guidi, ed. and tr., 'Les homiliae cathédrales de Sévère d'Antioche', *PO* 22 (Paris, 1930), 247.

5 *Digest* 34.2.19, *Corpus Iuris Civilis*, ed. T. Mommsen, P. Krueger et al., vol. 1 (Berlin, 1928–9); see also A. Watson, tr., *The Digest of Justinian*, 4 vols (Philadelphia, PA, 1985), 3.151–3.

Egypt (first century BC), Edessa in Mesopotamia (591–628) and Auxerre in Gaul (603–621/3), written in Greek, Syriac and Latin, respectively.[6]

The Sevso treasure

The Sevso treasure offers excellent preserved examples of individual items used at table for eating, drinking and hand-washing.[7] Their lavish decoration and large scale imply display. These objects were made to impress. Their decoration is assertive, calculated to increase the visual impact of the metal. Furthermore, at over half a metre high (0.528–0.573 m), three of the ewers are, with one exception, the largest Roman ewers ever found; at 0.642–0.72 m, the four plates (Figure 14.2a–d) are among the widest and one is the second heaviest (nearly 36 Roman lb, or 11,788 g) extant, causing, no doubt, attendants to pant.[8] However, the strategic location of ancient wear and repairs document their utilitarian use in the past, as will be described.[9] Seven of the treasure's fourteen objects can be identified as used at table, in the same way as illustrated by the third-century mosaic in the House of the Buffet Supper at Antioch (Figure 14.1) where silver dishes hold an entire meal from a starting course (*gustatio*) of artichokes, eggs and pigs' trotters, followed by the main meal (*cena*) of fish, then a ham hock and poultry, eventually ending with the *secunda mensa* and the dessert (*belloria*) – a cake.[10]

The other seven silver objects of the Sevso treasure were used elsewhere in the household and bath: two matching ewers and basin, a matching ewer and two situlas, and a casket.[11] The large copper cauldron (diameter 0.83 m)

6 EGYPT: A. Oliver and J. Shelton, 'Silver on papyrus', *Archaeology*, 32 (1979), 21–8; EDESSA: *Anonymi auctori chronicon ad A.C.1234 pertinens*, ed. J.-B. Chabot, CSCO 82, *Scriptores Syri* 37 (Paris, 1917), 222; tr. A. Abouna, CSCO 354, *Scriptores Syri* 154 (Louvain, 1974), 174–5; *Michel le Syrien, Chronique*, ed. and tr. J.-B. Chabot (1899–1905), 2.380 (translation), 390 (text); AUXERRE: J. Adhémar, 'Le trésor d'argenterie donné par Saint Didier aux églises d'Auxerre (VIIe siècle)', *RA*, series 6, 4 (1934), 44–54.

7 M. Mundell Mango and A. Bennett, *The Sevso Treasure*, vol. 1 (Ann Arbor, MI, 1994), 13. M. Mundell Mango, *The Sevso Treasure*, vol. 2 (in press) includes a chapter of the function of the individual objects.

8 Mundell Mango and Bennett, *Sevso*, 46–9.

9 See Bennett in Mundell Mango and Bennett, *Sevso*, 27–8 with comments below in note 13 regarding scratches and wear on the four plates. The size and elaborate decoration of these objects have led some scholars to conclude that they were not intended for use. So A. Kuttner in a recent lecture, 'Bringing splendour to the table: the archaeology of servitude on display in late antiquity'. I thank Fiona Greenland for bringing this paper to my attention and providing this reference. R. E. Leader-Newby, *Silver and Society in Late Antiquity: functions and meanings of silver plate in the fourth to seventh centuries* (Aldershot, 2004) examines the iconographic, rather than practical, function of domestic silver within contemporary visual culture. On recent studies, which consider the practicalities of dining, see note 21.

10 D. Levi, *Antioch Mosaic Pavements* (Princeton, NJ, 1957), 132–6.

11 Mundell Mango and Bennett, *Sevso*, 13, 319–473.

in which the objects were ultimately stored was undoubtedly used in the kitchen (see below). In the case of the silver, shape and decoration indicate function.

The silver for eating, namely, the four plates,[12] all have a network of scratches on their surfaces and are worn on their rims.[13] Among other themes, the narrative decoration of three of the plates illustrates and alludes to eating and drinking; that is, the procurement of game (boar, venison) and fish in the case of the Hunting (Figure 14.3) and Meleager (Figure 14.4) plates,[14] and the celebration of olive oil and wine on the Achilles plate (Figure 14.5).[15] The four treasure plates represent two types of serving plate specified by Apicius's cookery book of which the final compilation is contemporary (fourth–fifth century)[16] with the Sevso silver. Three of the plates (the Meleager, Achilles and Geometric plates), being concave, may be described as *lances* (Figure 14.2a–c),[17] the type used for sauced meat such as ostrich, other fowl, whole suckling pig, hare and fish.[18] The inlaid and raised decoration of these silver plates may have precluded direct contact with sauces which may have been served separately in bowls set on the plates as in the Antioch mosaic (Figure 14.1). The Hunting plate may be described as a flat *discus* (Figure 14.2d) a type which, according to Apicius, was used for drier food such as sausages, moulded foods, soufflés, roast lamb or peppered hare.[19]

The large size of three of the plates points to another possibility, namely that they were also used as tabletops (Figure 14.6d).[20] The increase in size and weight of silver plates during late antiquity may correspond to changes in configuration of couch and table. In the *triclinium*, three couches arranged at right angles and served by small plates on three tripods, gave way to the *sigma*-shaped bolster, the *stibadium* with a 'built-in' communal round or *sigma*

12 Ibid., 55–193.

13 Ibid., 27–8, 72–3, 110–11, 159–60, 186–7. Although the Meleager and Geometric plates are described on p. 27 as in 'almost mint condition' because little or not repaired in antiquity, all four plates are covered in scratches; see ibid., figs 1–4, 1–8 through 14, 1–18 through 21, 2–3, 2–14, 2–74 and 75, 3–1, 3–4 and 5, 4–3, 4–9, 4–13 and 4–19.

14 Ibid., 81–96, 121–47. Not all animals hunted are for food; see also Mundell Mango, *Sevso*, vol. 2.

15 Mundell Mango and Bennett, *Sevso*, 170–78; for interpretation, see Mundell Mango, *Sevso*, vol. 2.

16 B. Flower and E. Rosenbaum, *The Roman Cookery Book: a critical translation of the Art of Cookery by Apicius* (London, 1958), 12–13.

17 *Lanx* is the term now often applied to an oblong dish. More correctly, the term refers to its concave shape in section rather than in plan. When oblong, the *lanx* is specifically qualified as *quadrata* (*Digest* 34.2.19.4). On the latter, see M. Mundell Mango in D. Buckton, ed., *Byzantium. Treasures of Byzantine Art and Culture from British Collections* (London, 1994), no. 15.

18 Flower and Rosenbaum, *Apicius*, 4.5.1; 6.1.1, 2.1, 9.11–12; 8.7.16; 10.3.2.

19 Ibid., 4.2.16; 7.13.8; 8.6.9–10; 8.12.

20 See Mundell Mango, *Sevso*, vol. 2.

marble table (Figure 14.6a–c). This development is amply illustrated in Dido's banquet in the Roman Vergil, (Vatican, BAV MS lat. 3867, fol. 100v), Pharoah's banquet in the Vienna Genesis (Vienna, ON MS theol. gr. 31), in illustrations of picnics (in the Ambrosiana Iliad [Milan, Biblioteca Ambrosiana MS F, 205 inf.] and catacomb paintings) and elsewhere.[21] The seventy-seven marble tables that survive (some are fragmentary; some have been found in domestic contexts)[22] have broad borders with raised decoration and beaded rims (Figure 14.6a–b),[23] exactly corresponding to the decoration – and in some cases to the round shape – of the Meleager and Achilles plates (Figures 14.4–5). The marble tops measure 80 to 160 cm across; the plates are 72 and 69 cm in diameter. Given this discrepancy in size, it is possible that the silver plates were placed on top of marble tabletops, within the borders (Figure 14.6e). Furthermore, the figural friezes of both the two silver plates and all (with one exception) the marble tabletops face outwards (Figures 14.4–5, 6a–b) and those on the plates slope down (Figures 14.2b–c, 6e), and were thus to be viewed from the edge rather than across the surface, as in the case of earlier silver plates with inwardly facing border friezes, represented in the Sevso treasure by the Hunting plate (Figure 14.3). The wealth of narrative detail on the Meleager plate invited careful scrutiny at close range. That and the Achilles plate could have been rotated at intervals to reveal the next scene to each person reclining on the *stibadium*. Furthermore, certain iconographic details assumed prominence when viewed by individual guests, seated for example *cornu dextra* or *cornu sinistra*, the first and second most honoured positions in late antiquity.[24]

Now for drink. As stated above, John the Cappadocian's dishes were 'accompanied by various wines'.[25] Sidonius Apollinaris described how his guests after lunch at his villa 'sat over wine' and talked.[26] Katherine Dunbabin's recent study of drinking practices describes a transition from the Greek habit of mixing wine in a large communal crater to a Roman one of mixing wine with hot water drawn from a samovar, using individual cups and according

---

[21] K. Dunbabin, 'Triclinium and stibadium', in W. Slater, ed., *Dining in a Classical Context* (Ann Arbor, MI, 1991), 128–35; K. Weitzmann, *Late Antique and Early Christian Book Illumination* (London, 1977), pls 2, 13; K. Dunbabin, *The Roman Banquet: images of conviviality* (Cambridge, 2003), 141–8, 191–202, pls XII–XVI, figs 116–20. On imperial dining, see S. Malmberg, 'Dazzling dining: banquets as an expression of imperial legitimacy', (unpublished PhD dissertation, University of Uppsala, 2003) and his chapter in this volume.

[22] For example, C. Donnay-Rocmans and G. Donnay, 'La Maison de Cerf', in *Apamée de Syrie: Bilan des recherches anchéologiques, 1973–1979. Aspects de l'architecture domestique d'Apamée* (Brussels, 1984), 159, 162, fig. 6, pls LII.1–2.

[23] J. Dresken-Weiland, *Reliefierte Tischplatten aus Theodosianischer Zeit* (Vatican City, 1991).

[24] Sidonius Apollinaris, *Epistulae* 1.11.10; Dunbabin, *Banquet*, 192–3.

[25] See note 1 above.

[26] Sidonius Apollinaris, *Epistulae*, 2.457.6.

to personal taste. The water was carried in a ewer to the table where it was mixed with the wine in the goblet.[27]

The Sevso treasure's amphora and one ewer, both ornamented with Dionysiac figures,[28] were undoubtedly used for serving wine (Figures 14.7a, 14.8). The Dionysiac imagery including panther handles on the amphora combined with that of food: the game and fish alluded to in the top and bottom friezes of the amphora. Although worthy of display, both objects show signs of wear through use: namely loss of gilding. The amphora now has a rubbed and broken surface repaired in antiquity to keep it watertight.[29] Although not made as a matching pair of vessels they functioned together.

The amphora has a tall, stoppered neck to keep liquids warm and resembles in shape contemporary copper-alloy samovars (Figure 14.9).[30] While not operating as a samovar itself, it may have been used to carry warmed water to the table for mixing with wine. The amphora could have been filled by a funnel of the type now in the Getty Museum (Figure 14.7b).[31] The amphora's thick handles may have served to lessen the heat while being carried. Being relatively small (height 38.5 cm) and lightweight (5 lb, or 1,637 g) and having a small mouth, its contents could easily have been poured into the cup for mixing with wine dispensed from the Dionysiac ewer, thus used as an *oinochoe*. When the ewer, which has a capacity of 4 litres, was held in the right hand, the figure of Dionysos was visible (Figure 14.8). The elaborate octagonal upper rim of the ewer was attached to align one cusp with the front and to serve as a spout pouring into a cup (Figure 14.8b).

Another ewer of this treasure decorated with a grid of tiny animals and related images (Figure 14.10)[32] may also have been used at table for hand-washing as part of a set composed of ewer and handled basin, as illustrated at Dido's banquet. Much food was taken from serving platters and eaten by hand so that washing was a necessary part of the meal. Silver *aquiminaria* used for washing before meals are mentioned in Justinian's *Digest* and inventories.[33] The Animal ewer's lid kept water warm and the flamingo heads on the handle plates allude to its contents.[34] Although elaborately decorated with 120 engraved and inlaid images, the ewer was put to use as indicated by patterns of wear on body and lid where the metal is rubbed

---

27 K. Dunbabin, 'Wine and water at the Roman convivium', *JRA* 6 (1993), 116–41.

28 See Mundell Mango and Bennett, *Sevso*, 194–266.

29 Ibid., 27–8, 206–11, 250.

30 W. B. Emergy and L .P. Kirwan, *The Royal Tombs at Ballana and Qustul* (London, 1938), no. 790, pl. 93D; J. C. Waldbaum, *Metalwork from Sardis* (Cambridge, MA, 1983), no. 522.

31 'Aquisitions/1992', *Getty Museum Journal*, 21 (1993), no. 14.

32 See Mundell Mango and Bennett, *Sevso*, 267–318.

33 *Digest* 34.2.19, 21. See also Sidonius Apollinaris, *Epistulae* 1.11.14; Adhémar, 'Auxerre', 53–4.

34 Mundell Mango and Bennett, *Sevso*, 318, fig. 7-52a/b.

smooth (Figure 14.10a).[35] A weight inscription of 20 lb, or 6,549 g, on its base (Figure 14.10b) suggested – since it now weighs only 12 lb, or 3,929 g – that it once had a matching handled basin (weighing 8 lb, or 2,619 g), as is the case with a complete *cherniboxeston* or washing set (stamped 582–602) now in the Hermitage, with similar inscription and ewer shape (Figure 14.11).[36] Three types of silver washbasins are known from late antiquity. The first, that considered here, is a flat and broad *patera* with a horizontal handle; the second, the *trulla* of saucepan shape, also has a horizontal handle; the third, the *pelvis*, is a wide basin often with a pair of drop handles, which may have formed part of general household silver.[37] All three types often have aquatic decoration (fish, shellfish, waterbirds, fishermen, mythological marine characters).[38]

Stylistically, iconographically and technically the Animal ewer (Figure 14.10) has strong links with the Hunting plate (Figure 14.3), whose Latin inscription refers to *vascula*, a possible play on words for both 'small' silver vessels and hunting implements.[39] This could suggest that they formed part of a picnic service, which may have been legally classified as part of *argentum viatorium*,[40] silver used on journeys. Indeed, the 'portraits' of these objects may appear on the plate itself, spread out before the plate's owner Sevso and his fellow diners on the *stibadium* at the hunt picnic (Figure 14.3 centre): a large platter holds a fish while a washing set (ewer and handled basin) stands in front of it.

Moving from the *triclinium* and the picnic to the kitchen, it is very likely that the large copper cauldron in which the fourteen silver objects of the Sevso treasure were concealed belonged to their owner (Figure 14.12).[41] Being 0.83 m in diameter and having a capacity of c. 800 litres, it would have been suitable for use in a large household. Cauldrons of comparable dimensions have been found in military and monastic contexts where they were in the service of large numbers of people. Soot deposit on the base indicates that it was made to heat water or some other liquid over an open fire, in the preparation of food (boiling, braising and so forth) or for washing or both. Apicius gives

---

35 Ibid., 279–81.

36 Ibid., 282.

37 As in *Digest* 33.10.3. E. C. Dodd, *Byzantine Silver Stamps* (Washington, DC, 1961), nos 1, 30 (*patera*); 14, 77 (*trulla*). While the *patera* was used at table, the *trulla* may have been used in the bath. On the *pelvis*, see M. Mundell Mango in Buckton, *Byzantium*, no. 9.

38 K. J. Shelton, *The Esquiline Treasure* (London, 1981), 68 note 15, 78 no. 3; Dodd, *Stamps*, nos 1, 30.

39 *Haec Sevso tibi durent per secula multa posteris ut prosint vascula digna tuis*: 'Let these, O Sevso, yours for many ages be, small vessels fit to serve your offspring worthily'. See Mundell Mango and Bennett, *Sevso*, 77 and Mundell Mango, *Sevso*, vol. 2.

40 *Digest* 34.2.40.

41 On the cauldron, see Mundell Mango and Bennett, *Sevso*, 20–26, 474–80.

recipes for dishes made in a large cauldron (*ahenum*), both gourmet recipes for the wealthy and simpler dishes for lesser members of a large household;[42] a large cauldron is also seen in use at the picnic on the Hunting plate (Figure 14.3). The cauldron continued in use for some time, requiring thirty-two repair patches on its base and others on the sides. Eventually it may have been retired from heating and used for dry storage.

Other Late Antique domestic plate

Other Late Antique silver supplements the information gained from the objects in the Sevso treasure, particularly regarding smaller-scale vessels and utensils, now missing from that assemblage. Notable among these are sets of matching vessels, more characteristic, perhaps, of domestic than ecclesiastical silver where a single *diskopoterion* could furnish a small church or form a convenient single donation.[43] Plates with figural decoration, which may also have had a serving or other table use, are found or recorded singly, in pairs or in sets. The three Sevso plates of this type (Figures 14.3–5) were found together but made separately (see above). Other examples were manufactured as pairs or sets. These include a Dionysiac pair in the Mildenhall treasure, another pair with Hippolytus from Thebes in Egypt, a set of six plates with marine scenes found at Bubastis in Egypt and now in the Benaki Museum, Athens, and the set of nine plates from Cyprus with the cycle of David scenes.[44]

Many Roman silver treasures have plates and bowls of simple adornment (ornamented rims and central rosettes, swastikas or stars),[45] which clearly form part of a dinner service. Similar objects were made in late antiquity. The Esquiline treasure contains two sets of small plates bearing the owner's monogram within a wreath. The four round plates (diameters 16.1 cm) are identified as a set by the Latin weight inscription on one of them.[46] The other set is of four rectangular plates (20.2 by 14.6 cm) with an openwork

---

42 Flower and Rosenbaum, *Apicius*, 5.1.2; 6.2.1, 3; 7.1.1; 8.1.2, 10, 6.6, 11, 7.3, 4, 16; 8.6.11, 7.3; 9.4.2. Alternatively, the cauldron may have had an industrial or agricultural use, perhaps still within the household to which the silver belonged. See Mundell Mango, *Sevso*, vol. 2.

43 M. Mundell Mango, *Silver from Early Byzantium: the Kaper Koraon and related treasures* (Baltimore, MD, 1986), 3–6.

44 K. S. Painter, *The Mildenhall Treasure* (London, 1977), nos 2–3; M. C. Ross, *Catalogue of the Byzantine and Early Medieval Antiquities in the Dumbarton Oaks Collection, I: Metalwork, Ceramics, Glass, Glyptics, Painting* (Washington, DC, 1962), no. 7; S. Pelekanides, 'Ἀργυρὰ Πινάκια τοῦ Μουσείου Μπενάκη', *AE* 1942–44 (1948), 37–62; K. Weitzmann, ed., *Age of Spirituality* (New York, 1979), nos 425–32.

45 See, for example, the Chaource treasure: H. B. Walters, *Catalogue of the Silver Plate (Greek, Etruscan and Roman) in the British Museum* (London, 1921), nos 151-67.

46 Inscription: SCVT.IIII.P V, which reads '4 *scut*[*ellae*], 5 pounds'; Shelton, *Esquiline Treasure*, nos 5–8.

rim (Figure 14.13).[47] Similar small plates with minimal (cross monogram or cross) or no decoration have been found singly, in pairs or in sets in domestic treasures; the plates with a cross have often been mistaken for patens.[48] These simple plates occur in repeating dimensions (35–53 cm; 25–8 cm; 13–15 cm) within each treasure, which points to a serial production of extended sets.[49] Examples appear in several treasures: that of Canoscio (seven plates), Cyprus (six plates stamped 578-630), and Mytilene (four plates stamped 605-630),[50] and a set from Izmir (four plates stamped 613-629/30).[51] Comparable simple plates dated by stamps from 491 to 651 have also been found singly in Bulgaria, Asia Minor and Russia.[52]

Bowls used for sauces or condiments also belonged to dinner services: the Egyptian papyrus inventory lists sixty *oxybapha* (Figure 14.1 on right in centre) and twenty-four *boletaria*.[53] Late Antique bowls found singly and in treasures continue the tradition, even if their numbers are lower. Matched bowls in the Mildenhall and Carthage treasures are as richly ornamented as display objects.[54] Some more simply decorated Late Antique bowls (diameters 12–22 cm) have broad horizontal, sometimes beaded, rims, while others stand on a high foot and have a lid, a change in form which may correspond to a change in food served.[55]

The domestic spoons made in the sixth and seventh centuries are notably large and often elaborately decorated. It is known that Late Antique spoons were made in sets of twelve.[56] Such a set with inscribed handles formed part

47 Ibid., nos 9–12. On oblong dishes, see Mundell Mango in Buckton, *Byzantium*, no. 15.

48 See Mundell Mango, *Kaper Koraon*, nos 103–6; eadem, in Buckton, *Byzantium*, no. 96.

49 On these plain domestic plates, see, in addition to references in note 38, Mundell Mango, in Buckton, *Byzantium*, no. 51; eadem, 'The archaeological context of finds of silver in and beyond the Eastern Empire', in *Acta XIII Congressus Internationalis Archaeologiae Christiane* (Vatican City, 1998), 223; eadem, 'Byzantine, Sasanian and Central Asian silver', in C. Balint, ed., *Kontakte zwischen Iran, Byzanz und der Steppe im 6.–7. Jahrhundert* (Budapest, 2000), 274.

50 E. Giovagnoli, 'Una collezione di vasi eucaristici scoperti a Conoscio', *RACr* 12 (1935), 313–14, figs 2, 3, 5, 7 (Canoscio); Dodd, *Stamps*, nos 28, 33, 37-9, 54 (Cyprus); *Byzantine Art: an European art* (Athens, 1964), nos 500–503 (Mytilene).

51 Dodd, *Stamps*, nos 44–6; the fourth plate is in the Ortiz Collection, Geneva.

52 For example ibid., nos 5–6, 12, 15, 36, 51, 55, 67–9, 72–4, 76, 100.

53 Oliver and Shelton, 'Papyrus', 26.

54 Painter, *Mildenhall*, nos 5-8; O. M. Dalton, *Catalogue of Early Christian Antiquities in the British Museum* (London, 1901), nos 356–7.

55 H. A. Cahn and A. Kaufmann-Heinemann, *Der spätrömische Silberschatz von Kaiseraugst* (Derendingen, 1984), nos 47–51; Painter, *Mildenhall*, nos 9–12; Dodd, *Stamps*, nos 3, 23, 52–3, 81–3, 85; M. Mundell Mango, 'Continuity of fourth/fifth-century silver plate in the sixth/seventh centuries in the Eastern Empire', *AntT* 5 (1997), 89, fig. 3. On the changing shapes of dinnerware, see also Joanita Vroom's chapter in this volume.

56 M. Martin in Cahn and Kaufmann-Heinemann, *Kaiseraugst*, 56–96; S. R. Hauser, *Spätantike und frühbyzantinische Silberlöffel* (Münster, 1992), 94–7.

of a domestic silver service listed in the Auxerre inventory.[57] The Cyprus treasure contains a set of eleven (once twelve) spoons, each decorated on its bowl with a different animal. The Lampsacus treasure contains eight spoons preserved from a set inscribed with the owner's monogram (undeciphered) on the disc, and with a literary quotation to which amusing little afterthoughts have been added.[58] The quotations, which run down the length of the spoon's bowl and across the top and side of the square section of the handle, can be read when the spoon is held horizontally in the right hand, while eating (Figure 14.14).[59] Five spoons have quotations from the 'Greek Sayings of the Seven Sages' (Chilon, Pittakos, Solon, Bias, Periander: *Greek Anthology*, 9.366). Citations from the other sages (Cleobulus, Thales) undoubtedly adorned two of the four spoons now missing. To fill out the set of twelve, the other three surviving spoons have Latin verses from Vergil (*Eclogues* 2.17; 10.69), as did, probably, the two other spoons now missing. Whereas the verses are correctly copied and spelled, the shorter Greek witticisms ('Eat, you who are lovesick', 'Love those who mock you', 'You cannot be beautiful without money') that follow them contain some misspellings, which may suggest they were composed especially for the spoons.[60] A knife handle is similarly inscribed (see below).

These spoons may be seen as part of dining or feasting iconography. The 'Sayings of the Seven Sages' have been found inscribed on walls and on floors of rooms used for convivial gatherings, such as *triclinia* at Apamea and Baalbek,[61] an appropriate location, given that the 'Sayings' were delivered at the Banquet of the Sages. Other *triclinium* feasting imagery included mosaics of Ge (Earth) and the Seasons, hunting (as on the Sevso plates and Cyprus spoons) and *xenia* (common food and drink provisions), and the marble tables with figured rims considered above.

The Lampsacus treasure also contains a set of five spoons with the monogram of one Matthew on the disc and the names of Apostles on the upper handle.[62] Undoubtedly this set once numbered twelve. One may view

57 Adhémar, 'Auxerre', 52, no. 48.

58 Dalton, *Catalogue*, nos 387-92; Hauser, *Silberlöffel*, 31–6, nos 103–10; Mundell Mango, in Buckton, *Byzantium*, no. 133; F. Baratte, 'Vaisselle d'argent, souvenirs littéraires et manières de table: l'exemple des cuillers de Lampsaque', *CahArch* 40 (1992), 10–11.

59 This layout differs from the vertical placement of a cross on the bowl of spoons made for liturgical purposes; see Mundell Mango, *Kaper Koraon*, nos 18–21.

60 I owe this observation and the following translations to my husband, Cyril Mango. To the group of related short texts (without the literary quotations) on spoons elsewhere, already published (Hauser, *Silberlöffel*, 74), may be added those previously undeciphered on spoons from Touna el-Gebel in the Benaki Museum – 'Sorrow is untimely', 'Truth is simple' and 'Know thyself' – and another in a private collection – 'Blow so you don't get burnt'.

61 Mundell Mango, *Kaper Koraon*, 186–7, 218; Baratte, 'Vaisselle'.

62 The Antioch treasure has a set of seven spoons with the monogram of Domnos on the disc and, on the handle, a boar's head and the inscription Εὐλογία τοῦ ἁγίου ... followed by an

Apostle spoons as a christianized version of the Sages spoons, which served to remind the diners of the Communion of the Apostles, thus replacing the secular Banquet of the Sages.

Spoons were the only type of eating utensil regularly used at the Late Antique table. Food was cut in the kitchen so that table knives were unnecessary and, although a *fuscina* is included in the Auxerre inventory,[63] forks are relatively rare.[64] Known silver forks have spoon-like handles or form part a folding set of utensils.[65] A solid-silver knife handle with gold and niello inlay, said to be part of the Esquiline treasure, has a Greek inscription, *μὴ λύπει σεαυτὸν* ('Don't be despondent'), comparable to those on the Lampsacus and related spoons.[66] Other table knives generally have bone handles.[67] Those excavated at Corinth, attributed to the Byzantine period, have overall geometric ornament.[68]

Supplementing the Sevso amphora and Dionysiac ewer discussed above as wine-serving vessels are silver flasks in the Esquiline, Latakiya and other treasures and a large *scyphos* found at Tavas in Asia Minor – all decorated with Dionysiac or vintaging scenes – which may have been used in the serving of wine.[69] Extant Late Antique silver table services contain few drinking beakers,[70] goblets and bowls.[71] It is thought that in this period they may have been replaced by glass vessels.

Medieval Byzantium

Domestic silver continued to be made in quantity into the seventh century, as known from the presence of imperial control stamps on some silver until at least 663. The fact that in the seventh century only seven objects bearing control stamps are of church silver, while fifty-six (up from twenty-three in the sixth) are of domestic silver, would seem to indicate that domestic production

Apostle's name. Mundell Mango, *Kaper Koraon*, nos 49–55; Hauser, *Silberlöffel*, 43–5, nos 136–48.

63 Adhémar, 'Auxerre', 50, no. 25.

64 D. E. Strong, *Greek and Roman Gold and Silver Plate* (London, 1966), 129.

65 F. Baratte et al., *Le Trésor de la place Camille-Jouffray à Vienne (Isère)* (Paris, 1990), 80–81.

66 Mundell Mango, in Buckton, ed., *Byzantium*, no. 134.

67 As distinct from knives used as weapons and tools.

68 G. R. Davidson, *Corinth: Results of the Excavations Conducted by the American School of Classical Studies at Athens, XII: the minor objects* (Athens, 1952), no. 4144.

69 Shelton, *Esquiline Treasure*, 82–3; *Age of Spirituality*, no. 131; Ross, *Catalogue*, 1, no. 6.

70 Compared also with the great variety within each of the first- to second-century treasures of Hildesheim, Boscoreale and Berthouville; see Strong, *Plate*, 133–40, 163–5.

71 For example, the Kaiseraugst treasure has four conical goblets (Cahn and Kaufmann-Heinimann, *Kaiseraugst*, nos 43–6); the Mildenhall treasure has two goblets (Painter, *Mildenhall*, nos 13–14); the Lampsacus treasure has a small goblet (Dalton, *Catalogue*, no. 377).

was increasing rather than tapering off.[72] However, very little domestic silver can be convincingly dated after the year 700.

Silver plate made in the early period was treasured in the tenth century. Large silver plates (*missoria*) with relief decoration – comparable perhaps to two of the Sevso plates (Figures 14.4–5) – and inscribed with the name of the fifth-century general Jordanes, were still kept in the imperial palace in the tenth century.[73] Also preserved there at the time (and mentioned in 946, 971–5) were three large *missoria* (*apalarea, minsouria*) named, respectively, the *Likinios*, the Enemy-slayer (*Echthroktonos*) and the All-virtuous (*Panaretos*), which are considered to have been Late Antique imperial heirlooms. They were displayed, with the *Panaretos* in the centre, before a curtain at state banquets when the emperor and his company reclined in the old style in the *Chrysotriklinos*.[74] Thus, some early silver plate was still visible in the tenth century (and probably later) and may have exercised an influence on medieval plate.

While these earlier pieces were simply put on display, written sources refer to some specific types of domestic silver objects in use in medieval Byzantium, presumably of contemporary manufacture. A carved (relief-worked) silver service (*anaglyphon asemion*), heavy gold gem-encrusted plates (*skoutelia, minsouria)* and hand-washing sets (*cherniboxesta*) were all in use in the imperial palace in the tenth century.[75] Byzantine secular vessels given as diplomatic gifts to foreign rulers included one of rock crystal encrusted with gold and gems presented to Louis II the German in 872, and gold gem-encrusted plates (*skoutellia*) given to Arab ambassadors (946), the Russian queen Olga (957) and the Seljuk sultan Kiliç Arslan II (1161).[76] Two sets of gifts were sent to rulers by Romanos I in 935 and 938.[77] The first, given to the king of Italy, included three pieces of gilded silver plate (*ἔργα ἀργυρὰ διάχρυσα*) in addition to an onyx cup (*poterion*) and seventeen glass vessels, which may have been tableware. The inventory (preserved in Arabic) of the second set of gifts, sent to the caliph of Baghdad, al-Radi Billah, included flasks, a ewer, an amphora, cups, a 'tray' (platter?), knives and a casket, made of silver, gold and crystal, many set with precious stones and pearls. Following a military defeat in 1190, Isaac II used

72 Mundell Mango, 'Context', 208–10.

73 Constantine Porphyrogennetos, *De thematibus*, ed. A. Pertusi (Vatican, 1952), 61–2; C. Mango, 'The Palace of Marina, the poet Palladas and the Bath of Leo VI', in *Εὐφρόσυνον. Αφιέρωμα στον Μανόλη Χατζηδάκη*, vol. 1 (Athens, 1991), 330.

74 *De ceremoniis*, ed. J. J. Reiske, 2 vols (Bonn, 1829–1930), 587; Mango, 'Palace', 330; N. Oikonomides, *Les Listes de préséances byzantines des IXe et Xe siècles* (Paris, 1972), 274–5 and note 43.

75 Ibid., 277; J. Ebersolt, *Les Arts somptuaires de Byzance* (Paris, 1923), 68–9. On medieval imperial dining, see Malmberg, 'Dazzling dining' (see note 21 above).

76 Ebersolt, *Les Arts*, 61; *De ceremoniis*, ed. J. J. Reiske, 585, 597–8.

77 M. Mundell Mango, 'Hierarchies of rank and materials: diplomatic gifts sent by Romanus I in 935 and 938', *DChAE* 4 (2003), 365–73.

church silver and gold (*chrysion apephthon*) plate for his table, including ewers (*hydrochooi*) and basins (*cherniba*).[78] Among the aristocracy and other elites, more general references to precious-metal vessels may include silver table services. Around 890 Danielis brought from the Peloponnese 'many costly vessels of gold and silver of various kinds' to present to Basil I, while the will of Eustathios Boilas, dated 1059, twice mentions family silver plate (*asemion*), as distinct from its references to church plate.[79] A more specific text states that Constantine Dalassenos, *dux* of Antioch (1025) owned a gilded (*chrysokolletos*) silver wine *krater*.[80] In the fourteenth century, Theodore Metochites owned a drinking service, hand-washing basins (*cheroniptra*) and footbaths (*podoniptra*) in silver.[81]

The following discussion suggests that the middle Byzantine domestic silver that survives combines old and new stylistic elements. The earliest known extant secular silver objects of the medieval period are two drinking cups (Figure 14.15) and an inkpot. The silver cup dated c. 865 of the Grand Zhupan Sivin of Bulgaria (inscribed in Greek) excavated at Preslav, and another found at Gotland in Sweden, are decorated with three traditional scrolls,[82] but introduce the teacup shape known already in China and Central Asia that was to become common in Constantinople-produced White Ware pottery.[83] The conservatively decorated parcel-gilt silver inkpot in Padua is placed in the ninth or tenth century on the basis of the lettering of its inscription.[84] Several silver bowls recovered in Russia, used either as eating and/or drinking vessels, display so many oriental stylistic traits that opinion is divided as to their origin, although two bear integral Greek inscriptions.[85] Among the imperial and aristocratic objects taken from Constantinople

---

78 Ebersolt, *Les Arts*, 100.

79 Theophanes Continuatus, ed. I. Bekker (Bonn, 1838), 318; P. Lemerle, *Cinq études sur le XIe siècle byzantin* (Paris, 1977), 23, lines 91, 95; on the church plate, see M. Parani, B. Pitarakis and J.-M. Spieser, 'Un exemple d'inventaire d'objets liturgiques. Le testament d'Eustathios Boïlas (Avril 1059)', *REB* 61 (2003), 143–65.

80 S. G. Mercati, *Collectanea byzantina* (Bari, 1970), 458. I owe this reference to my husband.

81 Ebersolt, *Les Arts*, 109.

82 L. Praskov, ed., *Trésors d'art médieval bulgare. VIIe–XVIe siècle* (Geneva, 1988), no. 26; *Byzantine Art*, no. 515.

83 Mundell Mango, 'Central Asian', 271–2.

84 On the lid is a traditional apotropaic Medusa head and on the body mythological figures: H. C. Evans and W. D. Wixon, eds, *The Glory of Byzantium: art and culture of the Middle Byzantine era* A.D. *843–1261* (New York, 1997), 189–90; H. Maguire, 'Epigrams, art and the "Macedonian Renaissance"', *DOP* 48 (1994), 112–14.

85 B. P. Darkevic, *Svetskoe iskusstvo Vizantii. Proizvedeniya vizantiiskogo chudozhestvennogo remesla v vostochnoi Evrope X–XIII veka* (Moscow, 1975). This author (see ibid., English summary, 321–5) argues for an origin in Constantinople, while B. I. Marshak, 'Zur Toreutik der Kreuzfahrer', in A. Effenberger, ed., *Metallkunst von der Spätantike bis zum ausgehenden Mittelalter* (Berlin, 1982), 166–84, favours a source further east, such as Cilicia.

following the Fourth Crusade are some that may be domestic rather than ecclesiastical, as, for example, an alabaster bowl, a similar glass bowl, goblets and cups.[86]

Given the paucity of data pertaining to, and extant examples of, medieval Byzantine domestic silver services, the recent appearance of a new set of ten silver plates (Figures 14.16, 14.18–19), nine of which were purchased by the Greek state and are now exhibited permanently in Athens and Thessalonike, is certainly welcome, particularly as one plate names the medieval owner, Constantine the Alan, *proedros* (Figure 14.18).[87] This suggests an eleventh-century context. A Constantine the Alan, *magistros* was, according to Skylitzes, engaged in the battle of Dvin in 1047. This individual could well have subsequently acquired the more elevated title of *proedros*, first introduced in 963 by Nikephoros II Phokas who bestowed it on Basil the Nothos (Lekapenos).[88] The lettering of the plate's inscription compares well in general with that of the Brescia astrolabe (dated 1062) and that of Nikephoros III Botaneiates (dated 1078–81) on the serpentine roundel in London, while the knotted strokes appear for example already on the reverse of the ivory reliquary in Cortona dated to 963–69 and in the manuscript of 1042–50 at Sinai, showing Constantine IX, Zoe and Theodora.[89]

A recent article on these objects in the Benaki Museum journal unfortunately cites but disregards this evidence, dating the plates instead to the twelfth century.[90] It concentrates its artefactual commentary particularly on Islamic and Crusader-period metal and pottery comparanda, but omits technically relevant Byzantine metalwork such as the tinned copperware of the ninth to eleventh centuries and the inlaid brass doors manufactured at Constantinople between 1060 and 1089,[91] most of which employ engraving, as do the silver plates under discussion. Likewise, it ignores related metalware of the early

[86] Mundell Mango, 'Gifts', 366–71. On some of these, silver is combined or replaced by other materials, especially stones.

[87] When examining the newly found plates in 2002, Cyril Mango noted three monograms of a Nikephoros scratched onto the front, back and foot ring of the plate with trellis ornament.

[88] In the Escurial *Taktikon* the title is one rung below that of *zoste patrikia*. The title (*proedros* and *protoproedros*) was broadly granted in the eleventh century and disappeared after the mid-twelfth. See note 90 below.

[89] O. M. Dalton, 'The Byzantine astrolabe of Brescia', in *Proceedings of the British Academy* (London, 1926), 133–200; P. Williamson, ed., *The Medieval Treasury: the art of the Middle Ages in the Victoria & Albert Museum* (London, 1986), 90–91; A. Cutler and J.-M. Spieser, *Byzance médiévale, 700–1204* (Paris, 1996), pls 126, 263.

[90] A. Ballian and A. Drandaki, 'A Middle Byzantine silver treasure', *Benaki Museum*, 3 (2003), 47–80. This is followed by D. Kotzamane, 'Ο νέος θησαυρός των βυζαντινών ασημένιων δίσκων: τεχνική ανάλυση', ibid., 81–92.

[91] M. Mundell Mango, 'The significance of Byzantine tinned copper objects', in *Θυμίαμα στη μνήμη της Λασκαρίνας Μπούρα* (Athens, 1994), 221–7; G. Matthiae, *Le porte bronzee bizantine in Italia* (Rome, 1971).

period. To key Byzantine comparanda cited in the article (the three plates found in Bulgaria in 1903, now in Paris, and the dish with the Ascent of Alexander, found in Siberia, now in the Hermitage)[92] must be added an unpublished plate recently on display in the Metropolitan Museum of Art in New York (Figure 14.17).[93] Like one of Constantine's plates, this has a high foot, a cusped edge, a central medallion with a hunter surrounded by a scroll border and an outer border of running animals. It offers a closer comparison to the figural plates (Figure 14.16) than does the early thirteenth-century Hermitage plate, which is given too much weight in the discussion.

The new plates clearly form a decorative group and functional set. All ten have a central medallion. On one an empty medallion is formed by the circular inscription (Figure 14.18); on three the medallion contains figural decoration (Figure 14.16); on two it holds scrolled ornament; and on the other four, identical geometric ornament. Six plates (two figural, the four geometric) have an outer border. As regards shape, eight plates have a flat bottom and vertical walls. The other two (one figural and one with scrolled medallion) have a high foot, concave floor and cusped edge. The diameters of all ten are close, being of graduated sizes. On examining the plates in February 2002, I was able to stack all eight flat plates together (diameters 24–32.6 cm), fitting one inside the other – proof that they were made as a set (Figure 14.19). The top (smallest) plate was that with the inscription.

I was surprised to read, therefore, in the Benaki article that the plates 'were probably produced by different craftsmen or workshops'. And that, at any rate, the 'modern concept of the uniform "set" or "dinner service" played no part in Byzantium. Indeed, 'nothing of such a kind [sets of silver] has ever been noted even in the numerous treasure-hoards of late antiquity, where, on the contrary, silver vessels display a remarkable variety in shape, iconography and technique'.[94] But, as we have seen above, the manufacture of sets of silver for dinner services was standard practice in both the Roman and late Roman/Early Byzantine periods. The fact that all typological, decorative, iconographic and technical features of the ten plates have antecedents in late antiquity (see, for example, Figures 14.2 [high foot], 3 [layout, iconography], 10 [engraving], 13 [cusped rim]) further supports the argument that these plates should be viewed as a late example of a set used as part of a dinner service.

But what type of dinner service? On earlier plates, mythological heroes and personifications as well as the hunt were favoured subjects of decoration (for

---

92 G. Migeon, 'Orfèvrerie d'argent de style oriental trouvée en Bulgarie', *Syria* (1922), 141–4; B. Marshak in H. C. Evans and W. D. Wixon, eds, *The Glory of Byzantium: art and culture of the Middle Byzantine era A.D. 843–1261* (New York, 1997), no. 267.

93 The plate appeared in London in 1998 and is now in a private collection.

94 Ballian and Drandaki, 'Treasure', 68 and note 133.

example Figures 14.3–5), just as the set of medieval plates has a personification of the Sea, a soldier and a hunter. Do these types allude to Constantine the Alan's own military career and other interests? Does the fact that the eight plates stack compactly (Figure 14.19), making them portable, have a bearing on their use? Sevso, the owner of the fourteen pieces of silver considered above (who, coincidentally, is thought to have been a military man), used some of his silver (the Hunting plate, Figure 14.3, and Animal ewer, Figure 14.10) for a hunt picnic, according to the picture on his Hunting plate (see the analysis above). Constantine the Alan's silver is more compact, more easily carried, and may have been designed for use on military campaign when goods were carried by pack animals, perhaps as a medieval version of *argentum viatorium*. The imperial baggage train, whose equipping procedures dated back to the ninth century, included for imperial use plates (*skoutellia, minsourakia*) in gold (*holochrysa*) and wine/water coolers (*psychristaria*) and pails (*bedouria, sitlolekana*) in silver, with copies in baser materials – for example tinned copper (*chalka ganota*) – for subordinates.[95]

In sum, the Sevso treasure objects and other pieces of domestic plate, both Late Antique and medieval, combined with relevant written sources, offer tantalizing evidence of the active role that silver had – beyond mere display – in dining practices, within, and outside, the *triclinium*. This body of evidence deserves further, comprehensive study.

95 J. F. Haldon, ed. and tr., *Constantine Porphyrogenitus. Three Treatises on Imperial Military Expeditions: introduction, edition, translation and commentary*, CFHB 28 (Vienna, 1990), 106–13.

Figure 14.1: Antioch, House of the Buffet Supper: floor mosaic of silver service with meal displayed (Photo: Cyril Mango).

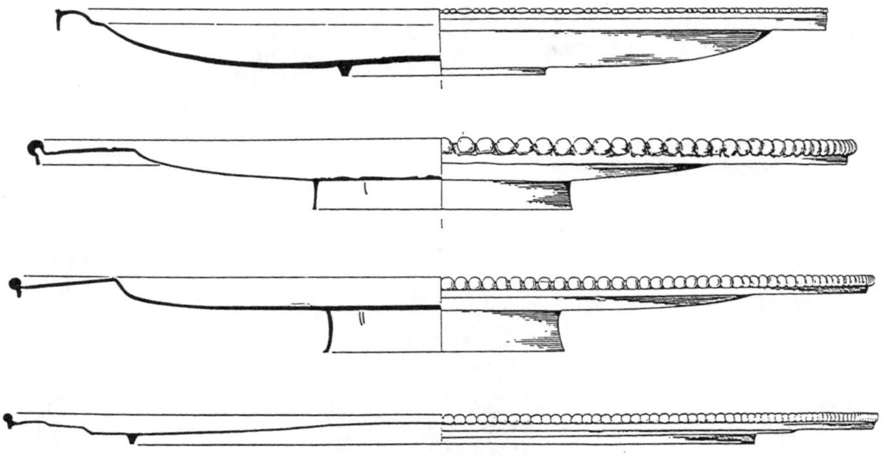

Figure 14.2: Private collection, Sevso treasure: profiles of four silver plates; *lanx*: a. Geometric plate; b. Meleager plate; c. Achilles plate; *discus*: d. Hunting Plate (Drawing: Miranda Scofield; courtesy of the Marquess of Northampton 1987 Settlement).

Figure 14.3: Private collection, Sevso treasure: the silver Hunting plate (Drawing: Miranda Scofield; courtesy of the Marquess of Northampton 1987 Settlement).

Figure 14.4: Private collection, Sevso treasure: the silver Meleager plate (Drawing: Rupert Cook and Miranda Scofield).

Figure 14.5: Private collection, Sevso treasure: the silver Achilles plate. (Drawing: Rupert Cook).

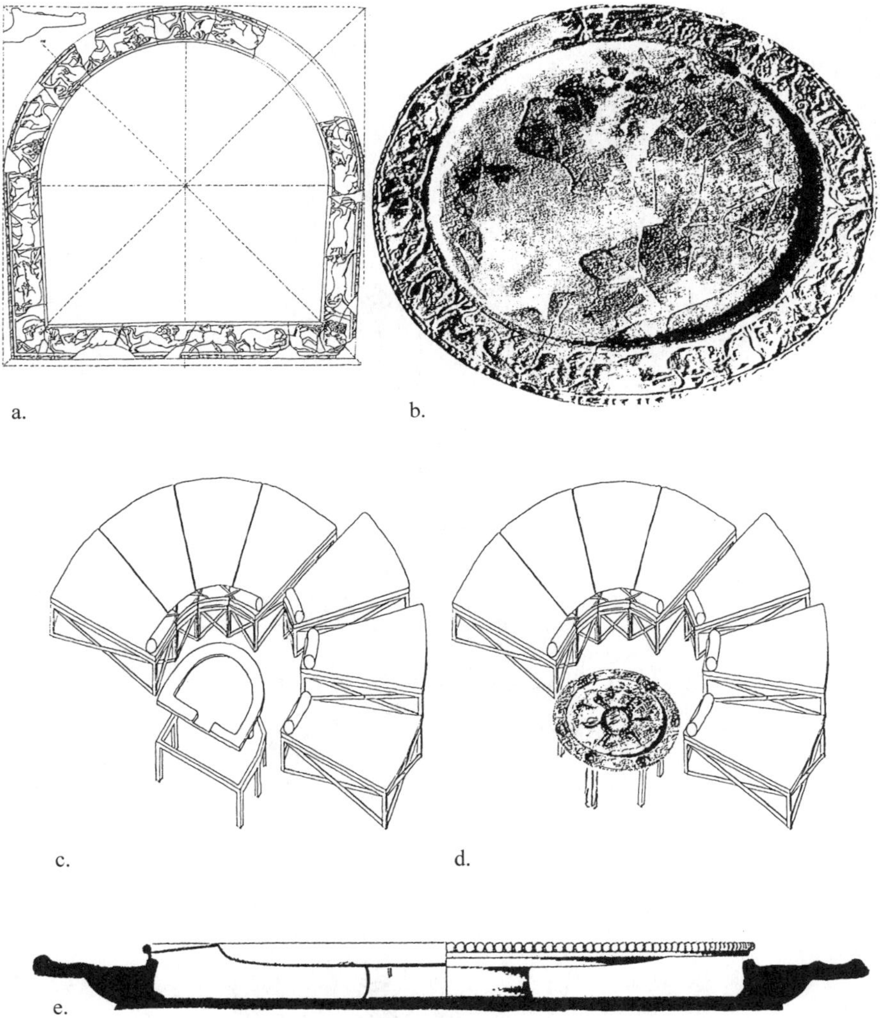

Figure 14.6: a–b. Marble tabletops; c. *stibadium* with marble tabletop; d. *stibadium* with silver Meleager plate as tabletop; e. silver Achilles plate set on top of marble tabletop (Drawings assembled by author).

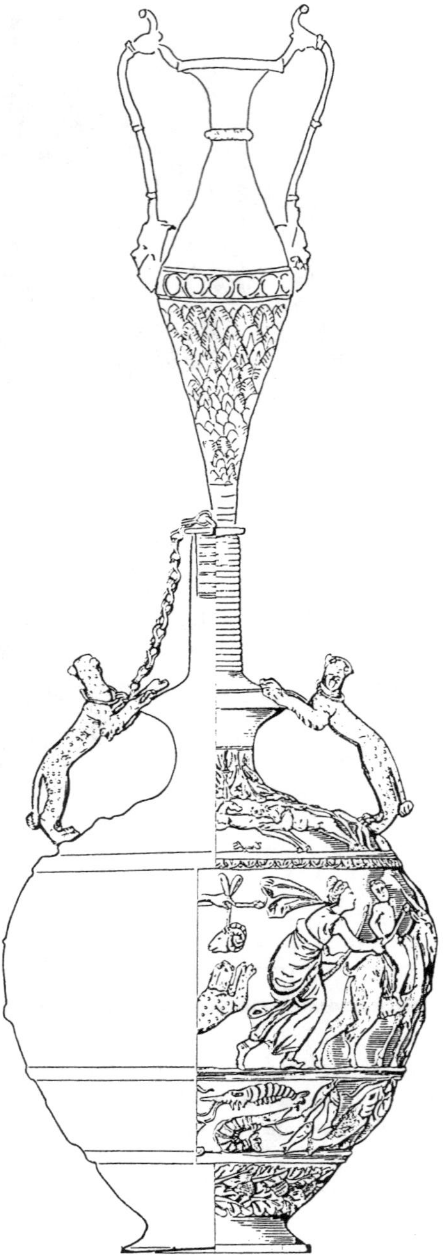

Figure 14.7: a. Private collection, Sevso treasure: silver amphora (Drawing: Miranda Scofield; courtesy of the Marquess of Northampton 1987 Settlement); b. Malibu, J. P. Getty Museum: silver funnel (Drawing: author).

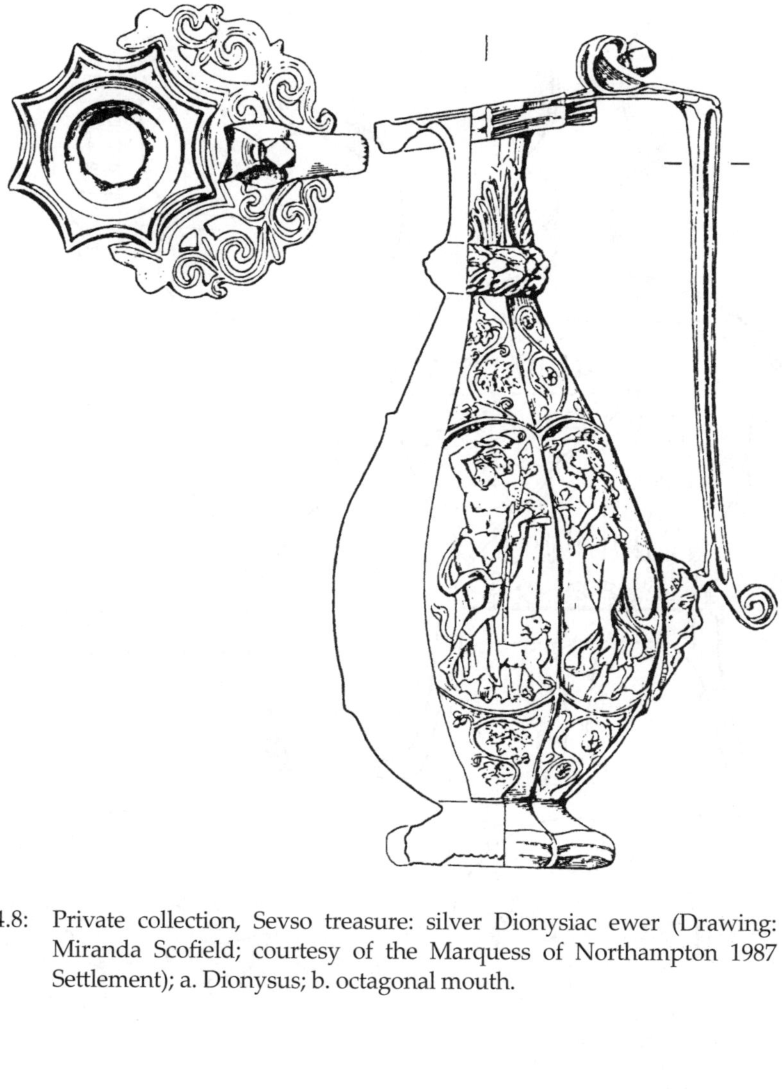

Figure 14.8: Private collection, Sevso treasure: silver Dionysiac ewer (Drawing: Miranda Scofield; courtesy of the Marquess of Northampton 1987 Settlement); a. Dionysus; b. octagonal mouth.

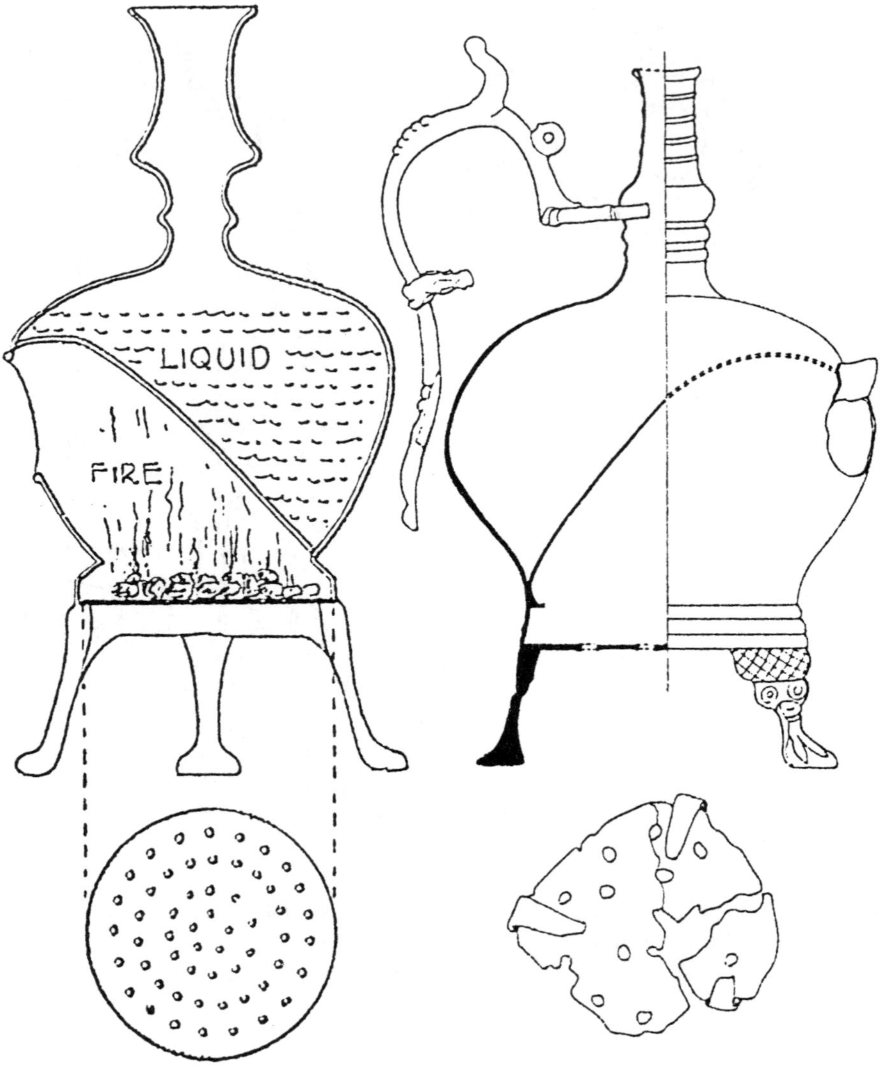

Figure 14.9: Copper-alloy samovars excavated at a. Sardis (After J. C. Waldbaum, *Metalwork from Sardis* [Cambridge, MA, 1983], pl. 34, no. 522); and b. Ballana, Nubia (After W. B. Emery and L. P. Kirwan, *The Royal Tombs at Ballana and Qustul* [London, 1938], pl. 93D).

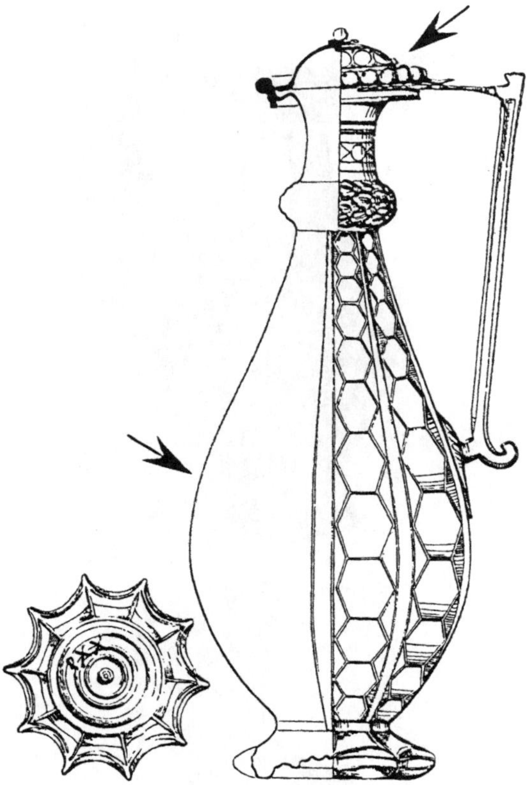

Figure 14.10: Private collection, Sevso treasure: silver Animal ewer (Drawing Miranda Scofield; courtesy of the Marquess of Northampton 1987 Settlement); a. wear marks on body; b. weight inscription on base.

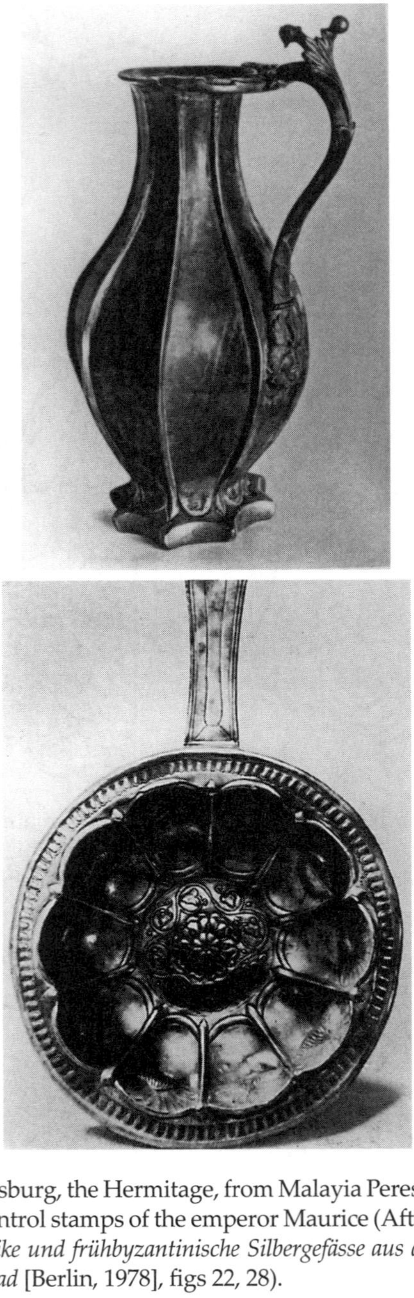

Figure 14.11: St Petersburg, the Hermitage, from Malayia Pereshchepina: washing set with control stamps of the emperor Maurice (After A. Effenberger et al., *Spätantike und frühbyzantinische Silbergefässe aus der Staatlichen Ermitage Leningrad* [Berlin, 1978], figs 22, 28).

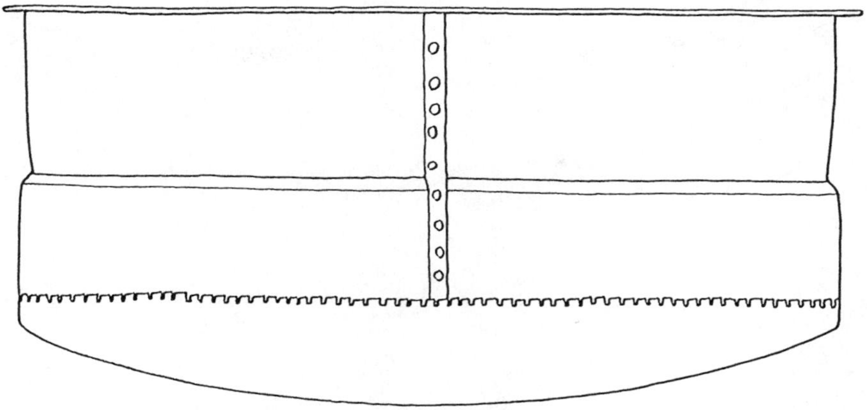

Figure 14.12: Private collection, Sevso treasure: copper cauldron (Drawing: Miranda Scofield; courtesy of the Marquess of Northampton 1987 Settlement).

Figure 14.13: British Museum, Esquiline treasure: silver plate (Courtesy of the British Museum).

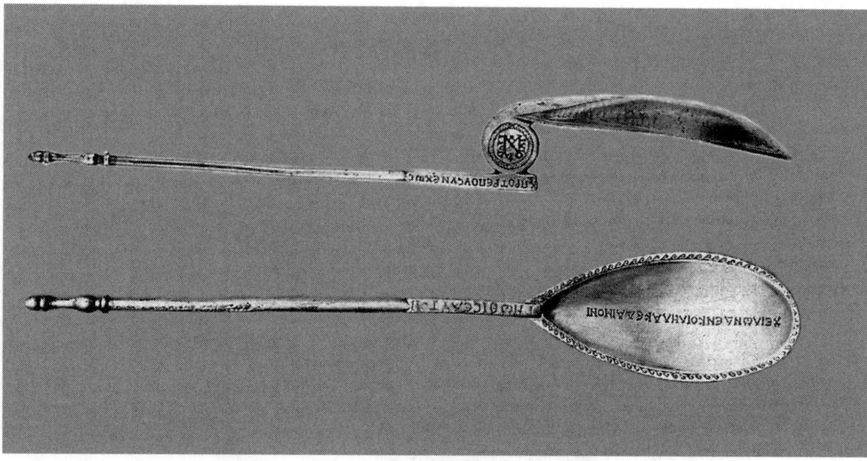

Figure 14.14: British Museum, Lampsacus treasure: silver spoon (Courtesy of the British Museum).

Figure 14.15: a. Preslav: silver cup of the Grand Zupan Sivin (c. 865); b. silver cup from Dune, Gotland, Sweden; now in Museum of National Antiquities, Stockholm (After: a. *Trésors d'art médieval bulgare* [Geneva, 1989], no. 26; b. *L'Art byzantin, art européen* [Athens, 1964], no. 515).

Figure 14.16: Athens, Benaki Museum: silver plate with hunter (Photo: R. Temple).

Figure 14.17: Private collection: silver plate with hunter (Photo: S. Fogg).

Figure 14.18: Private collection: silver plate with inscription (Photo: R. Temple).

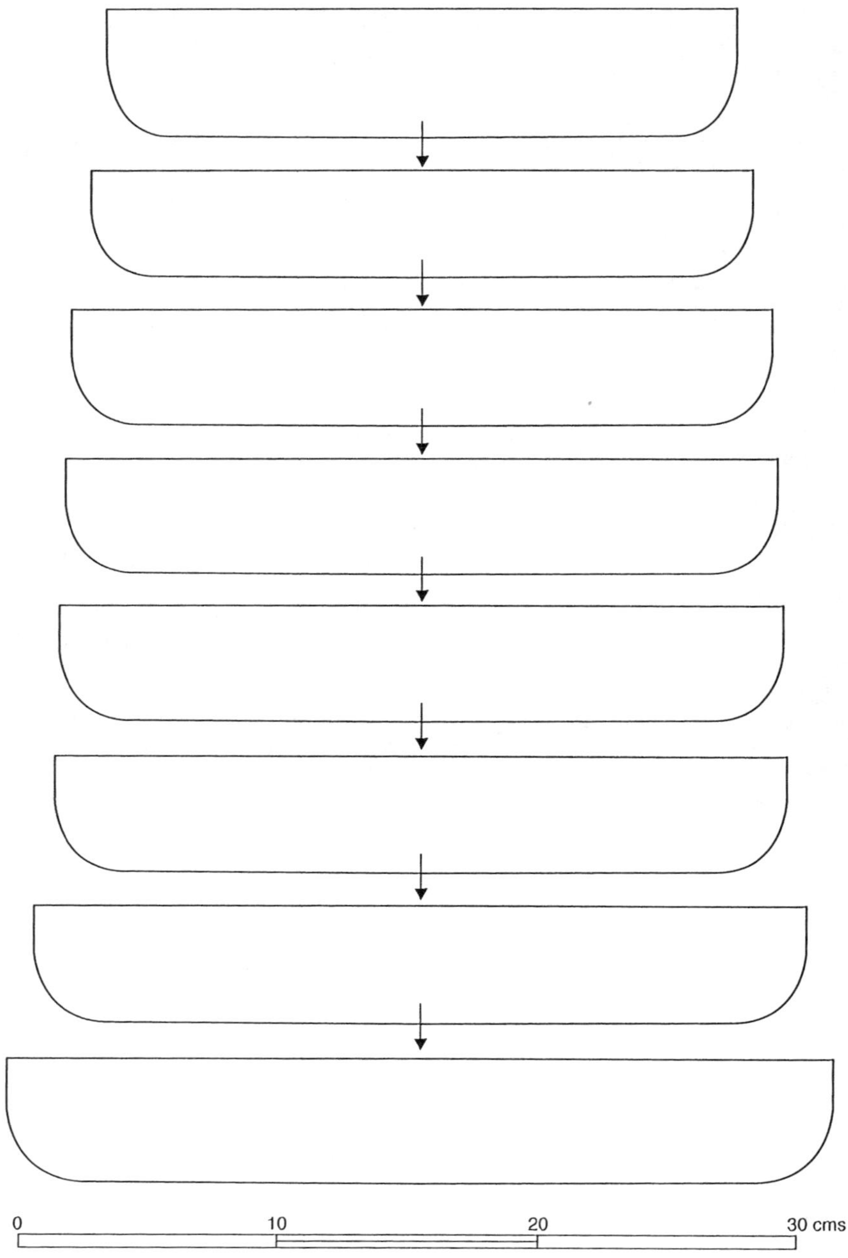

Figure 14.19a: Private collections: diagram showing eight silver plates being stacked together (Drawing: A. Wilkins).

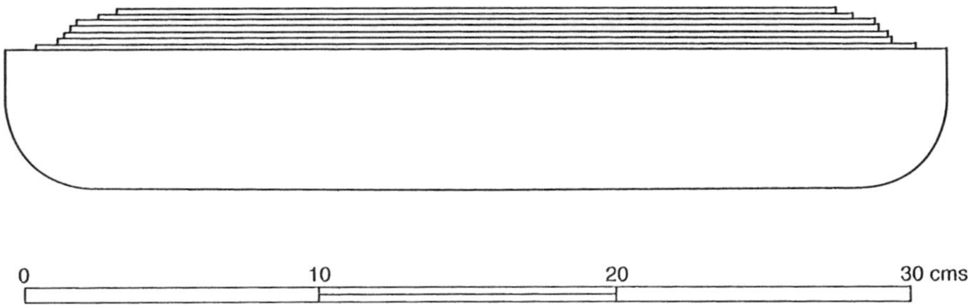

Figure 14.19b: Private collections: diagram showing eight silver plates stacked together (Drawing: A. Wilkins).

Section IV

Ideology and representation

15. What was kosher in Byzantium?

Barbara Crostini

The question of clean and unclean foods is rarely raised in a Byzantine context. This coherently reflects the enduring and consistent Christian position on the subject; namely that, because all creation is good, there cannot be any impediment to eating any of it (except, of course, human flesh) in any circumstance. Christianity is thus set apart from other religions in the choice of not proscribing certain foods as part of its self-definition.

This circumstantial silence was broken by a recent book, Tia Kolbaba's *The Byzantine Lists*, which devotes one chapter to the issue of 'unclean food'.[1] The polemical lists of 'errors of the Latins' analysed by Kolbaba raise this issue in the context of the para-theological debates between Greek and Latin Christians. Kolbaba explores the issue of 'unclean foods' from a number of perspectives, from the anthropological to the sociological to the theological, but in the end admits that her central question remains unanswered: why, despite the clear directives of the church about food, does the accusation of eating unclean foods appear in the medieval diatribes between Greeks and Latins?

The easy answer is, of course – and Kolbaba herself reluctantly allows for it – that attacking the Latins on the ground of their eating habits provides the polemicist with an easy way to be nasty. But whether this answer is appropriate and sufficient for these extremist texts in hand, Kolbaba's valiant attempt to give them a theological depth is not altogether misplaced. Even at the level of distaste, or disgust, rather than at that of unlawfulness, condemnation of other people's food habits reveals an ethnocentric attitude defining the 'us' to the detriment of the 'other'.[2] Despite seeing in food this added dimension, Kolbaba does not think that an explanation for the resurfacing of this question can be made 'by reference to the symbolism of Byzantine Christian culture', a line of thought that she adopts instead

1 T. M. Kolbaba, *The Byzantine Lists: errors of the Latins* (Urbana, IL, 2000), 145–69.

2 See Kolbaba, *Lists*, 150 and note 26, 151.

in the case of polemics about the form of the Eucharist.[3] In this paper, I would like to bring back the issue of 'unclean foods' to its symbolic import by looking closer at the scriptural basis for the church's pronouncements against eating discriminations.

In surveying the literature concerning this issue, Kolbaba mentions the letter of Peter of Antioch to the patriarch Keroularios, a document which is often held up as representative of the Greeks' goodwill towards the Latins advocated by this high prelate, though ultimately (and sadly) clashing against the patriarch's more intransigent mentality.[4] In this letter, a substantial section is devoted to countering Keroularios's attacks on the eating habits of the Latins.[5] Kolbaba's report of this key text is short and selective. The passage is chosen to represent 'those who explicitly repeat the canonical and patristic position'. So, for example, Peter of Antioch, in his reply to Keroularios, writes:

> As for the claim that they eat unclean things and their monks eat meat – lard – you will find, if you enquire about it, that these practices exist also among some of us [eastern Christians]. For Bithynians, Thracians, and Lydians eat magpies, crows, turtle-doves, and hedgehogs. The use of all of these the Fathers treated as indifferent. 'For everything created by God is good, and nothing is to be rejected if it is received with thanksgiving' (I Timothy 4.14)

Peter goes on to cite the canon of St Basil, thus supplementing his own opinion with both scriptural and patristic authority:[6]

> Even as we distinguish the harmful from the appropriate in vegetables and fruits, so also we distinguish the harmful from the beneficial in meats. For even hemlock is a vegetable and the flesh of a vulture is meat, but no one in his right mind would eat hen-bane or would touch dog-meat unless it were a matter of life and death. Yet he who ate it would not act unlawfully.[7]

Kolbaba's summary of Peter's letter omits the citation of the passage from Acts 10.11–15, which occurs between the citation of the letter of Timothy,[8] and the next paragraph citing Basil's canon. The omission is small, but

[3] Kolbaba, *Lists*, 158, rejects the possibility of explaining the phenomenon along these lines.

[4] S. Runciman, *The Eastern Schism: a study of the papacy and the eastern churches during the eleventh and twelfth centuries* (Oxford, 1955; repr. 1997), 65–6.

[5] *PG* 120.795B–816A.

[6] Kolbaba, *Lists*, 147–8 and notes 8 and 12.

[7] G. A. Rhalles and A. Potles, *Σύνταγμα τῶν θείων καὶ ἱερῶν κανόνων*, 6 vols (Athens, 1852–59; repr. 1966), 4.257.

[8] This biblical reference is not given in *PG* and may therefore have been identified by Kolbaba herself. Note, however, that her translation follows the biblical text, rather than the slightly modified version in Peter's text (see next quotation).

significant, because this is the scriptural text which lies at the basis of patristic teaching about foods. Nowhere does this *pièce justificative* appear in Kolbaba's chapter. Here is how Peter of Antioch uses it:

> 'For no creature of God is to be rejected, if it is received with thanksgiving.' And what convinces me of this is the bowl of cloth that came down from heaven, which contained all quadrupeds of the earth and wild beasts and reptiles, and the winged creatures of the sky, and Peter hearing from God, 'Rise up, Peter, kill and eat', and saying, 'Not at all, o Lord, because nothing common or impure ever entered into my mouth', and hearing again: 'What God has purified, you shall not call impure'.[9]

In order to examine here the significance of this passage, it is necessary to quote its contextualization in Acts 10.9–16:

> Peter went up on the roof to pray. He became hungry and wanted something to eat; and while it was being prepared, he fell into a trance. He saw the heaven opened and something like a large sheet coming down, being lowered to the ground by its four corners. In it were all kinds of four-footed creatures and reptiles and birds of the air. Then he heard a voice saying: 'Get up, Peter; kill and eat'. But Peter said: 'By no means, Lord; for I have never eaten anything which is profane or unclean'. The voice said to him again, a second time: 'What God has made clean, you will not call profane'. This happened three times, and the thing was suddenly taken up to heaven.

In this passage,[10] Peter is portrayed as an observant Jew, whose hunger at mealtimes – as the narrative framework emphasizes – is only satisfied through the consumption of 'clean foods', that is, foods that can be eaten according to the Levitical laws. In order to undo Peter's ingrained piety, no less than an ecstatic vision and a command coming directly from God to 'kill and eat' any animal are necessary. While Peter's mentality reflects the distinctions of clean and unclean animals made in Leviticus 11 and Deuteronomy 14, the language in which the vision is couched goes back to the Genesis narrative: the three categories of animals, standing for the whole of creation, echo Genesis 1.20–26, while the command to eat without distinctions recalls the covenant with Noah in Genesis 9.3.[11] The effect of these biblical resonances is that of portraying the 'new' command as in

[9] *PG* 120.800D–801A.

[10] The most recent commentary is the book by C. Lukasz, *Evangelizzazione e conflitto: indagine sulla coerenza letteraria e tematica della pericope di Cornelio (Atti 10, 1–11, 18)* (Frankfurt am Main, 1993), esp. 71–91.

[11] Lukasz, *Evangelizzazione e conflitto*, 75–8.

fact restoring the original order, 'to which Moses's "legislation" was only a provisional exception'.[12]

Although only the climactic dialogue of this passage is used in Peter of Antioch's letter, its background is surely implied. The broader context of the Acts narrative places Peter's experience as the centrepiece of his interaction with Cornelius, the Roman centurion who becomes the first 'pagan' convert to Christianity. The vision is thus understood to work in a twofold manner: practically, Peter can now freely eat with the gentiles, which he proceeds to do at the house of Cornelius (Acts 10.24–48) – and such conviviality has, of course, deeper cultural relevance; allegorically, the text proposes the interpretation of the animals in terms of the equality of all people before God. Together, these components contribute to the definition of the new *ecclesia* founded on Christ, in which Jews and gentiles are not separated by dietary distinctions. Rather, it is the criterion of virtue which characterizes 'Christian' men and women. In this new context issues concerning food return not in a specifically normative, but in a generically moralized manner, that is, as gluttony or fasting. This concept of ethical justice is uttered by Peter, who says: 'I truly understand that God shows no partiality, but in every nation anyone who fears him and does what is right is acceptable to him' (Acts 10.34–5).

The Christian attitude to food thus only partly originates in the direct confrontation with Judaism, along the path of progressive differentiation between these two religions. As a sect of Judaism, the new religion could well have kept the dietary laws, just as it kept the Old Testament from which they sprang. But it was not simply a matter of defining 'us' against 'them', because a third party, the 'pagans', had a key role to play in Christianity's self-identity. Lukasz's conclusions capture the entire significance of Peter's vision, considering that it was Luke's intention

> to problematize the conversion of the pagans to the end of emphasizing the need to eliminate those obstacles placed by the Judaeo-Christians against the evangelization of the gentiles and their being welcomed into the church … The pericope of Cornelius is basically designed as a conflict between the divine will for universal salvation and the Judaeo-Christian opposition to this, which must be overcome.[13]

---

12 Derrett, 'Clean and unclean animals', 217, quoted in Lukasz, *Evangelizzazione e conflitto*, 77 note 23.

13 Lukasz, *Evangelizzazione e conflitto*, 221: 'di problematizzare la conversione dei pagani allo scopo di dimostrare l'eliminazione degli ostacoli che da parte dei giudeocristiani vengono messi davanti all'evangelizzazione dei gentili e alla loro accoglienza nella chiesa. … La pericope di Cornelio è impostata come un conflitto tra la volontà divina di salvezza universale e l'opposizione giudeocristiana che deve essere sconfitta.'

In other words, the threefold interaction between Jews, Judaeo-Christians and 'pagans' required a radical lowering of the barriers of ethnic identity and segregation, particularly reflected in food laws, as well as a redefinition of the boundaries of Christian identity along purely spiritual lines.

By contrast, the upholding of Jewish identity within the Byzantine empire entailed the continuation of the Levitical laws, and the rabbis involved themselves with the particularities of defining the extent of the application of these laws according to the geopolitical situation of the Jewish communities, as Claudine Dauphin clearly showed in the case of late-antique Palestine.[14] The Jewish presence in the Byzantine empire, therefore, both territorially established and in the diaspora, kept alive the issue of clean and unclean foods as a marker of both ethnic and religious identity, further strengthened by the continuation of the 'kosher' mentality on the part of the Muslims. Thus, despite the church's canonical pronouncements on this question, the actual contingent experience of Byzantine Christians allowed them to apply 'negative' dietary distinctions and define the Christian as, unlike either Jew or Muslim, one 'who eats pork meat'.

Peter's vision, however, was not so easily forgotten. Peter of Antioch's use of Acts 10 as a proof text in defence of the Latins stands at the end of a long line of interpretations of this passage.[15] By using this text, Peter of Antioch reminds his colleague that it is not simply unfair, but profoundly unchristian to resort to food distinctions to support ethnocentric claims. In this sense, there is no real distinction between food mores and liturgical practice (particularly the debate over the use of unleavened bread for the Eucharist, known as the azymite controversy): both enter the eleventh-century contentions as symbolic of a deeper power struggle between Constantinople and Rome, a pitching of forces and mentalities concerning the definition of the *ecclesia* and its universality.

Two fragments of evidence allow us to penetrate further into the symbolic import of Acts 10 for medieval Byzantium: the first is the letter of Pope Nicholas I to Emperor Michael III in 865;[16] the second is a miniature of the 1066 Theodore Psalter.[17] The second of these fragments points to the Stoudite milieu at Constantinople, which was the hub of the 1054 debates,

---

[14] C. Dauphin, 'Interdits alimentaires et territorialité en Palestine byzantine', *TM* 14 (2002), 147–66; see pp. 148–9 and the bibliography cited therein for an introduction to the Jewish purity laws.

[15] For a full survey of the exegetical tradition, see F. Bovon, *De vocatione gentium. Histoire de l'interprétation d'Actes 10, 1–11, 18 dans les six premier siècles*, Beiträge zur Geschichte der biblischen Exegese 8 (Tübingen, 1967).

[16] *Epistolae carolini aevi* IV, MGH (Berlin, 1925), 477–8; see also H. Rahner, *L'Eglise et l'état dans le christianisme primitif* (Paris, 1964), 338–52.

[17] *Theodore Psalter: electronic facsimile*, ed. C. Barber (Champaign, 2000), miniature on fol. 138v; S. Der Nersessian, *L'Illustration des psautiers grecs du Moyen Age, II. Londres, Add. 19.352,*

and thus provides the key to understanding the resurgence of food issues in eleventh-century polemic.

The pope's letter was written in support of the legitimacy of Patriarch Ignatios against Photios and against the emperor's purported caesaro-papism. In it, Peter's vision was used to revindicate the *Libertas Ecclesiae* through Augustine's exegesis of the passage. According to this exegesis, the object descending from heaven and containing all species of animals – a vase, *skeuos* being translated as *vas* in both the Vulgate and the Vetus Latina – signified the Church; in it, all nations were united in baptism.[18] The papal letter ensured that Augustine's interpretation became known to at least some churchmen in Constantinople, and gave it a particularly Roman slant, by stressing the primacy of Rome over all Christendom. Presumably, both Augustine's exegesis and its Roman reading were circulated at the monastery of Stoudios, where the abbot Nicholas was leader of the Ignatian (pro-papal) faction. This pope's outspokenness about Roman primacy in his understanding of ecclesiology makes him into a kind of 'Gregorian reformer' *ante litteram*,[19] and it is therefore possible that the memory of his documents was relevant to the treatment of the question of church unity in the eleventh century.

Augustine's exegesis was originally part of his *Commentary on the Psalms*, where he linked the praise of creation in Psalm 103 with Peter's vision of God's creatures in Acts 10. Augustine interprets the beasts named in the Psalm as the 'ethne' (*Bestias silvae, gentes intellegimus*),[20] and the rock as Peter and, by reference to his obedience to God's command of slaying and eating all animals, as the Church (*omnes mactat et manducat Petrus; quia Petrus Petra, petra ecclesia*).[21] In the illustration of this Psalm devised at the Stoudios monastery in the 1060s, in the Theodore Psalter, this metaphorical and complex exegesis may still be at work.[22]

Bibliothèque des Cahiers archéologiques 5 (Paris, 1970), 49 and fig. 223. The chased animal is identified by Der Nersessian as a fox, by Barber as a rabbit.

18 P. Skubiszewski, '*Ecclesia, Christianitas, Regnum et Sacerdotium* dans l'art des Xe–XIe siècles: idées et structures des images', *CahCM* 28 (1985), 133–79, 142–3.

19 W. Ullmann, *The Growth of Papal Government in the Middle Ages: a study in the ideological relation of clerical to lay power* (London, 1955; 3rd edn, 1970), 191–209.

20 *Aurelii Augustini opera 10: Enarrationes in Psalmos*, ed. E. Dekkers and J. Fraipont, CCSL 38–40, 3 vols (Turnhout, 1990), Psalms 103, 40.10.3, pp. 1499–1500: 1499, line 12.

21 *Enarrationes*, 1500, lines 62–3.

22 The image in the Theodore Psalter is unlikely to be a representation of Peter's vision – above all, Peter is missing. Cf. the iconography which appears in University of Chicago Library MS 965, where Peter is kneeling in prayer and a bowl below the open heavens is placed before him: Luba Eleen, 'Acts illustration in Italy and Byzantium', *DOP* 31 (1977), 255–78, with fifty-two plates, pl. 26. My claim here is that the exegesis of Psalm 103 involving the Acts passage is behind the pictorial interpretation chosen in the Theodore Psalter.

The miniature illustrating verses 16–18 of Psalm 103 in the Theodore Psalter draws attention to itself by departing from the tradition of depicting at this point a stork's nest, as found in all other marginal psalters.[23] The variety of animals here shown instead appears closer to the biblical text:

> The trees of the Lord are watered abundantly,
> the cedars of Lebanon that he planted
> In them the sparrows (στρουθία) build their nests
> the stork (ἐρωδιός) has its home in the fir trees
> The high mountains are for the deer (ἔλαφοι)
> the rocks (πέτρα) are a refuge for the hares (λαγωοῖς in the Theodore Psalter text, substituting a more familiar word for the Septuagint's χοιρογρυλλίοις).

In the miniature, some sparrows and a stork are nesting on the branches of a tree; at the centre on a rock stands a deer; below the rock, a dark cave opens as a refuge for a hare that is being chased by a dog. And yet this illustration does not simply aim at literality; it chooses the representative animals from the Psalm's list, and arranges them meaningfully in a composition, adding the chasing scene at the bottom. The tradition of interpreting animals allegorically may thus function here as the key to unlock the illustrator's choice.

In fact, it is striking that nearly all the animals listed in the Psalm to praise God's creation were those regarded as 'unclean' according to the Jewish dietary laws.[24] Therefore, the beauty of creation emphasized in this Jewish prayer contrasts with the juridical relationship later established towards animals as food; rather, it is identical with Peter's reformed attitude after God's injunction through his vision, an attitude that effectively goes back to pre-Levitical times. It is significant that the only exception to unclean animals in this list is the deer, singled out in Deuteronomy as the paradigmatic animal 'that the unclean and the clean alike may eat' (Deuteronomy 12.22).[25] The image appears to exploit the contrast between clean and unclean animals by placing the deer at the top of the rock.[26]

The text of the *Physiologos* provides a symbolic interpretation for the deer, stating that just as the deer defeats evil dragons by pouring the water it has drunk into the crags where dragons hide, so Christ shed blood and

---

[23] Khludov Psalter, Moscow, Historical Museum MS 129, fol. 104r; Paris, BN MS 20, fol. 12r; BAV, Barberini MS 372, fol. 176r.

[24] See Leviticus 11 verse 6: χοιρογρύλλιον; verse 16: στρουθίον; verse 19: ἐρωδιόν and also Deuteronomy 14.

[25] See also Deuteronomy 12.15, 14.5, 15.22.

[26] In addition, the chasing scene may have a moral resonance: compare fols 28r and 190r, where other pursuing dogs assist the shepherd David in guarding sheep against wolves, inviting a metaphorical interpretation on the lines of the contrast between good and evil.

water from his side during his death on the cross, thereby freeing us from the dragon 'through his life-giving action of cleansing' – that is, he cleanses through the water from his sides and by his death grants resurrection – and destroying in us any diabolical inclination.[27] Since the illustration of the *Physiologos* text was carried out by the Stoudites at roughly the same time as the production of the Theodore Psalter, this interpretation of the deer as Christ could have been close to the mind of the artist.[28] The comparison in the *Physiologos* is based on the famous verse 'Like a deer yearns for running streams even so my soul' (Psalms 41 [42].2), illustrated in this Psalter with a deer drinking from the rock whence a stream flows (fol. 51r). This image, too, is an innovation of this Psalter if compared to its models and can be likened to the water-pouring rocks of Moses's water-miracles (fols 101v and 110r). In these scenes, the rock symbolizes the church which provides the waters of purification and salvation to its faithful, notably through the sacraments of baptism and the Eucharist.[29] The stately deer standing on the rock figuratively parallels Christ's position to that of Moses in the Moses image and symbolically represents Christ's presence in his church.

The ecclesiological import of this set of images, enhanced by the exegetical impact of Augustine's text filtered through the Roman perspective, leads us to conclude that, despite its apparent insignificance, even this image of a group of animals illustrating Psalm 103 in the Theodore Psalter is part of a wider discourse-in-images. In particular, its concerns fit well into the themes I have identified as being addressed in this book production, such as the definition of a Christian *oikoumene* beyond the laceration of the 1054 anathemas, and the position of Christianity with respect to the other 'ethne', and especially vis-à-vis Judaism.[30] Both at creation stage and in the second covenant with Noah in Genesis, just as later in the Christian *reprise*, food laws were not of central concern in regulating humanity's attitude to animals.

Both the distant, scriptural origin of the Christian debates on clean and unclean foods, and the contingent eleventh-century explicit or implicit comments on the topic, strongly suggest the symbolic dimension of food in defining, or denying, cross-cultural dialogue. To support the Church's

---

27 F. Zambon, tr., *Il Fisiologo* (Milan, 1975), 67: 'mediante il lavacro di rigenerazione'

28 M. Bernabò, G. Peers and R. Tarasconi, *Il Fisiologo di Smirne. Le miniature del perduto codice B.8 della Biblioteca della Scuola Evangelica di Smirne*, Millennio medievale 7 (Florence, 1998), 47.

29 A fuller commentary on these miniatures is in B. Crostini, 'Navigando per il Salterio: riflessioni intorno all'edizione elettronica del manoscritto Londra, British Library, Addit. 19.352', *BollBG* 56–7 (2002–2003), 133–209, 146–7.

30 For further elements of this discourse, see B. Crostini, 'Christianity and Judaism in eleventh-century Constantinople', in V. Ruggieri and L. Pieralli, eds, *EUKOSMIA. Miscellanea per il 75o di Padre Vincenzo Poggi S.J.* (Soveria Mannelli, 2003), 167–87.

claim that the non-enjoyment of food divorced from any ascetic motivation is wrong, Kolbaba quotes Apostolic Canon 51:

> If any bishop, priest, or deacon, or any clergyman at all, abstains from marriage, meat, or wine, not for mortification but because he abhors these things, forgetting that all things are exceedingly good … either let him repent or let him be deposed from office and expelled from the Church. Let a layman be treated likewise.[31]

This forceful reminder of the goodness of all creation, joining together food and sex, is appropriate to the many concerns for 'purity' that characterize the reformist mentality of the eleventh century, including among other things the debate over clerical celibacy,[32] as much as to its original one of fighting dualist sects. While at one level the question, internal to Christianity, consisted of a struggle for authority in defining whether or by whom uniformity of practice was to be established; at another, the deeper ecclesiological issue re-emerging with questions such as that of unclean foods affected the understanding of the basis for this religion.

In conclusion, Christianity appears in this matter not just to uphold cultural relativism – different people eat different foods – but consciously to attempt to forestall the drive to ethnocentrism that, defining one's own diet as the best possible and holding onto it with exclusive passion, as Kolbaba reminds us, justifies the rejection of the other. Thus, the bishop, priest, or layman raised on pasta – forgive the anachronism – is not only forbidden to abhor the ostrich-eating of another culture, but even required to enjoy it. Clearly, the requirement is not primarily for one's own benefit, but for the ostrich-eater's, who by this token cannot be discriminated against along behavioural divides. By separating, in effect, religious belief from everyday practice, and thus religious belonging from ethnic identity, Christianity has sought to define itself as a universal faith.

It is, therefore, precisely the factor eliminated from Kolbaba's discussion, namely the symbolism of Byzantine Christian culture (see note 3), against which the renewed interest in the issue of clean and unclean foods in the Greek–Latin debates around 1054 must be read. That discussion over 'kosher' food was present at the beginning of the Keroularian attack against Latin orthodoxy, as Peter of Antioch's letter to the patriarch attests, is probably sufficient in explaining the later resurfacing of this theme in the continuing polemic among Christians.

---

31 G. A. Rhalles and A. Potles, *Σύνταγμα*, 2.67. I reproduce the translation from p. 147.

32 See the essays in M. Frassetto, ed., *Medieval Purity and Piety: essays on medieval clerical celibacy and religious reform* (New York, 1998).

16. Eat, drink ... and pay the price

Antony Eastmond and Liz James[1]

Food and drink, not unnaturally, recur as themes throughout Byzantine literature and art, and the consequences of eating and drinking are often upheld in both as warnings to the unwary. From the fall of Adam and Eve as the result of eating, to the salvation of humanity through the body and blood of Christ at the Last Supper, re-enacted during the liturgy, food and drink symbolized both evil and good. The language of consumption pervades hell. Bodies were eaten into hell and the torments of evildoers, along with the gnashing of teeth, the outer darkness and the unquenchable fire, included the worm that sleepeth not and being eaten for eternity. At the forefront of the damned was the rich man who would not share his food with Lazarus, and is now and forever consumed by fire (Figure 16.1).

The danger of food formed a consistent theme in monastic literature. Monks were consistently reminded of food, of what not to eat, how little to eat of it, when to eat it and the need to share it.[2] Heaven was gained through abstinence. Even the visions of paradise described in saints' lives and other texts make little reference to food: when the saintly Euphrosynos, the despised and lowly cook of a monastery, was seen in a dream by a monk to be in charge of a garden of delights, this garden featured little food, other than a wondrous apple.[3] On the other hand, however, consumption, in the form of the bread and wine in the Eucharist, leads to salvation. Nevertheless, despite the centrality of the Eucharist in the deliverance of humanity and as a means of entry to heaven, food and consumption were not perceived as readily available for the saved. There are no images of banquets in heaven. Rather, over-consumption and its consequences were pictured more readily and vividly than the pleasures of the table. This paradoxical combination

[1] For Bryer, in memory of octopus ice cream and hamzi.

[2] See, for example, throughout John Moschos, *Pratum spirituale*, *PG* 87.2851–3116; J. Wortley, tr., *The Spiritual Meadow of John Moschos* (Kalamazoo, 1992); the index to *BMFD* 5.1890–91 devotes no less than forty-three lines of references to dietary rules and regulations.

[3] *De Euphrosyno coquo* (*BHG* 628c), in H. Delehaye, ed., *Synaxarium ecclesiae Constantinopolitanae. Propylaeum ad AASS Novembris* (Brussels, 1902), 35–6.

of salvation through general abstinence, and at the same time through consumption of the Eucharist, is most evident in the frequent depiction of the skeletal figure of St Mary of Egypt at the forefront of the saved in images of the Last Judgement (Figure 16.2), whose real nourishment in the desert had been the Eucharist she received from St Zosimos.[4]

Here, we shall consider two of the results of overindulgence in food and wine: obesity and vomiting. One of the most immediate consequences of all that eating was fatness, and the Byzantines' view of the overweight was not flattering. Indeed, to describe someone as corpulent was, on the whole, to abuse them. Prokopios in the *Secret History* was certainly not intending to compliment Justinian when he described him as 'neither tall nor unusually short ... not at all skinny but rather plump, with a round face that was not unattractive' and as bearing a strong resemblance to the monstrous Domitian.[5] The western bishop, Liudprand of Cremona, was similarly not well disposed towards the emperor Nikephoros II Phokas: describing him as 'a monstrosity of a man ... a dwarf ... fat-headed ... with a big belly' is only a small part of Liudprand's abuse.[6] For Michael Psellos, Constantine VIII, not an emperor for whom he had much praise, was a man of enormous size, over nine feet tall, with remarkable digestive powers and dominated by his gluttony and sexual passions, which had resulted in arthritis.[7] Terms of abuse revolving around the fuller figure were employed enthusiastically by any Byzantine author looking for a stick to beat the villains of their pieces. As Alexander Kazhdan showed, unpleasant fatness is a unifying theme in the varying accounts of that would-be usurper, John Komnenos, known as John the Fat.[8] For Nicholas Mesarites, John had coarse black hair, full, heavy shoulders and a fleshy bloated head. He looked weak and enfeebled and dripped with sweat. Stoutness here, coupled with coarse hair and a fat head, was clearly not meant as a compliment.[9] Nikephoros Chrysoberges

---

4 The *Life* of St Mary of Egypt, *PG* 87.3693–726, esp. chaps 19 and 21; B. Ward, tr., *Harlots of the Desert* (London, 1987), esp. 49–50, 52–4.

5 Prokopios, *Anekdota*, ed. J. Haury, revisions G. Wirth (Leipzig, 1963), vol. 3, 8.12–14; G. A. Williamson, tr., *Procopius: The Secret History* (London, 1966), 78–9.

6 'Relatio de legatione Constantinopolitana', chap. 3: Liudprandi Cremonensis, *Antapodosis, Homelia Paschalis, Historia Ottonia, Relatio*, ed. P. Chiesa (Turnholt, 1988), 188; F.A. Wright, tr., *The Works of Liutprand of Cremona* (London, 1930), 236–7.

7 Michael Psellos, *Chronographia*, tr. E. R. A. Sewter (London, 1953), 2.7.

8 A. Kazhdan with S. Franklin, *Studies on Byzantine Literature of the Eleventh and Twelfth Centuries* (Cambridge, 1984) devotes chapter 6 to a comparative study of the four accounts of the revolt of John by the four authors mentioned here, discussing John's fatness as a unifying theme.

9 Nicholas Mesarites, *Die Palastrevolution des Johannes Komnenos*, ed. A. Heisenberg (Würzburg, 1907), p. 27, lines 5–10 and p. 28, lines 11–13; Kazhdan with Franklin, *Studies*, 251.

similarly described the unfortunate John as corpulent, and also as ape-like.[10] Euthymios Tornikes abused him as fleshy, a puffed-up ox carcass, a bloated wineskin, inflated in mind and body; and Niketas Choniates additionally assaults John's figure as pot-bellied and barrel-shaped.[11] These authors all enjoyed using vivid, weight-related imagery to convey their loathing of John. Chrysoberges's metaphor of the 'sickle of punishment' slashing to pieces the corpulence of the usurper and destroying his puffed-up flesh is particularly vivid.[12] Very simply, fatness, like sexual depravity and other forms of excess, was one of the criteria employed within the rhetoric of invective to mark out the villain.

This contrasts with the categories of acceptable male beauty: the beautifully proportioned blond and white-skinned Digenes Akritas, for example.[13] Thinness, in contrast to fatness, was a sign of good looks and beauty, especially in men. Indeed, excessive thinness in both men and women was a sign of great piety and virtue. Mary of Egypt lost her womanly figure as a result of twenty years of living on just three loaves and Nikon the Metanoeite was described approvingly as tall, with shrivelled limbs and a face withered by fasting: 'his face changed due to his excessive asceticism and became emaciated'; his hair and beard were black and the appearance of his head squalid.[14]

That fat could be used as a term of abuse perhaps derives from gluttony's place as one of the eight vices, and taste's position as the 'mother of all vice'.[15] In the western tradition, the seven deadly sins are pride, avarice, envy, lust, sloth, anger and gluttony. In the eastern tradition, however, Origen developed the concept of ranking sins by their gravity, and categorized them either as mortal sins or as pardonable vices perpetrated without the full use of reason and free will. By the end of the fourth century, murder, idolatry and fornication were defined as the three capital sins.[16] Evagrios Pontikos

---

[10] The account comes in Nikephoros Chrysoberges's speech addressed to Alexios III Angelos, published in Nikephoros Chrysoberges, *Ad Angelos orationes tres*, ed. M. Treu (Breslau, 1892) and discussed in Kazhdan with Franklin, *Studies*, 244–5.

[11] Euthymios Tornikes, 'Discours I', in J. Darrrouzès, 'Les discours d'Euthyme Tornikès', *REB* 26 (1968), 49–72, especially, for example, 15.68–9; and Kazhdan with Franklin, *Studies*, 246–7; Niketas Choniates, *Historia*, ed. J. L. van Dieten (Berlin, 1975), 526; see also Kazhdan with Franklin, *Studies*, 247.

[12] See Kazhdan with Franklin, *Studies*, 245.

[13] *Digenes Akrites* [MS G], ed. J. Mavrogordato (Oxford, 1956), for example, IV.1178.

[14] For Mary of Egypt, see *PG* 87.3693–726, chap. 7; Ward, tr., *Harlots*, 41; for Nikon, see D. F. Sullivan, ed. and tr., *The Life of St Nikon* (Brookline, MA, 1987), 44.

[15] Gregory of Nyssa, *Traité de la virginité*, ed. and tr. M. Aubineau, SC 119 (Paris, 1966), 504–10.

[16] See I. Hausherr, 'L'origine de la théorie orientale des huit péchés capitaux', *OCA* 30 (1933), 164–75, also published in Hausherr, *Etudes de spiritualité orientale* (Rome, 1969), 11–22.

developed this into a system of eight vices, or sinful desires.[17] Gluttony was the first of the eight, followed by fornication (often as a result of gluttony), avarice, grief or despair, anger, sloth, vainglory and pride. Even after Evagrios was condemned for Origenism, his eight vices remained within monastic literature. A vice, in contrast to a sin, represented a weakness and an inclination to do evil, an explicit predilection towards certain sins, and even a habitually evil disposition. A vice and its corresponding virtue could not exist at the same time in the same person: it was not possible to be both gluttonous and abstemious. However, a man of vice could, as long as other virtuous inclinations were present, still perform good works in place of or next to the chief sin: one could, for example, be gluttonous but chaste.

Evagrios's system was linked to his belief in asceticism as the main path to salvation. His identification of the eight vices highlighted these as the temptations that the pious man needed to struggle against in order to contemplate divine wisdom. Thus the system of vices was specially developed in the first instance for monks, with listings of categories of special temptations instigated by demons, and then applied to laymen. Gluttony was one of the first of all temptations to assail the monk, for gluttony and lust reflected the coarse desires of the body. It was also the first of the three temptations of Christ. The summit of monastic achievement, for both men and women, was to achieve a completely immaterial state of being, like that of the angels, and one route to this was by abstention from food. Next to their emphasis on sexual temptation, texts such as John Moschos's *Spiritual Meadow* and Theodoret of Cyrrhus's *Lives of the Monks of Syria* place insistent and repeated emphasis on just how little ascetics ate; the less, the holier.[18]

A few surviving images attempt to convey the seriousness of sins, and the punishments that they would earn. This they represent through displays of consumption. In the narthex of the early tenth-century Yılanlı Kilise in the Ihlara gorge in Cappadocia, four naked women are bitten by serpents according to their sins: she 'who does not nourish her children' is bitten on

---

Also useful is S. Wenzel, 'The seven deadly sins: some problems of research', *Speculum*, 43 (1968), 1–22, though this is largely concerned with the west.

[17] See J. Driscoll, *The Ad Monachos of Evagrius Ponticus: its structure and a select commentary* (Rome, 1991), 13–15. For examples of the evils and dangers of gluttony, and the links between gluttony and lust, see his translation of the *Ad Monachos* in the same work, sections 6, 11, 38, 82, 97, 102.

[18] See, for example, John Moschos, *Spiritual Meadow*, for example p. 86 on the very holy anchorite who only ate wild vegetation and p. 184 on the monk who refused to drink. Theodoret of Cyrrhus, *Histoire des moines de Syrie*, ed. and tr. P. Canivet and A. Leroy-Molinghen, SC 234 and 257 (Paris, 1977–79), moves from Julian, who ate one meal of bread and salt per week (vol. 1, p. 196) to Salamanes who blocked himself into a windowless and doorless cell to emerge for food once a year (vol. 2, pp. 58–60).

her breasts; she 'who slanders' is bitten on the mouth; she 'who does not obey' is bitten on the ears; the fourth woman, who is bitten all over by eight serpents, now lacks the inscription to identify her particular, but literally overwhelming, sins (Figure 16.3).[19] A similar row, but this time of seven naked women and men being eaten by serpents, appears in the thirteenth-century narthex at Sopoćani in Serbia.[20]

Gluttony was also a cardinal theme in classical and Byzantine satire, where fatness and overeating were linked to comic effect, underlining both the vice and its ridiculousness. In the *Timarion*, Timarion discovers in the underworld that many of the dead are as concerned with food as the living. Among them is his old teacher, Theodore of Smyrna, at one time the 'biggest' sophist in Constantinople, who in his prime of life had to be carried about and was riddled with arthritis as a result of his gluttony. Now he is tall, white-haired and shrivelled, for a nourishing diet of mallow, cress and asphodel has restored him to life, but Theodore still hankers after pork fat, chicken and lamb.[21]

The same disapproval of obesity is shown in images of the fat. Sometimes, though not invariably, the Rich Man in hell is shown as obese, and some of the damned roasting away in images of the Last Judgement also appear overweight (Figure 16.1). However, the figure most regularly depicted as fat was Hades, keeper of the underworld, as shown in scenes of the Anastasis, especially in the ninth-century marginal psalters.

Originally, Hades, a combination of the underworld and of death, was depicted as a pagan god, venerable but dark-skinned. However, in the ninth century, above all in the group of manuscripts known as the marginal psalters, he was regularly depicted as fat and old, bald and dark, often a giant and often in a loincloth. After the ninth century, representations generally returned to the original slimmer and more sinuous type of image.[22] Images from the Khludov Psalter, for example, show Hades as a great fat being, with a wide mouth, a glutton swallowing up good and bad alike (fols 8v, 102v, which relate to the texts of Psalms 9 and 102 respectively). He is a corpulent figure with the bristly hair and beard and fat head already noted in literary accounts of unpleasant fatness. In these images, Hades does not appear interested in the torture and punishment of sinners, only that none escape him. Anna Kartsonis suggests that such images of Hades were

---

19 J.-M. and N. Thierry, *Nouvelles églises rupestres de Cappadoce. Region de Hasan Daği* (Paris, 1963), 100–101; for a good colour image, see N. Thierry, *La Cappadoce de l'antiquité au Moyen Age*, Bibliothèque de l'Antiquité Tardive 4 (Turnhout, 2002), pl. 56.

20 They are most clearly visible in schemas of the paintings: B. Zhivković, *Sopoćani. Tsrtezhi freska*, Spomenitsi Srpskog slikarstva srednjeg veka 3 (Belgrade, 1984), 27. No inscriptions identify the sins being punished here.

21 *Timarion*, tr. B. Baldwin (Detroit, MI, 1984), sections 23–4, pp. 58–9.

22 A. Kartsonis, *Anastasis. The Making of an Image* (Princeton, NJ, 1986), 139–40.

idiosyncratic, compared to the traditional representation of his lithe figure, but that the fat omnivorous giant would have been 'familiar to everyone from religious folklore'. She also proposes that the grotesque nature of the figure added insult to injury to the iconoclasts who objected to the representation of Hades in the first place.[23]

In the Old Testament, Hades was described as having ravenous jaws and an insatiable belly, swallowing young and old alike: 'Therefore Hades has enlarged its appetite and opened its mouth beyond measure …' (Isaiah 5.14) and 'Hades and Abbadon are never satisfied …' (Proverbs 27.20) are only two examples. In hymns and homilies from the fourth century, into the sixth and beyond, descriptions of Hades match the biblical testimony. Athanasios of Alexandria described Hades as having ravenous jaws and an insatiable belly, swallowing old and young alike; Andrew of Crete marked him as an insatiable eater. It was Hades's belly that came in for divine assault in Christ's descent to the underworld. In the *Gospel of Bartholomew*, Satan instructs Hades to make sure his gates are safe and his bars strengthened to keep Christ out. Hades replies: 'My belly is rent and my inward parts are pained; it cannot be but that God cometh hither.'[24] As Ephrem the Syrian put it, with the cross here serving as a weapon, Christ 'tore apart the voracious stomach of Hades and blocked the treacherous fully-opened jaws of Satan'.[25] Romanos the Melode used similar imagery in his hymns on the resurrection. In Hymn 20, Hades says: 'In his descent, he has attacked my stomach / so that I vomit forth those whom I formerly devoured'.[26] Romanos used this image of Christ piercing Hades's stomach and forcing him to vomit forth the dead on several occasions. It becomes clear that Hades's bulk depicted in the images of the Khludov Psalter was the result of his gluttony, devouring all who came his way. Death is the last great fatty: eat, drink and be merry, for tomorrow we must die.

But, of course, what goes in must come out again, and, as Romanos's *Hymns* show, it was a natural corollary of Christianity's interest in consumption and over-consumption that it also showed an interest in regurgitation, or vomit. Vomit recurs throughout the Bible (there are at least fifteen references) and consequently it comes up regularly in Byzantine exegesis. As a literal Second Coming, vomit features at the centre of the Second Coming of Christ. The status of vomit might be described as liminal: it is neither in nor out – or,

23 Kartsonis, *Anastasis*, 141.

24 *Gospel of Bartholomew*, in M. R. James, *The Apocryphal New Testament* (Oxford, 1924), 168.

25 Ephrem the Syrian, 'Sermo in pretiosam et vivificam crucem', *Sancti patris nostri Ephraem Syri, opera omnia* II (Rome, 1743), 249; and M .E. Frazer, 'Hades stabbed by the Cross of Christ', *Metropolitan Museum Journal*, 9 (1974), 157–8.

26 *Kontakia of Romanos, Byzantine Melodist*, ed. and tr. M. Carpenter (Columbia, MI, 1970), Hymn 20, 304.

rather, it has been both. It thus anticipates the status of the souls awaiting judgement, who are similarly in limbo, awaiting regurgitation.

Unlike fatness, however, vomit could be a good thing. The usual medieval medical analogy for vomit was that of the good expelling the bad.[27] The good body forcibly removed from itself its bad contents. As Revelation 3.16 declared, 'because you are lukewarm – neither hot nor cold – I shall spew you out of my mouth.' Biblical hermeneutics and Old Testament prefigurations reversed this in the figure of Jonah. In this case, an apostate prophet fleeing God's commands entered the whale, but a reformed preacher emerged. Here, the Byzantine moral was that what came out was considerably better than what went in. The whale's decorous regurgitation acted as the most celebrated antetype of the descent of Christ into Hades and his subsequent resurrection. In Christian terms, then, the very nature of regurgitation and vomit were inverted. Rather than the bad contents being purged from the good body and abhorred, the good contents were purged from the bad body and worshipped.

The transfer of such ideas into New Testament exegesis did not take long. By the sixth century, Romanos the Melode had effectively reduced Christ from the saviour of humanity to a particularly powerful emetic. Romanos's hymns show an interesting obsession with the gastric problems of Hades. In Romanos's 'Third Hymn on the Resurrection', strophes 7 and 9, Hades himself described his symptoms, and the inevitable result: 'I am pierced in the stomach; I do not digest the one whom I devoured. What I have devoured gave me strange eating. Not one of those whom I have eaten hitherto has troubled me ... Just as on the third day the whale disgorged Jonah, So now I disgorge Christ'.[28] Romanos returned to his theme in other hymns, such as his 'First Hymn on the Raising of Lazarus', where Death warns Hades that Christ 'searches for the contents of your belly. He has come, he who will purge you.'[29]

This grisly vision was echoed in an epigram on a now-lost image from the church of the Virgin at Pege (restored by Basil I, Constantine and Leo after 869). The epigram by Ignatios, magister of the secretaries under Basil I, and preserved in the *Greek Anthology*, may have accompanied an image of the Crucifixion: 'The dead Hades vomits up the dead / After having been

[27] For an introduction to the exegesis of vomit in the medieval west, see L. Smith, 'William of Auvergne and Confession', in P. Biller and A. J. Minnis, eds, *Handling Sin: confession in the Middle Ages*, York Studies in Medieval Theology 2 (York, 1998), 95–107.

[28] *Kontakia of Romanos*, 'Third Hymn on the Resurrection', strophes 7–9; see also similar comments in his 'Second Hymn on the Resurrection', strophes 2–3, and his 'Fifth Hymn on the Resurrection', strophe 2.

[29] *Kontakia of Romanos*, 'On the Raising of Lazarus I', strophe 11.

purged by the flesh of the Lord.'[30] The potential link of this epigram to the Crucifixion rather than to the Anastasis, when the assault on Hades's bloated belly actually takes place, shifts the emphasis away from the literal to the metaphorical.[31] There is a surviving visual match to this idea in a tenth-century ivory of the Crucifixion, published by Margaret Frazer.[32] This shows the cross of Christ spearing Hades in the stomach, with blood welling out all around (Figure 16.4). The ivory takes up the interest in the belly and has an inscription reading: 'The cross implanted in the stomach of Hades'. In the fourteenth century, these visual and textual ideas were combined in the image of the Crucifixion in the church of St George at Pološko in Macedonia. Here, 'the insatiable Hades' is stabbed in his voluminous belly by a sharp, pointed crucifix, and the scene is accompanied by an inscription taken from Romanos the Melode's 'Hymn on the Triumph of the Cross': 'My children, a wooden spear has suddenly pierced my heart; I am frightened and my entrails are suffering and my belly aches'.[33]

The metaphorical image of purging is depicted quite literally in the Khludov Psalter (Moscow, Historical Museum MS 129). On fol. 102v, accompanying Psalm 102.15–17, a soul is forcibly regurgitated from the mouth of Hades and into the arms of a waiting angel.[34] The link to the accompanying psalm is unclear as the text makes no reference to this idea but the association with the hymns of Romanos the Melode is obvious. On fol. 48r of the eleventh-century Barberini Psalter (BAV, Barberini MS 372), the imagery is even more graphic, as Hades clutches his stomach, such is his bellyaching, whilst the soul of Lazarus is purged by Christ back from it to the land of the living (Figure 16.5).[35]

The Last Judgement is a final area of display for vomit. The desire to show the physical resurrection of the body is pursued in Byzantine art in much greater detail than in the west. Unlike in the west, where, usually, whole bodies are depicted rising up out of their graves for judgement, in

---

30 *Anthologia Graeca*, 1.111, ed. H. Beckby (Munich, 1957). The translation is taken from M. D. Lauxtermann, *Byzantine Poetry from Pisides to Geometres. Texts and contexts, I*, Verlag der Österreichischen Akademie der Wissenschaften (Vienna, 2003), 182–3.

31 See Kartsonis, Anastasis, 146–8 for the link with the Anastasis and Lauxtermann, *Byzantine Poetry*, 183–4, for the suggestion that the link between the Crucifixion and the epigram is a scribal error.

32 Frazer, 'Hades stabbed', 153–61.

33 Z. Gavrilović, 'Eve or the Waters of Marah at Pološko', *Zograf* 25 (1996), 51–6, reprinted in her *Studies in Byzantine and Serbian Medieval Art* (London, 1991), no. 15; *Kontakia of Romanos*, 'Hymn on the Triumph of the Cross', strophe 1.

34 Psalm 102.15–17.

35 This is a considerable visual embellishment of the more straightforward image in the ninth-century Pantokrator Psalter on which it is based (Mount Athos, Pantokrator Monastery MS 61, fol. 29r); see S. Dufrenne, *L'Illustration des psautiers grecs du moyen âge*, Bibliothèque des Cahiers Archéologiques 1 (Paris, 1966), 23 and pl. IV.

Byzantium, the main preoccupation is with the imagery of regurgitation of body parts.[36] The images of the land and sea regurgitating the dead lie at the centre of many Byzantine Last Judgements. Arms, legs and other body parts emerge from the mouths of all kinds of beasts, including some unlikely candidates, notably the vegetarian elephants in the early thirteenth-century Last Judgement at Timotesubani in Georgia (Figure 16.6).[37] The whole is relegated to the fringes, and the parts come to the fore.

It is interesting that this imagery of fragmentation is divorced from the human division of bodies that fuelled the cult of saints and their relics in the west.[38] The reasons seem complex. It was certainly to remind all of the corporeality of resurrection: it really was about flesh, whole or part. It may have been that, in visual terms, it was all too easy to confuse whole bodies with souls, but less so the odd hand or foot. Most importantly, this emphasis on actual bodies gave the punishments of the damned their real terror. They were inflicted on real bodies producing real pains that all can understand, rather than spiritual punishments that might have seemed more distant from observers. This produced one slight paradox: denial of the flesh and thinness are among the main guarantees to enter heaven, as is evident from Mary of Egypt's prominence in depictions of the Last Judgement, but the Last Judgement is really a celebration of the flesh.

It is perhaps unsurprising that with all this loathing of gluttony, abuse of fatness and emphasis on vomit and regurgitation at the end of the world, there seems to be little desire or interest in the joy of food itself in the afterlife. Whilst worms consume all in hell, those in heaven, if not queasy at the thought of eating, certainly appear rather sombre and not in the mood for a feast. And remember: while gluttonous death waits to devour you, there is no room for fat people in heaven.

---

36 See, to take just one example, the Raising of the Dead and Last Judgement in the Pericope Book of Henry II of 1012 (Munich, Staatsbibliothek, MS Clm4452, fols 201v–202r): H. Fillitz, R. Kahsnitz and U. Kuder, *Zierde für ewige Zeit: das Perikopenbuch Heinrichs II* (Frankfurt am Main, 1994).

37 E. Privalova, *Rospis' Timotesubani* (Tbilisi, 1980), 92–4, pl. XXXV.

38 For which, see C. W. Bynum, 'Material continuity, personal survival and the resurrection of the body: a scholastic discussion in its medieval and modern contexts', in Bynum, *Fragmentation and Redemption; essays on gender and the human body in medieval religion* (New York, 1991), 239–98.

Figure 16.1: Italy, Torcello, west wall: detail of the damned from the Last Judgement, eleventh century (© Studio Bohm).

Figure 16.2: Georgia, Ateni, west conch: detail of the saved from the Last Judgement, c. 1090 (After A. Eastmond, *Royal Imagery in Medieval Georgia* [University Park, PA, 1998], plate VII).

Figure 16.3: Cappadocia, Yılanlı kilise, north wall of narthex: sinners suffering according to their sins; tenth century (After N. Thierry, *La Cappadoce de l'Antiquité au Moyen Âge*, Bibliothèque de l'Antiquité Tardive 4 [Turnhout, 2002], pl. 56).

Figure 16.4: New York, The Metropolitan Museum of Art: Byzantine ivory of the Crucifixion with Hades stabbed by the cross; tenth century (Photo: The Metropolitan Museum of Art).

Figure 16.5: Vatican City, BAV MS Barberini 372, fol. 48r (Psalter): The Raising of Lazarus; eleventh century (Photo: Biblioteca Apostolica Vaticana).

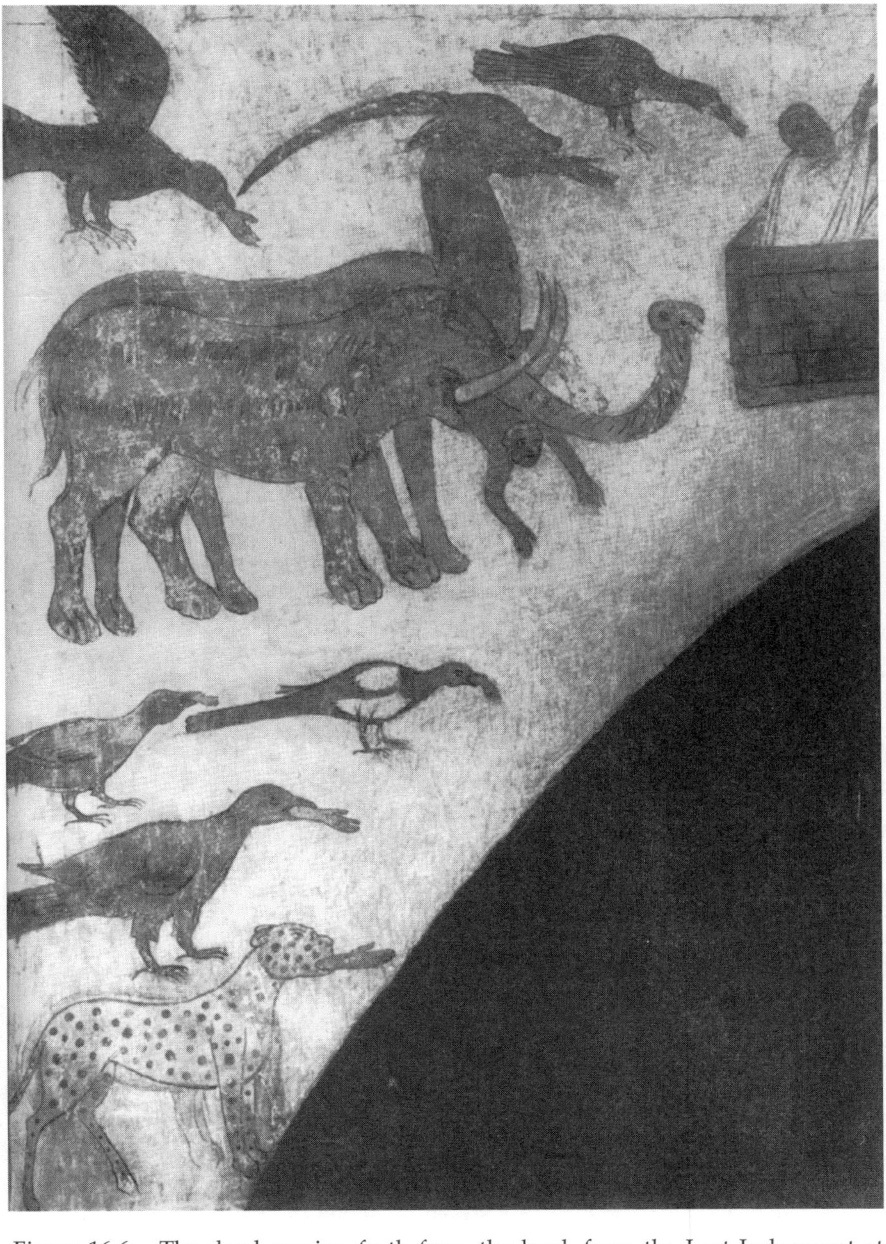

Figure 16.6: The dead coming forth from the land, from the Last Judgement at Timotesubani, Georgia, c. 1220 (After E. Privalova, *Rospis' Timotesubani* [Tbilisi, 1980], pl. XXV).

17. The changing dining habits at Christ's table

Joanita Vroom

In his work on the sociological aspects of food and meals the French scholar Roland Barthes has shown convincingly that food and dining habits are worthy of study.[1] According to Barthes, how and what people eat and drink in a society can be understood as a form of communication or, in his words, as 'a system of communication, a body of images, a protocol of usages, situations and behaviour'.[2] In this paper I will try to follow this perspective in my attempt to concentrate on the 'how' of dining practices in the Byzantine world (the 'what' is left for others elsewhere, including other chapters in this volume).

Consequently, I will present here a preliminary survey of the use of table equipment (for example, pottery, glass and cutlery) in the eastern Mediterranean from the fifth to the fifteenth century. In doing so, I will use two sources of information: pictorial representations of dining scenes in Byzantine art alongside textual evidence. Furthermore, I will present excavated examples of table equipment, which will underline my arguments. The aim of this survey is to establish whether the pictorial and written sources can contribute to an understanding of the changes in form and function of table utensils, and of the changes in dining habits in the Byzantine world – at least, for the well-to-do.

I do not claim in any way to strive for completeness in this survey, but rather to establish whether this is a fruitful line of approach to help us explain long-term changes in the utensils used on the table. As far as the pictorial sources are concerned, I will look at dining scenes from religious Byzantine art only, and at pictures of the Last Supper in particular.[3]

---

[1] R. Barthes, 'Pour une psycho-sociologie de l'alimentation contemporaine', *Annales E-S-C*, 16.5 (1961), 977–86; English translation: 'Toward a psychosociology of contemporary food consumption', in R. Forster and O. Ranum, eds, *Food and Drink in History: selections from the Annales E-S-C vol. 5* (Baltimore, MD, 1979), 166–73.

[2] Barthes, 'Toward a psychosociology of contemporary food consumption', 167.

[3] See J. Vroom, *After Antiquity. Ceramics and Society in the Aegean from the 7th to the 20th Century A.C.: a case study from Boeotia, Central Greece* (Leiden, 2003), 303–34, for more dining

Specifically, my attention will be focused on the depiction of the Last Supper in the Byzantine east as an actual meal (and not as a liturgical act) from the fifth century onwards. However, it is not my intention to discuss here all the known representations of the Last Supper in Byzantine art. I will concentrate my discussion upon those pictures in which the depicted scene has relevance for the understanding of the relation between changes in shape and changes in function of ceramics, glass and cutlery found at excavations.

Problems and possibilities in iconographical interpretation

One may wonder whether depictions of the Last Supper are suitable as illustrations of changing dining habits, as some scholars consider the scene to be the most conservatively treated in the Byzantine repertoire.[4] However, a closer look at apparently similar-looking depictions of the Last Supper from various periods can reveal clear developments over time. It will be, therefore, argued that the scene of the Last Supper as a representation of a meal is not one of the most conservative depictions in Byzantine iconography, but can show quite fundamental changes in key details of dining habits.[5] The consensus among most art historians seems to be that the Last Supper as a meal is of great interest because it is the only dining scene in Byzantine art (especially in illustrated manuscripts) which can be seen with a high frequency over a long period of time, even in those centuries for which we have little visual evidence (such as the eighth and ninth centuries).[6]

Here, I will pose the question of whether we can indeed observe a clear long-term development of dining habits in scenes of the Last Supper from late antiquity onwards by looking at the dining furniture, the tablecloth and above all the dining equipment on the table. In doing so, I will occasionally use other depictions of dining scenes in Byzantine religious art (among them Job's children banquet or the Hospitality of Abraham) to support my arguments.

---

scenes in Late Antique and Byzantine art.

4 For example, E. Dauterman Maguire and H. Maguire, 'Byzantine pottery in the history of art', in D. Papanikola-Bakirtzis, E. Dauterman Maguire and H. Maguire, eds, *Ceramic Art from Byzantine Serres* (Urbana, IL,1992), 2–3.

5 See also E. Dobbert, 'Das Abendmahl Christi in der bildenden Kunst bis gegen den Schluss des 14. Jahrhunderts', *RK* 14 (1891), 175–203, 451–62; G. Millet, *Recherches sur l'iconographie de l'évangile aux XIVe, XVe et XVIe siècles d'après les monuments de Mistra, de Macedoine et du Mont-Athos* (Paris, 1916), and K. Wessel, *Abendmahl und Apostelkommunion* (Recklinghausen, 1964), for this discussion.

6 Dobbert, 'Das Abendmahl', 382; Millet, *Recherches*; L. H. Loomis, 'The table of the Last Supper in religious and secular iconography', *AS* 5 (1927), 71–88; Wessel, *Abendmahl und Apostelkommunion*, 46.

Pictures of the Late Antique and Early Byzantine period (fifth to seventh century)

According to the art historian Eduard Dobbert, the oldest Last Supper meal in Byzantine art can be found on a fifth-century ivory diptych in the treasury of the cathedral of Milan (Figure 17.1).[7] On the Milan diptych we can distinguish four persons reclining on a high, semicircular couch (in late antiquity known as the *sigma*- or *stibadium*-couch). The couch has a crescent cushion or bolster on the front, and surrounds a small, semicircular table.

At the centre of the table we see a flat, wide plate with curved walls, containing a fish. Around the plate one can discern five or six small, cross-marked bread loaves. There are no knives, spoons or individual plates on the table. It appears as if the second diner on the left of the couch is holding a drinking cup (made of glass or metal?) in his hand, but the image is not clear. The person sitting next to him is reclining on the left side of the semicircular couch.

There are two other sixth-century images of the Last Supper which show the same characteristics as that in Milan. The first of these, which provides a classic prototype for later depictions, is a mosaic at San Apollinare Nuovo in Ravenna (dated to c. 500; Figure 17.2).[8] The second example is an illustration from the Codex Purpureus Rossanensis, a manuscript of Near Eastern or Constantinopolitan origin (Figure 17.3).[9]

Both pictures portray Jesus with a nimbus reclining on his left elbow on the extreme left side of a raised, cushioned couch. The twelve Apostles recline on their left arms as well. The semicircular table is covered with a tablecloth that is decorated with embroidered or woven decorative motifs; in the case of the Rossano Gospels, the tablecloth is decorated with birds. In the centre of the table one can discern one plate or dish with some bread rolls around it. In the Ravenna mosaic the six bread rolls seem to have a pyramidal shape; in the Rossano Gospels the two bread rolls are crescent-shaped. Neither image shows cutlery, individual plates or individual cups or beakers. The diners seem to eat their food from a centrally placed wide plate or dish with their fingers, which seems to suggest simple and communal dining.

---

7 Milan, Tesoro del Duomo: see Dobbert, 'Das Abendmahl', 183, fig. 18.

8 Ravenna, San Apollinare Nuovo: see A. Carile, ed., *Storia di Ravenna, II.1. Dall'età bizantina all'età ottoniana. Territorio, economia e società* (Venice, 1991), pl. 12; Dobbert, 'Das Abendmahl', fig. 19.

9 Rossano, Museo dell'Archivescovado, Codex Purpureus Rossanensis, fol. 3r, Gospels: G. Cavallo and W. Loerke, eds, *Codex Purpureus Rossanensis. Facsimile edition of MS Museo dell'Archivescovado*, Codices Selecti 81, 2 vols (Graz, 1985–87). See also A. Haseloff, *Codex Purpureus Rossanensis: die Miniaturen der griechischen Evengelien-Handschrift in Rossano* (Berlin, 1898), 22, pl. 5 and Dobbert, 'Das Abendmahl', fig. 22.

The meals represented in all three Last Supper scenes appear to be in accordance with dining habits in late antiquity. Written and pictorial sources confirm that from the late fourth century onwards the curved *sigma*- or *stibadium*-couch, adorned with a decorated bolster on the front, became the setting for formal and luxurious banquets, both indoors and outdoors.[10] One aspect of the protocol was that diners reclined to eat, which was an indication of high status, with their left arm supported on a bolster, taking food from a table with the right hand. The diners were placed in a hierarchical order, with the guest of honour (in the case of Last Supper scenes, Jesus) usually reclining in the right corner (*in dextro cornu*) and the second most important figure of the banquet in the left corner (*in sinistro cornu*).[11]

Archaeological finds complement the pictorial and written sources. In fact, masonry and marble examples of semicircular *stibadium*-couches and semicircular tables have been recovered in various parts of the Mediterranean, particularly in Albania, Greece, Turkey and Syria.[12]

The embroidered tablecloths depicted in the Last Supper scenes from Ravenna and in the Rossano Gospels are similar to Coptic textiles of the sixth century excavated in burial grounds in Egypt (Figures 17.2 and 17.3). Such textiles were often decorated with applied tapestry – woven or embroidered square ornamental motifs, or bands in wool or silk on a natural linen background, as we can see along the hemline of the tablecloth in the Last Supper mosaic from Ravenna. Furthermore, birds of all kinds (as on the tablecloth of the Rossano illustration) were very popular as a decorative theme on Coptic textiles of the sixth century.[13]

The shapes of the bread loaves in all Last Supper scenes were also known in antiquity. On Greek reliefs of the fifth century bc, one can already notice pyramid-shaped bread loaves in funerary-meal scenes. Examples of crescent-shaped bread rolls can be seen in Late Antique dining scenes of the mid fourth to late fifth century ad.14 The round cross-marked loaves

---

[10] J. Marquardt, *Das Privatleben der Römer* (Leipzig, 1864; 2nd edn revised by A. Mau in 1886), 308–9.

[11] Marquardt–Mau, *Das Privatleben der Römer*, 304. See further Simon Malmberg's chapter in this volume.

[12] For example K. M. D. Dunbabin, *The Roman Banquet: images of conviviality* (Cambridge, 2003), 193–5, figs 112–13; see also J. Vroom, 'The archaeology of late-antique dining habits in the Eastern Mediterranean: a preliminary survey of the evidence', in A. Gutteridge, E. Swift and M. Guidetti, eds, *Objects in Context, Objects in Use: the archaeology of everyday life* (Leiden, forthcoming).

[13] See D. Buckton, ed., *Byzantium. Treasures of Byzantine Art and Culture from British Collections* (London, 1994), 101–3, nos 111–12.

[14] See F. J. Dölger, *Ichtus IV. Die Fish-Denkmäler in der frühchristlichen Plastik, Malerei und Kleinkunst* (Münster, 1927), pl. 233 for pyramid-shaped bread rolls; and Dunbabin, *The Roman Banquet*, pls 13–14 and 16 for examples of crescent-shaped bread rolls in Late Antique dining

on the Milan diptych look similar to representations of bread on Pompeian frescoes and Late Antique sarcophagi and mosaics, as well as to excavated examples from bakeries in Pompeii (Figure 17.1). It has been suggested that, from antiquity onwards, these round loaves were incised in four or eight parts to simplify the breaking of the bread during the meal (and were therefore, known as quadrae or artes quadrati).15 Both in religious and secular art the number of bread loaves often corresponds with the number of diners, which seems to imply that each guest was served one loaf of bread during the meal.16

In the Milan diptych and Ravenna mosaic the large dish in the centre of the table has a broad flat base with curved upper wall (Figures 17.1 and 17.2). The shape of these dishes resembles contemporary dishes and plates of so-called 'Late Roman Red Slip Ware', which can be found at excavations all over the Mediterranean. These fine-textured Red Slip Wares – roughly dated between the fourth and seventh century – were specifically intended for use on the dining table, and were finished with a smooth reddish slip on both the inner and outer surfaces. They were meant as cheap imitations of gold and silver plates and consequently they were decorated only with rather simple designs, often stamped or rouletted. Especially forms 61 to 64 of Hayes's classification of African Red Slip Ware, made in Tunisia, look very similar to the plates shown on the diptych and mosaic (Figure 17.4).[17] In the Rossano Gospels, on the contrary, the chalice-like dish in the centre of the table looks very different from the previous Last Supper pictures: it has convex walls and a high pedestal ring foot (Figure 17.3).

The drinking cup of the Milan diptych appears to be quite similar to excavated examples of transparent or slightly green glass (Figure 17.1). In fact, many glass bowls and cups with a shallow or conical shape have survived from late antiquity; their form and thin walls seem to have been appropriate for drinking. Especially during the fourth century, luxurious glass tableware was gilded, engraved or cut with rich decoration. In excavated contexts cheaper equivalents of glass beakers, goblets and cups became quite common from the fifth to the seventh century.[18]

---

scenes. According to Dunbabin, *The Roman Banquet*, chap. 6, note 75, fig. 119, the two crescent-shaped bread rolls on the surface of the decorated tablecloth in the Rossano Gospels are a standard motif in late antiquity.

[15] F. J. Dölger, 'Unser tägliches Brot. Das eine Brot als Tagesbedarf und das halbe Brot des Einsiedlers Paulus', in *Antike und Christentum* (Bonn, 1936), pls 13–16; H. Blumner, *Technologie und Terminologie der Gewerbe und Künste bei Griechen und Römern* (Hildesheim, 1969), 88.

[16] Dölger, 'Unser tägliches Brot', 208 with textual references.

[17] J. W. Hayes, *Late Roman Pottery* (London, 1972), 107–111, forms 62–4, figs 17–18.

[18] J. W. Hayes, *Excavations at Saraçhane in Istanbul, vol. II: The Pottery* (Princeton, NJ, 1992), 400; Dunbabin, *The Roman Banquet*, 163, fig. 96; see also Buckton, *Byzantium*, 41, no. 18 for a fourth-century example of a transparent blown-glass bowl from Cyprus.

Representations from the Macedonian period (c. 850–1050)

A rare example of a Byzantine Last Supper scene from the ninth century can be found in a miniature of the Lectionary no. 21 in the Library of St Petersburg (Figure 17.5).[19] Jesus and the Apostles recline on a *stibadium*-couch with a crescent bolster around a semi-oval table covered with a tablecloth. A new feature in this composition is the figure of Judas sitting alone at the front of the table, and thrusting his hand into a centrally placed communal dish containing a fish. The wide dish has convex walls and a high pedestal ring foot, like the one in the miniature of the Rossano Gospels of the sixth century, although most of the previous plates in Late Antique dining scenes were depicted as flat with curved walls. Two large lamp-stands behind the dining table at the back of the picture seem to refer to the evening hour of the meal.

A similar arrangement can be seen in a miniature of the Khludov Psalter from the mid ninth century, now in Moscow,[20] as well as in a tenth-century Last Supper fresco in the church of San Bastianello at Pallara in Rome (Figure 17.6).[21] However, in both pictures the Apostles are depicted seated instead of reclining around the semicircular table. The change in Judas's position is again remarkable: he sits in front of the table as he tries to grasp food from a centrally placed communal dish, or as he eats with his hand in his mouth. Since antiquity, sitting, as opposed to reclining, at the dinner table had been the normal practice only for those of inferior social status. Knives, forks, individual plates, drinking cups or beakers are not represented in these three Last Supper scenes.

Lamp-stands (or *candelabra*) similar to those in the St Petersburg lectionary miniature are known from late antiquity. Lamps are usually made of metal and are supported by lamp-stands, as is nicely exemplified by a bronze lamp on a stand of the sixth or seventh century that is now in the British Museum in London.[22] However, less wealthy households would have probably used cheaper clay imitations. Noteworthy is the total absence of glass lamps and glass tableware in archaeological contexts from the eighth to the eleventh century.

---

19 St Petersburg, Biblioteka Publičnaja MS 21, Lectionary: see Dobbert, 'Das Abendmahl', fig. 23.

20 Khludov Psalter, Moscow, Historical Museum MS 129: M. V. Ščepkina, *Miniaturi Khludovskoi Psalt'iri* (Moscow, 1977); see also E. Dobbert, 'Das Abendmahl Christi in der bildenden Kunst bis gegen den Schluss des 14. Jahrhunderts', *RK* 15 (1892), fig. 31.

21 Unfortunately, this fresco is now lost, but is reproduced as an aquarelle in BAV MS lat. 9071, fol. 237: see also Dobbert, 'Das Abendmahl', fig. 24.

22 Buckton, *Byzantium*, 108, no. 119; see also 109, no. 120 'bronze lamp in the form of a peacock', sixth–seventh century from Egypt (?), which looks quite similar to the bird lamp on the Bastianello picture.

The large dish with high pedestal ring foot in the Last Supper scenes of the ninth and tenth centuries could be either of metal or clay: it is difficult to determine which, if either, medium the painter intended to simulate. The shape of these vessels is similar to the so-called 'fruit stand', a typical form found in so-called 'Glazed White Ware', which was exclusively produced in Constantinople during that period (Figure 17.7).[23] The use of these glazed dishes implies the care invested in the elegant presentation of food. The 'fruit stands' with interior relief decoration probably imitate metal prototypes. In fact, there is a remarkable continuity and uniformity in the production of metal vessels from the seventh to the eleventh century, and many metal dishes excavated in Europe resemble the ones in the Last Supper scenes.[24]

Pictures of the Komnenian era (c. 1050–1204)

By the eleventh century, several miniatures representing the Last Supper show Jesus and Peter as the only participants reclining as guests of honour on the right and left corners of the table (Figure 17.8).[25] The other Apostles sit around a large oval table covered with an embroidered tablecloth. Two cups or chalices are repeatedly placed next to the wide dish located as usual in the centre of the table.

The combination of one centrally placed dish flanked by two ceramic cups can be seen in many images of the Last Supper and other dining scenes of the Middle Byzantine period.[26] An eleventh-century miniature from an illustrated Book of Job at St Catherine's Monastery on Mount Sinai, which represents Job's children, exemplifies the manner of eating; a large communal plate and two communal cups are set on the table and five out of the ten diners reach with their hands towards and into the centrally placed dish (Figure 17.9).[27] This seems to confirm that people were dining in a

---

[23] C. Morgan, *Excavations at Corinth XI: the Byzantine pottery* (Cambridge, MA, 1942), 45, fig. 31, pl. V; U. Peschlow, 'Byzantinische Keramik aus Istanbul. Ein Fundkomplex bei der Irenenkirche', *IstMitt* 27/28 (1977/78), figs 3–5, 9, 12 and Hayes, *Excavations at Saraçhane in Istanbul*, fig. 7; see also J. Vroom, *Byzantine to Modern Pottery in the Aegean: an introduction and field guide* (Utrecht, 2005), 74–5.

[24] See M. Mundell Mango, 'Beyond the amphora: non-ceramic evidence for Late Antique industry and trade', in S. Kingsley and M. Decker, eds, *Economy and Exchange in the East Mediterranean during Late Antiquity* (Oxford, 2001), 93.

[25] Paris, BN MS 74, fol. 82, Gospels: H. Omont, *Évangiles avec peintures byzantines de 11e siècle: reproduction des 361 miniatures du manuscrit grec 74 de la Bibliothèque nationale* (Paris, 1908), seperate plate of fol. 82.

[26] Vroom, *After Antiquity*, figs 11.14–27.

[27] Mount Sinai, Monastery of St Catherine MS 3, fol. 17v, Book of Job with catenae: see K. Weitzman and G. Galavaris, *The Monastery of Saint Catherine at Mount Sinai: the illuminated Greek manuscripts* (Princeton, NJ, 1990), 37. See also the recent facsimile edition of the manuscript:

communal way and ate with their fingers.[28] We can, therefore, assume that since the well-to-do classes were apparently eating with their hands, the less wealthy were not doing otherwise.

The miniatures of this period also reveal the proliferation of bread loaves on the table of the Last Supper. Pictures often show round cross-marked loaves as well as round or oval slices of bread along the semicircular edge of the table. The appearance of 'pretzels' made out of bread is also noteworthy. Examples of this combination of bread rolls and bread 'pretzels' are to be found on a twelfth-century enamel plaque from the Pala d'Oro at San Marco in Venice (Figure 17.10),[29] as well as in a twelfth-century Gospel book in the National Library in Athens.[30]

If we look at the eleventh-century Last Supper fresco in the crypt of the monastery of Hosios Loukas in Greece, we see just one large communal dish placed centrally on the table (Figure 17.11).[31] This open dish is used by Christ and the Apostles who are seated around a *sigma*-shaped marble table. There are no knives, spoons or forks on the table, which implies that all diners use only their fingers to eat directly from the plate. Two ceramic cups flanking the communal plate are apparently also shared by all diners. A long, snake-like folded napkin on the right side of the table is provided during the meal, indicating that, by this period, napkins appear on the Last Supper table. For example, we can see three folded white napkins on a twelfth-century enamel plaque of the Pala d'Oro in Venice (Figure 17.10).

Most remarkable in this period is the sudden appearance of cutlery in Last Supper scenes. In miniatures of the eleventh century one often notes knives as part of the dining equipment. Moreover, it seems that in the east the introduction of forks in Last Supper scenes occurs unmistakably during this period. The forks usually have two points, as is shown on the Pala d'Oro plaque (Figure 17.10). A similar cutlery set (knife with matching fork) can be seen in a twelfth-century fresco in the church of Panagia Phorbiotissa at Asinou on Cyprus.[32] In a wall-painting in Karanlık kilise at Göreme in

G. Galavaris et al., eds, *Sinai, St Catherine's Monastery Codex Graecus 3. The Book of Job, facsimile edition*, 3 vols (Athens, 2002).

28 N. Oikonomides, 'The contents of the Byzantine house from the eleventh to the fifteenth century', *DOP* 44 (1990), 205–14, esp. 212.

29 Venice, Pala d'Oro, San Marco: see H. R. Hahnloser and R. Palacco, *La pala d'oro* (Venice, 1994), pl. 31.

30 Athens, NL MS 93, fol. 135v, Gospels: A. Marava-Chatzinicolaou and C. Toufexi-Paschou, *Catalogue of the Illuminated Byzantine Manuscripts of the National Library of Greece I. New Testament Manuscripts 10th–12th Century* (Athens, 1978), fig. 646; see also A. Delatte, *Les Manuscripts à miniatures et à ornaments des bibliothèques d'Athènes* (Liège, 1926), 82f.

31 Phokis, Crypt of Hosios Loukas: see N. Chatzidakis, ed., *Hosios Loukas* (Athens, 1997), 70–71, fig. 79.

32 Asinou, Panagia Phorbiotissa: see M. Sacopolou, *Asinou en 1106 et sa contribution à l'iconographie* (Brussels, 1966), pl. 8.

Cappadocia dated to c. 1200–1210, one can even distinguish three sets of matching knives and forks on the table (Figure 17.12).[33] It is interesting to note that in this last scene we witness the introduction of a high square table, a western feature that gradually will become a common piece of furniture in wealthy Byzantine households of this period.

The use of knives and forks as table and kitchen utensils during this period seems to be supported by the archaeological evidence. For example, the excavations at Corinth yielded a two-pronged iron fork of the eleventh century, as well as several knives with bone handles and iron blades of the tenth to thirteenth century. Furthermore, four iron knives and an iron fork with a bone handle of the mid twelfth to early thirteenth century were excavated at the medieval site of Braničevo in Serbia.[34]

The shape of the cups depicted in Last Supper scenes of the period recalls similar excavated ceramic examples, especially small cups and bowls in 'Glazed White Ware II' of the tenth to twelfth century (Figure 17.13).[35] The increased use of earthenware cups during this period may reflect the decline of the use of glassware on the table, a practice well documented during late antiquity. Additionally, the wide shallow dishes of most Last Supper scenes of this period exhibit much similarity with shapes of excavated decorated tablewares of the eleventh and twelfth centuries.[36] These bowls and dishes are wide (sometimes their rim diameter reaches up to 30 cm), and must have been quite practical for communal dining.

Documentary evidence corroborates many of these observations. Nicholas Oikonomides, who has studied inventories that list household goods of the middle and lower strata of the population in the Byzantine provinces, suggested that unlike the Byzantine court in Constantinople, the average Byzantine household in the eleventh century maintained rather simple eating procedures.[37] He noticed, for instance, that flat individual plates and cups are rarely mentioned, while drinking glasses appear only

[33] Cappadocia, Karanlık kilise, Göreme: see M. Restle, *Die Byzantinische Wandmalerei in Kleinasien*, vol. 2 (Recklinghausen, 1967), pl. 235.

[34] For example G. R. Davidson, *Corinth XII: the minor objects* (Princeton, NJ, 1952), 194, no. 1461, pls 88 and 189, nos 1410–21, pls 85–6; M. Popović and V. Ivanišević, 'Braničevo, cité médiévale', *Starinar*, 39 (1988), 125–79, fig. 31, nos 7–10, and fig. 32 (in Serbian with French summary). I would like to thank Dr Maria Parani for this last reference. More eleventh- to thirteenth-century knives were found during excavations on Byzantine sites in Bulgaria (for example Djadovo, Kovačevo), in Greece (for example Nichoria) and in Turkey (for example Tille, Gritille, Aşvan Kale); see also B. Pitarakis, 'Témoignage des objets métalliques dans le village médiéval (Xe–XIVe siècle)', in J. Lefort, C. Morrisson and J.-P. Sodini, eds, *Les Villages dans l'Empire byzantin (IVe–XVe siècle)* (Paris, 2005), 251 with further literature.

[35] Morgan, *Excavations at Corinth XI*, figs 30a, 36–7, pls VI, Xa; Peschlow, 'Byzantinische Keramik aus Istanbul', figs 7, 16, and Hayes, *Excavations at Saraçhane in Istanbul*, 25–7, fig. 9.

[36] See Vroom, *After Antiquity*, figs 3.7–3.9 and 234, table 7.3 on the left.

[37] Oikonomides, 'The contents of the Byzantine house', 205–14.

in monasteries. Furthermore, no knives or forks are mentioned; spoons, tables and seats are equally rare. He concluded, therefore, that 'people often, if not always, ate with their fingers from a large serving plate and drank from a common cup or jar.'[38]

Representations of the Palaiologan era (c. 1250–1453)

A remarkable feature of this period is the abrupt shift towards a greater variety and a larger number of vessels, jugs and cutlery on the Last Supper table. For instance, a *croce dipinta* in the Museo Nazionale di San Matteo in Pisa of the late twelfth or thirteenth century includes five bowls on the Last Supper table, which is laid with a white tablecloth (Figure 17.14).[39] In this way the participants shared one bowl between two or three men. The diners were, therefore, expected to eat from the same bowl, but now only with their immediate neighbours. Furthermore, the food was eaten with a knife as well as and with the fingers.

A late fourteenth-century fresco of the Last Supper at Mount Athos provides evidence for the distribution of food in several bowls, as well as for the use of jugs and glass beakers (Figure 17.15).[40] The distribution of food and wine or water in separate dishes and vessels respectively was not a regular practice on the dining table. The guests were apparently expected to share the dishes and utensils amongst themselves, although they appear to have had individual bread rolls. Together, the pictorial and archaeological evidence confirms the distribution of food in several small bowls during this period, which were apparently shared by three or four guests at the table.[41]

The long sharply pointed knives in the Athos fresco were probably intended to cut food into manageable pieces, which could then be picked up by hand. Alternatively, their pointed end could serve as a fork to lift food to the mouth. Three or four knives to be shared by all diners were often documented in Last Supper scenes of this period. A sharp knife resembling those in the Mount Athos fresco has been recently discovered during excavations at the medieval site of Panakton in Boeotia. This rural site yielded a number of knives, including a sharply pointed example

---

38 Oikonomides, 'The contents of the Byzantine house', 212.

39 Pisa, Museo Nazionale di San Matteo: see E. Sandberg-Vavalá, *La croce dipinta italiana e l'iconografia della passione* (Verona, 1929), fig. 164.

40 Mount Athos, Docheiariou Monastery: see A. Simonopetritis, *Holy Mountain: bulwark of Orthodoxy and of the Greek nation* (Thessalonike, c. 1970), 96.

41 Vroom, *After Antiquity*, figs 3.10–11 and 234, table 7.3 in the centre.

with a bone handle, which were stratigraphically dated to the fourteenth century.[42]

The depiction of glass cups or beakers is still uncommon in thirteenth-century Last Supper scenes from the east. The first glass beakers (actually in use!) are found in western religious art at the beginning of the fourteenth century; for instance, in a Last Supper by Duccio in the Opera del Duomo in Siena from 1308–11, and in Giotto's *Marriage at Cana* in the Arena Chapel at Padua from 1305–07.[43] In the same period, glass beakers of an Italian style were depicted in the Aegean, as in a fourteenth-century fresco of the Last Supper in the church of Panagia Kera at Merambello in eastern Crete.[44] The drinking scenes in these frescoes seem to correspond with the archaeological record. At excavations in Istanbul, Thessalonike and Corinth, glassware finds reappear in archaeological contexts from the eleventh century onwards. These finds include mostly drinking utensils such as bowls, goblets, beakers, cups, bottles and jugs, usually made of transparent glass of a pale greenish colour.[45] Furthermore, Byzantine written sources testify to a tendency to consume more wine after the twelfth century.[46]

Another interesting feature of this period is the rapid introduction of realistic details such as representations of tin-glazed pottery, namely a blue-and-white painted jug of archaic maiolica in Duccio's fourteenth-century Last Supper scene. At the same time, one can discern similar-looking blue-and-white painted jugs and glass vessels in a fourteenth-century icon depicting the Hospitality of Abraham in the Benaki Museum in Athens (Figure 17.16).[47]

---

42 S. E. J. Gerstel, M. Munn, H. E. Grossman, E. Barnes, A. H. Rohn and M. Kiel, 'A Late Medieval settlement at Panakton', *Hesperia*, 72 (2003), 165, fig. 12 with further literature; note also the appearance of a fourteenth-century metal spoon at excavations in Thessalonike: see *Θεσσαλονίκη. Ιστορία και Τέχνη* (Athens, 1986), 87, no. 24.3.

43 Siena, Opera del Duomo; Padua, Arena Chapel. See also R. Francovich and M. Valenti, *C'era una volta. La ceramica medievale nel convento del Carmine* (Florence, 2002), 74–5, for more depictions of glass in Italian art of the fourteenth century.

44 See Angeliki Lymberopoulou's chapter in this volume.

45 For example Davidson, *Corinth XII: the minor objects*, 83–90, figs 12–18, and Hayes, *Excavations at Saraçhane in Istanbul*, 401–9.

46 E. Kislinger, 'Dall'ubriacone al krasopateras: consume del vino a Bisanzio', in G. Archetti and P. Vila, eds, *La civilità del vino. Fonti, temi e produzioni vitivinicole dal medioevo al novecento* (Brescia, 2003), 173–96.

47 Athens, Benaki Museum: see A. Delivorias, *Οδηγός του Μουσείου Μπενάκη* (Athens, 1980), 41, fig. 29; H. C. Evans, ed., *Byzantium: faith and power (1261–1557)* (The Metropolitan Museum of Art, New York, 2004), 187, no. 107 (catalogue entry by A. Drandaki). Various depictions of archaic maiolica in fourteenth-century Italian art are shown in R. Francovich, 'Le fonti iconografiche', in idem, *La ceramica medievale a Siena e nella Toscana meridionale (sec. XIV–XV): materiali per una tipologia,* Ricerche di archeologia altomedievale e medievale 5/6 (Florence, 1982), 51–62 with further literature.

Apart from fish and bread, meat is frequently represented in Late Byzantine religious art. Specifically, roasted lamb, probably implying a link with Jewish tradition (see below), was often served on a large plate in one piece (with the head of the animal included). Such representations exemplify the growing importance of meat in dining scenes. However, in several examples, such as the Feast of Herod and the Wedding at Cana, the most frequently represented meat was poultry. In a wall-painting in the church of St Niketa at Čucer in Macedonia from c. 1315, one can actually see the host cutting a chicken into eatable pieces for his guests with a knife.[48]

In addition to fish and meat, some Late Byzantine dining scenes represent various types of food such as soups in the vessels depicted. We also find dishes filled with small round balls (perhaps fruits, chickpeas or lentils?) in, for example, a thirteenth-century miniature in a manuscript of the Bibliothèque nationale in Paris, as well as in a fourteenth-century fresco in the church of St Andrew near Skopje in Macedonia.[49]

Another interesting feature in Late Byzantine Last Supper scenes is the presence of white edible roots lying among the tableware. This vegetable makes its sudden appearance in many religious and secular wall-paintings, icons and miniatures in Byzantine art from the thirteenth century onwards.[50] A detailed study of the roots, known in Greek as *rapani*, in these dining scenes suggests that they are root vegetables.

In a Last Supper scene found in a thirteenth-century church at Bojana in Bulgaria, one can even distinguish three different types of roots (Figure 17.17).[51] The first type has swollen bulbils, thick stems and multiple roots, and presumably represents spring onions. The remaining two types are characterized by the following three features: 1. some have a sinuous single/double root ending; 2. some have multiple emergent stems; 3. and others have either single or perhaps double pinnate leaves (these could be either radishes or members of the *Apiaceae* family – carrots and celeriac).[52] According to Klaus Wessel, the inclusion of the roots in this particular

---

48 Macedonia, St Niketa, Čucer: O. Bihalji-Merin, *Byzantine Frescoes and Icons in Yugoslavia* (London, 1958), pl. 49.

49 Paris, BN MS 54, Gospels: see Wessel, *Abendmahl und Apostelkommunion*, 49; Macedonia, church of St Andrew near Skopje: see O. Bihalji-Merin, *Byzantine Frescoes and Icons*, 65. See also the wall-painting of the Wedding at Cana in the church of St Nicholas Orphanos, Thessalonike: A. Xyngopoulos, *Οι Τοιχογραφίες του Αγίου Νικολάου Ορφανού Θεσσαλονίκης*, Δημοσιεύματα του Αρχαιολογικού Δελτίου 4 (Athens, 1964), fig. 92.

50 Vroom, *After Antiquity*, figs 11.25, 11.28–9 and 11.32–7.

51 Bulgaria, Bojana: see A. Boschkov, *Monumentale Wandmalereien Bulgariens* (Mainz, 1969), 46.

52 I would like to thank Professor Martin Jones and George Pitt-Rivers, Professor of Archaeological Science at the University of Cambridge (UK) for this information. See also S. G. Harrison, G. B. Masefield and M. Wallis, *The Oxford Book of Food Plants* (Oxford, 1969), 180–81, 184–5.

composition at Bojana could be inspired by the everyday eating habits of the Balkans.[53] He also observed that in the same painting the Apostles keep a long white cloth decorated with black stripes on their knees. Such pieces of cloth are still in use as napkins during dinner in Bulgaria.

If some of the illustrated roots are indeed radishes, they may refer to the *maròr*, the bitter flavours that the Jews normally consumed during their Seder: a ritual paschal meal (Pesach) during which the Jews tasted symbolic foods.[54] The Last Supper, which Jesus shared with his Apostles in a house in Jerusalem, took place at the time of the Jewish feast of Passover. On the other hand, the white roots appear so frequently in pictures of a non-Pesach context that their presence may simply indicate a new ingredient on the dining table. Perhaps the radish-like roots were used against intoxication during excessive wine-drinking.[55] It has also been suggested that these white roots were perhaps refreshing for the mouth, and may have been used as a substitute for toothpaste or toothpicks in order to clean the teeth after and during meals.[56] These vegetables would indeed have a refreshing effect on the palate, rather like the horseradish (wasabi) and pickled ginger that the Japanese eat with sushi. In the terms of the sociologist Mary Douglas, they would each serve to 'punctuate' a menu of distinct courses.[57]

Discussion

This preliminary survey of the use of table equipment (pottery and cutlery) in Last Supper scenes from the Early Byzantine period to the Palaiologan era leads to several observations (see Table 17.1). Last Supper scenes of the fifth to the sixth century seem to represent dining habits which were identical to those prevailing in late antiquity. Diners reclined on a cushioned semicircular *stibadium*-couch around a semicircular table. In most eastern pictures from the fifth to the seventh century, Jesus is reclining on the extreme right side of the couch (*in dextro cornu*), which was the guest's of

53 Wessel, *Abendmahl und Apostelkommunion*, 48 and idem, *Reallexikon zur Byzantinischen Kunst* (Stuttgart, 1966), 10.

54 I would like to thank Professor Johanna Maria van Winter of the University of Utrecht (NL) for this suggestion.

55 H. Anagnostakis and T. Papamastorakis, ' "... and radishes for appetizers". On banquets, radishes and wine', in D. Papanikola-Bakirtzi, ed., *Food and Cooking in Byzantium. Proceedings of the Symposium 'On Food in Byzantium', Thessaloniki Museum of Byzantine Culture, 4 November 2001* (Athens, 2005), 147–72.

56 J. Koder, *Gemüse in Byzanz. Die Versorgung Konstantinopels mit Frischgemüse im Lichte der Geoponika*, Byzantinische Geschichtsschreiber, Ergänzungsband 3 (Vienna, 1993), 88 and note 12.

57 M. Douglas, 'Food as a system of communication', in eadem, *In the Active Voice* (London, 1982).

honour place already in Late Antique times (the so-called 'consul's spot' or place of the host).

There are no individual plates, knives or spoons on the table. The diners apparently ate their food with their fingers in a communal way, from a centrally placed dish. The shape of this dish resembles plates of the Late-Roman Red Slip Ware found at excavations. Around the communal dish (usually containing a fish), one can often discern some loaves of bread, one for each guest, which could have been used as a sort of spoon to mop up food and convey it to the mouth. Thus, the illustrations of the Last Supper seem to confirm an abundant use of bread in the Byzantine diet.

The pictorial and textual evidence indicates that across the eighth, ninth and tenth centuries customs in the Byzantine empire were slowly beginning to change, at least for the well-to-do classes. The Last Supper scenes from this period show that the diners now eschew the Late Antique habit of reclining around a table, and instead follow the western medieval habit of sitting upright. This shift from the reclining posture to the seated one implies major changes in dining manners.

In pictures of this period one can also recognize one communal large pedestal dish (either made of metal or of earthenware) on the table, which was shared by all diners. The shape of this dish with a high ring foot and convex walls recalls the so-called 'fruit stands' of Glazed White Ware, which were exclusively produced in Constantinople at that time. Furthermore, one can notice realistic-looking lamp-stands (*candelabra*), indicating the nightly hour of the meal (but probably not giving much light on the table). Cutlery, individual plates and individual cups were not yet depicted.

In Last Supper scenes of the Komnenian period, open shallow ring-footed dishes (without a lip) dominate, usually flanked by two ceramic drinking cups. These large dishes were obviously used communally by all diners for the main course. In short, the communal character of the meal persisted. The wide dishes display some similarities with the shapes of decorated tablewares of the eleventh to the twelfth century. These thick-walled vessels have large rim diameters and must have been quite practical for communal rather than individual use. It is highly probable that the Byzantines consumed the food in these communal dishes with their hands rather than with cutlery, just as the well-to-do in the pictures of dining.

It is equally noteworthy that there are always two ceramic drinking cups depicted in the pictures next to the communal bowl, perhaps simulating Glazed White Ware. The increased representation of drinking cups made of earthenware may respond to the substitution of ceramic cups for the drinking glasses of the Roman period.

During the twelfth to thirteenth century knives and forks suddenly make their appearance in the Last Supper scenes. From this time on there is regularly at least one knife depicted on the table. Sometimes a single large knife is the only available utensil for all the guests. In other instances several small knives are shared by three or four diners. Excavated examples of iron knives and forks seem to confirm the accuracy of this picture.

This period also sees the introduction of high square tables, usually laid with a white cloth. The table equipment expands to include folded napkins, and bread 'pretzels' make their debut on the Byzantine table. From the late twelfth century onwards the Last Supper scenes demonstrate an increased interest in the representation of a variety of foodstuffs. Several types of bread appear on the table as well as multiple dishes of fish and meat, while white root vegetables (carrots, radishes and spring onions) are introduced, apparently as a sort of side dish to the main course.

In addition to this change in the representation of eating habits, Palaiologan painters document the fragmentation of communal eating. In Last Supper scenes of the period one finds the separation of food into numerous bowls shared by two or three diners rather than the whole table. Glass beakers and jugs, as well as maiolica, appear along with an increasing variety of vessels. All this suggests the spread of wealth, consumerism and the prevalence of dining in smaller groups with more food in several smaller bowls on the table. This seems to be reflected in the ceramics found at excavations and surveys, where the rim diameters of the ceramic vessels of the Late Byzantine/ Frankish period are much smaller than their Byzantine predecessors.

In conclusion, the depiction of the meal in Last Supper scenes is not static. Furthermore, the written sources indicate that the use of food (for example bread, wine, fish, olive oil) and dining habits were not persistent from late antiquity into the Late Byzantine period, which seems to be supported by the pictorial and archaeological evidence. This is especially visible in the slow and gradual changes in the Last Supper scenes in Byzantine art, which may be taken to represent contemporary dining habits – at least, for the well-to-do.

The pictorial evidence and the textual sources corroborate the clear trend in the archaeological evidence, a change from shallow, open vessels during the Late Antique/Early and Middle Byzantine periods to smaller, deeper bowls during the Late Byzantine/Frankish period. I would suggest that in Greece at least there were gradual changes from exclusively communal dining in Late Antique and Byzantine times (focused on sharing food together) to a more western form of non-communal, small-group dining in the Late Byzantine/ Frankish period (perhaps marking the beginning of personal consumerism). There was probably no sudden, clear break in dining habits or in the use of table equipment, but rather a slow and gradual transition that took place at a different pace in different parts of the eastern Mediterranean.

Representations of the Late Antique – Early Byzantine period (fifth to seventh century)
Semicircular table
Semicircular couch with bolster
Reclining dining position at the table
Embroidered tablecloth
Flat, centrally placed plate/dish on the table
Only one drinking beaker/glass, shared by all diners
No cutlery or individual plates
Loaves of bread on the table
→ *Communal dining*

Representations of the Macedonian period (c. 850–1050)
Semicircular table and couch
Introduction of sitting next to reclining at the table
Tablecloth as curtain in front of table
Introduction of high lamp-stands at the back of the dining room
Wide, centrally placed dish with high pedestal ring foot
No cutlery, no drinking beakers/cups or individual plates
→ *Communal dining*

Representations of the Komnenian era (c. 1050–1204)
Table sometimes decorated with groove for disposal of fat
Introduction of high square table
Introduction of folded napkins
Addition of two drinking cups to centrally placed dish
Introduction of cutlery: knives and forks
Introduction of bread 'pretzels'
→ *Communal dining*
Representations of the Palaiologan era (c. 1250–1453)
White table cloth
Only sitting at the table
Proliferation of various table wares and cutlery
Sharing deeper dishes/beakers by two or three diners
Introduction of glass beakers and jugs on the table
Introduction of Maiolica vessels on the table
Introduction of 'white roots' on the table
→ *Shift from communal to small-group dining*

Table 17.1. Dining habits in pictures of the Late Antique – Early Byzantine period to the Palaiologan period (c. fifth to fifteenth century).

Figure 17.1: Milan, Tesoro del Duomo: ivory diptych of the Last Supper; fifth-century (After E. Dobbert, 'Das Adendmahl Christi in der bildenden Kunst bis gegen den Schluss des 14. Jahrhunderts', *RK* 14 [1891], fig. 18).

Figure 17.2: Ravenna, Basilica San Apollinare Nuovo: mosaic of the Last Supper; c. 500 (After E. Dobbert, 'Das Adendmahl Christi in der bildenden Kunst bis gegen den Schluss des 14. Jahrhunderts', *RK* 14 [1891], fig. 19).

Figure 17.3: Italy, Rossano, Museo dell' Archivescovado, Codex Purpureus Rossanensis, fol. 3r: miniature of Last Supper; sixth century (After E. Dobbert, 'Das Adendmahl Christi in der bildenden Kunst bis gegen den Schluss des 14. Jahrhunderts', *RK* 14 [1891], fig. 22).

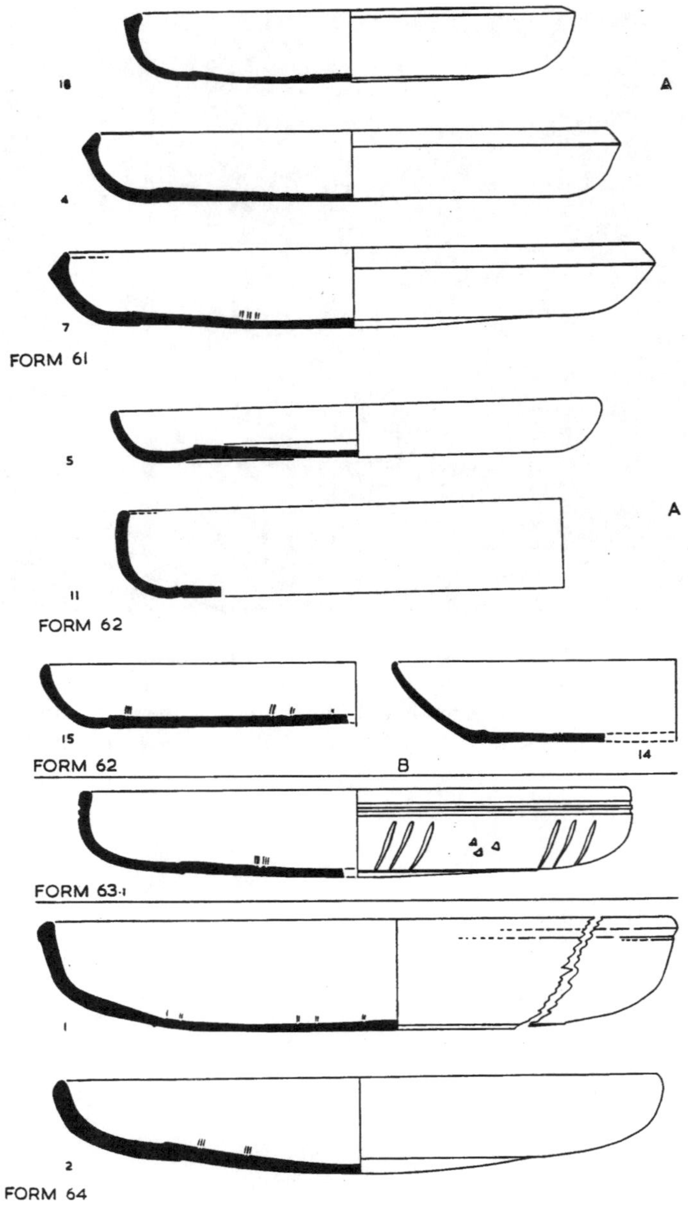

Figure 17.4: Hayes's forms 61–64 in African Red Slip Ware; c. late fourth to fifth century (After J. W. Hayes, *Late Roman Pottery* [London, 1972], figs 16–18).

Figure 17.5: St Petersburg, Biblioteka Publičnaja MS 21, Lectionary: miniature of the Last Supper; ninth century (After E. Dobbert, 'Das Adendmahl Christi in der bildenden Kunst bis gegen den Schluss des 14. Jahrhunderts', *RK* 14 [1891], fig. 23).

Figure 17.6: Vatican City, BAV MS lat. 9071, fol. 237: copy of a fresco of the Last Supper; c. eighth or tenth (?) century (After E. Dobbert, 'Das Adendmahl Christi in der bildenden Kunst bis gegen den Schluss des 14. Jahrhunderts', *RK* 14 [1891], fig. 24).

Figure 17.7: Large dish with high pedestal ring foot in Glazed White Ware; c. tenth to twelfth century (After C. Morgan, *Excavations at Corinth XI: the Byzantine pottery* [Cambridge, MA, 1942], pl. V).

Figure 17.8: Paris, BN MS 74, fol. 82, Gospels: miniature of the Last Supper; third quarter of the eleventh century (After H. Omont, *Evangiles avec peintures byzantines de 11e siècle: reproduction des 361 miniatures du manuscrit grec 74 de la Bibliothèque nationale* [Paris, 1908]).

Figure 17.9: Mount Sinai, St Catherine's Monastery MS 3, fol. 17v, Book of Job with catenae: miniature of Job's children; eleventh century (After K. Weitzman and G. Galavaris, *The Monastery of Saint Catherine at Mount Sinai: the illuminated Greek manuscripts* [Princeton, NJ, 1990], 37).

Figure 17.10: Venice, San Marco, Pala d'Oro: enamel of the Last Supper; c. 1105 (After H. R. Hahnloser and R. Palacco, *La pala d'oro* [Venice, 1994], pl. 31).

Figure 17.11: Greece, Phokis, crypt of Hosios Loukas: fresco of the Last Supper; eleventh century (Photo: J. Vroom).

Figure 17.12: Cappadocia, Göreme, Karanlık kilise: fresco of the Last Supper; c. 1200–1210 (After M. Restle, *Die Byzantinische Wandmalerei in Kleinasien*, vol. 2 [Recklinghausen, 1967], pl. 235).

Figure 17.13: Drinking cups and bowls in Glazed White Ware; c. tenth to twelfth century (After C. Morgan, *Excavations at Corinth XI: the Byzantine pottery* [Cambridge, MA, 1942], and J. W. Hayes, *Excavations at Saraçhane in Istanbul, vol. II: the pottery* [Princeton, NJ, 1992]).

Figure 17.14: Pisa, Museo Nazionale di San Matteo: miniature of the Last Supper in a *croce dipinta*; c. twelfth to thirteenth century (After E. Sandberg-Vavalá, *La croce dipinta italiana e l' iconografia della passione* [Verona, 1929], fig. 164).

Figure 17.15: Mount Athos, Docheiariou Monastery: fresco of the Last Supper; fourteenth century (After A. Simonopetritis, *Holy Mountain: bulwark of Orthodoxy and of the Greek nation* [Thessalonike, *c.* 1970], 96).

Figure 17.16: Athens, Benaki Museum: icon of the Hospitality of Abraham; fourteenth century (After A. Delivorias, *Οδηγός του Μουσείου Μπενάκη* [Athens, 1980], 41, fig. 29).

Figure 17.17: Bulgaria, church in Bojana: fresco of Last Supper; dated to 1259 (After A. Boschkov, *Monumentale Wandmalereien Bulgariens* [Mainz, 1969], 46).

18. 'Fish on a dish' and its table companions in fourteenth-century wall-paintings on Venetian-dominated Crete[1]

Angeliki Lymberopoulou

Certain table layouts in fourteenth-century wall-paintings from Crete have been tentatively labelled by some scholars as 'Venetian Layouts'.[2] Others have argued against this classification and have played down the significance of the Venetian element in the table displays.[3] The aim of this paper is to focus on what the appearance of certain specifically Venetian wares in an otherwise traditional Byzantine-Christian iconography says about the daily interaction of the Cretans and the Venetians during the fourteenth century, as well as about the status the Venetians and their artefacts enjoyed on the island. I have chosen two wall-paintings representing feasts from the church of the Panagia Kera, outside Kritsa at Merambello, in the prefecture of Lassithi, eastern Crete.[4] One is the Last Supper (Figure 18.1),[5] the other is Herod's Feast, which led to the beheading of John the Baptist (Figure 18.2).[6] The choice of examples from the church of the Panagia Kera was suggested by the appearance of two scenes with similar table layouts, one of which can be regarded as 'positive' evidence of the interaction between the Cretans and the Venetians (Last Supper); the other, however, appears in

1 Special thanks to Dr Rembrandt Duits for reading this paper and for his comments and suggestions.

2 M. Borboudakis, K. Gallas and K. Wessel, *Byzantinisches Kreta* (Munich, 1983), 116.

3 M. Vassilaki, 'Καθημερινή ζωή και πραγματικότητα στη Βενετοκρατούμενη Κρήτη: Η μαρτυρία των τοιχογραφημένων εκκλησιών', in S. Kaklamanis, A. Markopoulos and G. Mauromatis, eds, *Ενθύμησις Νικολάου Μ. Παναγιωτάκη* (Herakleion, 2000), 70 and note 27.

4 For the church: S. Papadaki-Ökland, 'Η Κερά της Κρίτσας. Παρατηρήσεις στη χρονολόγηση των τοιχογραφιών της', *AD* 22, Meletai (1967), 87–111; M. Borboudakis, *Panhagia Kera. Byzantinische Fresken in Kritsa* (Athens, n.d.); K.K. Mylopotamitaki, Ο Ναός της Παναγίας Κεράς Κριτσάς (Herakleion, 2005). For their location ibid., 93-95, nos 37 and 40 respectively.

5 Borboudakis, *Panhagia Kera*, fig. 25.

6 Borboudakis, *Panhagia Kera*, fig. 31.

a scene where the Venetian influences can be regarded as 'negative', since Herod's Feast led to the beheading of St John the Baptist.[7] Our wall-paintings belong to the second layer of the church, dated to the late thirteenth or early fourteenth century.[8]

In the Last Supper (Figure 18.1) we see in the background the assembly of the disciples, with Christ depicted to the far left, and Judas in the middle with his left hand in the large dish containing a fish, in the middle of the table. The table dominates the foreground of the wall-painting, covered with white cloth on top of a more elaborate tablecloth. The dish with the fish forms the centrepiece of an assembly of circular and triangular pieces of bread, white radishes, knives, jugs, cups, and decorated glasses. In Herod's Feast (Figure 18.2), the table occupies the largest part of the foreground, with the human assembly confined, again, mostly to the background and partly to the foreground on the right.

The table displays a layout almost identical to the one in the Last Supper, with a white cloth carrying circular and triangular pieces of bread, white radishes, knives, jugs, cups and identically decorated glasses. Only the large dish with the fish is lacking.

From all these objects I would like to concentrate on three: the dish with the fish, the white radishes and the decorated glasses. The representation of these objects combined on a table depicting a feast materialized for the first time on the island and became typical for such depictions in the churches of Venetian-dominated Crete.

To begin with, the dish with the fish is an element commonly found in representations of the Last Supper in both Byzantine[9] and western art.[10] Given the symbolism that the ancient Greek word for fish (ἰχθὺς) had acquired and its association with Christ, this is hardly surprising.[11] It also appears in western art in representations of feasts closely associated with

[7] A. Lymberopoulou, *The Church of the Archangel Michael at Kavalariana: art and society on fourteenth-century Venetian-dominated Crete* (London, 2006), 201–4.

[8] Papadaki-Őkland, 'Η Κερά της Κρίτσας', 95–105. The first layer is dated to the first half of the thirteenth century: ibid., 105-111.

[9] For example, in the church of Hagios Theodoros Tsopaka in Mane, dated to the last quarter of the thirteenth century: N. B. Drandakis, *Βυζαντινές τοιχογραφίες της Μέσα Μάνης* (Athens, 1995), 29–53, fig. 10 (on p. 43) and colour pl. 1.

[10] For example, Queen Mary's Psalter, London, BL Royal MS 2 B.VII, fol. 234r, dated to the fourteenth century: G. F. Warner, ed., *Queen Mary's Psalter: miniatures and drawings by an English artist of the 14th century reproduced from the Royal Ms. 2 B. VII in the British Museum* (London, 1912), pl. 240 (second row, miniature to the right).

[11] J. Geffcken, ed., *Die griechischen christlichen Schriftsteller der ersten drei Jahrhunderterte. Die Oracula Sibyllina* (Leipzig, 1902), 153. See also G. W. H. Lampe, ed., *A Patristic Greek Lexicon* (Oxford, 1961), 680 (no. 2).

Christ, such as the Marriage at Cana[12] and the Supper at Emmaus.[13] In other words, the dish with the fish, bearing a direct symbolical link to Christ, was equally familiar to both cultures, the Greek Orthodox and Venetian Catholic, which co-existed on the island at the time.

The same conclusion cannot be drawn for the remaining two objects. By the fourteenth century, the white radishes had become an element frequently represented on the table of the Last Supper in Byzantine iconography.[14] Western renditions of the scene, however, never included them. In fact, Byzantine iconography incorporated in the representation of the feast a 'real-life' element, since for Judaism, white radishes are a side dish served especially for Passover, the feast celebrated by Christ and his disciples at the Last Supper.[15] Even now in Greece they are considered a stimulant for appetite. However, the radishes can also be interpreted symbolically as referring to spring and redemption – in accordance, again, with Christ's Sacrifice.[16]

Finally, our third category of objects, the decorated glasses, have their roots certainly in western, most likely Venetian, glass production. Surviving examples of such glasses in a variety of shapes and forms are attested in the west (Figure 18.3),[17] but not in Byzantium, from the twelfth century onwards,

---

12 For example, Winchester Psalter, London BL Cotton Nero C.IV, fol. 17, dated to the twelfth century: K. E. Haney, *The Winchester Psalter: an iconographic study* (Leicester University Press, 1986), fig. 16.

13 For example, St Albans Psalter, dated to the twelfth century: O. Pächt, C. R. Dodwell and F. Wormald, *The St. Albans Psalter (Albani Psalter). 1. The full-page miniatures by Otto Pächt. 2. The initials, by C.R. Dodwell. 3. Preface and description of the manuscript by Francis Wormald* (London, 1960), pl. 39.

14 For example, in the church of St Nicholas Orphanos in Thessalonike, dated to the fourteenth century: A. Xyngopoulos, *Οι Τοιχογραφίες του Αγίου Νικολάου Ορφανού Θεσσαλονίκης*, Δημοσιεύματα του Αρχαιολογικού Δελτίου 4 (Athens, 1964), pl. 20, fig. 37; A. Tsitouridou, *Ο ζωγραφικός διάκοσμος του Αγίου Νικολάου Ορφανού στη Θεσσαλονίκη. Συμβολή στη μελέτη της Παλαιολόγειας ζωγραφικής κατά τον πρώιμο 14ο αιώνα*, Βυζαντινά Μνημεία 6 (Thessaloníki, 1986), pl. 32; K. Kirchhainer, *Die Bildausstattung der Nikolauskirche in Thessaloniki. Untersuchung zu Struktur und Programm der Malereien*, Marburger Studien zur Kunst- und Kulturgeschichte 3 (Weimar, 2001), pl. 29 (on p. 192). See further Joanita Vroom's chapter in this volume.

15 A. de Vries, *Dictionary of Symbols and Imagery* (Amsterdam, 1976), 379.

16 Vries, *Dictionary of Symbols*, 379. For a detailed analysis of the presence of radishes in Byzantine iconography and their significance, see H. Anagnostakis and T. Papamastorakis, ' "… and radishes for appetizers". On banquets, radishes and wine', in D. Papanikola-Bakirtzi, ed., *Food and Cooking in Byzantium. Proceedings of the Symposium 'On Food in Byzantium', Thessaloniki Museum of Byzantine Culture 4 November 2001* (Athens, 2005), 147–72, esp. 158–66. I would like to thank Dr Kallirroe Linardou for providing a photocopy of this article.

17 R. B. Mentasti, A. Dorigato, A. Gasparetto and T. Toninato, eds, *Mille anni di arte del vetro a Venezia* (Venice, 1982), 67, no. 45, fig. 45.

and are also depicted in western painting (Figure 18.4).[18] What is of great interest here is that the glasses depicted at Panagia Kera (Figure 18.1), with the frills along the bottom edges, belong to a specific and less common type of glasses, closely associated with Venetian production (Figure 18.5).[19] Furthermore, judging from surviving examples, it is possible that the Kera wall-paintings are the earliest representations of this specific type of glassware.[20] We can, therefore, assume not only that these particular glasses found their way to Cretan wall-painting under western (that is, Venetian) influence, but also that the artist saw the actual glasses rather than copied them from western iconography. However, their 'introduction' is not enough to classify the particular table layouts as 'Venetian'. Finally, unlike the preceding two objects, the glasses, other than pointing to a fashionable accessory of daily and practical use, do not bear any symbolical meaning.

The 'introduction' of a western element of a non-symbolical and, essentially, 'secondary' nature – these glasses point to daily practices only – into the conventional Byzantine iconography of the scene reflects, albeit on a small scale, the situation on the island of Crete during the fourteenth century.[21] Two of the multiple levels of interaction between the two civilizations, the social and the artistic, were making simultaneous progress but at different paces. On the social level, contrary to existing opinion, the native population, especially the upper classes, were happy to adopt western practices and commodities. This is confirmed by the taste for western fashion that was developed by the native population, as attested by the attire of a number of donors represented in fourteenth-century churches.

A telling example is the case of the male donors of the church of the Archangel Michael at Kavalariana, prefecture of Chania, south-west Crete,

---

[18] The frescoes in the cathedral of San Gimignano, dated to the second quarter of the fourteenth century, were formerly attributed to Barna da Siena but are presently assigned to the workshop of Lippo Memmi: G. C. Dini, A. Angelini and B. Sani, *Five Centuries of Sienese Painting: from Duccio to the birth of the baroque* (London, 1997), 106–9.

[19] *Mille anni*, 68–9, no. 48, fig. 48; E. Baumgartner and I. Krueger, *Phönix aus Sand und Asche. Glass des Mittelalters* (Munich, 1988), 198, no. 174 (fig. on p. 199). The most likely place of origin for these glasses was Venice: ibid., 192–3.

[20] Examples such as those in the San Gimignano fresco (fig.18.4) depict the simpler and more widely used form of the glasses, without the frills at the bottom. I would like to thank Dr Rembrandt Duits for providing this information.

[21] For a summary on the history of the island under the Venetians, see C. Maltezou, 'Η Κρήτη στη διάρκεια της περιόδου της Βενετοκρατίας (1211–1669)', in N. M. Panagiotakis, ed., *Κρήτη: Ιστορία και Πολιτισμός*, vol. 2 (Herakleion, 1988), 105–61. See also M. Georgopoulou, 'Venice and the Byzantine sphere', in H. C. Evans, ed., *Byzantium: faith and power (1261–1557)* (Metropolitan Museum of Art, New York, 2004), 489–94.

dated 1327–28.[22] The inscription of their church is very 'friendly' towards the Venetians, calling them 'great' and 'masters'.[23] The male donors are all depicted wearing fashionable western garments know as 'mi-partie' ('particoloured'),[24] which, in the west, often contained heraldic colours.[25] Furthermore, the dressmakers in the capital of the island, Candia, were creating clothes according to western fashion for their clients, while wealthy women were buying their (expensive) clothes directly from Venice.[26] The insertion of the Venetian glasses into Byzantine iconography falls into this category. A further link is established when we take into consideration that these glasses, just like the fashionable garments, were not cheap, and certainly not affordable by everybody. We can, thus, deduct that the adoption of western fashion and practices by the native Cretans in the fourteenth century was directly connected with expensive goods, in other words, goods that were indicative of wealth and social status. It has been suggested that the glasses seen in the wall-paintings of the Panagia Kera actually simulate cheaper, clay imitations.[27] However, there is no evidence that such clay imitations for these particular glasses existed. Moreover, the

---

[22] G. Gerola, *Monumenti Veneti nell' isola di Creta*, vol. 2, R. Istituto Veneto di Scienze, Lettere ed Arti (Venice, 1908), pl. 10, figs 3, 4.

[23] The inscription reads: 1... τρέχο(ν)τ(ος) του παρόντοσ |2 εόνοσ· ἔτουσ ϛωλϛ ἀφε(ν)τέβο(ν)τ(ος) ε<ν> τη Κρήτη τ(όν) με- |3 γάλον κέ ἀφέ<ν>τ(ον) ημ(όν) βενετήκ(ον)·ἐγεγώνη δέ·η παρούσα εκλη- |4 σήα τοῦ μέγάλου ταξηά<ρ>χου Μηχαήλ: τ(όν) άνο{ν ὁ}δηνάμεόν: δη ἐξόδου κέ ση<ν>- |5 δρομ(ής) Θεωτόκη τού Κότζη κε Μανού<η>λ του Μελησουργού· κε Νηκήτα του Σηδέρου κε Δημη- |6 τρήου κε τα τ(όν) τέκν(ον) αυτω<ν?>.|7 εὔχεσθε δη εμου αμάρτολου Ιω(άννου) |8 .ω τάχα κε ζουγράφου αμήν.

English translation: '... during the present century, in the year 6836 A.M. [= AD 1327/28], when Crete is ruled by the great Venetians our masters, this present church of the great archangel Michael of the heavenly hosts was made with the expenses and contributions by Theotokis Kotzis and Manuel Melisourgos and Niketas Sideres and Demetrios and their children. Pray for me the sinner Ioannes who happened to be the/a painter. Amen': Gerola, *Monumenti Veneti dell' isola di Creta*, vol. 4, R. Istituto Veneto di Scienze, Lettere ed Arti (Venice, 1932), 453–4 (no. 28); G. Gerola, *Τοπογραφικός κατάλογος των τοιχογραφημένων εκκλησιών της Κρήτης. Elenco topografico delle chiese affrescate di Creta*, ed. K. E. Lassithitakis (Herakleion, 1961), 38 (no. 146); A. Sucrow, *Die Wandmalereien des Ioannes Pagomenos in Kirchen der ersten Hälfte des 14. Jahrhunderts auf Kreta* (Berlin, 1994), 26–7; Lymberopoulou, *Archangel Michael at Kavalariana*, 170–71, 194–5.

[24] K. Mylopotamitaki, 'Η ενδυμασία της γυναίκας στην Κρήτη επί Βενετοκρατίας', *Archaiologia*, 21 (1986), 50; S. N. Maderakis, 'Η προσωπογραφία των δωρητών στις εκκλησίες της Κρήτης', in *Ετήσια έκδοση του Δήμου Χανίων* (Chania, 1988), 42.

[25] Heraldic colours were worn by people of social standing who had a private coat-of-arms as well as by people of military rank, by people belonging to the court of an aristocrat (i.e. servants) and by people who associated themselves with an aristocrat: R. Levi Pisetzky, *Storia del costume in Italia*, vol. 2 (Milan, 1964), 157–8.

[26] C. Maltezou, 'Βενετική μόδα στην Κρήτη (τα φορέματα μιας Καλογεροπούλας)', in N. A. Stratou, ed., *Βυζάντιον. Αφιέρωμα στον Ανδρέα Στράτο*, vol. 1 (Athens, 1986), 139–47.

[27] Vassilaki, 'Καθημερινή ζωή', 70 and note 27.

glasses in the painting might be interpreted as opaque (Figure 18.1), with the wine inside visible only through the opening at the top, but I believe that they were meant to be interpreted as transparent, since the glasses at the Memmi fresco (Figure 18.4) are also painted in the same way.

However, at the artistic level substantial western influences were kept at arm's length and were not allowed to interfere with the 'purity' of the character of the Byzantine iconography during the fourteenth century.[28] Artistically, Crete was still faithful to Constantinople. Such is the testimony of the wall-paintings of the Panagia Kera: the insertion of the glasses does not interfere or alter the essential and basic iconography with which its faithful Orthodox congregation was well acquainted. All it did was to add a part of the more expensive daily reality that had been on the island for about a century, elements of which were adopted by the wealthy Cretan aristocracy, primarily as status symbols.

[28] Lymberopoulou, *Archangel Michael at Kavalariana*, 8–10, 186, 203–4 and note 49, 217, 220–21.

Figure 18.1: Crete, Kritsa, Panagia Kera: Last Supper; late thirteenth/early fourteenth century (After M. Borboudakis, *Panhagia Kera. Byzantinische Fresken in Kritsa* [Athens, n.d.], fig. 25).

Figure 18.2: Crete, Kritsa, Panagia Kera: Herod's Feast; late thirteenth/early fourteenth century (After M. Borboudakis, *Panhagia Kera. Byzantinische Fresken in Kritsa* [Athens, n.d.], fig. 31).

Figure 18.3: Palermo, Archaeological Museum: drinking glass; twelfth century (After R. B. Mentasti, A. Dorigato, A. Gasparetto and T. Toninato, eds, *Mille Anni di Arte del Vetro a Venezia* [Venice, 1982], 67, no. 45, fig. 45).

Figure 18.4: Workshop of Lippo Memmi: Marriage at Cana (detail), San Gimignano, Cathedral; second quarter of the fourteenth century (formerly attributed to Barna da Siena). (Photo: courtesy of the Warburg Institute Photographic Collection).

Figure 18.5: Basel, Historisches Museum: drinking glass; thirteenth/fourteenth century (After E. Baumgartner and I. Krueger, *Phönix aus Sand und Asche. Glass des Mittelalters* [Munich, 1988], 198, no. 174 [fig. on 199]).

Section V

Food and the sacred

19. Divine banquet: the Theotokos as a source of spiritual nourishment

Mary B. Cunningham

In John 6.35, Jesus says to the disciples, 'I am the bread of life; he who comes to me shall not hunger, and he who believes in me shall never thirst.' Metaphors involving food – one has only to think of Christ as bread, the true vine (John 15.1), the living water (John 4.14) and so on – permeate the Gospels, especially that of John. These are in turn based on types in the Old Testament such as the manna which God sent down from heaven (Exodus 16.4, and following), the water which gushed forth from the rock when Moses struck it with his rod (Exodus 17.1–6), and many others. Anyone who had a chance to listen to the enthronement sermon of Rowan Williams, the current archbishop of Canterbury, may have noticed his sustained use of food metaphors, especially the image of God, or Truth, as the bread of life. 'The one great purpose of the Church's existence is to share that bread of life,' stated the archbishop, and 'the people who are in trouble are those who have seen everything and grasped nothing; who know everything about bread except that you are meant to eat it.'[1]

Throughout the Old and New Testaments, God's care and protection is expressed tangibly in his provision of food to his chosen people. This kind of imagery, even more than familial, erotic or militaristic symbolism evoking the attachment of Israel, and later the Christian church, to its God, expresses the complete physical and spiritual dependence of human beings on their Creator. Orthodoxy holds that, by his incarnation, God also made it possible for Christians to participate fully in his nature, as he participates in theirs. After 'putting on Christ'[2] in baptism, and partaking of his body

---

1 Enthronement sermon of the Archbishop of Canterbury, Rowan Williams, delivered in Canterbury Cathedral on 27 February 2003: *The Times* (28 February 2003), 47.

2 Galatians 3.27.

and blood in the Eucharist, a physical, as well as spiritual, restoration of the original state of blessedness is believed to take place.[3]

Byzantine preachers used metaphors involving food in many contexts, although in contrast to the biblical examples cited above, these may refer to intellectual refreshment rather than to the mystical experience of the Eucharist. Some festal homilies open with a call to the faithful to join the celebrations, comparing the feast to a banquet of which they will partake unstintingly. To take just one example, John of Damascus says near the beginning of his third homily on the *Koimesis* of the Virgin: '… I mean to serve a nourishing meal for the soul's health, appropriate for this holy night, and to provide spiritual joy for your hearts. We are usually faced with a dearth of nourishment, as you realize; so I am improvising a full-course banquet, and even if it is not very rich, or worthy of the invited company, at least it will be enough to satisfy our hunger.'[4] Various historians, including Peter Brown, have recently pointed out that food, or rather the lack of it, represented a far more important issue in late antiquity and the Middle Ages than it does among the affluent middle classes of western society today. Hunger took precedence over sexuality as the major preoccupation of monks.[5] In a society in which a smaller proportion of people could expect to be well fed on a daily basis, it is not surprising that imagery of food and drink features so prominently in spiritual and theological literature throughout the Byzantine period.

This paper will examine the theme of the Virgin Mary, or Theotokos, who, like her Son, came to represent a source of spiritual nourishment in Byzantine homilies and hymns. Whereas Christ himself represents the food

---

[3] See H. Wybrew, *The Orthodox Liturgy: the development of the Eucharistic liturgy in the Byzantine rite* (London, 1989), esp. 90–101; J. Meyendorff, *Byzantine Theology: historical trends and doctrinal themes* (New York, 2nd edn, 1979), 201–11. Meyendorff makes the important point that Byzantine theologians of the eighth century rejected the iconoclast view that the Eucharist represents an 'image' or 'symbol' of Christ: '… the Eucharist for them always remained fundamentally a mystery to be received as food and drink, and not to be "seen" through physical eyes … the Eucharist cannot reveal anything to the sense of vision; it is only the bread of heaven' (quote on p. 204).

[4] B. Kotter, ed., *Die Schriften des Johannes von Damaskos* V, Patristische Texte und Studien 29: *Opera homiletica et hagiographica* (Berlin, 1988), 548 (1), lines 4–7; B. E. Daley, S.J., tr., *On the Dormition of Mary: early patristic homilies* (Crestwood, NY, 1998), 231. John employs the *topos* of modesty here in accordance with Greek rhetorical tradition. Probably in the same period a less well-known preacher named John of Euboea stated, even more self-deprecatingly, '… I long that I may be a partaker at the table of the chosen ones, even if I am a partaker only of crumbs. For one may reach satiety even from a multitude of crumbs': *PG* 96.1461D.

[5] P. Brown, *The Body and Society: men, women, and sexual renunciation in Early Christianity* (London, 1990), 221. Other interesting studies of the relationship between food and medieval spirituality include C. W. Bynum, *Holy Feast and Holy Fast: the religious significance of food to medieval women* (Berkeley, CA, 1987); B. A. Heinisch, *Fast and Feast: food in medieval society* (University Park, PA, 1976).

of life or bread from heaven, as we saw above, Mary is pictured either as *his* source of nourishment, as the vehicle or receptacle by means of which the sustenance which is Christ reaches humanity, or, sometimes, as the reviving food or drink herself. Preachers and hymnographers consistently stress the relationship of the Theotokos to her Son, thereby limiting her salvific role in relation to humankind. Nevertheless, whether as the source of nourishment or its mediator, the Virgin Mary was increasingly viewed as an essential link in the interaction of God with his creation.[6] Ioli Kalavrezou has noted an increasing stress on the maternal qualities of the Theotokos by the end of the period of iconoclasm, both in texts and in images.[7] Linked to this is an emphasis on Mary's own completely natural (albeit miraculously induced) birth, although encomiasts also endlessly hailed her purity and sinlessness.[8] Eighth- and ninth-century homilists and hymnographers also continued to explore the typological dimensions of Mary's role as a link between humanity and divinity.[9] Some Old Testament types, such as the jar containing manna,[10] the table in the tabernacle,[11] and the oven in which the offering for Yahweh was baked,[12] reinforced the connection between nourishment and the incarnation of Christ.

The image of the Virgin Mary as a source of sustenance is most vividly conveyed in texts and images describing her nursing of Christ. Antony Cutler and others have catalogued many literary and artistic representations of this theme, thereby convincingly disproving the theory that this image was not initially a Byzantine one.[13] Fourth- and fifth-century monuments depict Mary's feeding of Christ at her breast, while in the sixth century

---

6 H. Graef, Mary, *A History of Doctrine and Devotion* (London, 1963; repr. 1987), esp. 101–61; J. Pelikan, *Mary through the Centuries: her place in the history of culture* (New Haven, 1996), 55–65.

7 I. Kalavrezou, 'When the Virgin Mary became *Meter Theou*', *DOP* 44 (1990), 165–72; eadem, 'The maternal side of the Virgin', in M. Vassilaki, ed., *Mother of God: representations of the Virgin in Byzantine art* (Athens, 2000), 41–5.

8 See, for example, Andrew of Crete's *Homily I on the Nativity of the Virgin, PG* 97.816C; idem, *Canon on the Conception of St Anna, PG* 97.1313A–B; John of Damascus (?), *Homily on the Nativity of the Virgin*, Kotter, *Die Schriften* V, 180 (10), line 18–181, line 1: Ἀλλ' οὐκ ἐκ μόνου πατρὸς ἢ ἐκ μόνης μητρὸς προήγαγεν, ἵνα τῷ μονογενεῖ φυλαχθῇ τὸ κατὰ πάντα μονογενές ...

9 M. Cunningham, 'The meeting of the old and the new: the typology of Mary the Theotokos in Byzantine homilies and hymns', in R. N. Swanson, ed., *The Church and Mary. Studies in Church History*, 39 (Woodbridge, 2004), 52–62.

10 Exodus 16.33.

11 Exodus 25.23.

12 Leviticus 2.4. This type is first cited by the sixth-century preacher Hesychios of Jerusalem in his Commentary on Leviticus 2.4: *PG* 93.807B.

13 A. Cutler, 'The cult of the *Galaktotrophousa* in Byzantium and Italy', *JÖB* 37 (1987), 335–50. See also G. Millet, *Recherches sur l'iconographie de l'Evangile* (Paris, 1916), 627; V. N. Lazarev, 'Studies in the iconography of the Virgin', *ArtB* 20 (1938), 26–65.

Romanos the Melode emphasizes the paradox that a Virgin could produce milk for her child.[14] Eighth-century preachers continued to meditate on this and related issues. Germanos, in his homily commemorating the deposition of Mary's belt and the swaddling clothes of Christ, writes with regard to the latter: 'She wrapped the great Lord in them as an infant with her motherly hands. She carried him with them at her bosom and suckled the One who gives breath and food to all nature.'[15] Even if, according to these accounts, the Theotokos only indirectly sustains the rest of humanity, the lyrical tone of some homilies suggests that Christians in this period regarded her increasingly as a source of maternal tenderness and support.[16] John of Damascus, if he is the author of one of the most eloquent yet theological Marian sermons to survive from this period,[17] evokes the loving, physical relationship between the Theotokos and her Son, as we see in the following passage:

> O ever-virginal little daughter who needed no man to conceive! He who has an eternal Father has been borne in the womb by you! O earth-born little daughter who carried the Creator in your God-bearing arms! […] His flesh is from your flesh and his blood is from your blood, and God suckled milk from your breasts, and your lips were united with the lips of God. O incomprehensible and ineffable miracles! The God of all things, knowing in advance your worth, loved you and because of this love, he predestined you [cf. Romans 8.12], and at the end of the ages [I Peter 1.20] he called you into being and revealed you as God-bearer, Mother, and Nurse of his own Son and Word.[18]

---

[14] P. Maas and C. A. Trypanis, eds, *Sancti Romani Melodi Cantica* (Oxford, 1963; repr. 1997), Kontakion on the Nativity I, stanza β, p. 2; Archimandrite E. Lash, tr., *Kontakia on the Life of Christ. St Romanos the Melodist* (San Francisco, CA, 1995), 4.

[15] *PG* 98.377A–B.

[16] Although Kalavrezou points to the increased emphasis on Mary's motherly qualities in the late ninth century, especially in the homilies of George of Nikomedeia and Photios, she does not focus on the corpus of early eighth-century homilies in which such lyricism is already present. See N. Tsironis, 'The Mother of God in the iconoclastic controversy', in Vassilaki, ed., *Mother of God*, 27–39.

[17] Kotter expresses doubts on the authenticity of this homily in the introduction to his edition, *Die Schriften* V, 149–50. See also J. Hoeck, 'Stand und Aufgaben der Damaskenos-Forschung', *OCP* 17 (1951), 37, note 2. A. Louth states that he is not entirely convinced of this homily's inauthenticity in *St John Damascene: tradition and originality in Byzantine theology* (Oxford, 2002), 226.

[18] Kotter, *Die Schriften* V, 177 (7), lines 20–33. See also the passage describing Mary's apprehension of Christ through all her senses later in the same homily: 'Your eyes are "continually before the Lord" [Psalm 24 (25).15], seeing eternal and unapproachable light [cf. I Timothy 6.16]. Your ears hear the divine word and delight in the harp of the Spirit; through them the Word entered that he might become flesh. Your nostrils are charmed with the Bridegroom's ointment, who is himself a divine ointment, which is poured out to anoint his own humanity, for "your name is ointment poured out" (Canticum 1.3), says the scripture. Your lips praise the Lord and are attached to his lips. Your tongue and throat discern the words

In another homily dating from roughly the same period, Andrew of Crete expresses doubts about whether the Virgin Mary really suckled Christ in the manner of other women, stating, 'I will not speak of her strange, miraculous way of nursing'.[19] This statement may reflect the preacher's view, as in the case of Romanos, that it is paradoxical for a virgin to give milk.

Byzantine homilists frequently use metaphor to suggest the role of the Theotokos as the link between Christ and the natural world. In this context we find metaphors evoking the earth and its cultivation. Andrew of Crete, perhaps inspired by his fifth-century predecessor Proklos of Constantinople,[20] writes, 'you are blessed among women, God-tilled earth ...who bore the unsown and unwatered ear of corn of our life in your womb.'[21] The seventh-century patriarch Modestos of Jerusalem calls her a 'field which [Christ] chose above all the earth; he grew up from her like an unplanted shoot, whose grain can neither be gathered nor thrown away, nourishing all things forever without being consumed, harvested only in the Father's bosom'.[22] Theoteknos of Livias, on the other hand, calls the Virgin herself 'the fruit that our earth has yielded',[23] while John of Damascus, inspired by the Song of Songs, compares her to the 'apple tree growing in the midst of the deep woods'.[24]

Typological treatment of the Virgin Mary began as early as the second century,[25] but it received fuller expression in the early fifth century, as evidenced especially in the homilies of Proklos of Constantinople.[26] Typology is the exegetical method which sees prefigurations of events or

---

of God and are filled with divine sweetness (cf. Psalm 118 [119].103). Your heart is pure and unblemished, seeing and desiring the unblemished God. A womb in which the Uncontained dwelt and breasts of milk from which God, the little child Jesus, was nourished!': Kotter, *Die Schriften* V, 179 (9), line 34–180, line 1. These translations are my own.

19 *PG* 97.1076A–B; Daley, tr., *On the Dormition of Mary*, 105. This is actually Andrew's first homily on the *Koimesis* (printed as his second in *PG*).

20 ὦ ἄρουρα ἐν ᾗ ὁ τῆς φύσεως γεωργὸς Χριστὸς ὡς στάχυς ἀσπόρως ἐβλάστησεν: 'O field, in which Christ himself, the nature's farmer, sprouted forth unsown as an ear of corn!', Homily I on the Theotokos, in N. Constas, *Proclus of Constantinople and the Cult of the Virgin in Late Antiquity* (Leiden, 2003), 138–9, III.

21 *PG* 97.865C.

22 *PG* 86.3288A–B; Daley, tr., *On the Dormition of Mary*, 87.

23 A. Wenger, *L'Assomption de la très sainte vierge dans la tradition byzantine du VIe au Xe siècle. Études et documents* (Paris, 1955), 272–91; Daley, tr., *On the Dormition of Mary*, 80.

24 Canticum 2.3. Kotter, *Die Schriften* V, 496 (10), lines 36–8; Daley, tr., *On the Dormition of Mary*, 195.

25 J. N. D. Kelly, *Early Christian Doctrines* (London, 5th edn, 1977), 69–75.

26 Studies include N. Constas, 'Weaving the body of God: Proclus of Constantinople, the Theotokos, and the loom of the flesh', *JECS* 3.2 (1995), 169–94; B. Marx, *Procliana. Untersuchungen über den homiletischen Nachlass des Patriarchen Proklos von Konstantinopel*, Münsterische Beiträge zur Theologie 23 (Münster, 1940); J. H. Barkhuizen, *Proclus, Bishop of Constantinople: Homilies on the Life of Christ*, Early Christian Studies 1 (Brisbane, 2001).

persons of the New Testament in the context of the Old. This approach does not eradicate the historical importance of the old and new covenants; as Sebastian Brock and Frances Young have shown; however, it transfers these figures into a sacred and eternal time frame in which their symbolic significance becomes preeminent.[27] Proklos was the first Byzantine preacher to establish many typological references for the Virgin, while reminding his audience that 'the entire miracle of the Virgin birth [is] hidden in the shadows [of the Old Testament]',[28] but it is clear that many more were added to the liturgical tradition in the course of the fifth through the eighth centuries.[29]

Perhaps one of the richest, although enigmatic, sources of typological treatment of the Virgin Mary is the anonymous Akathistos Hymn, which has been dated variously to the early fifth, sixth or seventh centuries.[30] Leaving aside the question of the hymn's date and provenance, it is important for the purposes of this paper to note its extensive use of both typological and poetic metaphors evoking food, drink and spiritual nourishment in relation to the Theotokos. Building on the agricultural imagery, which we noted earlier in various homilies, the hymnographer hails the Virgin in the fifth strophe:

> Hail, vine-twig of unfading bud;
> Hail, treasure of undying fruit;
> Hail, you who cultivate the cultivator of our life;
> Hail, earth that flourishes with a fertility of compassion;
> Hail, table that bears a wealth of mercy …[31]

Such imagery continues in the eleventh strophe, in the following lines:

> Hail, food, following after manna;
> Hail, minister of holy joy;
> Hail, promised land;
> Hail, from whom flow milk and honey;

---

27 S. Brock, *The Luminous Eye* (Rome, 1985), 17; F. Young, *Biblical Exegesis and the Formation of Christian Culture* (Cambridge, 1997), 152–5.

28 Constas, *Proclus of Constantinople*, 173.

29 I hope in the course of my current research, which focuses on Marian homilies and hymns of the eighth century, to establish a database of types and epithets describing the Theotokos. On the basis of my work so far, it is possible to state that later preachers and hymnographers added many new types to those which had been established by Proklos.

30 Using both literary and theological arguments, L. M. Peltomaa argues that the Akathistos was composed sometime between the Councils of Ephesus (431) and Chalcedon (451): *The Image of the Virgin Mary in the Akathistos Hymn* (Leiden, 2001). In this she challenges previous views, which located the hymn in the sixth or even seventh century. See, especially, E. Wellesz, 'The "Akathistos": a study in Byzantine hymnography', *DOP* 9–10 (1956), 143–74 and the bibliography cited in Peltomaa, *The Image*, 22–3, 40–48.

31 Peltomaa, *The Image*, 6–7, 5 (E).

Hail, bride unwedded.[32]

It is striking that in these separate passages, Mary is pictured both as the agent of nourishment ('earth', 'table', 'promised land') and as the food itself. This food is always linked to the primary object of veneration, Christ, but the metaphors convey as well the impression that the Virgin herself represents a source of succour. The stream of epithets, unbroken by theological commentary, which flows through the Akathistos, can only be understood if one possesses some knowledge of Early Christian liturgical and typological tradition.[33]

The last section of this paper will deal with an extended metaphor of a banquet which Andrew of Crete applies to the Theotokos in his first homily on the *Koimesis*.[34] This is a complex passage in which more than one scriptural allusion comes into play. In order that we may discuss the text in detail, it is necessary to quote the passage in full:

> To this perfect spiritual banquet of minds, the fleshly Mother of the eternal Mind invites us. The royal table is ready, and the subject of our discourse today is enlivened and swelled by God's mysterious action. All this radiant beauty, shining beyond the power of words in the faces of the guests at the banquet, suffuses our surroundings today. I, too, am a reveler here, though a stranger and a newcomer. Unworthy though I am, I am to lead our exalted contemplation. Let no one refuse to join this feast, on seeing our shabby wretchedness; the mystic story behind these inspired reflections was not prepared by us, but by the Mother of God herself. Since, then, the table is covered with such riches to allure its spiritual guests, let us go, as befits the Spirit, into the Spirit's depths. Already she, who begot Wisdom itself in the flesh, has imitated Wisdom in her own being and has offered herself completely as a mystical, heavenly banquet-table, prepared for those who are spiritually initiated in divine realities, and she invites us generously to the feast. We are not offered slaughtered victims of sacrifices or drinks from a mixing-bowl [cf. Proverbs 9.1–5] – not that blessed sacrifice from days gone by, nor that cup filled with God's own nectar – but meditations on *her* mysteries, supernatural and truly divine. She who presides at the feast, who invites us to share in it, shows us from her own experience how great the house is which Wisdom has built. She shows us herself as the holy table, bearing in her womb, through God's dispensation, our Lord and God Jesus Christ, who is nothing other than our life-giving bread – him who is eternal life, holding all creation together, made bread from the leaven of Adam's dough. Those who approach him in a holy way he leads to new life and transforms into divine reality, cleansing them and making them immortal by making them his own, through participation in a totally new kind of fellowship with him. This,

32 Peltomaa, *The Image*, 10–11, 11 (Λ).

33 See Peltomaa, *The Image*, esp. 139–205.

34 Andrew of Crete, *Homily I on the Dormition*, *PG* 97.1084–5.

> surely, is what refreshes those who love him, what constitutes their very life. It is an excellent, indescribable life; nothing we know in this creation is more exalted than this! He who is beyond all theology, by an incomprehensible self-emptying, bent down in pity for the human race, though he was the source of creation, and chose to come down a second time to share in our poverty, to be mixed into the dough of our race, 'to share in flesh and blood like us' [Hebrews 2.14] …
>
> … This, as far as I can understand it and put it into ready words, is the spiritual table of Wisdom to which God draws us. These are the 'orgies' mystically celebrated around her – sacred rites given by God![35]

Andrew begins this section in conventional rhetorical style by comparing his sermon to a banquet to which 'the Mother of the eternal Mind invites us. The royal table is ready, and the subject of our discourse today is enlivened and swelled by God's mysterious action …' The topos of the orator's unworthiness is duly employed, with the interesting addition that Andrew is a newcomer in these surroundings.[36] After this Andrew evokes the banquet prepared by the personification of Wisdom in Proverbs 9.1–5. A parallel between Mary and Wisdom can be drawn here, but the preacher reminds us that unlike Wisdom, who acted as hostess, the Theotokos offered *herself* 'as a mystical, heavenly banqueting table'. And unlike the Proverbial *trapeza*, which offered freshly killed meat and newly mixed wine, Andrew's banquet table, the Theotokos herself, contains 'nothing other than our life-giving bread – him who is eternal life, holding all creation together, made bread from the leaven of Adam's dough'. With these words we are brought back to the type of the table (*trapeza*) in the tabernacle or the temple (Exodus 25.23–30), which held the 'bread of the Presence'.[37] This represents a type of Christ himself who, as we saw at the beginning of this paper, is himself the 'bread of life'. The Eucharistic symbolism of all these images scarcely needs emphasizing.[38] In addition to these typological meanings, yet another idea may be extracted from this passage. The Virgin Mary, imitating Wisdom, offers the revelers 'meditations on her mysteries, supernatural and truly divine'. This phrase evokes the table of spiritual fare described by John

---

35 Daley, tr., *On the Dormition of Mary*, 111–12. Daley notes that this homily was erroneously published as the first in the trilogy of sermons on the *Koimesis* by F. Combefis and after him, J.-P. Migne.

36 Daley suggests that Andrew may have been acting as a guest preacher, perhaps even at the court liturgy at Constantinople, when he delivered this trilogy of sermons. See Daley, tr., *On the Dormition of Mary*, 116 note 20.

37 Margaret Barker, *The Gate of Heaven: the history and symbolism of the Temple in Jerusalem* (London, 1991), 29.

38 For a good introduction to Old Testament types of the Eucharist, see J. Daniélou, *The Bible and the Liturgy* (Notre Dame, 1956), esp. 142–61.

Chrysostom in a homily on Genesis.[39] As Chrysostom suggested in that text, Andrew proposes here that the nourishment received at the great Marian and dominical feasts is *intellectual* as well as Eucharistic; it is partly by listening to the sermons composed for these events that Christians receive spiritual nourishment.

Leena-Mari Peltomaa devotes one section of her study of the Akathistos Hymn to a perceptive analysis of metaphor, especially as applied by Byzantine hymnographers and preachers to the Virgin Mary.[40] Criticizing the unlikely conclusions reached by various scholars concerning the epithets contained in the *chairetismoi* sections of the Akathistos,[41] Peltomaa makes the important point that metaphor must be understood within its various contexts: the meaning of the text as a whole is important, as is the cultural and theological background of its author and intended audience. Although Peltomaa's first premise, that 'poetic language is in a logical relationship to the context in which it appears', is fully convincing,[42] her second proposition, that 'metaphor is a process of transfer which gives rise to only one meaning' seems unnecessarily restrictive.[43] The passage in Andrew of Crete's first homily on the *Koimesis* which we have been examining combines a number of metaphors and types, not just the most obvious one of the table laid by Wisdom in Proverbs 9.1–5. On the basis of this text, it seems clear that preachers were not afraid to pile type upon type, thus building up layers of meaning, all of which support the proposition that the Theotokos is a worthy receptacle of the divine offering, Christ himself. Such complex use of typology serves to weave together the Old and New Testaments, along with the homilies that interpret them, into a seamless tapestry, which testifies, by means of a theological and evocative

39 This table is illustrated in Athens, NL MS 211, fol. 56, at the beginning of John Chrysostom's Homily 7 on Genesis, *PG* 54.607–14. In the text of the homily, the preacher urges his audience to go home from church and to set up two tables. One should contain the normal gastronomical feast (pictured in this miniature with various meats and elaborately folded napkins), whereas the other (shown with a Gospel, a cross, the holy elements and a dove representing the Holy Spirit) should set forth the spiritual instruction received in church for the benefit of the whole household. See A. Marava-Chatzinicolaou and C. Toufexi-Paschou, eds, *Catalogue of the Illuminated Byzantine Manuscripts of the National Library of Greece III: Homilies of the Church Fathers and Menologia, 9th–12th Century* (Athens, 1997), fig. 17.

40 Peltomaa, *The Image*, 116-125.

41 Peltomaa criticizes a number of studies, including P. M. Addison, *Akathistos. Byzantine Hymn to the Mother of God, Translation for Chant and Choral Recitation* (Rome, 1983); V. Limberis, *Divine Heiress: the Virgin Mary and the creation of Christian Constantinople* (London, 1987); and N. B. Tomadakis, 'Ἀκάθιστος Ὕμνος, Κανών, Ἀκολουθία', in *Θρησκευτικὴ καὶ ἠθικὴ ἐγκυκλοπαίδεια*, vol. 1 (Athens, 1962), 1147–64.

42 Peltomaa, *The Image*, 116.

43 Peltomaa, *The Image*, 121.

use of imagery and metaphor, to the central doctrine of Christianity: the incarnation of Christ.

To conclude, let us recapitulate briefly some of the ways in which food imagery is applied to the Virgin Mary in Byzantine liturgical texts. As we have seen, Mary's role as the bearer and mother of Christ is implied in both poetic and typological references to bodily nourishment. As the Galaktotrophousa, the Virgin offers milk to the One who nourishes the whole of creation.[44] The typological epithets that we have seen, including the untilled earth, the promised land, the jar containing manna, and the table in the tabernacle, all express theologically Mary's essential role in the incarnation of Christ. The Virgin, from whom alone God took his human nature, is, in the words of Proklos, 'the only bridge for God towards humankind'.[45] In addition to their theological meaning, types of the Mother of God convey a sacramental symbolism, especially with reference to baptism and the Eucharist. Images of food and drink, which appear throughout the Old and New Testaments, denoting communion between God and his creation, are thus particularly appropriate as metaphors for the Virgin Mary who herself represents the final link in this great mystery.

44 A related iconographical motif, which conveys more literally the idea that Christ and his mother nourish the rest of humanity, is that of Christ offering food to the hungry while sitting in his mother's lap at the church of the Virgin Hodegetria in Peć (c. 1330). See also the thirteenth-century image of the Mother of God holding the Christ child on her right arm and a basket in her left hand at the church of the Virgin at Prizren, Kosovo. A fragment of an inscription in Old Serbian on the left of Christ reads 'krmitelj', 'the food provider', which corresponds to the Greek ὁ τροφεύς, referring to Christ. Tragically, this church was destroyed in March 2004 as a result of ethnic conflict in Kosovo. See G. Babić in D. Panić and G. Babić, *Bogorodica Ljeviska* (Belgrade, 1975), 54 and 96. I am very grateful to Zaga Gavrilović for providing me with slides and bibliography of these images.

45 Constas, *Proclus of Constantinople*, 136–7, lines 20 and 24.

20. Being a potential saint

Patricia Karlin-Hayter

Our subject is, very suitably, carousing, known principally from the deplorable indulgence in it attributed to iconoclast (or murdered[1]) emperors admittedly by their detractors. The two cases I have in mind come from a saint's Life.

I have never felt the obligation for a Byzantinist to read saint's Lives as very painful, nor their 'uniformity' all that uniform. Even so, I rate St Antony the Younger's pretty highly.[2] In fact, it is two Lives: Antony's *vita* is preceded by that of his guide to monastic life and sainthood, John, whose *Life*, inside the double structure, begins 'There was an arch-bandit in the mountains of Anatolia …' and continues with his career as such, until the urge to be saved and a monastic vocation take possession of this bandit. After many years of praying, fasting and so forth, he has become a famous saint and the parents of a little John drop the boy on him. John is destined to receive, many years later, along with the σχῆμα, a new name – Antonios.

St Basil the Great warned about parents who popped children into monasteries when they were too young. Whether familiar with St Basil or simply showing common sense, at some point the holy Father sent John off, with instructions to start with life in the world, and in due course come back and become a monk.

The two banquets belong to the future St Antony's worldly life. He has quite a brilliant career, and it is as ἐκ προσώπου (deputy) of the Kibyrraiot theme that he is summoned to Constantinople to give a report. Is he, prudently, travelling incognito? At all events, he has instructed his suite to say that he is a doctor, rather a good doctor. So on an occasion when they were settling down for the night in a very well-to-do house, the attendants of the *ek prosopou*, questioned by the personnel of the house, say he is a doctor

[1] For example Michael III.

[2] *Vita Antonii Iunioris*, ed. A. Papadopoulos-Kerameus, *Pravoslavnij Palestinskij Sbornik*, 19.3 (1907), 186–216 *e codice mutilo*.

who gives people absolutely everything that makes life good. Informed of this, the lord of the manor asks: 'Can he allow you to have a child?' They say: 'Oh yes. He's got a method for that too …' Full of joy, he prepares a splendid banquet. When all are seated at table, his guest, the *ek prosopou* – a doctor, the host thinks, says to him: 'Here's your table filled with all the good things in the world … and you have a big and beautiful house. But the best thing of all, you do not seem to have.' The host is rather injured: 'And what might that be?' John replies: 'You haven't got a child, have you?' The master of the house says: 'No, sir. For twenty-five years I've been married to my wife here (τῇ γυναικί μου ταύτῃ), and God has given us no offspring …' John says to the two of them in an engaging way (χαριέντως): 'And if something could be managed (ἐὰν γένηται τίποτε) and you were to have a child, what would I get?' The man answered: 'The third of all my possessions.' 'No, no,' says John, 'just ten warhorses, reared for me with care, and barley-fed' (the only precise information about food given). This having been agreed to, John says: 'Bring me some parchment.'[3] As they could not find any, he had them bring in a holy Gospel, tore off some of the last leaves and made a little tome of them on which he wrote a prayer. He then gave them the following instructions: 'Wash your bedclothes, wash yourselves too, wiping yourselves absolutely clean. With this prayer bound directly on the flesh, her ladyship will lie down next to you in the bed, and I trust in God who blesses fathers, and gives them the joy of begetting children, that it will be with you according to your desire.'

Needless to say the couple had their child 'and there was more joy in that house than had ever been seen there before'. Of course John would not take the horses.[4] He had just been joking, which, apparently, was allowed to him.

But you can go too far. He decided to get married. News reached the ex-ruffian saint, who promptly wrote an indignant letter, which reached John – St Antony-to-be – just as the wedding festivities were beginning. He got the message and deliberately stepped up that night's fun, and had laid before his friends and relations, at a late hour, a truly Syracusan banquet, with first-quality wine (οἴνου πρωτείου). He himself was drinking nothing but boiled onion juice, but had it brought to him in a purple glass, so that no one should notice. He kept the party going till the second watch, till Dionysos had knocked them all out for him.[5] No bed was needed, all slept just where they lay, and he slipped out unnoticed, and made for the column of his spiritual Father, and embarked on his monastic life.

---

[3] ἀφελόμενος ἐκ τῶν ἐσχάτων φύλλων, διατμήξας συνέρραψεν τόμον, ὅσον ἐδύνατο διαζῶσαι τὸν φορέσαι μέλλοντα.

[4] *Vita Antonii* 195.15–196.20.

[5] *Vita Antonii* 201.18.

Section VI

Outside the empire

21. More Malmsey, Your Grace? The export of Greek wine to England in the later Middle Ages

Jonathan Harris

In Act I, Scene IV of Shakespeare's *Richard III*, the duke of Clarence is famously done to death by being first stabbed and then, just to make sure, drowned in a 'Malmsey-butt'.[1] Malmsey was a type of sweet wine, which was originally associated with the Peloponnese, especially the area around Monemvasia. When the Franks took over Monemvasia after 1204, they called the city and the wine they found there 'Malvoisie'. Malvoisie was in turn anglicized into Malmsey. By the fifteenth century, the type of grape which produced Malmsey was also being cultivated on Crete and Cyprus and even in Spain in order to produce the quantities needed to satisfy the market.[2]

Malmsey was not the only Greek wine available in England during the fifteenth century. There was also 'Rumney', another rather sweet concoction, which came originally from Zakynthos and the Ionian islands. The name Rumney is another anglicization, this time from 'Romania', one of the names applied in the west to the Byzantine empire.[3] The merchant Richard Cely appears to have been fond of prescribing Rumney for his female friends and relatives. In 1482, he wrote to his brother that two ladies had visited him one Sunday morning after walking a mile. He thereupon gave them a

---

1 Shakespeare did not make up the story, which appears earlier in Thomas More, *The History of Richard III*, ed. R. S. Sylvester, in *The Yale Edition of the Complete Works of St Thomas More*, 16 vols (New Haven, CT, 1963–97), 2.7.

2 H. and R. Kahane, 'Byzantium's impact on the West: the linguistic evidence', *ICS* 6 (1981), 389–415, at 398; E. Sakellariou, 'Latin Morea in the Middle Ages: observations on its demography and economy', in C. Dendrinos, J. Harris, E. Harvalia-Crook and J. Herrin, eds, *Porphyrogenita: essays on the history and literature of Byzantium and the Latin East in honour of Julian Chrysostomides* (Aldershot, 2003), 301–16, at 310; A. D. Francis, *The Wine Trade* (London, 1972), 9, 15.

3 R. L. Wolff, 'Romania: the Latin empire of Constantinople', *Speculum*, 23 (1948), 1–34. By the fifteenth century, Rumney, like Malmsey, was also being produced in Spain: Francis, *Wine Trade*, 9, 15, 23.

'pottell of whyte romney' and was pleased to record that 'thay tooke hyt thankefully'. Between 1482 and 1484 he ordered no less than eighty-one gallons of the stuff for his mother's household.[4] Rumney was, however, a distinctly inferior brew to Malmsey and discerning customers like the duke of Clarence would not be seen dead in anything else.

Unlike Liudprand of Cremona, therefore, who proclaimed it to be undrinkable, the inhabitants of the British Isles appear to have had a taste for Greek wine. Two Irish Franciscans who passed through the Morea and Crete on their way to the Holy Land in 1322 commented on the excellence of the wine that they encountered on the way and we have Bryer to thank for pointing out that the members of an English delegation, who stayed at Trebizond in the summer of 1292, drank a modest fifteen aspers' worth of the local black wine on their first day. By the sixth day, they had acquired such a taste for it that they knocked back forty-eight aspers' worth.[5] Sir Richard Guylforde, who journeyed through the Peloponnese en route to Jerusalem in 1506, noted that 'there groweth moche Romney and Maluesey' and was pleased to come across 'a cyte called Malsasia, where firste grewe Malmasye and yet dothe; howbeit hit groweth nowe more plentuously in Candia and Modona, and no where ellys.'[6] For such gastronomic tourists, the returned pilgrim William Wey (c. 1407–76) produced a handy English–Greek phrasebook replete with useful items such as 'Woman, haue ye goyd wyne?' (translated as *Geneca, esse calocrasse*) and 'Bryng heder wyne' (*Fertodo crasse*). If all failed, the traveller could fall back on 'Wher ys the taverne?' (*Elle canawte*).[7]

One did not have to go so far to sample Greek wine, however. It was one of the commodities of the eastern Mediterranean which, from the late thirteenth century onwards, were shipped to the ports of London and Southampton by Genoese and Venetian merchants, operating from the areas of the former Byzantine empire dominated by their respective republics. By 1400 the Venetians alone were importing a thousand casks of

---

4 *The Cely Papers: selections from the correspondence and memoranda of the Cely Family, merchants of the staple, AD 1475–1488*, ed. H. Elliot Malden, Camden Society, Series 3.1 (London, 1900), 103; A. Hanham, *The Celys and Their World: an English merchant family of the fifteenth century* (Cambridge, 1985), 265.

5 Liudprand of Cremona, 'Relatio de Legatione Constantinopolitana', in P. Chiesa, ed., *Liudprandi Cremonensis Opera Omnia*, CCCM 156 (Turnhout, 1998), 185–218, at 187; G. Golubovich, *Biblioteca bio-biblografica della Terra Santa e dell'oriente francescano* (Florence, 1906–27), 3.254; A. A. M. Bryer, 'Edward I and the Mongols', *History Today*, 14 (1964), 696–704, at 703.

6 *The Pilgrimage of Sir Richard Guylforde to the Holy Land, A.D. 1506*, ed. H. Ellis (London, 1851), 12.

7 *The Itineraries of William Wey*, ed. G. Williams (London, 1857), 1.102.

sweet wine from Crete into England every year.[8] The supply was plentiful enough for wine from Greece to be found not only in London but all over England. Apparently, there was a good quantity in the larder of Durham abbey in about 1360.[9]

So lucrative was the trade in wine and spices from the eastern Mediterranean that the Venetians and Genoese vied with each other to dominate it, the Genoese resorting at one point to a drastic cut in their freight rates in an attempt to undercut the Venetians.[10] When it came to complete outsiders trying to break into the monopoly, both republics were prepared to take drastic and even violent action. When the English ship *Katherine Sturmy* voyaged to the Levant in 1457 with a cargo of tin, wool and cloth to exchange for spices, it was ambushed by the Genoese near Malta on the return journey and its cargo destroyed.[11] In 1488, alarmed by reports of foreign vessels loading wine at Cretan ports, the Venetian Senate placed a prohibitive duty of four ducats on each barrel of Malmsey loaded onto foreign ships bound for western Europe.[12] It was not until the second decade of the sixteenth century that English merchants finally broke into the Mediterranean trade.[13]

It was not just the supply of wine to England that was controlled by Italian merchants. In Constantinople, wine was a much more important part of everyday diet than in northern Europe and its import and sale had always been carefully regulated by law.[14] By the mid-fourteenth century, however,

[8] *The Second Book of the Travels of Nicander Nucius of Corcyra*, ed. J. A. Cramer, Camden Society, Series 1.17, (London, 1841), 12; A. A. Ruddock, *Italian Merchants and Shipping in Southampton, 1270–1600* (Southampton, 1951), 73; E. B. Fryde, 'Italian maritime trade with medieval England (c. 1270–c. 1530)', *Receuils de la Societé Jean Bodin* 32, 291–337, at 317, reprinted in idem, *Studies in Medieval Trade and Finance* (London, 1983), no. 14; Francis, *Wine Trade*, 9, 22; F. C. Lane, *Venice: a maritime republic* (Baltimore, MD, 1973), 67–73.

[9] *Extracts from the Account Rolls of the Abbey of Durham*, ed. J. T. Fowler, Surtees Society, 99, 100, 103 (London, 1898–1900), 2.563.

[10] F. C. Lane, *Venetian Ships and Shipbuilders of the Renaissance* (Baltimore, 1934), 46, 262.

[11] *Calendar of the Patent Rolls: 1452–1461*, ed. H. C. Maxwell-Lyte and A. E. Bland (London, 1910), 517; E. M. Carus-Wilson, *Medieval Merchant Venturers* (London, 1954), 70–71.

[12] *Calendar of State Papers and Manuscripts Relating to English Affairs Existing in the Archives and Collections of Venice, and in Other Libraries of Northern Italy. Vol. 1: 1202–1509*, ed. R. Brown (London, 1864), 175; Ruddock, *Italian Merchants*, 221–3.

[13] R. Hakluyt, *The Principal Navigations, Voyages, Traffiques and Discoveries of the English Nation*, 12 vols (Glasgow, 1903–5), 5.62; A. L. Simon, *The History of the Wine Trade in England*, 3 vols (London, 1906–9), 2.238–9.

[14] A. Karpozelos, 'Realia in Byzantine epistolography, X–XIIc', *BZ* 77 (1984), 20–37, at 26; A. M. Dembinska, 'Diet: a comparison of food consumption between some eastern and western monasteries in the 4th–12th centuries', *Byzantion*, 55 (1985), 431–62, at 447; G. Dagron, 'The urban economy, seventh–twelfth centuries', in A. E. Laiou, ed., *The Economic History of Byzantium from the Seventh through the Fifteenth Century*, 3 vols (Washington, DC, 2002), 2.393–461, at 459–60.

the Venetians and Genoese dominated the shipping of products from Crete and the Aegean to Constantinople as completely as they did everywhere else. The courtier and historian Nikephoros Gregoras complained that much of Constantinople's trade had been diverted through the Genoese colony of Galata on the opposite side of the Golden Horn, while the Venetians not only imported huge quantities of wine from Crete, free of duty thanks to earlier agreements with the Byzantine emperors, but even owned many of the taverns in the Byzantine capital where it was sold.[15]

On the face of it, therefore, it seems unlikely that merchants from what remained of the Byzantine empire before 1453 would have much opportunity to profit from this export trade and that any attempt to do so would lead to reprisals like that visited upon the *Katherine Sturmy*. Yet that was not, in fact, the case. As Angeliki Laiou, Nevra Necipoğlu and others have shown, Byzantine merchants were very active in the later Middle Ages, albeit in a secondary role. Italians controlled the prerequisites of international trade, namely shipping and banking, but although no other ships were allowed to participate in the trade, the Venetians and Genoese were perfectly happy for other people to use theirs.[16] Thus Byzantine merchants were able to operate by hiring Italian shipping and were particularly active in the Black Sea trade with Trebizond and the route up the Adriatic to Ragusa. Wine was among the commodities they traded.[17]

What has not been appreciated, however, is just how far afield these Byzantine merchants were able to venture in this secondary role, thanks to the ubiquitous Genoese and Venetian galleys. Two fifteenth-century English chronicles suggest that their operations extended as far as London. One records that when the emperor Manuel II Palaiologos was in London during the winter of 1400/1401, he was kept informed of events in the east by 'mercatores Graeci'. Another, the *Crowland Chronicle Continuations*,

---

15 Nikephoros Gregoras, *Byzantina Historia*, ed. L. Schopen, CSHB, 2 vols (Bonn, 1829–30), 2.841–2; J. Chrysostomides, 'Venetian commercial privileges under the Palaeologi', *StVen* 12 (1970), 267–356, at 298–9; D. M. Nicol, *Byzantium and Venice: a study in diplomatic and cultural relations* (Cambridge, 1988), 291–3; K.-P. Matschke, 'The Late Byzantine urban economy', in A Laiou, ed., *The Economic History of Byzantium*, 2.463–95, at 475–7.

16 Francis, *Wine Trade*, 22.

17 A. E. Laiou-Thomadakis, 'The Greek merchant of the Palaeologan Period: a collective portrait', in Πρακτικά της Ακαδημίας Αθηνών (Athens, 1982), 96–124, at 113, reprinted in A. E. Laiou, *Gender, Society and Economic Life in Byzantium* (Aldershot: Variorum 1992), no. 8; eadem, 'The Byzantine economy in the Mediterranean trade system: thirteenth–fifteenth centuries', *DOP* 34–5 (1980–81), 177–222, at 189–90, 196, 210; N. Necipoğlu, 'Constantinopolitan merchants and the question of their attitudes towards Italians and Ottomans in the late Palaeologan period', in C. Scholz and G. Makris, eds, *Polypleuros Nous: Miscellanea für Peter Schreiner zu seinem 60 Geburtstag*, Byzantinisches Archiv 19 (Munich, 2000), 251–63.

describes how King Edward IV (1461–83) indulged in trade with both Italian and Greek merchants.[18]

These chronicles should perhaps be treated with some caution, since their monastic authors may well not have had first-hand information about trading conditions of the time. There is, however, another body of evidence that is much more authoritative: the set of documents known as the *Exchequer Customs Accounts* or E122, which are preserved in the National Archives (formerly the Public Record Office) in London. The accounts recorded cargoes that were imported into or exported from London and the customs duty that was levied on them. One set, for the year 1445/1446, records that a cargo of sweet wine was imported into London by a certain George of Constantinople.[19] Thus the accounts make it clear that a Byzantine merchant was involved in the English wine trade in the last years before the fall of Constantinople, even if there is little likelihood that anything more will ever be known about the identity of this George.

We are on firmer ground with another example. The accounts tell us that, in November 1445, an Andronikos of Constantinople imported a total of fourteen barrels of sweet wine into the port of London, using vessels owned by an Italian, Marco da Pryole, and one belonging to an Englishman, John Cappell.[20] This individual is almost certainly Andronikos Effomatos, about whom we know a great deal from other sources. Along with his brother, Alexios, Andronikos had left Constantinople to settle in London in 1440 and lived there continuously for about thirty-five years.[21] Although a gold wire drawer by trade, Andronikos seems to have supplemented his income by importing various goods in Venetian and Genoese ships, no doubt reselling them at a handsome profit. In 1450 he brought in a number of daggers on the *Santa Consolata* of Genoa, commanded by Bartolomeo Doria, and a consignment of furs on another ship.[22] He also sent goods in the other direction, exporting a cargo of kerseys in 1449.[23]

Greeks from Constantinople were not the only ones to profit from the lucrative trade of shipping wine to northern Europe. Those living in areas under Latin rule were in a good position to take advantage of it. In 1396

---

18 J. Trokelowe and H. Blaneforde, *Chronica et Annales*, ed. H. T. Riley, Rolls Series 28 (London, 1866), 336; *The Crowland Chronicle Continuations*, ed. N. Pronay and J. Cox (London, 1986), 139.

19 National Archives, London, E122/203/3, fol. 13.

20 National Archives, London, E122/203/3, fols 14v, 16.

21 J. Harris, *Greek Emigrés in the West, 1400–1520* (Camberley, 1995), 34, 37, 185–7; idem, 'Two Byzantine craftsmen in fifteenth-century London', *JMedHist* 21 (1995), 387–403; J. L. Bolton, *The Alien Communities of London in the Fifteenth Century. The Subsidy Rolls of 1440 and 1483–4* (Stamford, 1998), 27.

22 National Archives, London, E122/73/25, fols 9, 16v.

23 National Archives, London, E122/73/23, fol. 40v.

John Nicolai of Crete sent a quantity of wine to England on the Venetian Flanders galleys, which were dispatched every year to London and Bruges.[24] Further afield, there was a merchant called Demetrios, from the Hospitaller-ruled island of Rhodes, who brought wine to Rouen during the 1470s, though interestingly it was Spanish wine that he dealing in.[25] Like Andronikos Effomatos, these Greek merchants would also have wanted to profit by bringing back English products. Thus, in April 1439, Manuel Sybianos exported English cloth and tin from London in the galley of Giovanni Barbarigo.[26]

One last, curious, point. The Constantinopolitan craftsman and merchant Andronikos Effomatos died in about 1473, but his younger brother, Alexios, lived on in London and was still alive in 1483.[27] There is, therefore, at least a theoretical possibility that it was a barrel of Malmsey imported by a Byzantine that brought about the untimely end of the duke of Clarence. That, of course, is to stray into the realms of fantasy.

---

24 B. Krekič, 'A note on the economic activities of some Greeks in the Latin Levant towards the end of the fourteenth century', *StVen* 9 (1961), 187–91, at 191.

25 Archives Départementales du Seine-maritime, Rouen, 6 BP1, fol. 60v; M. Mollat, *Le Commerce maritime normand à la fin du Moyen Age* (Paris, 1952), 509.

26 National Archives, London, E122/73/12, fol. 33v.

27 Harris, *Greek Emigrés*, 197.

22. Record of Byzantine food in Chinese texts

Chen Zhiqiang

In ancient and medieval Chinese texts the Byzantine state is called Da-qin (Ta-ts'in) and Fu-lin, and the identification of the source of these names has been an extremely controversial issue since the end of the nineteenth century. The name Ta-ts'in was first used in the *Bie-guo-dong-ming-ji,*[1] while Fu-lin was used in chronicles written after the Sui and the T'ang dynasties during the period between the seventh and ninth century. 'The country of Ta-ts'in', the *Hou-han-shu* says, 'has another name, Li-qian, ... and is also called Hai-xi-guo', or 'the country of the western part of the sea'.[2] The *Tang-shu* records: 'the country of Fu-lin is also called Ta-ts'in'.[3] We can infer from these historical records that a great amount of information is available in ancient and medieval Chinese texts about the Byzantine empire, under various names such as Li-qian, Li-chien, Li-hsuan, Ta-ts'in, H'ai-hsi and Fu-lin. The information is reasonably useful to researchers in the field of Byzantine studies. It is for this reason that since the end of the nineteenth century such Chinese texts have attracted the attention of many sinologists and historical-geographers – among them Visdelou, de Guignes, Wylie, Henry Yule, Bretschneider, Pelliot, Pauthier, Neumann and Hirth[4] – all of

[1] *Bie-guo-dong-ming-ji* (Notes on Interesting Things in Foreign Countries) was written by Guo Xian, who was a high official of the later H'an dynasty in the second century. He records many things that are not recounted in the dynastic annals. He is perhaps the first author who wrote something about the country named Ta-ts'in and later Fu-lin in the ancient and medieval Chinese texts.

[2] *Hou-han-shu* (Annals of the Later H'an Dynasty), covering the period AD 25–200, was written c. 420–72 by Fan Ye. He wrote the history based on new information and his work became the source of the later dynastic chronicles. The information used in the dynastic annals, as far as I can ascertain, perhaps derived from the earlier history book *Wei-lio* by Yu H'uan.

[3] *Xin-tang-shu* (The New Annals of the T'ang Dynasty), covering the period 618–907 and written by O-yang Xiu, a famous writer of the Sung dynasty, c. 1044–60, contains a reference to Fu-lin, which is regarded as the Byzantine empire. In the book, however, there is also new information about Fu-lin and records of events that took place during the T'ang dynasty.

[4] Translations of Chinese texts into western languages can be found in many works by European scholars. See, for example, E. Chamberlin, 'Les Pays d'Occident d'après le Wei-lio',

whom made excellent translations of passages of Chinese texts into western languages.

In Chinese texts there is also information about Byzantine food and drink, which is treated by Chinese writers as something strange, or at least different from food and drink in China. The most curious things to ancient Chinese eyes, however, were the different kinds of precious stones. *Hou-han-shu* mentions:

> The people of that country are tall and well proportioned, somewhat like the Chinese, whence they are called Ta-ts'in. In the country there is gold, silver, precious stones and strange things in plenty, especially the jewel that shines at night, the pearl under moonshine, the chicken-frightening rhinoceros, corals, amber, precious stones like pearls, cinnabar, green jadestone, gold-embroidered rugs, ready-made gold-embroidered felts, and fine silk-cloth of various colors. They make gold-coloured cloth and asbestos cloth.[5]

Ancient and medieval Chinese writers also mention the trees growing in the East Roman empire, such as pines, cypress, pagoda-trees and so on. A historical account of them follows:

> The country has trees: pines, cypress, pagoda-trees, catalpa, bamboo, reeds, poplars, parasol trees and all kinds of other plants. The people customarily plant all kinds of grain in the fields. Their domestic animals include the horse, the donkey, the mule, the camel. They cultivate the mulberry silkworm.[6]

It is reasonable to believe that some of the information contained here is mistaken. For example, the mulberry silkworm was not known to the

---

T'oung P'ao, 6 (1905), 519–71. M. P. Charlesworth, *Trade Route and Commerce of the Roman Empire* (Cambridge, 1936); E. Chavannes, 'Notes additionelles sur les Tou-Kiue Occidentaux', *T'oung P'ao*, 5 (1904), 1–97; F. Hirth, *China and the Roman Orient: researches into their ancient and medieval relations as represented in old Chinese records* (Shanghai, 1885); H. Yule, *Cathay and the Way Thither: being a collection of medieval notices of China* (London, 1915); P. Pelliot, 'Li-kien, autre nom du Ta-ts'in (Orient Mediterranean)', *T'oung P'ao*, 16 (1915), 609–91; idem, 'Deux itinéraires de la Chine en Inde à la fin du VIII siècle', *BEFEO* 4 (1904), 131–413; L. Boulnois, *The Silk Road* (London, 1966); I. M. Franck and D. M. Brownstone, *The Silk Road: a history* (New York, 1986); C. K. Papastathis, 'Silk trade and the Byzantine penetration in the state organization of South Arabia', in *Cultural and Commercial Exchanges between the Orient and the Greek World* (Athens, 1990), 111–21; Shen Fu-wei, *China and Africa: their exchanges for two thousand years* (Beijing, 1990), 228–9.

[5] Fan Ye , *Hou-han-shu*, Chinese Ancient Books Printing House (Shanghai, 1986), chap. 118.

[6] Pei Song-zhi, *San-guo-zhi* (The History of the Three Kingdoms), Chinese Ancient Books Printing House (Shanghai, 1986), chap. 30, written before AD 297, compiled c. 429, quotes, as a note, the *Wei-lue* (The Brief History of the Wei Kingdom), written by Yu Huan around the middle of the third century. The *Wei-lue* was a rich source of information for later authors.

Byzantines until the sixth century, when Justinian I allegedly sent two monks to learn the art of silk production in China.

In the seventh century, knowledge of the western countries, including Byzantium, in Chinese books increased as a result of more frequent commercial exchanges. A group of Chinese had the opportunity to visit the eastern Mediterranean and hence came to know more about the Byzantines. *Xing-jing-ji* records that:

> the country of Fu-lin lies several thousand li west of the country of Zham (Syria), separated by mountains. It is also called Ta-ts'in. The colour of their faces is red and white. The men all wear plain clothes and the women wear silk clothes beset with pearls. They enjoy wine and have a fancy for dry cakes. They are very skilled sexually, and clever at weaving … Cereal is scarce, and there are neither plants nor trees. They feed their horses on dried fish and they themselves live on ku-mang (Khurma). Ku-mang is the name of the Persian date. There are different kinds of Fa for the Ta-shih, the Ta-ts'in and Tz'im-tz'im. Of these, the Tz'im-tz'im Fa allows them to get married to their relatives, frequent among barbarians, and prohibits them from speaking while eating.[7]

The author is right in his remark about the wine and cakes, which were a completely different kind of food and drink compared to the most popular rice and broomcorn (gaoliang) cakes of China. The qualification 'neither plants nor trees' probably indicates that the writer was describing the desert of western Asia. *Xin-tang-shu* also mentions the same foods:

> Fu-lin is the ancient Ta-ts'in, and being situated on the western sea, is also called H'ai-hsi-kuo (Hai-xi-guo) or the country on the west of the sea. It is customary for them to enjoy wine and they have a fancy for dry cakes. On one of seven days, the lord and his subjects have a rest, when they refrain from doing any business and carouse all night.[8]

An interesting account on the emperor's dining circumstances reads as follows:

---

[7] Du You, *Tong-dian*, (Comprehensive Studies of History), Chinese Ancient Books Printing House (Beijing, 1988), chap. 193, written c. 766–801, contains some new sources regarding Ta-ts'in. The new information comes from the book *Jing-xing-ji* by Tu H'uan, who was Tu Yiou's nephew and had travelled in the western countries between 751 and 762. Tu H'uan's book has been lost, and we know it only from the *T'ung-tien*.

[8] *Xin-tang-shu* (The New History of the T'ang dynasty), Chinese Ancient Books Printing House (Shanghai, 1986), chap. 221b. It covers the period AD 618–907, and it was written by O-yang Xiu, a famous writer of the Sung dynasty, c. 1044–60. It contains an account of Fu-lin, which is a combination of the accounts of the *Chiu-t'ang-shu* and the *Wei-lio*. In this book, however, there are new pieces of information about Fu-lin and records of events that happened during the T'ang dynasty.

> There is a bird like a crane, with green feathers, which always sits on a cushion by the side of the king. If anything poisonous has been put into the king's meals, while eating, the bird will crow loudly.[9]

You-yang-za-zu (Notes on the Folklore in You-yang) was written by Duan Chien-shi (c. 847–59), a writer of the T'ang dynasty. It records many things regarding Fu-lin (the Byzantine state). A monk from the country of Fu-lin, who was a friend of the author of the book, gave him all the information.

> E-wei (asafoetida) grows in the country of Jia-ze-na, which is the state of Bei-tian-zhu. The people of Chia-ts'e-na call it Xing-yu. It also grows in the country of Persia, where it is called the tree of E-yu-jue. It has a height of eight or nine chang [c. 21.6 m] and an olive-yellow bark. It sprouts its new leaves, which are like the ears of a mouse, in the third month of every year, but without flowers and fruits. When its branches are cut, its sap oozes out of the wound. The sap is like maltose, and it coagulates after a long time, and this is what is called asafoetida. The monk Wan of the country of Fu-lin said the same about the plant as the monk Ti-p'o of the country of Me-jie-tuo. [chap. 18]
>
> … The tree of P'o-na-sa (jackfruit) grows in the country of Persia, as well as in the country of Fu-lin, where it is called the tree of E-pu-ch'an. It grows five or six chang high [c. 16.2 m], with an olive-green bark. Its leaves are very smooth and glossy, and do not wither in summer and winter. It bears fruits without flowers. The fruit grows out of the stem of the tree, as big as a wax gourd, within a shell, which has thorns. When the pulp of the fruit becomes sweet, it can be eaten. The core of the fruit is as big as the Chinese date. There are several hundred seeds in a fruit. The kernel in the pip is like the flesh of the chestnut, and is very tasty when eaten after being fried. [chap. 18]
>
> … The tree of Pan-nu-se grows in the country of Persia, as well as in the country of Fu-lin, where it is called the tree of Chun-h'an. It grows to a height of three chang [c. 8.1 m], and has a circumference of four or five ch'ih [c. 1.35 m]. Its flower is white, like the mandarin orange in shape. Its seeds are green, as big as the wild jujube, with an oily sweet taste, and can be eaten. The inhabitants of the western countries extract its oil, which can be used to smear on the body to cure urticaria. [chap. 18]
>
> … The tree of Qi-dun (olive) grows in the country of Persia, as well as in the country of Fu-lin, where it is called Chi-ti. It grows to a height of two or three chang [c. 8.1 m], with an olive-white bark. Its flowers are like those of the teak, very fragrant. Its seed seems to be like the carambola and is ripe in the fifth month of every year. The inhabitants of the western countries extract its oil to fry their cakes and fruit, just as the Chinese use oil. [chap. 18]

9 *T'ang-h'ui-yiao* (Important Documents of the T'ang Dynasty), Chinese Ancient Books Printing House (Beijing, 1976), chap 99. This was compiled in the reign of that dynasty and contains all kinds of official documents of the T'ang government. Its account of Fu-lin is based on the records of dynastic histories.

... Bi-bo (climbing fig) grows in the country of Mo-chia-to (ancient India), where it is called the pear of Pi-po; it is also called E-li-k'o-t'a in the country of Fu-lin. Its vine grows three or four chih high [c. 1.08 m], as thin as a chopstick. Its leaves are like those of the cordate houthuynia. Its seed is like the mulberry, picked in the eighth month of every year. [Text 71, chap. 18]

... Bei-qi grows in the country of Persia and is called Xu-bo-li-ta in the country of Fu-lin. It grows over a chang high [c. 2.70 m] and about a ch'ih in circumference [c. 0.27 m]. Its bark is green and thin, very smooth and glossy. Its leaves are like those of the asafoetida, three leaves on the end of every twig. It does not have flowers and fruits. The people of the western countries usually cut it in the eighth month of every year, and it sprouts new leaves by the twelfth month of every year, when it grows luxuriantly. Unless cut in the eighth month, it will wither. When its branches are cut in the seventh month of every year, its yellow sap oozes out and seems to be like honey, with a slight fragrance, and can be used as the ingredient of medicine to cure a disease. [chap.18]

... Persian Zao-jiao (Persian honey locust) grows in the country of Persia and is called Hu-yie-yan-mo; it is also called E-li-qu-fa in the country of Fu-lin. The tree grows three or four chang high [c. 8.1–10.8 m], four or five ch'ih in circumference [c. 1.08–1.35 m]. Its leaves are like those of the citron but shouter and smaller, and do not wither in winter. It bears fruit without flowers. The fruits are pods two ch'ih long [c. 0.54 m]. In the pod there are separate spaces, in each of which there is a seed. The seed is as big as a fingertip, red and hard, as black inside as Chinese ink, as sweet as maltose, and can be eaten or used as the ingredient of medicine. [chap. 18]

... The tree of Mo (myrrh) grows in the country of Persia and is called E-ch'ai in the county of Fu-lin. It grows to a height of about a chang [c. 2.70 m] with an olive-white bark. Its leaves seem like those of the Chinese scholar-tree, but linger. Its flower is like that of the orange tree, but bigger. Its seed is black, as big as the *Cornus officinalis*, is bitter and sweet, and can be eaten. [chap. 18]

... E-si (fig) is called E-ri in the country of Persia and Di-ri in the country of Fu-lin. The tree grows a chang and four or five ch'ih high [c. 3.51–3.78 m]. Its branches and leaves are very luxuriant. Its leaf has the shape of that of the castor-oil plant with five protruding parts around the edge. It bears fruit without flowers. Its fruits are crimson, somewhat like the small persimmon, and their taste is the same as the sweet persimmon. The fruits are ripe every month. [chap. 18]

... A-p'o-sen (balsam) grows in the country of Fu-lin. It has a height of over a chang [c. 2.70 m], and olive-white bark, opposite leaves, in pairs, which are thin. Its flowers seem to be those of the turnip, pure yellow. Its seed has the shape of the pepper, of crimson colour. When its branches are broken, its sap oozes out and is like oil. The sap can be used to smear on scabies, which will completely disappear. Its oil is very expensive, more valuable than gold. [Text 76, chap. 18]

> … Ye-xi-mi (jasmine) grows in the country of Fu-lin and also in the country of Persia. The plant has a height of seven or eight ch'ih [c. 1.89–2.16 m]. Its leaves seem to be like those of the plum. It grows luxuriantly all the year round. Its flowers are white, with five petals. It has no seed. When it blooms, the air of the fields will be heavy with the aroma of its flowers, somewhat like the Zhan-tang that grows in the district Ling-nan [hills to the north of the Kuang-tung and Kuang-hsi provinces in China] in the southern part of China. The inhabitants of the western countries usually pick its flowers to extract the oil, which is very fragrant and creamy. [chap. 18][10]

Wai-guo-zhuan (Account of Foreign Countries), written by K'ang T'ai (Kang Tai) of the Wu kingdom (222–80), was lost before the twelfth century. The information it contained on the country of Ta-ts'in is known only from later authors. At the time of the Wu kingdom, the Chinese seemed to learn more about Ta-ts'in. 'The book *Wai-guo-zhuan*', written during the time of the Wu kingdom, reports that the country of Ta-ts'in produces dates, hazelnuts, carambola, lotus roots and various fruits.'[11]

After the second half of the twelfth century, Chinese writers presented new information about Byzantine food. *Ling-wai-dai-da* (Answers to Questions about Foreign Countries) was written by Zhou Qu-fei, c. 1178, just after his return from Kui-lin, in south-western China, after his long tenure of office there. He wrote this book in order to answer the questions of his friends about foreign countries. The information contained therein is believed to have been derived from merchants frequenting the district: 'Their food mainly consists of rice, cakes and meat. They do not drink wine, and use golden and silver vessels, and spoons to help themselves. After meals they wash their hands in a golden bowl filled with water.'[12] Another ancient Chinese text, *Zhu-fan-zhi* (Essays on Foreign Countries), which was written by Zhao Ru-kuo c. 1208–25, contains a related account of Ta-ts'in: 'They do not drink wine, and use golden and silver vessels, and spoons to help themselves. After meals they wash their hands in a golden bowl filled with water.' The *Tu-h'uan-ching-hsing-chi* (Notes on Travelling by Tu H'uan) relates:

---

[10] Duan Chien-shi, *You-yang-za-zu*, Chinese Ancient Books Printing House (Beijing, 1987).

[11] *Wen-lei-chu* (*Yi-wen-lei-ju*) (The Collection of Books according to Subjects), compiled by O-yang Hsun c. 887–88, contains a piece of prose entitled *Chi-pu-fu* (*Qi-bu-fu*) (The Prose of the Marvelous Cloth), and its preface. The prose was written by Yin Chu, who was a poet of the Chin dynasty, and records the event when the country of Ta-ts'in offered asbestos cloth to a Chinese general (Text 81 chap. 87).

[12] Zhou Qu-fei, *Ling-wai-dai-da*, Chinese Ancient Books Printing House (Beijing, 1987), chap. 3.

> The country of Fu-lin lies to the west of the country of Zhan, and is called Ta'ts'in. The colour of their faces is red and white. The men all wear plain clothes and the women wear silk clothes set with pearls. They enjoy wine and have a fancy for dry cakes. They are very skilled in manufacturing and clever at weaving.[13]

After the end of the twelfth century, new information about Fu-lin appears:

> Ta-ts'in is also named Li-qian. The court of the later H'an dynasty was first to communicate with the country. This country, being situated on the western sea, is also called H'ai-hsi-ko (Hai-xi-guo) or 'the country of the western sea'. They make golden coins, on which they have an image of their king's face … the country produces gold, silver, pearls, foreign silk cloth, cows, sheep, horses, camels with a single hump, pears, apricots, dates that grow for one thousand years, olives, millet and wheat. They make wine from grapes.[14]

Sung-shih (History of the Sung Dynasty), written by T'o-t'o c. 1343–45, contains a similar account of Fu-lin, which was copied from the *Ssu-ch'ao-shih* (History of the First Four Emperors of the Sung Dynasty):

> He said: the climate of the country is very cold; their houses, made of earthen materials, have no tiles. The country produces gold, silver, pearls, foreign silk cloth, cows, sheep, horses, camels with a single hump, pears, apricots, dates that grow for one thousand years, olives, millet and wheat. They make wine from grapes.[15]

Ben-chao-gang-mu (Compendium of Materia Medica), written by Li Shi-zhen, a great doctor and pharmacologist of the Ming dynasty, describes 1,892 kinds of drugs and provides 11,000 prescriptions, among which many come from the country of Fu-lin (and Ta-ts'in). It mentions many ingredients for foods or medicine such as mercury, alum, coloured glaze, *Aucklandia costus*, nutmeg, *Curcuma aromatica*, tulip, *Rosmarinus officinalis*, *Commiphora molmol*, sensitive plant, *Hovenia dulcis*, the incense of wisteria,

---

[13] This book is based on the historical material from the *Ling-wai-dai-da* and repeats a number of *topoi* we have seen in earlier texts (see above).

[14] *Win-xian-tong-kao* (The Comprehensive Study of Chinese Historical Documents), Chinese Ancient Books Printing House (Beijing, 1987), chap. 339; it was written by Ma Tuan-lin after 1195 and is based on former dynastic histories and other documents. It is the second comprehensive study of Chinese documents and borrows considerable material from the first such book, the *T'ung-tien*.

[15] T'o-t'o, *Sung-shih*, Chinese Ancient Books Printing House (Shanghai, 1986), chap. 490.

frankincense, honey locust, storax,[16] turnip, marmot, white elephant, ostrich, jackfruit, and so on.

We cannot list all Chinese historical accounts and texts in this short article, but hope that those passages we have cited here help us to comprehend the dietary behavior of the Byzantines, at least as it was recorded by people to whom the Greek diet was an 'exotic' subject that aroused considerable curiosity.

[16] On which see Andrew Dalby's chapter in this volume.

Index

The enkomia included in the first section of the volume have not been indexed.